Studies in Celtic History XXV

SAINTS' CULTS IN THE CELTIC WORLD

STUDIES IN CELTIC HISTORY

ISSN 0261–9865

Studies in Celtic History aims to provide a forum for new research into all aspects of the history of Celtic-speaking peoples throughout the whole of the medieval period. The term 'history' is inderstood broadly: any study, regardless of discipline, which advances our knowledge and understanding of the history of Celtic-speaking peoples will be considered. Studies of primary sources, and of new methods of exploiting such sources, are encouraged.

Founded by Professor David Dumville, the series was relaunched under new editorship in 1997. Proposals or queries may be sent directly to the editors at the addresses given below; all submissions will receive prompt and informed consideration before being sent to expert readers.

Prof. Dauvit Broun, Department of History (Scottish), University of Glasgow, 9 University Gardens, Glasgow G12 8QH

Dr Máire Ní Mhaonaigh, St John's College, Cambridge, CB2 1TP

Prof. Huw Pryce, Department of History and Welsh History, Bangor University, Gwynedd LL57 2DG

For titles already published in this series
see the end of this volume

SAINTS' CULTS IN THE CELTIC WORLD

Edited by
STEVE BOARDMAN, JOHN REUBEN DAVIES AND
EILA WILLIAMSON

THE BOYDELL PRESS

First published 2009
The Boydell Press, Woodbridge
Paperback edition 2013

ISBN 978 1 84383 432 8 hardback
ISBN 978 1 84383 845 6 paperback

Transferred to digital printing

The Boydell Press is an imprint of Boydell & Brewer Ltd
PO Box 9, Woodbridge, Suffolk IP12 3DF, UK
and of Boydell & Brewer Inc.
668 Mt Hope Avenue, Rochester, NY 14620–2731, USA
website: www.boydellandbrewer.com

A CIP catalogue record for this book is available
from the British Library

This publication is printed on acid-free paper

CONTENTS

List of Illustrations vi
List of Contributors vii
Abbreviations ix
Editors' Preface xi

1 Rochester, Hexham and Cennrígmonaid: the movements of St Andrew in Britain, 604–747 1
James E. Fraser

2 The cults of Saints Patrick and Palladius in early medieval Scotland 18
Thomas Owen Clancy

3 Personal names and the cult of Patrick in eleventh-century Strathclyde and Northumbria 42
Fiona Edmonds

4 Bishop Kentigern among the Britons 66
John Reuben Davies

5 Adjacent saints' dedications and early Celtic History 91
Karen Jankulak

6 Cuthbert the cross-border saint in the twelfth century 119
Sally Crumplin

7 David of Scotland: 'Vir tam necessarius mundo' 130
Joanna Huntington

8 The cult of Saint George in Scotland 146
Steve Boardman

9 The cult of the Three Kings of Cologne in Scotland 160
Eila Williamson

10 The medieval and early modern cult of St Brendan 180
Jonathan M. Wooding

General Index 205

LIST OF ILLUSTRATIONS

Map

Churches dedicated to St Patrick in the kingdom of Strathclyde and surrounding areas 41

Table

Gospatrics in the house of Bamburgh 43

LIST OF CONTRIBUTORS

STEVE BOARDMAN is Reader in Scottish History, School of History, Classics and Archaeology, University of Edinburgh

THOMAS OWEN CLANCY is Professor of Celtic, Department of Celtic, University of Glasgow

SALLY CRUMPLIN is Research Assistant for the Sites and Monuments Record of Aberdeen City Council

JOHN REUBEN DAVIES is Research Fellow in Scottish History, School of History, Classics and Archaeology, University of Edinburgh

FIONA EDMONDS is Lecturer in Celtic History, Department of Anglo-Saxon, Norse, and Celtic, University of Cambridge, and a Fellow of Clare College, Cambridge

JAMES E. FRASER is Lecturer in Early Scottish History and Culture, School of History, Classics and Archaeology (Scottish History), and School of Languages, Literatures and Cultures (Celtic and Scottish Studies), University of Edinburgh

JOANNA HUNTINGTON is a Leverhulme Early Career Fellow, School of Historical Studies, University of Newcastle

KAREN JANKULAK is Lecturer in Medieval History, Department of History, University of Wales, Lampeter

EILA WILLIAMSON is Research Fellow in Scottish History, School of History, Classics and Archaeology, University of Edinburgh

JONATHAN M. WOODING is Director of the Centre for the Study of Religion in Celtic Societies, University of Wales, Lampeter

ABBREVIATIONS

AC (A)	*Annales Cambriae*, A-text: 'The *Annales Cambriæ* and Old-Welsh Genealogies from *Harleian MS. 3859*', ed. Egerton Phillimore, *Y Cymmrodor* 9 (1888), 141–83, reprinted in *Arthurian Period Sources: Genealogies and Texts*, ed. John Morris, Arthurian Period Sources 5 (Chichester, 1995), 13–55
ASC	*The Anglo-Saxon Chronicle: A Collaborative Edition*, general eds David. N. Dumville and S. D. Keynes, 23 vols (Cambridge and Woodbridge, 1983–)
AU	*The Annals of Ulster (to AD 1131)*, ed. and trans. Séan Mac Airt and G. Mac Niocaill (Dublin, 1983)
Bede, *HE*	Bede the Venerable, *Historia ecclesiastica gentis Anglorum*, ed. Bertram Colgrave and R. A. B. Mynors, *Bede's Ecclesiastical History of the English People* (Oxford, 1969)
BL	British Library, London
Boece, *Chronicles*	Hector Boece, *The Chronicles of Scotland Compiled by Hector Boece. Translated into Scots by John Bellenden, 1531*, ed. R. W. Chambers, Edith C. Batho and H. Winifred Husbands, Scottish Text Society, 3rd series 10 and 15, 2 vols (Edinburgh, 1938–41)
Book of Llan Dâv	*The Text of the Book of Llan Dâv reproduced from the Gwysaney Manuscript*, ed. J. Gwenogvryn Evans (Oxford, 1893; rev. impr. Aberystwyth, 1979)
Chron. Bower	Walter Bower, *Scotichronicon*, ed. D. E. R. Watt *et al.*, 9 vols (Aberdeen and Edinburgh, 1987–98)
Chron. Fordun	Johannis de Fordun, *Chronica Gentis Scotorum*, ed. W. F. Skene, The Historians of Scotland 1 and 4, 2 vols (Edinburgh, 1871)
CWAAS	Cumberland and Westmorland Antiquarian and Archaeo-logical Society
EHD 1	*English Historical Documents, c. 500–1042*, ed. Dorothy Whitelock, English Historical Documents 1 (2nd edn, London, 1979)
EHR	*English Historical Review*
IR	*Innes Review*
LBS	S. Baring-Gould and John Fisher, *The Lives of the British Saints: The Saints of Wales, Cornwall and Irish Saints*, 4 vols (London, 1907–13)
NLS	National Library of Scotland, Edinburgh

ODNB	*Oxford Dictionary of National Biography*, ed. H. C. G. Matthew and Brian Harrison, 60 vols (Oxford, 2004); also online at http://www.oxforddnb.com/
PL	*Patrologiae cursus completes. Series Latina*, 221 vols (Paris 1844–64)
PSAS	*Proceedings of the Society of Antiquaries of Scotland*
RMS	*Registrum Magni Sigilli Regum Scotorum. The Register of the Great Seal of Scotland*, ed. John Maitland Thomson *et al.*, Scottish Record Society, 11 vols (Edinburgh, 1882–1914; reprinted 1984)
RS	Rolls Series
RSCHS	*Records of the Scottish Church History Society*
St Nich. Cart.	*Cartularium ecclesiae Sancti Nicholai Aberdonensis*, ed. J. Cooper, New Spalding Club 2 and 7, 2 vols (Aberdeen, 1888–92)
SHR	*Scottish Historical Review*
Symeonis opera	*Symeonis Monachi Opera Omnia*, ed. Thomas Arnold, Rolls Series 75, 2 vols (London, 1882–5)
TA	*Accounts of the Lord High Treasurer of Scotland*, ed. Thomas Dickson *et al.*, 13 vols (1877–1978)
TCWAAS	*Transactions of the Cumberland and Westmorland Antiquarian and Archaeological Society*
VCH	*Victoria County History*

EDITORS' PREFACE

The origins of this volume lie in a series of papers delivered during two sessions of the Leeds International Medieval Congress in July 2006, supplemented by further invited contributions. The two sessions were organised under the auspices of the Survey of Dedications to Saints in Medieval Scotland, a project funded by a Major Research Grant from the Arts and Humanities Research Council. The project is designed to record and collate acts of dedication to saints (loosely defined to include all forms of commemoration and veneration) within the boundaries of the Scottish realm from the early medieval period to 1560.[1]

The aim of the Leeds papers was collectively to address the way in which devotion to particular saints might transcend or cross linguistic, cultural and political boundaries. The emphasis of the papers collected here is therefore on the issue of transmission, that is, why certain saints' cults spread beyond their original points or communities of origin to achieve a wider and more diverse following and the mechanisms by which this occurred. Many of the chapters have an Insular, and particularly north-British, focus. For this reason the volume was originally to have been entitled *Saints' Cults in the Insular World*, but the wider scope of some of the essays, particularly the inclusion of material on Brittany and Breton cults, persuaded the publishers and editors to opt for the current title. The editors acknowledge that the implication that the cults examined in the volume grew and developed in a cultural, linguistic, devotional or political environment that could be described as distinctively or significantly 'Celtic' is potentially unhelpful.[2] Most obviously, a number of contributions deal with societies, such as late medieval lowland Scotland and northern England, which were most assuredly not part of any wider 'Celtic World', if such could be said to have existed. Here, then, 'Celtic' is being used solely as a geographical shorthand to indicate that the studies that make up the volume concentrate on saints' cults in a northern British context where interaction between Irish, Welsh and Scottish devotional traditions was extensive (particularly in the early medieval period).

Aside from the principal concern with tracing and explaining the spread of cults into new areas or social contexts, the collected essays have thrown up a variety of interesting sub themes. The contributions of Crumplin, Huntington and Boardman suggest, in varying ways, the importance and durability of Anglo-Scottish interaction from the twelfth to the fifteenth century. St Cuthbert was a figure venerated across a great swathe of northern England and southern Scotland, his cult assiduously cultivated throughout this wide spiritual hinterland by the guardians of his

1 A searchable database of the project's results may be found online at http://www.shc.ed.ac.uk/Research/saints/index.htm

2 The warning of Patrick Sims-Williams ('Celtomania and Celtoscepticism', *Cambrian Medieval Celtic Studies* 36 (1998), 1–35) to make fewer assumptions about non-linguistic Celtic unity is in the editors' minds.

shrine at Durham. Although he came to be presented as a protector of Durham, and the north of England in general, from the depredations of the Scots in the fourteenth century, Cuthbert remained a focus for devotion in the northern kingdom. The same can be said of St George, whose cult enjoyed a meteoric rise in popularity in England in the fourteenth century through the saint's identification as the military patron of English kings. Despite the political hostility said to characterise Anglo-Scottish relations in the late medieval period, George also attracted devotees within Scotland, men drawn by the saint's universal appeal as a protector of knights and men-at-arms. Huntington's study of David I (1124–53) deals with a man whose sanctity was never fully established, but who certainly became a model of kingly virtues for both the Scottish and English monarchies in later periods. These points of Anglo-Scottish contact in areas of devotion and moral authority chime well with recent re-evaluations of the relationship between the two realms in the late medieval period, which have pointed to areas of continued social and cultural interaction.

A similar situation of communication and exchange across political and linguistic frontiers can be found in the early medieval period as shown in Fraser's consideration of the origins of the cult of St Andrew at Cennrígmonaid (St Andrews). This gives the Pictish kingdom and its ecclesiastical life not only a Northumbrian perspective, but also a wider British, not to say European one, reinforcing the view presented by Bede in *Historia Ecclesiastica*, v.21. The transplantation to Scotland of non-native cults of a different kind is explained by Clancy in his uncovering of early medieval evidence for interest in St Palladius and St Patrick, saints whose veneration is usually identified with Ireland. The cults of both these saints link churchmen from north Britain – both Britons and Picts – with scholars in Ireland before 900. While Clancy has pondered why Britons and Picts both saw fit to patronise the cults of saints associated most closely with Irish religious origins, Edmonds asks why Northumbrian aristocrats should have identified with the cult of St Patrick through their personal names: that Patrick's cult had such a diverse constituency meant that it was accessible to the Northumbrians, who adopted some of the cultural and religious markers of the people and lands they sought to dominate politically.

Davies also makes a connection between Northumbrian magnates and another cult that came to spread through Strathclyde–Cumbria, that of St Kentigern. By the eleventh century, three important ethnically British saints, Kentigern, Patrick and Gildas, were being linked historically with Strathclyde. By the twelfth century, the kingdom of Scots was undergoing a process of historiographical definition as something of a melting-pot of all-comers – British, Gaelic and Angles. The most striking aspect of this process is that the historians whose works we can identify were all English, making the *regnum Scottorum* a place where they could maintain their Englishness in the face of Norman political and cultural dominance further south.

Thus, an important theme throughout this collection is the way in which northern England and southern Scotland formed a region of natural interaction in the early medieval period – a 'unity' in diversity that in many ways survived the emergence of a bi-polar political frontier in the late medieval period.

Another theme at the heart of three of the chapters is the influence of historical and hagiographical writing of all eras on modern understanding of the spread of saints' cults. Davies argues that the spread of the cult of St Kentigern through

Cumberland, North Wales, and even to Brittany, is a combined product of twelfth-century churchmen, their legendary hagiographies, and the modern imagination. Jankulak takes the theme further, and unpicks the influential work of G. H. Doble, Charles Henderson, E. G. Bowen and others, showing that apparently recurrent cult-sites across Wales, Cornwall and Brittany, of single saints, and of pairs or groups of saints, are nearly always more apparent than real. Wooding's survey of the evidence for the growth of the cult of St Brendan, meanwhile, acknowledges the importance of the hugely popular ninth-century account of Brendan's maritime wanderings, the *Nauigatio Sancti Brendani abbatis*, in providing a 'literary impetus' for the generation of dedications in the later medieval period, but also suggests a genuinely early transfer of the cult from Ireland to Scotland and South Wales shortly after the saint's death.

The continued receptiveness of late medieval Scotland to cults and devotional habits originating elsewhere is suggested not only by Boardman's study of St George, but especially by Williamson's article on the cult of the Magi. Williamson outlines the increased popularity within Scotland of the 'Three Kings of Cologne', and maps out the possible routes by which the cult became familiar to new devotees. The spread of interest in the Magi as figures of supernatural power (whose names might be invoked on protective amulets and charms) seems to reflect the growing late medieval concern with devotions centred on Christ and the Holy Family. That Scottish engagement with George and the 'Three Kings' seems entirely consistent with European trends might be worth stressing, since recent work by David Ditchburn has suggested that the overall tendency in the late medieval period was indeed for the localised cults of Gaelic or British saints to be superseded or supplemented by new pan-European devotions introduced through dynastic, commercial and cultural contacts with the Low Countries, England and the Baltic.[3]

On the whole, the essays assembled here point to the difficulty of treating the development of medieval saints' cults within the confines of 'national' historiographies. It is hoped that, individually and in combination, these articles will make a useful contribution to the study of saints' cults in, across and beyond the Celtic-speaking territories of the British Isles and Ireland in the middle ages.

The editors would like to thank all those who attended the conference sessions at Leeds, particularly those who contributed to the post-paper discussions there. Caroline Palmer of Boydell & Brewer must also be thanked for her help and patience at various points in the production of the volume and for her calm acceptance of our failure to deliver the promised white Parisian gloves and Sparrowhawk. The editors would also like to acknowledge the financial assistance of the Doctor Jamie Cameron Trust in the production of the volume's dust-jacket.

3 David Ditchburn, *Scotland and Europe: The Medieval Kingdom and its contacts with Christendom, 1214–1560* (East Linton, 2001), 49–57.

1

ROCHESTER, HEXHAM AND CENNRÍGMONAID: THE MOVEMENTS OF ST ANDREW IN BRITAIN, 604–747[1]

James E. Fraser

It is well known that two twelfth-century versions of a foundation legend with common elements claim that the establishment of the cult of the apostle Andrew at Cennrígmonaid, now St Andrews,[2] took place during the reign of a *rex Pictorum* called *Ungus filius Urguist* in the shorter, so-called A version of the legend, and *Hungus filius Ferlon* (*recte Forgus*) in the longer Version B.[3] The pseudo-historical tendencies of Scottish ecclesiastical foundation legends of this epoch are increasingly widely appreciated. The question of the Andrean dedication at

1 At various points in this chapter, certain dates, name-forms, etc. have been adopted in silent conformity with J. E. Fraser, *From Caledonia to Pictland: Scotland to 795* (Edinburgh, forthcoming), where further explanation of such adoptions is provided.

2 On the place-name *Cennrígmonaid*, 'king's-muir-head', see S. Taylor, introduction, in S. Taylor (ed.), *The Uses of Place-Names* (Edinburgh, 1998), 1–11, at 3; see also W. J. Watson, *The History of the Celtic Place-Names of Scotland* (Edinburgh and London, 1926), 397.

3 W. F. Skene (ed.), *Chronicles of the Picts, Chronicles of the Scots, and Other Early Memorials of Scottish History* (Edinburgh, 1867), 138–40 ('Version A'), 183–93 ('Version B'). The most recent discussions of these two texts are D. Broun, 'The Church of St Andrews and Its Foundation Legend in the Early Twelfth Century: Recovering the Full Text of Version A of the Foundation Legend', in S. Taylor (ed.), *Kings, Clerics and Chronicles in Scotland 500–1297* (Dublin, 2000), 108–14; and S. Taylor, 'The Coming of the Augustinians to St Andrews and Version B of the St Andrews Foundation Legend', in *ibid.*, 115–23. Earlier discussions include U. Hall, *St Andrew and Scotland* (St Andrews, 1994), 60–77; M. Ash and D. Broun, 'The Adoption of St Andrew as Patron Saint of Scotland', in J. Higgitt (ed.), *Medieval Art and Architecture in the Diocese of St Andrews* (British Archaeological Association, 1994), 16–24; M. O. Anderson, 'The Celtic Church in Kinrimund', in D. McRoberts (ed.), *The Medieval Church of St Andrews* (Glasgow, 1976), 1–10; M. Anderson, 'St Andrews before Alexander I', in G. W. S. Barrow (ed.), *The Scottish Tradition: Essays in Honour of Ronald Gordon Cant* (Edinburgh, 1974), 1–13; W. F. Skene, 'Notice of the Early Ecclesiastical Settlements at St Andrews', *PSAS* 4 (1860–62), 300–21, at 302–7.

Cennrígmonaid, then, cannot be answered without the help of historians of twelfth-century Scotland. The rest of us have learned, from sneak previews provided in the commemorative volume for the late Marjorie Anderson, that Dauvit Broun and Simon Taylor are in the process of seeking answers, as they work away at new editions of these two foundation legends.[4] This chapter is thus avowedly a hostage to fortune. Under consideration will be some circumstantial evidence that the twelfth-century claim that the founder of Cennrígmonaid was a Pictish king called *(H)Ungus* is unlikely to be pseudo-historical, whatever one makes of the rest of each legend.

Two Pictish kings attested in contemporary records bore this name. The second of these, Onuist son of Vurguist, was king of Picts for some fourteen years from 820 until 834.[5] The earlier king, also Onuist son of Vurguist, was king of Picts for some thirty years from 732 until 761.[6] Both have had their proponents among past advocates of the partial or entire historicity of the twelfth-century material. The earliest proponent may have been whoever copied the thirteenth-century exemplar of the shorter version of the Pictish king-list, which identified the second Onuist as he who *aedificavit Kilremonth* (with variants).[7] This identification does not, however, close the case, for Cennrígmonaid is first attested in contemporary records as early as 747, in the obit of its abbot Túathalán *ab Cindrighmonaidh*.[8]

This eighth-century attestation of a monastery at Cennrígmonaid is invaluable for a number of reasons. For example, it establishes chronological priority in name-forms. It has thus been established that the king-list's *Kilremonth* is much later in form than *Cennrígmonaid*, belonging to the twelfth century.[9] The king-list's evidence accordingly becomes unlikely to be much earlier than the

4 Broun, 'Church of St Andrews', 112–14, and Taylor, 'Coming of the Augustinians', 116–19, discuss some pseudo-historical aspects of the two foundation legends.

5 Onuist II is *Oengus m. Fergusa rex Fortrenn* at *Annals of Ulster* 834.1; S. Mac Airt and G. Mac Niocaill (eds.), *The Annals of Ulster (to A.D. 1131)* (Dublin, 1983), henceforth *AU*. *Rex Pictorum* is inferred from his inclusion in the Pictish king-list.

6 Onuist I is *Oengus Pictorum rex* in the *Chronicle of 766*; B. Colgrave and R. A. B. Mynors (eds), *Bede's Ecclesiastical History of the English People* (Oxford, 1969), 576. In referring to the 'continuation of Bede' as the *Chronicle of 766*, I follow A. Woolf, 'Onuist son of Uurguist: *Tyrannus carnifex* or a David for the Picts?', in D. Hill and M. Worthington (eds), *Æthelbald and Offa: Two Eighth-century Kings of Mercia* (BAR British Series 383: Oxford, 2005), 35–42. Onuist is *Oengus m. Fergusso rex Pictorum* at *AU* 736.1 and *AU* 761.4 (similarly in *Annals of Tigernach*; W. Stokes (ed.), *The Annals of Tigernach*, 1 (Felinfach, 1993), henceforth *AT*). On the first year of his reign, see now A. Woolf, 'AU 729.2 and the Last Years of Nechtan mac Der-Ilei', *SHR* 85 (2006), 131–4.

7 King-lists D, F and K; M. O. Anderson, *Kings and Kingship in Early Scotland* (2nd edn: Edinburgh and London, 1980), 266, 273, 287. King-list I (*ibid*., 281) records that Custantín his brother and predecessor *primo edificauit ecclesiam Sancti Andree*. Anderson (*ibid*., 62–3) showed that the scribe streamlined his Pictish material, and concluded that he 'was not particularly interested in the Pictish period'; the transfer of credit for building *Kilremonth* is a slip of this editing process.

8 *AU* 747.10; *AT* 747.11. A. A. M. Duncan, *Scotland: The Making of the Kingdom* (Edinburgh, 1975), 71, noticed this evidence, but went on (p. 104) to place the foundation in the ninth century.

9 Anderson, 'St Andrews', 1.

thirteenth-century date of its exemplar, and nothing like a contemporary witness to the foundation of the monastery.[10] Attempts have been made to get round this awkward evidence. Smyth, for example, watered down the king-list's *aedificavit* to the vaguer 'associated with', and spoke of 'a refounding' of St Andrews, or 'a change in its status' from the eighth century.[11] This is special pleading. The eighth-century obit of Abbot Túathalán demonstrates that Cennrígmonaid was in existence seventy-three years prior to the accession of the second Onuist, who cannot therefore have *aedificavit Kilremonth*. We are bound to conclude that he was erroneously identified as the founder in the twelfth century or later, and that this error is preserved in the shorter king-list. It is notable, indeed, that the thirteenth-century exemplar of this list seems also to have misplaced the foundation of Abernethy, attributing it to a Pictish king who flourished c.600, while the longer version probably preserves the genuine (but pseudo-historical) attribution to a king of similar name who flourished some eighty years earlier.[12]

Pending the findings of Broun and Taylor, we must work from Broun's earlier conclusion, in conjunction with Marinell Ash, that the two twelfth-century versions of the foundation legend need not have shared a substantial narrative in common, and may indeed have shared little more than the knowledge of the names of the king and the cleric involved in the foundation.[13] One possibility is that the founder-king's name had formerly been chosen by a pseudo-historian essentially at random (or perhaps according to some lost set of criteria) from a king-list, and was subsequently learned by the twelfth-century pseudo-historians whose accounts survive. In that event, the possibility would loom that the foundation of church and cult in the Pictish period is entirely pseudo-historical. Such a conclusion is made problematic, however, by the independent evidence of the Chronicle of Ireland c.911, using contemporary records, that there was a monastery flourishing at Cennrígmonaid in the eighth century, and indeed in the middle years, no less, of the reign of the earlier Onuist.[14] This striking coincidence from independent evidence, associating this king with Cennrígmonaid, is surely a stroke in favour of the possibility that a skeleton of historicity supports the foundation stories of St Andrews, fleshed out in different pseudo-historical ways by two twelfth-century writers, who at the time may simply have had to guess which *(H)Ungus* in the Pictish king-list had been the founder.

10 For discussion, see Ash and Broun, 'Adoption of St Andrew', 17.

11 A. P. Smyth, *Warlords and Holy Men: Scotland AD 80–1000* (London, 1984), 180, 186–7. A. O. Anderson, *Early Sources of Scottish History 500–1286*, 1 (Edinburgh, 1922), 267, seems to have had something similar in mind. See now A. Woolf, *From Pictland to Alba, 789–1070* (Edinburgh, 2007), 65–6. For the possibility of Ionan involvement in this (putative) re-founding, see T. O. Clancy, 'Iona, Scotland, and the Céli Dé', in B. E. Crawford (ed.), *Scotland in Dark Age Britain* (St Andrews, 1996), 111–30, at 113–15, 117–18.

12 Anderson, *Kings and Kingship*, 246–7 (A), 262 (B), versus 266 (D), 272 (F), 287 (K).

13 Ash and Broun, 'Adoption of St Andrew', 18–19; see Anderson, 'St Andrews', 7, for the earlier view that their common source material may have been more substantial.

14 Anderson, 'St Andrews', 7, pointed out that the gaelicised genitive *Forgusso*, as the B Version of the foundation legend renders the king's patronymic, ought to belong to a linguistic context significantly earlier than the twelfth century. A later pseudo-historian could have copied the name from a much earlier king-list.

It is certain that Cennrígmonaid was a functioning monastery during the reign of the first Onuist son of Vurguist. Nevertheless, it is quite uncertain whether the place was founded in the target period 732 × 747, for there is nothing outwith the foundation legends to rule out an earlier foundation.[15] Nor can we know to whom the eighth-century church there was dedicated, whether St Andrew or any other patron (or indeed any patron at all). The earliest explicit attestations of the Andrean dedication at Cennrígmonaid cluster round about 1100, in various texts with provenances in different parts of Britain and Ireland.[16] Before this, we have only the tantalising evidence of the pilgrimage of one Irishman, Áed mac Máel Mithig, to Cennrígmonaid in 965 (further confirmation of the priority of this name-form in *cenn-*).[17] A Scots chronicle from the middle of the sixteenth century, appended to a manuscript of the chronicle of Andrew of Wyntoun, dates the coming of St Andrew's relics to Scotland to 761, seemingly oblivious to the fact that this was, strikingly, the year of the first Onuist's death.[18] This curious record is unusable without further research into this fascinating text. Nothing in this paper makes certain either the date of the foundation of Cennrígmonaid or the antiquity of the Andrean dedication there. Instead, I propose only to raise one or two points for consideration that have not hitherto been brought out in connection with this question. In so doing, I claim no more than to make firmer the possibility that there is something genuine underlying the twelfth-century foundation legends.

The first point to be raised is actually what drew me to this subject in the first place. It extends from work on the Pictish origin story outlined in the first chapter

15 For possibilities relating to earlier activity, see Hall, *St Andrew*, 55–7. E. Proudfoot, 'Excavations at the Long-Cist Cemetery at the Hallow Hill, St Andrews, Fife, 1975–7', *PSAS* 126 (1996), 387–454, at 440–2, suggests that decline in burials at the Hallow Hill after the seventh century relates to the foundation and rise of Cennrígmonaid in the eighth. Otherwise archaeology has yet to establish a foundation-date at St Andrews proper; for a summary, see S. M. Foster, 'Discovery, Recovery, Context and Display', in S. M. Foster (ed.), *The St Andrews Sarcophagus: A Pictish Masterpiece and its International Connections* (Dublin, 1998), 36–62, at 43–5, 48–50.

16 Anderson, 'St Andrews', 5. Texts include the *Prophecy of Berchán* [B. T. Hudson (ed.), *Prophecy of Berchan: Irish and Scottish High-kings of the Early Middle Ages* (Westport CT and London, 1996)], § 156 (*tech an apstail*, 'house of the apostle'); Lifris, *Vita Sancti Cadoci* [A. W. Wade-Evans (ed.), *Vita Sanctorum Britanniae et Genealogiae* (Cardiff, 1944), 24–141], § 26 (*basilica sancti Andree Apostoli*, 'the church of St Andrew the Apostle') [J. R. Davies, *The Book of Llandaf and the Norman Church in Wales* (Woodbridge, 2003), 76n.2, has argued for a narrowing of the date of composition of Lifris's Life to 1091 × 1104]; *Vita Sanctae Margaretae Scotorum Reginae* [W. M. Metcalfe (ed.), *Pinkerton's Lives of the Scottish Saints* 2 (Paisley, 1889), 159–96], §§ 7, 20 [§§ 4, 9, in A. O. Anderson, *Early Sources of Scottish History 500–1286*, 2 (Edinburgh, 1922), 59–88] (*ecclesia S. Andreae*, 'church of St Andrew').

17 *Chronicon Scotorum*, 965.1 (*Aodh mac Maoilmithidh in perigrinatione moritur .i. hi Cind Ri Monaidh*); W. M. Hennessy (ed.), *Chronicum Scotorum: A Chronicle of Irish Affairs from the Earliest Times to A.D. 1135* (London, 1866), henceforth *CS*.

18 Skene, *Chron. Picts and Scots*, 387 (*the ȝere of God sevynn hundir lxj þe relikis of Sanct Androw þe Apostle com in Scotland*). I am grateful to Steve Boardman for assistance with this chronicle, and in particular with his facsimile of the manuscript (BL Reg. 17 D.xx).

of Bede's History, establishing that Duncan and others were correct to conclude that Bede's source was a Pictish text.[19] What these scholars did not know, which we now know, is that the Pictish kings who reigned from 697 to 724 may be identified as Dalriadic Gaels on their father's side and (probably Verturian) Picts on their mother's.[20] This revelation by Clancy proves to have major repercussions for understanding the origin story. Its most famous element is its conclusion, which is also its climax. Here the reader is told that it is currently the case that *in dubium*, 'in uncertain cases', it is customary for the Picts to choose their kings on the basis of maternal, rather than paternal heritage, and that this custom goes back to the dawn of Pictish history. This claim is the principal basis for the famous paradigm of matrilineal inheritance among the Picts. Clancy's work reveals this passage to be something rather different. After all, we know that, not only did the royal brothers, who reigned in Pictavia during Bede's adulthood, claim the kingship in the described way themselves, but the earlier one also captured the kingship from someone else, a case of 'uncertain' legitimacy if ever there was one. Thus, we find strong indications, by considering it against its immediate context, that this myth is aetiological like so many other origin myths of early medieval times, concerned with explaining aspects of immediate political realities c.700 by way of pseudo-history. Once this presentist character of the origin myth is appreciated, it is impossible to remain unfascinated by its presentation of Picts who are all descended from unions between a Pictish parent and a Gaelic one (like the one that produced these contemporary kings), and Picts who, in distress, should call upon Gaelic military support (did these contemporary kings do the same in seizing the kingship for themselves?). The bottom line here is that the myth is steeped in the political realities of the early eighth century, and was surely composed c.700.

Bede thus had it from Pictish contemporaries, and not necessarily from ancient tradition, that the *gens Pictorum* originated in Scythia. Now, St Andrew too had a Scythian connection, which ought to have been well known to any studious Pict at the time of composition, as it was certainly known centuries later to the author of Version A of the foundation legend.[21] Quoting from Origen, Eusebius of Caesarea wrote in his seminal *Historia ecclesiastica*, a text well known to Bede in Latin translation, that, after the brutal Flavian suppression of rebellious Judaea, the apostle Andrew went to Scythia, having obtained it by lot as his mission field.[22] Origen had been informed by apocryphal 'Acts of Andrew' and derivative texts composed c.200, and the apostle's Scythian connection was repeated by, amongst others, Isidore of Seville and the *Martyrologium Romanum*, becoming widely known in the West by the end of the seventh century.[23] The Pictish author and

19 K. Jackson, 'On the Northern British Section of Nennius', in N. Chadwick (ed.), *Celt and Saxon: Studies in the Early British Border* (Cambridge, 1963), 20–62, at 40, can be added to the list of such scholars.

20 T. O. Clancy, 'Philosopher-King: Nechtan mac Der-Ilei', *SHR* 83 (2004), 125–49.

21 Skene, *Chron. Picts and Scots*, 138.

22 Eusebius, *Historia ecclesiastica*, iii.1; K. Lake (ed.), *Eusebius, the Ecclesiastical History*, I (Loeb Classical Library, London and Cambridge MA, 1926). For a discussion of Eusebius's Andrean sources, see P. M. Peterson, *Andrew, Brother of Simon Peter: His History and his Legends* (Leiden, 1958), 7–8.

23 Peterson, *Andrew*, 14–15, 24–9; see also Hall, *St Andrew*, 3–6.

readers of the origin story may well have experienced a heightened interest in the cult of St Andrew once their imagined Scythian heritage had been established as history.[24] The extent to which such interest can have been a driving force behind an Andrean dedication at Cennrígmonaid, however, is questionable, and impossible to test.

A more promising line of enquiry may be dedication patterns involving St Andrew in seventh-century Britain, and in particular in Anglo-Saxon England. Bede mentions two major Andrean dedications in his History. One was at Rochester in west Kent, founded in the early years of the Cantuarian mission to England.[25] The other was at Hexham on the River Tyne.[26] The idea of a tenuous link between these two dedications has been raised before, formed by the person of Gregory the Great, the pope who sent Augustine and his fellow missionaries to Kent. Gregory dedicated the monastic church he established at his family home on the Caelian Hill at Rome to St Andrew, and Augustine was resident there when he was chosen to head up the pope's Anglo-Saxon mission. It has accordingly been suggested that the Rochester Andrean dedication by his missionaries represents a nod to Gregory by Augustine, and to their shared Caelian Hill origins.[27] Moreover, Stephen's *Vita Sancti Wilfrithi* says that Wilfrid, at his first arrival at Rome – where 'this lowly spark of fire, kindled in our *gens*, was fanned to flame by God' – prayed 'in the oratory dedicated to St Andrew' for the apostle's intercession, possibly having in mind the same Gregorian house on the Caelian Hill:

> In the oratory dedicated to St Andrew the apostle he humbly knelt before the altar above which the four gospels had been placed, and besought the apostle, in the name of the Lord God for whom he suffered, that the Lord, by his intercession, would grant him a ready mind both to read and to teach the words of the Gospels amongst the nations.[28]

Stephen's hagiographical purpose in this chapter is principally to establish the quality and authority of Wilfrid's learning on the one hand, and his zeal to teach on the other. His technique involves repeated references to apostolic saints. The quality of the learning available at Rome is established by invoking the image of 'the most excellent teacher of the gentiles' St Paul, and by quoting from his letter to the Galatians. The authority of that teaching is established by invoking St Peter, 'apostle and chief of apostles', and by alleging that Wilfrid was given a papal blessing. The invocation of St Andrew here establishes Wilfrid's zeal to teach

24 Hall, *St Andrew*, 65, raised this possibility, having considered (pp. 33–4) the potentially parallel case of the Andrean church established in Ravenna by Theodoric the Great.

25 Bede, *Historia ecclesiastica gentis Anglorum*, ii.3; Colgrave and Mynors (eds), *Bede's Ecclesiastical History*; henceforth *HE*. Translations follow Colgrave's, with occasional modifications by the present writer.

26 Bede, *HE*, v.20.

27 J. McClure and R. Collins (eds), *Bede: The Ecclesiastical History of the English People; The Greater Chronicle; Bede's Letter to Egbert* (Oxford, 1994), 376.

28 Stephen, *Vita Sancti Wilfrithi*, § 5; B. Colgrave (ed.), *The Life of Bishop Wilfrid by Eddius Stephanus* (Cambridge, 1927), henceforth *V. Sanct. Wilfrithi*. Translations follow Colgrave's, with occasional modifications by the present writer. There were several Andrean churches in Rome at this time; see Hall, *St Andrew*, 36.

what he had learned 'among the nations' (*in gentibus*).[29] This possible link between Wilfrid and the Caelian Hill allows for a Gregorian link with Hexham, which, according to Stephen, Wilfrid founded in the 670s 'for the Lord, in honour of St Andrew the apostle',[30] many years after he had sought the saint's intercession at what may have been Gregory's church in Rome.

One possible explanation of these two Anglo-Saxon Andrean dedications, then, is that they represent different expressions of appreciation of Gregory the Great, whom eighth-century Whitby in particular promoted as the apostle of the Anglo-Saxons.[31] It is not insignificant, however, that neither Stephen nor Bede makes any explicit Gregorian connections in either case. Bede mentions no Gregorian dedication to St Andrew in his summary of the pope's career, and Stephen does not mention Gregory or the Caelian Hill in his discussion of the Andrean oratory visited by Wilfrid at Rome.

A second possibility for understanding the dedications is to follow Patrick Wormald in seeing the Andrean dedications at Rochester and Hexham as expressions of missionary zeal. After all, in the apocryphal *Acts of Andrew and Matthias*, of which a tenth-century Anglo-Saxon verse translation from Latin survives (the orthodoxy of which had been rejected in the fourth century), St Andrew was 'the missionary *par excellence*'.[32] He acquired this aspect of his dossier in pre-Nicaean writings, of course, because of the part Andrew plays in the gospel attributed to John. Here, quite at variance with the synoptic gospels, he is portrayed as one of two disciples of John the Baptist to whom their master reveals that Jesus is the Christ, and, having seen the truth for himself, as having fetched his brother Simon (i.e. St Peter), thus becoming both the first apostle of Jesus and the first Christian evangelist.[33] However, commemoration reflecting missionary zeal is somewhat awkward for 670s Hexham, unless one extends the meaning of 'missionary' to include reformation in favour of the Continental apostolicist orthodoxies embraced at the Synod of Whitby several years earlier. Even in that event, a dedication reflecting the authority of the papacy, to St Peter or St Paul, would probably have made more sense. Indeed, we have seen Stephen using these apostles in that very way in *Vita Sancti Wilfrithi*. Moreover (and as Wormald perceived) Stephen's concern to link Wilfrid with evangelisation revolved around the Northumbrian Continental missions of the eighth century.[34] Thus we find Stephen associating the efforts of his contemporary Willibrord, a product of his

29 Stephen, *V. Sanct. Wilfrithi*, § 5.

30 Stephen, *V. Sanct. Wilfrithi*, § 22.

31 *De vita atque virtutibus Gregorii Papae*, §§ 9–14; B. Colgrave (ed.), *The Earliest Life of Gregory the Great* (Lawrence KS, 1968); followed by Bede, *HE*, ii.1. It is worth noting that it is really only in Bede's retelling of this material that Gregory becomes apostle of the Anglo-Saxons; in the Whitby *De vita*, it is arguably the case that the author regarded him as apostle of the Deirans very specifically.

32 P. Wormald, in J. Campbell (ed.), *The Anglo-Saxons* (London, 1991), 89. See also Peterson, *Andrew*, 6–13, 32–3; Hall, *St Andrew*, 6.

33 John 1: 35–42. For discussion, see for example Peterson, *Andrew*, 4–5. The author of Version A of the foundation legend elected to open the text with reference to these chapters of John; Skene, *Chron. Picts and Scots*, 138.

34 Wormald, in Campbell (ed.), *Anglo-Saxons*, 89.

own monastery, with an alleged evangelisation of the Frisians by Wilfrid in the 670s.[35]

A third possibility for understanding the Andrean dedications at Rochester and Hexham has nothing to do with missionary zeal, and is also alluded to by Version A of the St Andrews foundation legend. By Jerome's time, St Andrew had become associated hagiographically with the foundation of the earliest church at Byzantium, at or even before its transformation into Constantinople. This tradition enabled Constantinople to take its place alongside the other apostolic sees of its empire, like Jerusalem and Antioch. As David Farmer observed, however, it also came to act as a kind of 'counterweight' to Rome's traditional associations with St Peter and St Paul.[36] As the brother of Peter (and indeed as his evangelist), Andrew was a logical choice to act as a Petrine counterweight, and his association with Scythia and other areas of the Greek East conveniently placed him in the orbit of Constantinople. Presumably it was in order to make him a plausible counterweight to Paul, Rome's other great apostolic saint, that Andrew's calling of Peter became the basis of the developing notion of Andrew as 'missionary *par excellence*' in certain pre-Nicaean writings. This weight of tradition was firmly in place by the twelfth century, when Version A of the St Andrews foundation legend clearly picked up on it. As Broun's précis of the recovered full text indicates, the author wrote of St Andrews that, 'in relation to the first Rome, this is the second', a line that must surely be lifted verbatim from some Constantinopolitan text. In this extravagant way Bishop Giric, who lies behind this legend, sought to establish the metropolitan credentials of twelfth-century Cennrígmonaid.[37] Broun has pointed, at least preliminarily, to papal recognition of York's claim to supremacy over Scotia in the last decades of the eleventh century as the probable impetus for such a bold counter-claim.[38]

York was dedicated to St Peter by Bede's day, and the establishment of an Andrean 'invent-a-cult' at Cennrígmonaid c.1100 could make sense, establishing 'St Andrews' as Constantinople to York's Rome.[39] However, from the all-important papal perspective there must have been something of the junior partner about St Andrew mobilised in this manner, whether at Constantinople or at Cennrígmonaid. A similar perspective may have obtained in twelfth-century Britain. Having parted company with his first English appointee to the see of St Andrews for persisting in regarding himself as a suffragan of York, Alexander I made a second appointment in 1120. The bishop-elect Eadmer of Canterbury arranged for the date of his uptake of the see to fall upon the feast-day of St Peter and St Paul. Did Alexander take the same point that has been made here about the trumping of St Andrew by his brother? For no reason that seems to have been obvious to Eadmer, whose account survives, the king refused the new bishop the

[35] Stephen, *V. Sanct. Wilfrithi*, § 26.

[36] D. H. Farmer, *The Oxford Dictionary of Saints* (4th edn, Oxford, 1997), 21. See also Hall, *St Andrew*, 28–9, who questions the earliness of the Roman dimension.

[37] Broun, 'Church of St Andrews', 111. This section of the recovered text is not in Skene's edition.

[38] Broun, 'Church of St Andrews', 113.

[39] Ash and Broun, 'Adoption of St Andrew', 21–2, though the argument here is that the adoption of St Andrew as patron saint dates from this period, not that the cult itself does.

pastoral staff and the ring of office, and no homage was done. On the next day Eadmer confirmed the king's fears, revealing that St Andrews was to his mind a suffragan of Canterbury. Furious, Alexander restored the see to custodianship, refused to allow Eadmer to assume the episcopate or to seek consecration elsewhere, and, as Eadmer relates, embarked upon a campaign of bullying and intimidation that saw Eadmer return to Canterbury in 1121.[40] This chain of events seems to confirm that a Petrine 'invent-a-cult' would have served Bishop Giric far better than an Andrean one. It therefore seems likely that the Andrean dedication at Cennrígmonaid was not an invention of the twelfth century, but something not altogether convenient that was already established by then. As we have seen, the presence of significant relics at Cennrígmonaid by the middle of the tenth century is confirmed by Áed's pilgrimage to the place from Ireland in 965.[41] Further circumstantial evidence, in the form of the accession to the Pictish kingship of a Custantín in 789, has been adduced to suggest that the Andrean cult had been imported in the middle of the eighth century, when Byzantium was ruled by the iconoclastic Constantine V (741–75).[42] And then there is that bewildering sixteenth-century dating of the coming of Andrew's relics to 761.

With all this in mind, the relationship of our two major Andrean dedications in Anglo-Saxon England with certain Petrine ones may be further instructive in exploring the possibility that the Andrean dedication at Cennrígmonaid belongs to the eighth century. Sub-Roman East Kent and West Kent are quite distinct archaeologically, and it has been shown that, in fact, Bede's *regnum Cantuariorum* was 'an amalgam of two kingdoms that had once been distinct', and continued to reflect such diphyletic origins, in the form of joint kingships, into the eighth century.[43] The famous Kentish origin story in which the kingdom was founded by two brothers, Hengist and Horsa, surely reflects the same bipartite political reality.[44] The diphyletic character of this *regnum* is also reflected by the very early establishment of separate sees in Kent at Canterbury in the east, and Rochester in the west. At Canterbury, Augustine dedicated his episcopal church to Christ, but he also founded an influential monastery outside the city, and the church there was

40 See for example Duncan, *Scotland*, 130–1. For Eadmer's version of events, see Eadmer, *Historia Novorum*; A. O. Anderson, *Scottish Annals from English Chroniclers A.D. 500 to 1286* (London, 1908), 138–42.

41 Taylor, 'Coming of the Augustinians', 120–1, shows that the twelfth-century 'Augustinian Account' from Cennrígmonaid, half a century later in date than Version A of the foundation legend, approached the matter of the see's supremacy rather differently, but with no less conviction.

42 Ash and Broun, 'Adoption of St Andrew', 17–18; building on Smyth, *Warlords*, 187, whose attention, however, remained fixed on the ninth century.

43 N. Brooks, 'The Creation and Early Structure of the Kingdom of Kent', in S. Bassett (ed.), *The Origins of Anglo-Saxon Kingdoms* (London and New York, 1989), 55–74, at 68–9; see also B. Yorke, *Kings and Kingdoms of Early Anglo-Saxon England* (London and New York, 1990), 27, 32–4.

44 Bede, *HE*, i.15. Bede's equation of Æthelbert's ancestor Oeric with Oisc, the eponymous ancestors of the Oiscingas (*ibid.*, ii.5), may further reflect a bipartite kingdom rationalising itself as a single polity, here using a different pseudo-historical strategy to link the descendants of Hengist and Oisc. For discussion of this material, see Brooks, 'Creation and Early Structure of the Kingdom of Kent', 58–64.

dedicated to St Peter and St Paul.[45] Then in 604 he established the see of Rochester in West Kent, and dedicated its episcopal church to St Andrew.[46] These two major dedications, separated by a significant political cleavage, thus seem to replicate the pattern observed between Rome and Constantinople, with the senior ecclesiastical centre bearing a Petrine dedication, and its most eminent counterpart on the other side of the cleavage bearing an Andrean one.

At Hexham the situation is more complex, but no less compelling as regards this pattern. As previously indicated, the church there was founded in the 670s by Wilfrid, who at the time was bishop of York. After 664 York was the chief church in Northumbria, another diphyletic Anglo-Saxon *regnum*, consisting of the mighty northern kingdom of Bernicia and the southern Deiran kingdom, within which York lay. Twenty years earlier, upon completing his ecclesiastical training abroad, Wilfrid had received Ripon in Yorkshire from Alchfrith, king of the Deirans. It was Wilfrid's first ecclesiastical foothold in the *regnum Nordanhymbrorum*; Stephen says, 'the door of this world was being opened wide [for him] by the Lord and by the holy apostle Peter'.[47] Here the hagiographer foreshadows Ripon's Petrine dedication. He informs us that this commemoration did not actually take place until some twenty years later, apparently not long before the foundation and dedication of Hexham.[48] Our understanding of this lengthy delay is clarified by Bede's prose *Vita Sancti Cuthberti*: Wilfrid was given an existing monastery at Ripon, which had been founded some years before by Ionan monks from Melrose, who had probably given their church some other dedication.[49] It was only when he had acquired the means as bishop to build a grand new church at Ripon that Wilfrid took the opportunity to commemorate St Peter there. Within a matter of years he had founded Hexham in Bernicia, and dedicated its grand church to St Andrew.

It may be noted in passing that Wilfrid may also have been responsible for the Petrine dedication at York itself. Stephen indicates that the church there was undergoing restoration by him at the same time as the new Petrine church was being built at Ripon. The hagiographer surely intended the restoration programme at York to be a metaphor for the bishop's restoration of the Northumbrian Church writ large to the orthodox condition it had enjoyed under Paulinus in the 620s, the Cantuarian missionary who had founded the church (and the Church).[50] Thus Stephen invokes that very memory here: the church was 'first founded by St Paulinus the bishop and dedicated to God in the days of Edwini, once a most Christian king'. The hagiographer says *dedicatae Deo* here, but does not mention a Petrine dedication by Paulinus. It thus seems possible, given events at contemporary Ripon, that Wilfrid bestowed York's Petrine dedication himself, upon the restored church. As suited his hagiographical purpose, Stephen implied that the church (and so the Church) had been allowed to decay into ruin, but Bede says rather that Paulinus had not managed to complete the church. That had been the

45 Bede, *HE*, i.33.

46 Bede, *HE*, ii.3.

47 Stephen, *V. Sanct. Wilfrithi*, § 8.

48 Stephen, *V. Sanct. Wilfrithi*, § 17.

49 Bede, *Vita Sancti Cuthberti*, § 8; B. Colgrave (ed.), *Two* Lives *of Saint Cuthbert* (Cambridge, 1940).

50 Stephen, *V. Sanct. Wilfrithi*, § 16; on Paulinus's mission, see Bede, *HE*, *lib.* ii.

work of Oswald, whose ecclesiastical allegiances were Gaelic and Ionan.[51] This information may be historically true, but no doubt Bede had perceived Stephen's metaphor, and was speaking to that as well.

At any rate, the commemorative pattern at Ripon and Hexham again mirrors the relationship between Canterbury and Rochester, save in that neither Northumbrian monastery was an episcopal seat during Wilfrid's episcopate (though both became so soon afterwards). Rather, they derived their sense of linkage, as well as their relative senior and junior status, as houses within the Wilfridian monastic *familia*. Petrine Ripon was Wilfrid's first monastery and his first abbatial appointment; he was ordained a priest there, and skulked there after being denied the see of York in the 660s.[52] Stephen placed him at Ripon for the receipt of extensive royal donations of land, establishing hagiographically that the saint's eventual expulsion from York in no way sullied his claim to these lands in later years.[53] It was Ripon alone that the Northumbrian Church-in-council could be persuaded to restore to the expelled Wilfrid's keeping after much negotiation in the first years of the eighth century.[54] As he approached death a few years later, it was Ripon's treasury that Wilfrid opened in order to distribute alms.[55] He also took great care (and with some ceremony) to name his successor at Ripon, and it was there that he was buried after his death in Mercia.[56] Stephen's recourse to original documents in *Vita Sancti Wilfrithi* demonstrates that not all of this is hagiographical hindsight associated with the place of the saint's burial, nor a function of the hagiographer's chauvinism regarding his own monastery. There can be little doubt that Ripon was for Wilfrid foremost among all the places he regarded as his own property. In Columban terms, it was, in effect, his Iona. Indeed, this fact presumably explains why *Vita Sancti Wilfrithi* was composed there, in which text Stephen likens the dedication of the church to the consecration of the temple by Solomon.[57]

Like Ripon, Hexham was a royal foundation.[58] It seems, however, to have been neither as near nor as dear to Wilfrid's heart as Ripon. Although Stephen does say that the saint named his Hexham successor, as he had done for Ripon, he places this nomination not at Hexham itself, but rather on Wilfrid's death-bed in Mercia, and some time after Ripon had been bequeathed as part of an elaborate private ceremony. In addition, *Vita Sancti Wilfrithi* makes no mention of any bequests made from Hexham's treasury; instead, the abbot there receives a bequest from Ripon's

51 Bede, *HE*, ii.14.

52 Stephen, *V. Sanct. Wilfrithi*, §§ 8–9, 14. It is acknowledged here that, in fact, Wilfrid was frequently (and perhaps almost entirely) in Mercia in this period.

53 Stephen, *V. Sanct. Wilfrithi*, § 17. For explicit land-claims surrounding Ripon, see *ibid.*, § 45; see also M. Roper, 'Wilfrid's Landholdings in Northumbria', in D. P. Kirby (ed.), *Saint Wilfrid at Hexham* (Newcastle, 1974), 61–79, at 63.

54 Stephen, *V. Sanct. Wilfrithi*, § 47.

55 Stephen, *V. Sanct. Wilfrithi*, § 63.

56 Stephen, *V. Sanct. Wilfrithi*, §§ 63, 66.

57 Stephen, *V. Sanct. Wilfrithi*, § 17. For a discussion of the centrality of Ripon to Wilfrid, albeit with a different emphasis, see R. L. Poole, 'St. Wilfrid and the See of Ripon', *EHR* 34 (1919), 1–24.

58 Stephen, *V. Sanct. Wilfrithi*, § 22. It was donated by Queen Aeðilthryð, wife of Ecgfrith. For discussion, see Roper, 'Wilfrid's Landholdings', 72–4.

treasury.[59] Nevertheless, Stephen provided a due sense of connection between them, not least by describing the magnificence of the two churches built under Wilfrid's episcopal direction. The junior and senior status of Andrean Hexham and Petrine Ripon respectively within the Wilfridian *familia* thus seems to replicate the pattern we have noted for Andrean Rochester and Petrine Canterbury in Kent. The parallel is intensified, moreover, by the fact that Ripon and Hexham lay to either side of Northumbria's diphyletic cleavage, the one in the Deiran kingdom, and the other in Bernicia.

Destiny had in store for Northumbria's major Petrine and Andrean dedications at York and Hexham respectively a still closer parallel with Kent. At the Synod of Whitby in 664, Wilfrid's episcopal seat at York had been confirmed as the foremost church in the whole of the Northumbrian province, and indeed, if Stephen is to be believed, as the metropolitan seat for the whole of northern Britain.[60] Wilfrid's Andrean church at Hexham became the second-rank church in the Northumbrian province after he was expelled from York in 678 by Archbishop Theodore of Canterbury. The archbishop now established separate sees for the Bernicians and the Deirans, and elevated Hexham to episcopal status as the seat of the former, York being maintained as the seat of the Deiran see.[61] With this act Archbishop Theodore fully brought about between the two dominant churches in the *regnum Nordanhymbrorum* the same pattern we have observed in the *regnum Cantuariorum* after 604, and indeed at Rome and Constantinople.[62]

There were a great many (more than twenty) Petrine dedications of Anglo-Saxon churches in the seventh century. Andrean ones were not confined to the churches mentioned here, but they were much rarer than Petrine ones (less than ten), so that the prominence of these examples seems notable.[63] The perceptible commemorative pattern, in which three different Continentally minded bishops linked the senior or dominant ecclesiastical centre within a province to a Petrine dedication, and the most eminent of its suffragan centres to an Andrean one, offers something of an explanation. An important additional facet of this putative pattern is that the junior partner was often located on the other side of a major political cleavage within the province. With this pattern in mind, its three independent examples in Augustine's Kent, the Wilfridian monastic *familia* and Theodore's

59 Stephen, *V. Sanct. Wilfrithi*, §§ 63, 65.

60 Stephen, *V. Sanct. Wilfrithi*, § 16. That Stephen is to be believed was argued by M. Gibbs, 'The Decrees of Agatho and the Gregorian Plan for York', *Speculum* 48 (1973), 213–46. For more recent reflections on the evidence, see T. M. Charles-Edwards, *Early Christian Ireland* (Cambridge, 2000), 431–2; J. E. Fraser, ' "All the Northern Part of Britain": The Metropolitan Episcopate of Wilfrid of York, 669–78', in D. Petts and S. Turner (eds), *Early Medieval Northumbria: Recent Research and New Directions* (Turnhout, forthcoming).

61 Bede, *HE*, iv.12; Stephen, *V. Sanct. Wilfrithi*, § 24.

62 Gibbs, 'Decrees of Agatho', 229, argued that Wilfrid had intended all along that Hexham should become an episcopal seat.

63 Hall, *St Andrew*, 38–9. Stephen, *V. Sanct. Wilfrithi*, § 65, informs us that Wilfrid's monastery at Oundle in Mercia had a church dedicated to Andrew.

Northumbria (not to mention Rome and Constantinople), we may return at last to the question of Cennrígmonaid in the eighth century.[64]

In returning to Cennrígmonaid in the reign of the first Onuist son of Vurguist, it must be stated at the outset that we move into the realm of informed conjecture, or perhaps informed expectation. The *regnum Pictorum* in this period was envisioned by Bede, at least, as diphyletic, or at least bipartite like Kent and Northumbria had been, with northern and southern Pictish zones boasting different ecclesiastical histories.[65] If it were possible to prove that the Pictish kings and ecclesiastical leaders of the early eighth century were conscious of the commemorative pattern in question, one could expect that, having embraced Continental reforms c.715, they might have established a dedication to St Peter at their most senior and eminent episcopal church, and, in the other half of Pictavia, they might have dedicated the most senior and eminent episcopal church to St Andrew.[66] Were they conscious of Anglo-Saxon, or indeed Northumbrian commemorative patterns? We cannot know the answer to this question, but there are two suggestive pieces of evidence.

The first has to do with royal chapels. According to Bede, there was one at the principal royal stronghold of the Bernician kings at Bamburgh, dedicated to St Peter.[67] The parish of Duffus on the Moray coast, containing the massive Pictish promontory fort of Burghead, was dedicated to St Peter, as was Ogstoun, the adjoining parish to the east. Archaeology suggests moreover that a chapel had been established at Burghead by the eighth century,[68] and Alasdair Ross has found onomastic evidence that 'a very important pre-parochial mother church' stood somewhere in Duffus parish in the earlier medieval period.[69] Of course, that Burghead was the principal royal stronghold of the kings of Fortriu is nothing more than inference.[70] Isabel and George Henderson have likened the quality of ornamentation on Pictish ecclesiastical sculpture from nearby Kinneddar with the best examples at the major ecclesiastical centres at Portmahomack and St Andrews.[71] What is more, St Andrews and Kinneddar share an image in common

64 Other examples of the pattern, in different times and places, have been kindly brought to my attention by different audiences at oral presentations of this research, but need not detain us.

65 Bede, *HE*, iii.4.

66 That the foundation of Cennrígmonaid represented the replication of a Northumbrian pattern occurred to Skene, 'Notice of the Early Ecclesiastical Settlements', 313, though his conception of the circumstances was rather different from the one presented here. See also Hall, *St Andrew*, 58, 65–6, who envisioned the Andrean cult being introduced 'in development of, even in rivalry with, a cult of St Peter in Pictland'.

67 Bede, *HE*, iii.6.

68 I. Ralston, *The Hill-Forts of Pictland Since 'The Problem of the Picts'* (Groam House Lecture, 2004), 31.

69 A. Ross, pers. comm., to whom I am very grateful for this information from his unpublished PhD thesis.

70 That the *regnum Fortrenn* lay in northern Pictland, and not south of the Mounth as long surmised, has been comprehensively shown by A. Woolf, 'Dún Nechtain, Fortriu and the Geography of the Picts', *SHR* 85 (2006), 182–201, at 188–200.

71 G. Henderson and I. Henderson, *The Art of the Picts: Sculpture and Metalwork in Early Medieval Scotland* (London, 2004), 49, 130, 203, 216, 218.

of King David rending the jaws of a lion, which Thomas Charles-Edwards has shown to have imperial overtones redolent of precocious high-kingship.[72] However likely, it nevertheless remains conjecture that Burghead was the Bamburgh of the *regnum Pictorum*, and more so that the Petrine dedication of the parish dates from Pictish times. Even if these propositions are accepted, we have no way of determining whether the situation at Bamburgh was being emulated.

Our second suggestive piece of evidence that Pictish leaders were aware of Northumbrian commemorative patterns is furnished by Bede. One of the few things we know about the Pictish reformation (*correctio*) implemented by the Pictish king Naiton son of Der-Ilei c.715 is that, having embraced reform, the king undertook to build a new church somewhere in his kingdom, and to bestow upon it a dedication to St Peter.[73] At best this knowledge establishes only half the desired pattern – hardly decisive where a pattern has only two components! What is more, it does so only if we assume that the Petrine church in question was built at the predominant episcopal seat in the Pictish kingdom. In the *regnum Cantuariorum* the Petrine church was established in East Kent, the dominant part of the kingdom at the time of Augustine.[74] If this also happened in the *regnum Pictorum*, we now know to look for such a seat c.715 in the northern Pictish zone. It need not have happened, however. In Bernician-dominated Northumbria after 664, the dominant Petrine church was established in Deira, at York, the seniority of which church was unimpeachable. Famously, Bede informs us from Pictish sources that the southern Pictish zone received Christianity before the (dominant) northern one did, allowing for the possibility that here, as in Northumbria, the senior ecclesiastical centre was reckoned to lie within the junior kingdom of the diphyletic *regnum*.[75]

There are hints that Hexham sought to beef up its status in Northumbria in the face of York's exalted historic position. For example, it associated itself quite intimately with the cult of the martyr-king St Oswald. Bede described pilgrimages by the monks at Hexham to nearby Heavenfield on Hadrian's Wall, to the wooden cross that was said to have been put up there a century earlier by Oswald, as he said his prayers before his victory at Hexham, which brought him to power in 634. The Hexham community also held a vigil at Heavenfield on St Oswald's Eve, and eventually built a church there dedicated to the martyr-king.[76] Oswald, the son of a Bernician father and a Deiran mother, was credited by Bede with the unification of Northumbria;[77] at Hexham he had secured the liberty (and future greatness) of the Bernicians, as well as their christianisation under his auspices. One could certainly appreciate how his cult, presided over by Hexham, may have been infused with a 'national' flavour. If the dominant episcopal see in Pictavia was not in Fortriu, the

72 T. M. Charles-Edwards, ' "The Continuation of Bede", *s.a.* 750: High-kings, Kings of Tara and "Bretwaldas" ', in A. P. Smyth (ed.), *Seanchas: Studies in Early and Medieval Irish Archaeology, History and Literature in Honour of Francis J. Byrne* (Dublin, 1999), 137–45, at 142–3. Intriguingly, Duffus was given by David I to the Fleming Freskin, who built there Moray's greatest motte, and whose family took the name *de Moravia* 'as a sign that they were greatest in that land', Duncan, *Scotland*, 189.

73 Bede, *HE*, v.21.

74 Yorke, *Kings and Kingdoms*, 27, discusses the relative status of East and West Kent.

75 Bede, *HE*, iii.4.

76 Bede, *HE*, iii.2.

77 Bede, *HE*, iii.6.

main Verturian church could have made similar attempts – perhaps with the cult of St Columba – to compensate for its junior status.

We have a slight indication that the most powerful bishop in Pictland in the early eighth century was, however, based in Fortriu like the dominant kings. Adomnán's *Lex innocentium* of 697 was endorsed by the *rex Pictorum*, Naiton's brother and predecessor Bridei, and by two Pictish bishops, Curetán and Cóeti, the latter being bishop of Iona.[78] These two men would appear to have been the chief bishops of the Picts in 697.[79] Curetán is *Curitanus sanctus episcopus et abbas Ruis Mind Bairend* in the Martyrology of Tallaght, but later martyrologies show that two separate commemorations are combined here. These later texts are probably mistaken, however, in naming the second saint commemorated here as Barrfind; it is surely Menn Bairenn instead, an abbot of Aghaboe who died in 695 (*quies Minn Bairenn abbatis Achaid Bo*).[80] Setting his commemoration aside leaves Curetán as *episcopus et abbas Ruis*, bishop and abbot of Ross (*Ros*).

Early Ross seems to have excluded Wester Ross and to have extended from the River Beauly west of Inverness to the Tarbat peninsula, where in the 1990s the remains of an Early Historic monastery were discovered. One might have imagined that Ross took its name from that great peninsula, Scottish Gaelic *ros* usually referring to a promontory. However, William Watson observed that promontories take the article in Gaelic (*an ros*), and concluded that the name was probably borrowed from Pictish British, and denoted a moor (*rhos* in modern Welsh).[81] The place-name Fortrose in the Black Isle seems to denote 'lower Ross', implying that the *rhos* or moor in question was the Black Isle. Thus Watson contrasted the flat plain of *Machair Rois* with the Black Isle, 'sloping gently to both firths' that define that peninsula.[82] Having decided that the Black Isle was the moor from which Ross took its name, Watson proposed that Fortrose, 'lower Ross', may have been a name given 'to a part of the [*rhos*], in contradistinction' to Rosemarkie, *Ros Maircnidh*, also in the Black Isle and associated with a burn-name.[83] This place-name evidence is striking for our purposes, for it was with Rosemarkie that Curetán, bishop of Ross, was associated by his medieval cult. His see may be thought to have encompassed the Black Isle in heart of Fortriu, and to have had its seat at Rosemarkie, which has produced Pictish ecclesiastical sculpture. Even more striking is the fact that Rosemarkie, on this evidence the chief episcopal

78 M. Ní Dhonnchadha, 'The Guarantor List of Cáin Adomnáin, 697', *Peritia* 1 (1982), 178–215, at 191, 214 (and §§ 21, 22 and 91 of the list).

79 That Iona was regarded in Pictland as a Pictish monastery is revealed by Bede, *HE*, iii.4; for further discussion, see Fraser, *From Caledonia to Pictland*, forthcoming. For Walahfrid Strabo's description of Iona as *insula Pictorum* in the ninth century, see T. O. Clancy, 'Iona in the Kingdom of the Picts: A Note', *IR* 55 (2004), 73–6.

80 R. I. Best and H. J. Lawlor (eds), *The Martyrology of Tallaght* (Henry Bradshaw Society 68: London, 1931), 24; *AU* 695.3. The abbot's name means 'halidom of Barrfind'. I am grateful to Gilbert Márkus for discussing this evidence with me.

81 W. J. Watson, *Place-Names of Ross and Cromarty* (Inverness, 1904), xxi.

82 *Ibid.*, xi, 128–9.

83 *Ibid.*, xi, 128–9; Watson, *Celtic Place-Names*, 441. Watson suggests in the latter work that the Gaelic burn-names *Marcaidh* and *Maircnidh* reflect Welsh *Marchnant*, 'horse burn'. I have profited from discussing this evidence with Alex Woolf and Simon Taylor.

church in the northern Pictish zone, bore a Petrine dedication. Here again there are problems, however. We may accept that Curetán's seat was at Rosemarkie, but we cannot be certain of the date of its Petrine dedication. To suggest that King Naiton built his new Petrine church at Rosemarkie because it was the dominant episcopate in the Pictish kingdom is perfectly plausible, but involves adding a few more fragile threads to the web that has been constructed with regard to the tantalising Burghead evidence. It makes good sense of the evidence we have, but even the most orderly cobweb is easily swept away. It would be helpful if we could trust the fifteenth-century testimony of Andrew of Wyntoun, who observed in his chronicle, under the year 716, that Naiton 'foundit' Rosemarkie in Ross:

> Sewyn hundyr wyntyr and sexteyn
> Qwhen lichtar was þe Uirgyne cleyn ...
> Nettan Derlynge þan regnande
> Our þe Peychtis in Scotlande.
> In Rosse he foundit Rosmarkyn,
> Þat dowit was withe kyngis syne,
> And made was a plasse chathedralle
> Be northe Murrawe seweralle.[84]

We are therefore left with 'what ifs'. If Naiton's Petrine church was built in Fortriu, perhaps at Rosemarkie, and if he and his advisors were aware of our commemorative pattern and sought to emulate it – both plausible enough as propositions, given our evidence – we would expect an Andrean dedication at the most prominent church in southern Pictland. The two versions of the St Andrews foundation legend give us a candidate at Cennrígmonaid, crediting its foundation to a king who bore the name of Naiton's successor and avenger, Onuist son of Vurguist.[85] There are faint indications that the place was significant during Naiton's reign as a base of operations for Ionan clergy.[86] As William Skene first perceived, aspects of the foundation legend smack of this Onuist's genuine historical context, while Ash and Broun have fortified the claim of Version B that a

84 Andrew of Wyntoun, *Original Chronicle*, v.14, lines 5797–5808 (MS Cott); F. J. Amours (ed.), *The Original Chronicle of Andrew of Wyntoun*, IV (Edinburgh and London, 1906). The main versions of this complex chronicle go on to confuse matters by dating 'þis fundacion' to c.600, but material in two MSS shows that this earlier date, extracted from Bonifacian hagiography, belongs to Restenneth, not to Rosemarkie.

85 The notion of the twinning of Cennrígmonaid with a church in the north calls to mind the Scottish origin story in the Life of St Catroe of Metz, in which the Scots settle in Ross, whence they proceed to occupy 'the cities of *Rigmonath* and *Bellethor*, situated far apart' (Anderson, *Early Sources* 1, 44n). Just as *Rigmonath* signifies Cennrígmonaid, *Bellethor* must signify the *palacium Cinnbelachoir* where Domnall mac Ailpín died in April 862 (*Chronicle of the Kings of Alba*, § 9; Anderson, *Kings and Kingship*, 149–53; King-list D, *ibid.*, 267, says he died *in Rathinueramon*). It has been suggested that this palatial monastery be placed at the head of the Pass of Ballater on Deeside, and identified with Tullich, where the church bore a dedication to St Nechtan, probably a Pictish abbot who died in 678 [*AU* 679.4; T. O. Clancy, 'Deer and the Early Church in the North-East', in K. Forsyth (ed.), *This Splendid Little Book: Studies in the Book of Deer* (Dublin, forthcoming)].

86 S. Taylor, 'Place-Names and the Early Church in Eastern Scotland', in B. E. Crawford (ed.), *Scotland in Dark Age Britain* (St Andrews, 1996), 93–110, at 98–100.

version of the legend was composed for a Pictish king in the middle of the ninth century,[87] when its author's distance from this Onuist was no greater than Bede's from the Synod of Whitby. We know that Cennrígmonaid had been founded by the middle of Onuist's reign, and, as we have seen, the Pictish monumental sculpture recovered from it shows the monastery to have been a major centre with royal connections.[88] In addition, of course, the archdeaconry of St Andrews, as it becomes documented in the twelfth and thirteenth centuries, extended from the Firth of Forth to the Mounth, the two frontiers of the southern Pictish zone known to Bede.

This final assemblage of evidence of varying quality sits very well alongside the general proposition that, as a result of the Pictish *correctio* c.715, a new church was built at the northern episcopal seat at Rosemarkie and dedicated to St Peter, and that an Andrean dedication followed at Cennrígmonaid, perhaps with a new church building as well. This proposition is in line with the commemorative pattern outlined above, with its two Northumbrian examples just across the frontier from Pictavia. The leap of faith involved in accepting such a proposition may not be great, but remains a leap all the same. The case is circumstantial, and proof is distinctly lacking at various key points, apart from striking notices in two late medieval vernacular chronicles of uncertain value. In the final analysis, at best this paper can but nudge what might have been true – an hypothesis already accepted by many – another rung or two up the ladder of likelihood.[89] At the very least, it seems that an eighth-century dedication to St Andrew at Cennrígmonaid is not just far from an impossibility, but could in fact make a great deal of sense.

87 Skene, 'Notice of the Early Ecclesiastical Settlements', 308–9; Ash and Broun, 'Adoption of St Andrew', 19–20. Skene associated Hungus's son Owen in this legend with *Ougen rex Pictorum*, whose obit s.a. 736 occurs in *Annales Cambriae*; E. Faral (ed.), *La Légende Arthurienne: études et documents*, 3 (Paris, 1929), 44–50. In addition, he called attention (pp. 313–15) to the exile of Acca, bishop of Hexham, after 732, and proposed that he fled to Pictland and established a new see at Cennrígmonaid. A modified version of these thoughts was put forward in W. F. Skene, *Celtic Scotland: a history of ancient Alban*, Vol. II: Church and Culture (2nd edn, Edinburgh, 1887), 261–75, especially 272–4. Skene's hypothesis gained popular currency [e.g. R. K. Hannay, *St Andrew of Scotland* (Edinburgh and London, 1934), 29]. It was rejected by I. Henderson, *The Picts* (London, 1967), 87, and cited without enthusiasm by A. Macquarrie, *The Saints of Scotland: Essays in Scottish Church History AD 450–1093* (Edinburgh, 1997), 182–3, but more recently has been embraced by Woolf, 'Onuist son of Uurguist', 38.

88 For discussion of the sculpture, see for example L. Alcock, *Kings and Warriors, Craftsmen and Priests in Northern Britain AD 550–850* (Edinburgh, 2003), 229; Henderson and Henderson, *Art of the Picts*, 129–30, 192–3.

89 For example, Woolf, 'Onuist son of Uurguist', 37–8, where a case is outlined that is further suggestive – circumstantially – of an eighth-century foundation.

2

THE CULTS OF SAINTS PATRICK AND PALLADIUS IN EARLY MEDIEVAL SCOTLAND

Thomas Owen Clancy

The two churchmen who stand 'at the door of Irish history' have received much scholarly attention over the years, amounting to a sizeable sub-discipline within Irish history and Celtic studies.[1] The two are mirror images one of the other: for Patrick we possess his own impressive and moving words, from the twin documents called the Confession and the Letter to Coroticus.[2] He is the earliest insular churchman for whom we can frame any real biographical and personal detail. Alas, this is unmatched by any chronological security, or contemporary documents external to his own writings, and the historical and autobiographical Patrick thus floats relatively free in a troubled sea of time that includes most of the fifth century. Palladius is the opposite. To some extent, he is merely a chronological datum, fixed in time, but otherwise disembodied. In AD 431, according to Prosper of Aquitaine, the bishop Palladius was sent to be the first bishop of the Irish Christians. We know little more than this, although recent work, especially by Thomas Charles-Edwards and Dáibhí Ó Cróinín, has helped to flesh out his world and the anti-Pelagian context of his mission, and Ó Cróinín has made a convincing case for identifying with Palladius a historical character in an important early fifth-century poem, which reveals something of his (misspent?) youth and background.[3]

For all the uncertainties surrounding Ireland's Christian foundations, Scotland can feel entitled to a bit of righteous jealousy. The evidence for these two, and what

1 For useful summaries, see David N. Dumville *et al.*, *Saint Patrick, A.D. 493–1993* (Woodbridge, 1993); Thomas Charles-Edwards, *Early Christian Ireland* (Cambridge, 2000), 202–33.

2 Numerous editions and translations exist. The most readily accessible are A. B. E. Hood, *St Patrick: His Writings and Muirchu's Life* (Chichester, 1978); Thomas O'Loughlin, *St Patrick, The Man and His Works* (London, 1999); see also Ludwig Bieler and Fergus Kelly, *The Patrician Texts in the Book of Armagh* (Dublin, 1979).

3 T. M. Charles-Edwards, 'Palladius, Prosper, and Leo the Great: Mission and Primatial Authority', in Dumville, *Saint Patrick*, 1–12; *idem*, *Early Christian Ireland*, 202–14; D. Ó Cróinín, 'New light on Palladius', *Peritia* 5 (1986), 276–83; *idem*, 'Who was Palladius "First Bishop of the Irish"?', *Peritia* 14 (2000), 205–37.

it reveals, is certainly much more than we know about anything contemporarily in Scotland. At some point in the middle ages, scholars put that righteous jealousy into action, and brought both these churchmen into contact with Scotland in writings about them. These writings have tended to fall victim to the perennial attitude towards hagiography in modern Scottish historiography, which views it as a quarry for historical facts. In this context, the claim made in lives of St Patrick that his birthplace was near Dumbarton has been noticed, but even while acknowledging that the list of candidates for Patrick's birthplace is inexhaustible, and establishing even a good short-list implausible, few would support its historicity, and so it is passed over fairly quickly. The claim in the same lives of St Patrick that Palladius died in the land of the Picts, and had a chapel dedicated to him at Fordoun in the Mearns, has, not unreasonably, tended to be dismissed as a late fabrication, on the presumption that it is a late confusion of the meaning of 'Scots', in the 431 entry on Palladius's mission *ad Scottos in Christum credentes*.[4] Thus in the one case these traditions have gained a certain respectability in scholarly circles, and in the other have received little attention at all.

To date no one has seemed interested in exactly why hagiographical traditions about Patrick and Palladius were claiming a connection with regions in northern Britain, nor in establishing when to any satisfaction, still less in the significance of these claims. I would like to rectify this situation in what follows.[5]

The sources

It is possible to gain a fairly precise sense of when northern British data enters the traditions of Patrick and Palladius, or at least, a sense of when it was not there, and perhaps one can suggest some of the circumstances for the creation of some of this material. The starting point here must be the Life of Patrick composed by Muirchú maccu Machthéni c.700.[6] We must presuppose that at some time in the seventh century, churchmen of Patrick's churches had gained hold of Prosper of Aquitaine's account of Palladius as first bishop of the Irish believing in Christ, and had to square this with their own traditions concerning Patrick as apostle of Ireland. In Muirchú's Life, he disposed of the awkward figure of Palladius, 'first bishop of the Irish', by making him unpopular in Ireland upon his arrival. Through God's will, no one would listen to Palladius, or believe in Christ, and so he set off for his homeland, but never got there:

> Revertente vero eo hinc et primo mari transito coeptoque terrarum itenere in [Pictorum] finibus vita functus est.

4 For example, A. Boyle, 'Notes on Scottish Saints', *IR* 32 (1981), 59–82, at 71.

5 I should note that a brief summary of what follows concerning Palladius appeared as part of the discussion in T. O. Clancy, 'Scotland, the "Nennian" Recension of the *Historia Brittonum*, and the *Lebor Bretnach*', in *Kings, Clerics and Chronicles in Scotland, 500–1297. Studies in Honour of Marjorie Ogilvie Anderson on the Occasion of her 90th Birthday* (Dublin, 2000), 87–107, at 95–7.

6 Hood, *St Patrick*, 64, 85 for the sections on Palladius, and see 78 for variant readings, including the main reading *Pictorum* against the Book of Armagh's *Britonum*, which I have supplied in the quote below.

[But on his return journey from here, after making the first sea crossing and proceeding by land, he died in the land of the [Picts].[7]]

It may be, as has been suggested, that Muirchú here transmuted data that had described Palladius returning to Gaul and dying in the region of the Poitou (*Pictonia*).[8] In the Book of Armagh, c.800, uncertainty about this description led the scribes to write *in Britonum finibus* instead.[9] That other scholars around 800, in possession of Muirchú's Life, were still prepared to believe in Palladius dying in Pictland is revealed by the text in Latin, written in Wales in AD 829/30, called *Historia Brittonum*. There, the tradition that Palladius died *in terra Pictorum* is repeated in all the early recensions.[10]

Muirchú's influential text was thus a starting point for traditions connecting Palladius to the Pictish regions of Scotland; he may also be the partial (if perhaps inadvertent) originator of the idea that Patrick was born in the region of Dumbarton. Problems with the manuscript transmission of the relevant chapter of the Life prevent absolute certainty about the form of the name he gave, but it is clear that Muirchú was confident that he could identify the town in which Patrick says he was born (*Bannavem Taburniae*) with a town not far from the Irish Sea called, perhaps *Ventre*, but more likely *Nemthor*. As Francis John Byrne notes, 'All the indirect witnesses to Muirchú's text point conclusively to *Nemtor* or *Nemthor*' as having been the form in Muirchú's original, and certainly the eighth-century hymn *Génair Pátraicc i nNemthur*, and all subsequent Irish expansions of Muirchú's Life, thought this was the form (and not *Ventre*, on which most of the effort at identification has been expended).[11] Nowhere in Muirchú, however, is the direct impression given that Patrick had come from the region around Dumbarton – merely that Muirchú knew he had come from a place now called Nemthor.

The material from Muirchú is somewhat jejune. Rather startling then is the development of both these traditions by, at the latest, c.1000 (but plausibly, as we shall see, in the eighth and ninth centuries). In texts subsequent to Muirchú, Nemthor, Patrick's putative birthplace, is identified as being in the region of Strathclyde, and the vague references to Palladius's death among the Picts crystallise into his death and enshrining at Fordoun. This material has generally been investigated from the Irish end, and the manner in which the traditions relating to Scotland have been augmented has not been of much interest.[12] But as we shall

7 *ibid.*, and see L. Bieler, 'The Mission of Palladius: A Comparative Study of Sources', *Traditio* 6 (1948), 1–32, at 31. This article helpfully reviews the Palladian tradition in Irish texts and gives in an Appendix (27–32) the relevant texts; this is to some extent replicated in Dumville, *Saint Patrick*, 65–84.

8 Ó Cróinín, 'Who was Palladius?', 237.

9 Bieler, 'Mission of Palladius', 31; Dumville, *Saint Patrick*, 67.

10 Dumville, *St Patrick*, 221–32 (at 223, 227, 230).

11 F. J. Byrne and P. Francis, 'Two Lives of Saint Patrick', *Journal of the Royal Society of Antiquaries of Ireland* 124 (1994), 5–117, at 69. There is a discussion at 68–70 that outlines the historiographical and textual arguments regarding this place-name, and references to earlier literature on the subject may be found there. Byrne's important point concerning the underlying form has not been sufficiently noticed.

12 For some comment, see Boyle, 'Notes', 71; A. Macquarrie, 'Lives of the Saints in the

see, both traditions can provide important contributions towards our understanding the development of the church, and saints' cults, in Scotland.

The main texts that develop these traditions all seem to be linked in some fashion, but the relationship among them has proved to be difficult to pin down.[13] Two Latin Lives of Patrick, generally called *Vita II* and *Vita IV* (the numbers given by John Colgan in *Acta Sanctorum*), and another Life, largely in Irish with Latin admixture, generally called the 'Tripartite Life' (these three Lives ultimately going back to a common original), all include augmented traditions about Patrick's birthplace and childhood, and the place of Palladius's death.[14] They are joined in this by the scholiastic glosses on the eighth-century Old Irish hymn *Génair Patraicc i nNemthur* ('Patrick was born in Nemthor').[15] This hymn is essentially a verse retelling of Muirchú's Life, and is found in the two manuscripts of the Irish *Liber Hymnorum*, dating to the eleventh century. The glosses on the hymn are close to the three later Lives in the information they relate, though not so close that clear dependence can be shown either way text to text, and other explanations may need to be sought for their relationship. The dates of the Lives after Muirchú are somewhat contentious. The *Vita II* is found in a manuscript of the mid-eleventh century; the *Vita IV* in a manuscript of c.1100, although since that manuscript is not the original, it must have originated at an earlier date. The manuscripts of the Tripartite Life are not very old, but the language is a mixture of Old and Middle Irish, and so it belongs to somewhat the same period as our other texts.[16] We may

Aberdeen Breviary: Some Problems of Sources for Strathclyde Saints', *RSCHS* 26 (1996), 31–54, at 44–50. Simon Taylor has recently reviewed the evidence for Patrick in 'The Early History and Languages of West Dunbartonshire', in *Changing Identities, Ancient Roots. The History of West Dunbartonshire from Earliest Times*, ed. Ian Brown (Edinburgh, 2006), 12–41.

13 The pioneer at trying to construct a stemma for the Patrician texts was Ludwig Bieler, especially in his introduction to *Four Latin Lives of St Patrick* (Dublin, 1971), and his article 'Bethu Phátraic. Versuch einer Grundlegung des Verhältnisses der iriscchen Patriciusviten zu den lateinischen', *Anzeiger der österreichischen Akademie der Wissenschaften*, philosophisch-historische Klasse 111 (1974), 251–73. For more recent attempts, see the detailed discussion of Byrne and Francis, 'Two Latin Lives', and the more succinct summary of his understanding of the textual tradition by Thomas Charles-Edwards, *Early Christian Ireland*, 11–13. The discussions of both Macquarrie and Taylor (see n. 12 above) do not take sufficient account of the complexities of the textual tradition.

14 *Vita II* and *Vita IV* are edited in Bieler, *Four Latin Lives*, and translated with extensive notes and discussion by Byrne and Francis, 'Two Latin Lives'. The 'Tripartite Life' was edited and translated by Whitley Stokes, *The Tripartite Life of Patrick* (London, 1887). A more recent edition by Kathleen Mulchrone, *Bethu Phátraic. The Tripartite Life of Patrick* (Dublin, 1939) never received the planned second volume of translation and notes.

15 *The Irish Liber Hymnorum*, ed. and trans. J. H. Bernard and R. Atkinson, 2 vols (London, 1898), I.99; *Thesaurus Palaeo-Hibernicus*, ed. and trans. W. Stokes and J. Strachan, 2 vols (Cambridge, 1901–3), II.312–13.

16 For a not entirely satisfactory summary of the historiography relating to the 'Tripartite Life', see Dumville, *Saint Patrick*, 255–8. There has been considerable disagreement about the linguistic date of the text, and scholars have been divided over whether to prefer the historical or the linguistic evidence. Discussion has not been helped by

add to this the evidence from a translation of the *Historia Brittonum* made in Scotland before 1093, which also repeats the information about Palladius's death in Fordoun, and adds the detail that the location of this was in the Mearns.[17] Crucial to all this is the date of the Tripartite Life. Argument has gone on for over a century on this topic. Linguistic examination has led some to conclude that it belongs to the tenth or the eleventh century; but the historical reference-points in it, most particularly reference to an early precursor-kindred of the family that later became the powerful Dál Cais, suggest a date of around 900. The Dál Cais had coalesced, and acquired their name, by 934, the first annalistic reference to a king of theirs.

The most recent detailed study of these linked sources has concluded a number of things, not all of which I feel able to support, but cannot for the present improve on. Byrne and Francis argue for a date of 'not later than c.830' for the Tripartite Life; and thus date the exemplar of it and the *Vita II* and *Vita IV* to the eighth century. (As Thomas Charles-Edwards points out, the *Notulae* in the Book of Armagh show that something like it was in existence by 800.[18]) They associate the text lying behind all these lives, an augmented version of Muirchú, with the churchman called Colmán na mBretan, abbot of the northern Brega monastery of Sláne (†751), indeed its earliest recorded abbot, and sire of a whole dynasty of churchmen in Sláne.[19] Crucially, they focus on this character because of what they call his 'familiarity with Welsh language and topography'. It is doubtful whether there need be anything relating specifically to Wales itself in the text lying behind these lives, but there is certainly knowledge of a British language, and the topography of northern Britain.[20]

For our purposes it is not essential to home in on one church or individual for the composition of the exemplar of these diverse hagiographical productions. I would be happier to take the period between c.700 (the date of Muirchú), and 1000 (a date related to the earliest manuscripts of *Vita II* and the Old Irish hymn *Genair*

Bieler's decision to label the ancestor text he saw as underlying the *Vita II, Vita IV* and Tripartite Life as *BPh*, and another closely related postulated Latin text as *W*. He was followed in this by Byrne and Francis. The summary by Charles-Edwards cuts through much of the murk, but because of the nature of the venue does not show the underlying argument.

17 A. G. van Hamel, *Lebor Bretnach* (Dublin, [1932]), 68; for the dating and provenance of this text, see Clancy, 'Nennian Recension'. One may note that in giving this more detailed information it augments its own base text, as the original *Historia Brittonum* knew only that Palladius had died among the Picts; see *ibid.*, 95–7.

18 Charles-Edwards, *Early Christian Ireland*, 11.

19 Byrne and Francis, 'Two Lives', 5–16; 14–15 for identification of Colmán; for Colmán and his family, see K. Hughes, *The Church in Early Irish Society* (London, 1966), 162–3. Charles-Edwards, *Early Christian Ireland*, 12, quotes the suggestion with guarded approval. While Byrne and Francis may be correct in dating the ancestor text to the eighth century, c.830 seems remarkably early for the date of the Tripartite Life as we have it; Charles-Edwards puts it at 900–950 (*ibid.*, 13).

20 But see their discussion of the Welsh place-name Mathafarn in relation to one rendition of Patrick's birthplace as *campus Tabern* or *campus tabernaculorum*: 'Two Lives', 13, 71–2. Just as we know this to have been a reasonably common name in Wales, we cannot exclude the name having been present elsewhere in Brittonic-speaking territory, such as Strathclyde.

Pátraic) as the base-line for the point at which northern British traditions came into the Patrician hagiographical family, and then suggest a few possible scenarios in which this might have happened. But first it is necessary to scrutinise more closely what each of these witnesses tells us about Palladius and Patrick.

Palladius

There are two separate, but perhaps linked, strands to the augmentation of traditions about Palladius in the Patrician texts. One involves his foundation of three churches in Leinster before he leaves Ireland. This may be found in the *Vita II* (§§ 23–24), the *Vita IV* (§§ 27–29), the Tripartite Life,[21] and the scholia in the *Liber Hymnorum* on Fiacc's Hymn:[22] Appendix 1, below, provides translations of the relevant texts.[23] The other involves the information about where in Scotland Palladius worked and/or died and/or was buried. Information regarding this can be found in the *Vita II*, the scholia in the *Liber Hymnorum*, and the *Lebor Bretnach* (see Appendix 1, below). The fact that both these strands of augmentation are not found together in either the *Vita IV* or the Tripartite Life may suggest that the two strands did not arrive in the tradition from the same sources. Moreover, unlike the information on the three Leinster churches, which is fairly consistent in those texts that preserve it, there are curious differences among the three texts providing information on Palladius's sojourn in Scotland. In the *Vita II*, Palladius is specified as having died in *campus Girgin*, a plain well known as a Pictish place-name in various Irish sources, and generally associated with Angus and the Mearns.[24] This text further clarifies that he died in *Forddun*. In the scholia, the only text that mentions a storm, Palladius is blown to 'the south-east extremity of Modaibg', where he founds Fordoun.[25] This also informs us of his name in this region, 'Pledius'. Finally *Lebor Bretnach*, translated in Scotland in any case, only refers to him as *Pledias*, and we are simply told 'he came and served God in Fordoun in the Mearns'. All three of these references, and the fact that they may be decoupled in terms of their transmission from the Leinster information, suggest a Scottish source, or perhaps sources.[26] Can we get any more specific than this?

21 Stokes, *Tripartite Life*, 30–1.

22 Stokes and Strachan, *Thesaurus Palaeo-Hibernicus*, 312–13.

23 And see n. 7 above.

24 See e.g. William J. Watson, *The History of the Celtic Place-Names of Scotland* (Edinburgh, 1926), 108–9.

25 'Modaibg' is an impenetrable name or form of a name. I would presume that some form of the name lying behind the Mounth (*Monad*) lies behind it. Certainly Fordoun can be said to lie to the south-east of the Mounth.

26 My impression is that *Lebor Bretnach* adds information when it specifies that Fordun is in the Mearns – as I have discussed elsewhere, it adds and innovates on the basis of an extensive knowledge of Scottish traditions and geography: Clancy, 'Nennian Recension', 95–7. Our options are then: 1) that there was a supplementary set of information telling us that Palladius died at Fordun in Mag Girginn, to the south-east of 'Modaibg', having been blown there by a storm; or 2) that individual items from this set of information had been supplied at different times from different sources. The latter

The strange reference in the twelfth-century glosses on the Martyrology of Oengus may help. Here Palladius is identified with a certain saint Torannán. Torrannán is the Gaelic name of the Scottish saint Ternan. That he was thought of in Ireland as having come from Scotland is suggested by the main text of the Martyrology of Oengus, which describes him as having come across the wide sea.[27] He is also one of seven men linked as brothers by a late tradition, who appear to be saints of Scottish extraction working in Ireland.[28] At least one of these saints may plausibly be identified with the St Drostan who died in Ardbraccan in 719.[29] If these seven men were roughly contemporary, then Torannán too might be of the early eighth century.

But why is he fused with Palladius here? Ternan's main Scottish church seems to have been Banchory-Ternan, but he also had a dedication at Arbuthnott, which is contiguous with the parish of Fordoun, Palladius's own.[30] The glosses to the Martyrology of Oengus are not the only place the two saints were associated. In the Martyrology of Aberdeen, which dates from the end of the fifteenth century, we are told that Ternan was Palladius's apostle, who helped him convert many Scots to Christ.[31] The entry here notes that Palladius's body was at 'Fordoune' where 'in our days they have been translated into a certain chapel'.[32] I have also argued elsewhere that in the Life of St Lawrence of Canterbury, by the journalistic hagiographer Goscelin, a scene that has Ternan, 'archbishop of Ireland' visit Lawrence in his church in the Mearns, at either Lawrencekirk or Fordoun, is a misappropriation of a legend of the meeting of Palladius and Ternan, such as can be found in the Aberdeen Breviary.[33] There I argued further that the Lawrence culted in Lawrencekirk was St Lawrence the Martyr, and not he of Canterbury. Alan Macquarrie, who first drew attention to this source, had previously argued that

option would rely on a number of interventions of Scottish-based research in the Patrician tradition – by no means an unlikely scenario.

27 *Félire Óengusso Céili Dé. The Martyrology of Oengus*, ed. and trans. W. Stokes (Dublin, 1905), 140 (core text), 148–9 (glosses).

28 P. Ó Riain, *Corpus Genealogiarum Sacntorum Hiberniae* (Dublin, 1985), §§ 209, 701; Watson, *Celtic Place-Names*, 298; D. Ó Cróinín, 'The Oldest Irish Names for the Days of the Week?', *Ériu* 32 (1981), 104–8, 112–14.

29 T. O. Clancy, 'Deer and the Early Church in North-Eastern Scotland', in *Studies in the Book of Deer*, ed. Katherine Forsyth (forthcoming, Dublin, 2008); for the annal entry, see, *AU* 719.2.

30 J. M. Mackinlay, *Ancient Church Dedications in Scotland: Non-Scriptural Dedications* (Edinburgh, 1914), 105–8, for discussion of both saints. As noted there, W. F. Skene, *Celtic Scotland: A History of Ancient Alban. Volume 2, Church and Culture* (Edinburgh, 1877), 226–31, discusses the related notices of Palladius and Ternan.

31 Alexander Penrose Forbes, *Kalendars of Scottish Saints* (Edinburgh, 1872), 133; see also 131.

32 Further references to the late medieval cult of Palladius may be found in the *Database of Dedications to Saints in Medieval Scotland* [available online at http://www.shca.ed.ac.uk/research/saints]. It is worth adding (as noted by Bieler, 'Mission of Palladius', 20), that the *Aberdeen Breviary* (pars estivalis, fos 24v–25v, Lectio IV) places Palladius's relics '*apud Langforgund in Mernis*', i.e. Longforgan rather than Fordun.

33 T. O. Clancy, 'The Foundation of Laurencekirk Revisited', *IR* 50 (1999), 83–8.

there was some connection here with Irish tradition, possibly from as early as the eighth century.[34]

The origins, then, of the connection between Palladius and Ternan might well be simply one of geography. However, we might want to venture a hypothesis that connects him with the transmission of information about Palladius to Ireland; or alternatively, the importation of the Patrician texts, such as a version of Muirchú's Life, which might spark the cult of a saint who Muirchú said had died among the Picts. It is worth stressing that there are really two acts of intellectual transmission we need to explain: why there was a cult of Palladius in the Mearns in the early middle ages, and how scholars in Ireland came to know about it. Perhaps a useful lead to follow in connecting Ternan to one of these acts of transmission is the tradition linking him to a small church in Leinster, much as Palladius is also linked to three such Leinster churches.[35]

On the other hand, following a different and equally tentative clue, it may seem likely that the information about Palladius's death among the Picts came to Pictland from Armagh. The reason for suggesting this is the proximity of the cults of St Lawrence and St Palladius, in the parishes of Fordoun and Lawrencekirk (formerly Conveth). We know that by the mid-seventh century Armagh was in possession of relics of St Lawrence, portions of which it would on occasion give out to subordinate churches.[36] What I would tentatively suggest, then, is that the arrival in the Mearns of the cult of Lawrence, and the arrival of the Patrician texts, which would give rise to the cult of Palladius, happened at about the same time. I would further suggest that these should be linked in some way to the activities of the Pictish saint Ternan (Torannán). That said, I would not like this suggestion to obscure the core observation here, that one way or another a cult of Palladius was present in the Mearns from an early date, that the impetus for establishing it came from Ireland, and that Irish churchmen knew about it.

A further route to explore is the presence of Pictish churchmen at work in Ireland at various points during our period 700 × 1000. Two points during this period stand out in my mind. One is the early eighth century. This was a period of ecclesiastical reform in Pictland, and at least at a minor level saw a looking away from Iona as the main provider of church infrastructure and personnel. Although, following Bede's references to this period, we may suspect that this involved closer ties to Northumbria, reinforced ties with other Irish houses need not be ruled out.[37] In this context the presence in Ireland of a Pictish bishop called Fergus, who attended a council in Rome in 721, is surely of some import.[38] Equally, as noted above, I have argued that the Drostan who died in Ardbraccan in 719 is the same

34 A. Macquarrie, 'An Eleventh-century Account of the Foundation Legend of Laurencekirk, and of Queen Margaret's Pilgrimage there', *IR* 47 (1996), 95–109.

35 See n. 27 above for Torannán's churches; for Palladius's churches, see Appendix, and for discussion and locations, see Byrne and Francis, 'Two Latin Lives', 87–90.

36 Charles Doherty, 'The uses of relics in early Ireland', in *Irland und Europa: Die Kirche im Frühmittelalter. Ireland and Europe: The Early Church*, ed. P. Ní Chatháin and M. Richter (Tübingen, 1984), 89–101, esp. 93.

37 Bede, *HE*, v.25.

38 *Sacrorum Conciliorum nova et amplissima Collectio*, ed. J. D. Mansi (repr. Graz, 1960–2), XII.261–6. He is described as *Fergustus Episcopus Scotiae Pictus*.

individual as St Drostan of Deer and Aberdour in north-east Scotland.[39] For one reason or another, then, some major Pictish churchmen appear to have been active in Ireland at this time. We cannot connect them with Armagh, but the point is nonetheless significant. We may wish to remember, moreover, that with some notable exceptions, the written Patrician texts we have are far from being, strictly speaking, Armagh products; for instance, Byrne and Francis associate the evolution of the text lying behind the Tripartite Life, *Vita II*, and *Vita IV* with a churchman based not in Armagh but in Sláne, working in the mid-eighth century. This time period also suits well one in which the Pictish church appears to have been thinking in terms of reform and change, and have been making contact with the Europe-conscious Northumbrian church. In this context, one in which churches were being dedicated to saints like Peter and John,[40] the cult of the first (although failed) bishop of Ireland, with his Roman background and papal commission, may have been attractive among Pictish churchmen.

Links are appreciable from later on, however, and certainty is impossible. A Pictish bishop in the Orkneys in the ninth century could communicate with an escaped Irish captive because he had been trained in Ireland.[41] In the Life of St Cathroe (a tenth-century work), that saint goes to Ireland for his higher education: indeed, Armagh is specified here.[42] As Dauvit Broun has pointed out too, someone in Armagh was well enough connected with Pictland around 900 to change the nomenclature to 'Alba' at about the same time as it happened in Pictland itself.[43] It may be possible to join the dots here, and suggest that developments in the tenth century, which saw young men from eastern Scotland receiving their training in Armagh, had their beginnings as early as the early eighth century.

Patrick

Patrick's cult in Strathclyde is another matter, but just as significant. Here the sources seem rather more consistent.[44] The main part of the material relating to Patrick in 'Nemthor' involves a series of miracle stories, including ones about the

39 Clancy, 'Deer and the Early Church'.

40 See Bede, *HE*, v.21; Barrow, 'The Childhood of Scottish Christianity: A Note on Some Place-name Evidence', *Scottish Studies* 27 (1983), 1–15.

41 Reidar Th. Christiansen, 'The People of the North (including edition and translation of *Vita Findani* by T. O'Nolan)', *Lochlann: A Review of Celtic Studies* 2 (1962), 137–64, at 151, 159.

42 A. O. Anderson, *Early Sources for Scottish History, A.D. 500 to 1286*, rev. edn (Stamford, 1990), 436–7; see also David N. Dumville, 'St Cathróe of Metz and the Hagiography of Exoticism', in *Studies in Irish Hagiography. Saints and Scholars*, ed. J. Carey, M. Herbert and P. Ó Riain (Dublin, 2001), 172–88, at 176.

43 D. Broun, 'Dunkeld and the Origin of Scottish Identity', in *Spes Scotorum, Hope of Scots. Saint Columba, Iona and Scotland*, ed. D. Broun and T. O. Clancy (Edinburgh, 1999), 95–111, esp. 107.

44 These are usefully summarised by Taylor, 'Early History and Languages', 40–1, though this is based only on the Tripartite Life. His discussion of the date and origin of these traditions approaches them only through the Tripartite Life, and does not consider the implications of their wider textual representation.

stone on which he was born and the well at the place where he was baptised. Examination of this material in detail suggests that we could reconstruct the original dossier of material about Patrick's British origins. This series of childhood hagiographical anecdotes includes information about a church built over the well at his baptism, and its shape, 'according to those who know the place'.[45] In the *Vita II* there is no explicit linkage of this material, or the name Nemthor, to any other location. In the *Vita IV*, however, Patrick's parents are said to be from Strathclyde (*Strato Cluade*). The vernacular sources, the scholia in the *Liber Hymnorum*, and the Tripartite Life are clearer yet. They link the name Nemthor to the early medieval fortress of Ail Cluaide, the 'Rock of Clyde', now Dumbarton Rock. The Tripartite Life further specifies that Patrick's parents originated among the Strathclyde Britons.

There is, nonetheless, a certain amount of confusion and difference brought about by attempts at clarification. This is best revealed in the mangling of the ideas, told fairly straightforwardly, about the links between the Britons of Armorica and the Britons of Strathclyde. The story in the *Vita IV* is strange, and seems to be a learned mixing of ideas about his origins, while the stories in the scholia and the Tripartite Life are about the circumstances of Patrick's kidnapping by 'the seven sons of Sevensome'. It is curious that none of this appears in the *Vita II*. Byrne may be right to suggest that this is deliberate omission rather than anything else.[46]

All the Lives share the miracle of stone, well and church. It must be that the church referred to is that of Kilpatrick (now Old Kilpatrick), near to Dumbarton Rock.[47] We know from thirteenth-century charters that Kilpatrick was a major shrine and pilgrimage site, in possession of extensive lands in the area, which were subject to dispute.[48] Alan Macquarrie has drawn attention to the presence of a well-endowed pilgrim house here, all suggestive of the fact that Kilpatrick had been a fairly major church.[49] He points in the same direction that I have taken: that the association of Patrick with the area must date from the period between the Book of Armagh and the writing of the Tripartite Life, though I would push the earlier barrier back to the composition of Muirchú's Life, and emphasise that the end date for this is the composition of the Life underlying not just the Tripartite Life but also *Vita II* and *Quarta*, and thus may pre-date the Tripartite Life, perhaps even by a considerable amount of time. He suggests that it was the presence of Kilpatrick, a church dedicated to Patrick, which drew the legends to it. This rather begs the question of why there was a church dedicated to Patrick there in the first place, and I suspect that we are dealing with a slightly different sequence of events. I would prefer to suggest that local traditions about St Patrick led to the building of a church at a site associated with his birthplace (indeed, the Lives can be read as saying as much).

45 *Vita IV*, § 3: Byrne and Francis, 'Two Lives', 21 ('as the experts (*periti*) say', *Vita II*).

46 Byrne and Francis, 'Two Lives', 68.

47 On Kilpatrick, see Macquarrie, 'Lives of Scottish Saints', 44–50; Taylor, 'Early History and Languages'.

48 See Taylor, 'Early History and Languages', and *Registrum Monasterii de Passelet*, ed. Cosmo Innes, Maitland Club 17 (Edinburgh, 1832), 113–15, 157–73, and Appendix 3.

49 Macquarrie, 'Lives of Scottish Saints', 44–50.

Once again we are left with questions of why, how and when. The why would seem to be answered by paying attention to the *datum* that triggers this material, that is, the association of the name Nemthor with Dumbarton. It may be that this was indeed another name among the Britons for Dumbarton Rock; one might also point to the nearby Rosneath as a place containing the element *nemed-*, which lies beneath the name Nemthor.[50] It may even be that this was where Muirchú had in mind. Either way, a local link between his place-name and that of one in the vicinity of Ail Cluaide, if not the Rock itself, is the best explanation. Having made this connection between Nemthor and the hinterland of Dumbarton, further legends were built up associating Patrick with the area. Again, then, we must be dealing with a text of Muirchú reaching the kingdom of Dumbarton at some stage in the early middle ages and spawning this set of legends about Patrick.

We can get some control over when these legends came into existence by determining when the dossier of material came into the possession of Irish scholars. Three factors may help to do this. One is the use of the name *Ail Cluaide* in both the scholia and the Tripartite Life. Ail Cluaide, the Rock of the Clyde, was well and truly sacked after a four-month siege by a coalition of Vikings in 870,[51] and after that it is never mentioned in the annals, or much of anywhere else, until the thirteenth century. That the site lasted in poetic memory in Wales is apparent from the poem *Armes Prydain*, but I doubt Irish scholars would have had such long-standing literary associations.[52] Of course, there are indications from material remains that the site was still in use in some form afterwards, though perhaps not as a fortress or a royal seat, which is certainly how our texts depict it. All this may suggest that our dossier came to Irish Patrician scholars before 870, at a time when *Ail Cluaide* was still a functioning and thriving fortress. On the other hand, the mentioning of Strathclyde (*Strato Cluade, Bretnaib Sratha Clúathe*) in both the *Vita IV* and the Tripartite Life send the opposite signals. The first appearances of this collocation in annals begin simultaneously in Ireland and in Wessex; in the Annals of Ulster for 872, where Arthgal is called king of the Britons of Strathclyde; and in 875 for the Anglo-Saxon Chronicle, which speaks of the *Straetclaed Wealas*.[53] This could suggest a date after 870 for the dossier. Backing up the idea of a post-870 origin for the dossier is the fact that one of the main strands of Patrick dedications is in those regions that became incorporated into the

50 See most recently Taylor, 'Early History', 18, although he seems to accept *Ventre* as having been the underlying form, despite Byrne and Francis's persuasive arguments (see n. 11 above). For earlier comments on *Nemthor* and its possible etymology, see Watson, *Celtic Place-Names*, 246–7. On the element *nemed-*, see G. W. S. Barrow, 'Religion in Scotland on the Eve of Christianity', in *Forschungen zur Reichs-, Papst- und Landesgeschichte*, ed. K. Borchardt and E. Bünz, part 1 (Stuttgart, 1998), 25–32; *idem*, 'The Uses of Place-names and Scottish History – Pointers and Pitfalls', in *The Uses of Place-Names*, ed. S. Taylor (Edinburgh, 1998), 54–74.

51 *AU* 870.6.

52 *Armes Prydein. The Prophecy of Britain from the Book of Taliesin*, ed. Ifor Williams, English version by R. Bromwich (Dublin, 1972), lines 11, 151.

53 *AU* 872.5; *The Anglo-Saxon Chronicle*, trans. and ed. M. J. Swanton (London, 1997), s.a. 875 (variant manuscripts have other forms); and for a summary of the data and further references, see T. O. Clancy, 'Ystrad Clud', in *Celtic Culture: An Historical Encyclopedia*, ed. J. T. Koch (Santa Barbara CA, 2006).

kingdom of Strathclyde/Cumbria. There are a series of Patrick dedications up the Clyde (Dumbarton itself, Dalziel, Dalpatrick – see map, p. 41); equally, in Dumfriesshire the presence of dedications at Kirkpatrick-Fleming, Renpatrick, and Kirkpatrick-Iuxta, as well as others further west, suggests to me that, like other saints such as Constantine of Govan and Kentigern of Glasgow, his cult was exported south with the expansion of Strathclyde in the period after 870.[54] That said, I find it hard to believe it was invented at this period. It seems more reasonable to suggest that a close association of Patrick with the previous 'royal church' of the Dumbarton dynasty had much to do with the exportation of his cult into the new expanded kingdom of Strathclyde. The prominence of the name Gospatrick in the eleventh century in Cumbria and beyond should also be remembered in this context (see table, p. 43), though Fiona Edmonds's discussion (below) sees other potential influences on this development, in particular the importance of Patrick among the Hiberno-Norse settlers of the western seaboard. It is helpful, in this context, to be assured by the textual transmission we have been examining that the cult of Patrick was present on the Clyde at an earlier date. The foundation of Kilpatrick, then, and the evolution of his cult, may plausibly date from before 870, even if the use of the term Strathclyde may date the dossier or its arrival in Ireland to after that date.

It may be worth adding the linguistic context of the name Kilpatrick into this discussion. Although I have stressed that the childhood miracle stories give Patrick a firmly British background in British Strathclyde, the place-name itself is Gaelic, one of many names employing the Gaelic element *cill-* 'church', followed by a saint's name. One of the pioneering place-name scholars, Bill Nicolaisen, derived a date of usage for this term as a live toponymic element of before c.800, on the basis of the limited distribution of the element in eastern Scotland.[55] This may be a reasonable deduction for eastern Scotland, but scholars are increasingly cautious about its application elsewhere.[56] In Argyll and the south-west of Scotland, the situation is manifestly different, especially as Gaelic continued to be spoken in some of these areas well into the later middle ages or modern period; and in others is unlikely to have reached these areas before 800. Kilpatrick, on the other hand, belongs to a more selective group of *cill-* names situated around the lower Clyde, in Dumbartonshire and Renfrewshire. These include a lost *Kilmahew*, Kilmaronock, a lost *Kilmaloog*, Kilpeter (now Houston), Killellan, Kilmacolm, Kilbarchan.[57] The presence of Peter, Patrick and Columba in this group is especially interesting. The precise cultural context for the creation of these names is still undecided: did Gaels gradually penetrate Strathclyde from Cowal in the early

54 Cf. Davies, 'Bishop Kentigern', below, who takes a different view.

55 W. F. H. Nicolaisen, *Scottish Place-Names*, 2nd edn (London, 1979), 130, 144.

56 Macquarrie, 'Some Scottish Saints', 49, n. 56, has seen the problem, though his solution depends upon his understanding of there having been a Gaelic conquest of Strathclyde by the kingdom of Alba in the tenth century; and also his understanding of how Gaelic comes into the area, neither of which I share.

57 It may be that we should treat as a large dispersed cluster all the *cill-* place-names in the northern part of south-west Scotland, and so include those in Cunninghame (e.g. Kilwinning, Kilmarnock), and Lanarkshire (East Kilbride). This collection of names and dedications could do with a close study.

middle ages? Had the church in the Firth of Clyde region long been serviced by Gaelic churchmen (as suggested recently by James Fraser's researches on Kingarth)? Or did these *cill-* names arrive with the takeover of the whole Clyde seaboard by Gall-Gháidheil in the eleventh century, as tentatively mooted by Dauvit Broun?[58] A close study of this discreet grouping of ecclesiastical place-names may reveal some of the answers, but equally may not. At present, then, the fact that Patrick's birthplace bears a Gaelic name cannot help refine our understanding of the evolution of the tradition.

Returning to the traditions regarding Patrick's birthplace on the Clyde, it remains to consider how these came about. The initial question must relate to the arrival of a Life of Patrick, a version of Muirchú probably, in the Strathclyde region. Once again there are several contexts in which contacts between northern Britons and Ireland in this period are visible. The most impressive is the often mentioned presence, alongside Fergus the Pict, bishop of Ireland at the council in Rome in 721, of an Irish (or at any rate Gaelic) bishop of the Britons called Sedulius, probably for Siadal.[59] This could easily be a bishop from Wales, but the association with Fergus makes the territory of the northern Britons, at this date virtually confined to the kingdom of Dumbarton, quite attractive for this bishop's zone of operation. An Irish bishop in Strathclyde in the 720s might be just the person to introduce the cult of his native saint, indeed, perhaps even to make the associative leaps necessary. However, it is clear that there had been links between Gaelic churchmen and the kingdom of Dumbarton for a long while in any case – Adomnán (who refers to 'our father Patrick') tells a story about communications between Columba and a king of Dumbarton. James Fraser has recently been constructing a fairly persuasive picture of a long-term Gaelic dimension to the Firth of Clyde in the sixth to eighth centuries, particularly in an ecclesiastical context, and this could also be a route through which Patrician material reached the Clyde.[60]

Another profitable link to pursue is the churchman favoured by Byrne as having been responsible for the forging of the document underlying all the later Lives of Patrick we have been discussing. This is the man called Colmán na mBretan, abbot of Sláne in Brega, who died in 751.[61] Byrne associates him with the Welsh, but I suspect the contents of these lives, if he is indeed linked with their base-text, means that he was a Briton from the kingdom of Dumbarton. Even if Colmán has nothing

58 Dauvit Broun, 'The Welsh Identity of the Kingdom of Strathclyde *c.*900–*c.*1200', *IR* 55 (2004), 111–80, at 136–40. For the context, see further Alex Woolf, *From Pictland to Alba, 789–1070*, New Edinburgh History of Scotland 2 (Edinburgh, 2007), 252–5; T. O. Clancy, 'The Gall-Gaidheil and Galloway', in *Gall-Ghaidheil: The Vikings in the Western Isles*, ed. C. Batey (forthcoming).

59 *Sacrorum Conciliorum*, XII.261–6. The name is given as *Sedulius episcopus Britanniae de genere Scotorum*. I have suggested his potential identification with either *Sidal* of Druim Laidggin whose death is noted at *AU* 722.7, or *Siadhail mac Luaith, doctor*, whose death is noted at *AU* 759.1: see Clancy, 'Deer and the Early Church'.

60 Adomnán, *Vita S. Columbae*, I.15: *Adomnán's Life of Columba*, ed. A. O. Anderson and M. O. Anderson, rev. edn (Oxford, 1991), 238. See James E. Fraser, 'Strangers on the Clyde: Cenél Comgaill, Clyde Rock and the Bishops of Kingarth', *IR* 56 (2005), 102–20.

61 See n. 19 above.

to do with the Patrician texts, it would be well for scholars to remember the territory of the northern Britons as a possibility – perhaps even a probability given his Gaelic name – for Colmán's origins.

Whatever the sequence of events that gave rise to Patrick's church, it seems that Patrician scholars in Ireland came into possession of a strand of tradition linking Patrick's birth, baptism, and childhood deeds with the area around Dumbarton and Kilpatrick. We may also see, from some of the linking themes in the stories (ice, snow, fire), that this was a relatively coherent dossier of material. That such a dossier, with its knowledge of the religious landscape of the Clyde, must have come from British sources, laying claim to Patrick's birthplace, is also apparent.

Conclusions

Although it is difficult to be conclusive about many of these matters, a number of important and fairly firm points do emerge. One is that the evidence for these two 'external', i.e. non-native, cults in Scotland is early medieval evidence. Even if we do not agree with Byrne that the original text underlying these traditions need be from the 730s or 740s, this information belongs to the period before c.1000. Indeed, in both cases, the information seems to point to the underlying text or texts having been created before 900. This is so in the case of the Palladius material, since it has him dying in the region of the Picts; after 900, such a designation would have less relevance. Similarly, various factors point to a linkage between Dumbarton Rock, when it was thriving, and the cult of Patrick, i.e. before its destruction in 870. It probably needs emphasising that our evidence for church dedications in the period pre-1000 is slim in the extreme, and those to non-native saints like Patrick and Palladius are always suspected of being introduced at a later stage. In these two cases, we may be considerably more confident that they are early medieval cults.

Both these cults also link churchmen from the north of Britain with Patrician scholars in Ireland, whether they be in Armagh, or Sláne, or elsewhere. Neither in Pictland, nor in Dumbarton/Strathclyde, have the ecclesiastical links with Ireland as a whole, as opposed to the Columban *familia*, been sufficiently explored.[62] We should remember, as I have been suggesting, that in each case there are two episodes of contact being demonstrated: one when Picts or Britons receive and become interested in Muirchú's Life and its contents (i.e. its references to Nemthor, and to Palladius's death in Pictland); the other when the local cult reactions to this impetus in Scotland is transmitted back to Ireland. Excitingly in both cases we can also see, to a limited extent, the later medieval developments of these cults and their connections with other local sites. The early medieval starting points, however, allow us to build a fuller and longer picture of development than we would originally have been prompted to do.

In the case of the Patrick dossier, it also seems that we can recover a small slice of Clydeside hagiography, with a local flavour, from the pre-1000 period. This is unique, and certainly more than we can do with any confidence for St Kentigern or

62 This is a point James Fraser has been stressing in recent work, see e.g. 'Strangers on the Clyde'.

the other local Strathclyde saints, given the nature of their twelfth-century or later hagiographical texts. This material gives incidental details of local religious landscape (the stone – perhaps the Patrick's Rock that is still in the Clyde; his well; the church); of social structure like the king's steward, and the tax of butter and cheese. Indeed, we may wish to speculate about the link made between 'Campus Taburniae' and a Roman camp in these sources (see, for instance, *Vita II* and *Vita IV*) as being connected with the fact that Kilpatrick was indeed one terminus of the Antonine Wall.

Finally, all this material gives us the hagiographical background to one of the most interesting series of texts preserved in the Paisley Register, that concerning the lands of Kilpatrick. This dispute, the nature of its settlement, the names and backgrounds of the witnesses called, the testimonies they give, the situation of Kilpatrick in the 1170s and thereafter, with its extensive lands being eaten away by local noblemen; the hospitaller Beda Ferdan, with his intriguing name and his great house made of twigs: all these provide one of the most vivid snapshots of the changing nature of church, culture and language around the River Clyde in an age of great transformation. It is a text that would repay much more attention; I append a translation here in the hope that it will spark further research (see Appendix 3).[63]

So although the historical Patrick and Palladius are, alas, unlikely ever to have had much to do with Scotland, their cults were indeed present in the early middle ages, they were locally important, and internationally known. Perhaps the most intriguing historical question they raise is why we find these cults most prominently in non-Gaelic areas of Scotland, as Britons and Picts both saw fit to patronise the cults of saints associated most closely with Irish religious origins.[64]

63 The legal proceedings regarding these lands are summarised and reviewed by Lord Cooper in his *Select Scottish Cases of the Thirteenth Century* (Edinburgh and London, 1944), 32–40, with a translation of part of the text I give below. Cooper surveys the proceedings into the late thirteenth century.

64 This article is based on a paper previously presented in different forms to the Irish Conference of Medievalists, Maynooth and the Scottish Place-Name Society in Glasgow, and I am grateful to participants at both for helpful suggestions. A number of scholars have provided either input or encouragement during the long evolution of this article, and I am particularly grateful to Dauvit Broun, Rachel Butter, James Fraser, Gilbert Márkus, Simon Taylor and Alex Woolf, and more recently Fiona Edmonds and Sarah Erskine, for their contributions. I am alone responsible for the final product. The written article was completed during my period as Snell Visitor from the University of Glasgow to Balliol College, Oxford, and I am grateful to both institutions for the opportunity thus provided.

APPENDICES

Traditions of Palladius and Patrick in Britain – main texts

APPENDIX 1

Traditions of Palladius

Vita II S. Patricii (before the eleventh century)
Translation by Byrne and Francis, 'Two Lives'; edited by Bieler in *Four Latin Lives*.

§ 23. So at a suitable time, God's counsel commanding him, he [Patrick] went on the way he had started towards the task for which he had long been prepared, that is the preaching of the Gospel. And Germanus sent a senior with him, the priest Segitius, so that he might have a suitable witness and companion; and he had not yet been consecrated in episcopal orders by Saint Germanus.

And indeed they were also aware that Palladius, an archdeacon of Pope Celestinus of the city of Rome who then held the apostolic see as forty-fifth in line from the apostle Peter, had been ordained and sent by the holy pope to convert that island lying in wintry cold.

But God forbade him to do so, because no-one can receive anything on earth unless it be given him in heaven. For neither did those fierce men accept his teaching, nor did he want to spend time in a land not his own, but he returned to him by whom he had been sent. So he turned back, and making the first seacrossing from here, as he began the land journey he died in the territory of the Picts.

§ 24. For the most blessed Pope Celestinus of the church of Rome consecrated as bishop an archdeacon called Palladius and sent him to the island of Ireland having consigned to him relics of the blessed Peter and Paul and other saints, having also given him volumes of the Old and New Testaments.

So Palladius entering the land of the Irish arrived at the territory of the Lagenenses [Leinstermen], in which Nathi filius Garrchon was ruler, who was hostile to him.

But through the divine mercy other men were baptised into the worship of God by the blessed Palladius in the name of the Holy Trinity, and three churches in that country were built: one which is called Cell Fine, in which are held until today with great veneration his books, which he received from Saint Celestine, and a box of relics of the blessed Peter and Paul and other saints, and the tablets on which he used to write, which later after Palaldius himself are called *pallere* in Irish, that is, 'the burden of Palladius'.

And indeed the second church is named after the disciples of Palladius, that is Thech na Róman; the third church, that is Domnach Arte, in which are Silvester and Solonius, holy men of the family of Palladius, and afterwards their relics <were taken> to Inis Baitheni and there they are revered with the relics of Baithenus.

Finally after a small interval, Palladius having died in the plain of Girgin in a place which is called Forddun – for some say that he received the martyr's crown there –

§ 25. Patrick, sent by the same Pope Celestinus to Ireland, arrived …

Vita IV S. Patricii (before 1100)
Translation by Byrne and Francis, 'Two Lives'; edited by Bieler in *Four Latin Lives*.

§ 27. … So at a suitable time, at God's inspiration, he [Patrick] went on the way he had started towards the task for which he had long been prepared, that is the preaching of the Gospel. And Saint Germanus sent a senior priest Segitius, with him so that he might have a suitable witness and companion. But he had not yet been consecrated in episcopal orders by Saint Germanus.

For he knew that Palladius, an archdeacon of Pope Celestinus, the bishop of the city of Rome who then held the apostolic see as forty-fifth in line from the apostle Peter, had been ordained by that pope and been sent to preach in Ireland.

§ 28. So when he arrived there, he began to preach the word of the Lord in the territory of the Laginenses. But because the Almighty Lord did not decree beforehand that the Irish peoples should be brought by him from the error of paganism to an inviolable faith in the holy and undivided Trinity, he stayed there for just a few days.

Nevertheless a few believed through him, and in that country he built three churches: one of which is called the church of Fine, in which are held until today his books, which he received from Saint Celestinus, and a box with relics of the blessed apostles Peter and Paul and other saints, and the tablets on which he used to write, which after Palladius himself are called *palladiae* (that is, 'the burden of Palladius'), and are held in great veneration.

The second church was built by the disciples of Palladius, which is called Domus Romanorum; the third is the church which is called Dominica Archa, in which are holy men of the companions of Palladius, Silvester and Solinus, whose relics were carried after some time to the island of Boethenus and they are held there with great honour.

However, Saint Palladius seeing that he could not advance much there, wanting to return to Rome he departed to the Lord in the land of the Picti. However others say that he received a martyr's crown in Ireland.

Tripartite Life (by c.900) Latin/Gaelic
Translation by Stokes, *Tripartite Life*, I.30–2; edited by Mulchrone, *Bethu Phátraic*, 19–20.

Now the chief who was in Rome at that time was Celestinus, the forty-second man from Peter. He sent Palladius, an archdeacon, with twelve men, to preach to the Gaels – for it belongs to Peter's successor to benefit Europe – in like manner as Barnabas went from Peter to preach to the Romans etc. When Palladius came to the territory of Leinster, namely to Inber Déa, Nathi son of Garrchú opposed him and expelled him. And he baptised a few in that place, and founded three churches, Cell

Fine, in which he let his books, and the casket with relics of Paul and Peter, and the board on which he used to write, and Tech na Róman, and Domnach Airte, wherein are Sylvester and Solonius. As, then, he was returning, sickness seized him in the lands of the Picts, so that he died thereof.

Scholia on 'Fiacc's Hymn' ('Génair Pátraicc i nNemthur'), Gaelic/Latin, from the *Liber Hymnorum* (before the eleventh century)
Translation from *Thesaurus Palaeo-Hibernicus*, ed. Stokes and Strachan, 312–13.

Now after Patrick had studied with German the canon and the ecclesiastical order, he said to German that he had often been invited in heavenly visions, and that he had heard the voice of the children '... to Celestinus, that he may ordain you, for he is proper to do so.' Patrick therefore went to him and he did not give him the honour, for he had sent Palladius before to Ireland that he might teach them. Palladius therefore went into Ireland and landed in Uí Garrchon in the Fortuatha of Leinster, and he founded churches therein, to wit, Tech na Rómanach and Cell Fine and others. Now no good welcome was given to him there, so he went thence to go round Ireland ... to the north, and a mighty storm came upon him, and he was driven to the south-east extremity of Modaibg (?) and he founded there a church called Fordun and his name there is Pledius.

Lebor Bretnach, Gaelic, before 1093 (earliest manuscript, late eleventh century).
Lebor Bretnach: The Irish Version of the Historia Britonum Ascribed to Nennius, ed. A. G. van Hamel (Dublin [1932]), 68.

At that time, Pledias [Palladius] was sent to Ireland to preach to them. Patraic went to the south to study, and he read the canons with Germanus. Pledius was expelled from Ireland, and he came and served God in Fordun in the Mearns.

APPENDIX 2

Patrick's Birth and Childhood

This dossier of material appears in the Tripartite Life, and *Vita II* and *Vita IV*. I have here mainly outlined the contents, and only given text where discussed in the body of the article above, or where there are interesting variants. For citations from the Tripartite Life, Mulchrone's edition is referred to as 'M', Stokes's as 'S'; translations, where applicable, are from Stokes.

Descent and Origin
Tripartite Life (M, 5; S, I.8)
As to Patrick, then, of the Britons of Ail Cluaide [Dumbarton] was his origin. Calpurn was his father's name, an archpriest was he. Fotid [= Potitus] was his grandfather's name: a deacon was he. Concess was the name of his mother: of the Franks was she, and she was a kinswoman of [St] Martin's.

Vita IV, § 1
Some say that Saint Patrick was descended from the Jews. For after Our Lord suffered for the salvation of the human race, the Roman army devastated Judaea in revenge for his passion, and the Jews were led away captive and scattered throughout the world; and some of them settled among the Armorican Britons, from whom it is said Saint Patrick traced his race. This can be learnt from the *Books of Epistles* which he wrote himself, where he says: 'We were scattered to the ends of the earth because of our sins, because we did not keep the rules of the Lord and did not observe his commandments.'

However, it is certainly nearer to the truth and more certain that he is speaking of the diaspora that the Britons suffered at the hands of the Romans, as a result of which some of them occupied that land called Armorica next to the Tyrrhene Sea.

It was from that diaspora then that his parents went to the region of Strato Cluade, where Patrick was conceived and born, his father being Kalfurnus and his mother Concessa.

From the glosses on 'Genair Pátraicc i n-Nemthur'
Translation from *Thesaurus Palaeohibernicus*, ed. Stokes and Strachan, II.310–11.
Nemthor: i.e. a city in north Britain, namely Ail Cluaide.
This is the cause of his bondage. Patrick and his father, namely Calpurn, Concess his mother, a daughter of Ocmus, and his five sisters, … all went from the Britons of Ail Cluaide over the sea of Wight southwards on a journey to the Britons of Armorica, that is to the Letavian Britons; for they had relatives there at that time, and moreover, the mother of the children, i.e. Concess, was of the Franks, and she was a near relative of Martin's. That was the time at which seven sons of Sectmaide [= 'Sevensome'], king of the Britons, were in exile from the Britons. So they made a great foray among the Britons of Armorica, where Patrick was with his family, and they slew Calpurn there, and they brought Patrick and Lupait with them to Ireland…

Birth (all three Lives)
Tripartite Life (M, 5; S, I.8); also *Vita II*, *Vita IV*, § 1.1–3.
In Nemthor, however, was holy this Patrick born; and the flagstone whereon he was born, when anyone commits perjury under it, [it] pours forth water as if it were bewailing the false testimony. But if his oath be true the stone remains in its proper nature ...

Vita II, § 1–2
He was born then in that town called *Nemthor* [*Vita IV*: which may be translated into Latin as 'heavenly tower'] ... Patrick was born in *Campus Taburne*. That plain was called 'of the tents', since the Roman army once set up their tents there one cold winter, and from this it was called Campus Tabern ... [*Vita IV*: But in the British language it is called *Campus Tabern* [? = *Mathafarn*], that is 'The Plain of the Tents'.]

Here then he was born upon a stone which is still held in honour ...

Baptism (all three Lives)
Tripartite Life (M, 5; S, I.8); *Vita II*, *Vita IV*, § 3.
A church, moreover, was founded over that well in which Patrick was baptised, and there stands the well by the altar, and it has the form of the cross, as the wise declare.

Miracles (all three lives)

Miracle of flood and fire in wintertime (*Vitae*, § 5; Tripartite Life, M, 6; S, I.10)
Miracle of firewood in winter cold (*Vitae*, § 6; Tripartite Life, M, 6–7; S, I.10–12)
Heals his sister after she strikes her head on stone: she retains scar. [Later in the Life Patrick recognises her by this scar.] (*Vitae*, § 7; Tripartite Life, M, 7; S, I.12)
Miracles of sheep and wolf (*Vitae*, § 8; Tripartite Life, M, 7; S, I.12)
He cures a mad cow (*Vitae*, § 9; Tripartite Life, M, 7–8; S, I.12)
Heals his foster-father in the middle of an assembly of the Britons (*Vitae*, § 10; Tripartite Life, M, 8; S, I.14)
Raises boy from the dead with drink of milk (only in *Vita IV*, § 11, and later Irish Lives)

Miracles (only in Tripartite Life and *Vita IV*)

Turns water to honey (*Vita IV*, § 12; Tripartite Life M, 8; S, I.14)
Miracle of the palace hearth (*Vita IV*, § 13; Tripartite Life, M, 8–9; S, I.14–16)
Once the steward [*rechtairi*] of the king of the Britons went to announce to Patrick and his fostermother that they should go to cleanse the hearth of the palace of Ail Cluaide. [Patrick prays, and the fire burns without ashes.]
Miracle of the butter and cheese (*Vita IV* § 14; Tripartite Life, M, 9; S, I.16)
At another time the reeve [*rechtairi*] of the king of the Britons came to Patrick's fostermother to seek tribute of curd and butter. [Patrick makes these out of snow.]

Circumstance of Captivity
Tripartite Life (M, 9; S, I.16).
Now this is the cause of Patrick's coming at first to Ireland. There were in exile seven sons of Fechtmaide, to wit, seven sons of the king of the Britons, and they went to ravage in Armorica. It came to pass that some Britons of Strath Clyde were on a journey to their brethren, that is, to the Britons of Armorica; and in the ravaging were slain Calpurn, son of Potitus the father of Patrick, and his mother Concess, daughter of Ocbass of Gaul. Patrick, then, is taken in the ravaging ...

Vita II, § 11 [*Vita IV*, § 15].
The following was the reason for his first exile and his arrival in Ireland. [*Vita IV*: For the good providence of Almighty God had led him to that nation ... so that while still young he might learn the language of the nation whose apostle he would afterwards be.] The Irish army being assembled and gathered together in a fleet with a great number of ships would often sail across to Britain and take many prisoners away from there. And doing this as they were accustomed to, it so came to them that the boy and his sister were captured and brought to Ireland with other prisoners, of whom there were a hundred of either sex. He was then seven years old.

APPENDIX 3

Kilpatrick in the Thirteenth Century

From the Register of Paisley Abbey, c.1233; *Registrum Monasterii de Passelet*, ed. Innes, 113–15, 157–73.
THE INTENTION of the Abbot and community of Paisley is to prove that all that land of *Monachkennaran* [= Boquhanran] above the river Clyde was unjustly alienated to Gilbert son of Samuel [of Renfrew], which by right ought to belong to their church of *Kylpatrik*; wherefore they requested that that Gilbert should be removed from the said land, and that land should be legally recalled to the right and property of the said church.

FIRST presentation of the witnesses by the Abbot and community against the said Gilbert, Monday just before the feast of St Matthew [21 September], in the parish kirk of Irvine, in the year of grace 1233. Alexander son of Hugo having sworn, says that, sixty years and more previously, he saw a certain man named *Beda Ferdan* [? from G. *fer dána*] living in a certain great house made of branches next to the church of Kilpatrick facing east. And he held that land of Monachkennaran which Gilbert son of Samuel now holds. Asked in whose name he possessed the said land, he says that it was solely in the name of the church, providing no other service for the said land except receiving and feeding guests who were coming there. He says moreover that when he was a boy, he had once been received there with his father as a guest, and that the said Beda held by the same right and service the land of *Cultbuthe* [= Kilbowie] and of *Dumtechglunan* [= Duntiglennan]. Thomas Gaskel having sworn, said that he saw the said Beda Ferdan staying in the same house situated in the land of the church of Saint Patrick, holding the same lands in the same manner, by the same right, and providing the same service as Alexander had testified: he adds moreover that he saw afterwards *Cristinus* son of the said Beda possessing the same lands by the same right by which his father possessed them, and that all the land of the church was divided into four parts, of which the said Beda Ferdan possessed one part, and three others [possessed] the three other parts, any one of whom, in the name of the church, would respond to guests, shared out among themselves. Asked about the time, he says that more than forty years had passed, because he was raised there from infancy. Questioned which other lands belonged to the church, he says that *Cochmanach* [= Cochno], *Fimbelach* [= Faifley], *Edinbernan* [= Edinbarnet], and *Craguentalach* [= Craigbanzo], and certain other lands which Dufgall son of the Mormaer [*filius Comitis*; i.e. of the Lennox] now holds. Dufgall son of the Mormaer having sworn, says entirely the same as Thomas Gaskel, and adds that the said land of Monachkennaran and many other lands became alienated from the said church through his own wrong and negligence, because he did not wish to offend his father or brother or his forebears.

THE SECOND presentation of the witnesses by the Abbot and community of Paisley against the said Gilbert son of Samuel, the next Saturday after the feast of St Martin [11 November], in the parish kirk of Ayr, in the aforesaid year. *Malcolmus Beg* having sworn says that he saw Beda Ferdan inhabiting his house situated next to the cemetery of the church of Kilpatrick to the east side, and he held in the name of the church that land of Monachkenneran which Gilbert son of Samuel now holds, and for the said land and others which he held of the church he received guests coming to the church, making no other service for them [i.e. the lands]. Asked in the time of which mormaer he saw this, he says that it was in the time of Mormaer Alwin, and that the same mormaer gave to Saint Patrick and to the church that land of *Kachconnen* which he, Malcolm, held afterwards and sold through fear; and he says that all the lands of the church which the said Beda held and which Dufgall and others now hold, were free and quit from all temporal service, and that the men remaining and living on those lands were always protected by the church and were in the care of the church against everyone. *Anekol* having sworn, he says entirely the same as Malcolm Beg, and adds that Earl David the brother of King William, in the time when he held and possessed the mormaerdom of the Lennox, wanted to have assistance from those lands as from other lands of the mormaerdom, and he was not able to [get it], because they were defended by the church. *Gilon* having sworn, says entirely the same as Malcolm Beg. *Gilbethoc* having sworn, agrees with Malcolm and Anecol in everything, and adds that the said Beda was killed for the right and freedom of the church. *Fergus* son of [perhaps a mistake for *de* 'of'] Cunigham having sworn, agrees with Gilbethoc in everything. *Hilarius* having sworn, says entirely the same as Fergus and Gilbethoc. *Nemias* [= Nehemiah?] having sworn, says entirely the same as Anecol, and adds concerning the time [when this took place], that fifty years and more had passed since he saw that, and for sure he had that which he says, for he was born in that parish. *Ressin* having sworn, says entirely the same as Nemias. *Gillemor* having sworn, says entirely the same as Ressin and Nemias. *Rotheric Beg* of Carrick having sworn, agrees in everything with Malcolm Beg his brother. Asked how he knows, he says that he saw that from his adolescence, since he was born and raised in the parish of Kilpatrick. *Rathel* having sworn, he agrees in everything with the aforementioned Rotheric. *Gilkonel Manthac* [= *Gille-Conaill mantach*, 'stammering'], brother of the earl of Carrick, having sworn, says entirely the same as Malcolm Beg.

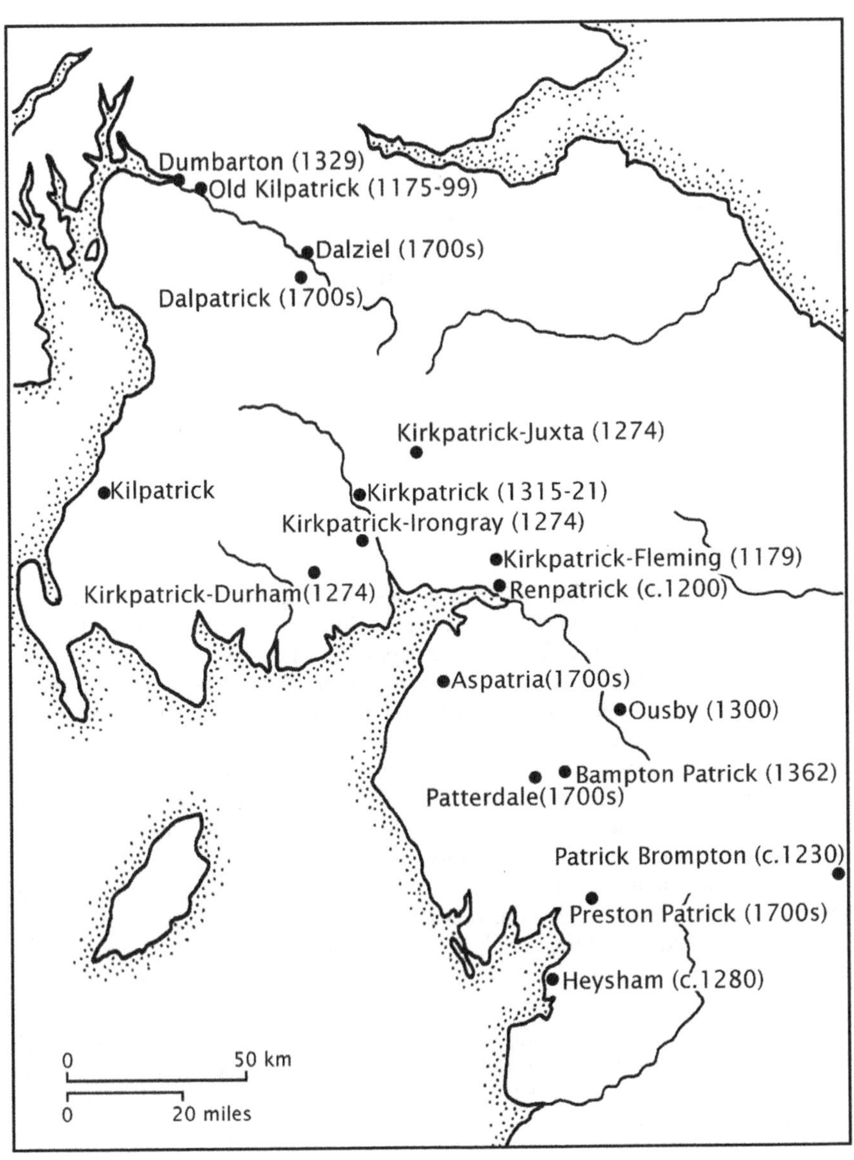

Churches dedicated to St Patrick in the kingdom of Strathclyde and surrounding areas

3

PERSONAL NAMES AND THE CULT OF PATRICK IN ELEVENTH-CENTURY STRATHCLYDE AND NORTHUMBRIA

Fiona Edmonds

It has long been known that personal names shed light on aspects of medieval society that might otherwise be obscure, including cultural identity, familial connections and religious affinities. The personal names that I shall discuss here, which describe the bearer as the devotee of a saint, can be placed in all three of these contexts.[1] The Gaelic versions of such names feature a saint's name in the genitive after the elements *máel-*, 'tonsured one', or *gille-*, 'servant' or 'devotee'.[2] A Brittonic equivalent of the *gille-* names existed too: names in *gwas-*, 'servant'.[3] The focus of this chapter, then, will be the *Gwas-Patric* and *Gille Pátraic* names that were used in the kingdom of Strathclyde and the former kingdom of Northumbria during the eleventh century.[4]

Although it is tempting to link the use of these names with the presence of St Patrick's cult in northern Britain, this equation cannot automatically be made. Other factors conditioned the popularity of the name *Gwas-Patric*, which became

1 I am grateful to the following for providing information, references, or access to their unpublished work: Dr Andrew Bell, Professor Thomas Charles-Edwards, Professor Thomas Clancy, Mr Hugh Doherty, Mr Owain Jones, Dr Oliver Padel, Dr Paul Russell and Mr Alex Woolf.

2 *Dictionary of the Irish Language based mainly on Old and Middle Irish Materials: Compact Edition* (Dublin, 1998), 361 (esp. *gilla* e), 449 (esp. *3 mael II*); M. A. O'Brien, 'Old Irish Personal Names', ed. Rolf Baumgarten, *Celtica* 10 (1973), 211–36, at 229–30.

3 *Geiriadur Prifysgol Cymru: A Dictionary of the Welsh Language*, 4 vols (Cardiff, 1950–99), II.1590–1 (esp. *gwas* 1.2b); Melville Richards, 'Gwŷr, Gwragedd a Gwehelyth', *Transactions of the Honourable Society of Cymmrodorion* (1965), 27–45, at 40–1.

4 For the sake of clarity I shall use the form *Gwas-Patric* since it is not clear which form was normal in eleventh-century Strathclyde and Northumbria (see Appendix). I shall use the form *Gospatric*, however, for the individuals who are conventionally referred to as such by scholars. The Modern Welsh form is Gwas Padrig.

Gospatrics in the house of Bamburgh

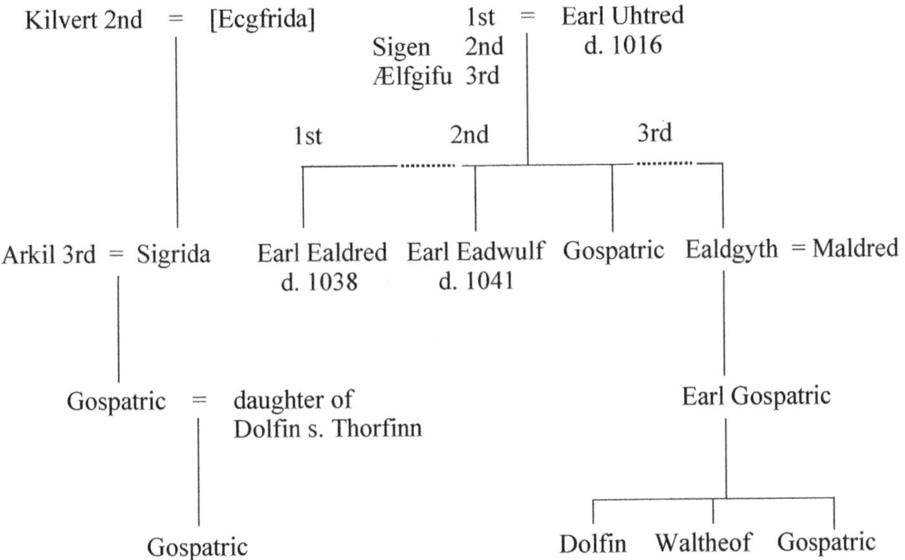

widely used in the form *Gospatric* during the twelfth century.[5] I shall nevertheless argue here that the Patrician connotation of *Gwas-Patric* was significant when the name was adopted by the house of Bamburgh during the mid-eleventh century. The Bamburgh dynasty was solidly Northumbrian, so its adoption of and adherence to a Brittonic name, which connoted devotion to a saint most widely venerated in Ireland, requires explanation.

It has previously been suggested that the earliest bearers of the name *Gwas-Patric* had links with the Brittonic-speaking territory of Strathclyde.[6] The Bamburgh dynasty's adoption of the name, however, has never been explained. I therefore aim to show that at precisely the time when the name started to be used by members of the house of Bamburgh, this family was extending its power into Strathclyde, where Patrick was venerated. Some members of the family put down roots in Strathclyde, and their interest in the cult of Patrick most probably resulted from their integration into the region. The first member of the dynasty to bear the name was Gospatric, son of Uhtred (d. 1064). The next generation of the family contained two Gospatrics: the sons of Maldred and Arkil. These men may have been named after Gospatric, son of Uhtred, but I will argue that the Strathclyde connections of the name remained significant in their generation.

Before this argument is constructed, it is necessary to explain the territorial and

5 See below, note 18.

6 William F. Skene, *Celtic Scotland: A History of Ancient Alban*, 2nd edn, 2 vols (Edinburgh, 1886–7), I.395; Charles Phythian-Adams, *Land of the Cumbrians: A Study in British Provincial Origins A.D. 400–1120* (Aldershot, 1996), 136–7.

political terms which will be used in this chapter. The kingdom of Northumbria had imploded in the later ninth century, but Northumbrian culture persisted in places, notably in the earldom centred on Bamburgh.[7] Thus the term 'Northumbrian' will be applied both to the former kingdom and to the northern earldom. By the tenth century, the kingdom of Strathclyde had absorbed territory that had belonged to the Brittonic-speaking kingdom of Dumbarton, although Strathclyde's heartlands lay further south than those of the earlier kingdom.[8] Strathclyde subsequently expanded into Dumfriesshire, and to the south of the present border with England, into modern-day Cumberland. It has been suggested that the name *Cumbra land*, and its Latin equivalent *Cumbria*, applied only to this newly acquired southern territory,[9] but it is clear that these names related to Strathclyde as a whole.[10] Some commentators have argued that Cumberland was a distinct sub-kingdom of a wider Cumbria,[11] or that Cumberland was detached from Strathclyde by the English during the tenth century.[12] Nevertheless, there are hints that the kingdom of Strathclyde remained intact during the mid-eleventh century, when the earls of Northumbria sought to exercise power there.[13] Thus in this chapter the terms 'Strathclyde' and 'Cumbria' will be applied to the territory between and including Clydesdale and Cumberland.

Gwas-, máel- *and* gille- *names*

In order to argue that the Patrician connotations of the name *Gwas-Patric* appealed to the house of Bamburgh, it is necessary to show that the name was interpreted etymologically. The etymologies of personal names, however, can quickly become irrelevant. As Cecily Clark noted, 'the meaning of a name is always

7 David Rollason, *Northumbria, 500–1100. Creation and Destruction of a Kingdom* (Cambridge, 2003), 211–90.

8 Dauvit Broun, 'The Welsh Identity of the Kingdom of Strathclyde c.900–c.1200', *IR* 55 (2004), 111–80, at 111–12; Thomas Owen Clancy, 'Ystrad Clud', in *Celtic Culture: A Historical Encyclopedia*, ed. John T. Koch, 5 vols (Santa Barbara CA and Oxford, 2006), v.1818–21; Simon Taylor, 'The Early History and Languages of West Dunbartonshire', in *Changing Identities, Ancient Roots: The History of West Dunbartonshire from Earliest Times*, ed. Ian Brown (Edinburgh, 2006), 12–41, at 25–6.

9 D. P. Kirby, 'Strathclyde and Cumbria: A Survey of Historical Developments to 1092', *TCWAAS*, 2nd series 62 (1962), 77–94, at 86–8.

10 For example, see David's Inquest, *The Charters of King David I: The Written Acts of David I King of Scots, 1124–53 and of his Son Henry Earl of Northumberland, 1139–52*, ed. G. W. S. Barrow (Woodbridge, 1999), 60–1; P. A. Wilson, 'On the Use of the Terms "Strathclyde" and "Cumbria" ', *TCWAAS* 2nd series 66 (1966), 57–92. For recent discussions of Strathclyde's extent, see D. N. Dumville, *The Churches of North Britain in the First Viking-Age*, Whithorn Lecture 5 (1997), 3 note 7, 31–2; Clare Downham, *Viking Kings of Britain and Ireland: The Dynasty of Ívarr to A.D. 1014* (Edinburgh, 2007), 159–61.

11 Phythian-Adams, *Cumbrians*, 109–29.

12 A. A. M. Duncan, *Scotland: The Making of the Kingdom* (Edinburgh, 1975; repr. 1996), 93; *idem*, *The Kingship of the Scots, 842–1292: Succession and Independence* (Edinburgh, 2002), 23–5.

13 See below.

extra-linguistic, that of a personal name being primarily a social one'.[14] The 'meaning' of the *gwas-*, *máel-* and *gille-* names is particularly hard to ascertain because these descriptive phrases were not only used as given-names, but also as epithets. For example, the epithet *Gwas Padrig*, 'devotee of Patrick', was applied to Ieuan, a patron saint of Cerrigydrudion, Denbighshire, Wales.[15] According to *Buchedd Ieuan Gwas Padrig*, Ieuan had earned the epithet in his youth, when he was a disciple of St Patrick.[16] There is no doubt that the sense of Ieuan's epithet was appreciated by the author of the text, which survives in a sixteenth- or seventeenth-century manuscript.[17]

In contrast, the lexical origins of given-names often become less important than the social connotations that the names acquire. Insley and Barrow have argued that the name *Gospatric* achieved popularity in the twelfth century because of its prestigious associations with the comital house of Bamburgh, and the offshoot of that dynasty at Dunbar[18] (Máel Coluim III granted Dunbar to Gospatric, son of Maldred, c.1072.[19]) This process of emulation was already under way in the first couple of decades of the twelfth century, when Gospatric, sheriff of Roxburgh, was active.[20] The sheriff was not closely related to the earls of Bamburgh and Dunbar; his father and grandfather had been provosts of Hexham.[21] The social connotations of the name *Gospatric* would have carried great weight in Hexhamshire. By contrast, the name's Brittonic etymology would have been less meaningful in this primarily English-speaking zone. On the other hand, the twelfth-century prestige of the name *Gospatric* cannot explain the Bamburgh dynasty's

14 Cecily Clark, 'Socio-Economic Status and Individual Identity: Essential Factors in the Analysis of Middle English Personal-Naming', in *Naming, Society and Regional Identity*, ed. David Postles (Oxford, 2002), 99–121, repr. in *Words, Names and History: Selected Writings of Cecily Clark*, ed. Peter Jackson (Cambridge, 1995), 100–13, at 101; cf. 110–11.

15 D. R. Thomas, *A History of the Diocese of St Asaph, General, Cathedral and Parochial* (London, 1870), 532–6; *LBS*, III.295–8.

16 For an edition, see *LBS*, IV.425–6.

17 J. Gwenogvryn Evans, *Report on Manuscripts in the Welsh Language*, 2 vols in 6 (London, 1898–1910), II.474, 476.

18 G. W. S. Barrow, 'Northern English Society in the Twelfth and Thirteenth Centuries', *Northern History* 4 (1969), 1–28, at 9; John Insley, 'Some Aspects of Regional Variation in Early Middle English Personal Nomenclature', *Leeds Studies in English*, new series 18 (1987), 183–99; repr. with alterations in *Studies on the Personal Name in Later Medieval England and Wales*, ed. Dave Postles and Joel T. Rosenthal, Studies in Medieval Culture 44 (Kalamazoo MI, 2006), 191–209, at 191–3, 198–201.

19 *Historia regum*: *Symeonis opera*, II.3–283, at 199; W. Greenwell, 'The House of Gospatric', in *A History of Northumberland*, ed. John Crawford Hodgson *et al.*, 3 vols in 7 (1893–1940), VII.14–106, at 36–93.

20 A. S. Ellis, 'Gospatrick', *Notes and Queries* 55.3 (1875), 131–2; G. W. S. Barrow, *Kingship and Unity: Scotland 1000–1306* (London, 1981), 7, 16; Insley, 'Some Aspects', 192.

21 James Raine, *The Priory of Hexham, its Chronicles, Endowments and Annals*, 2 vols, Surtees Society 44, 46 (Durham, 1864–5), I, appendix viii. The text that Raine provides is from BL, MS Yates Thompson 26, fol. 149r. The MS dates from the late twelfth century: Bertram Colgrave, *Two Lives of Saint Cuthbert: a Life by an Anonymous Monk of Lindisfarne and Bede's Prose Life* (Cambridge, 1940), 31–2.

adoption of the name in the eleventh century. It is likely that members of the house of Bamburgh appreciated the Patrician association of *Gwas-Patric*, even if the precise meaning of the first element was unclear to English-speakers.

The linguistic connotations of personal names also had variable significance. Lewis has noted that certain personal names 'originated in other countries and were first adopted in England in particular cultural circumstances' but that such names 'can and do naturalise within a generation of their arrival in a culture'.[22] Thus, names that were once alien to the English naming-stock could become assimilated to the point where they no longer seemed unusual. This process no doubt explains the fact that the Brittonic name *Gwas-Patric* became popular in English-speaking as well as Brittonic-speaking contexts. Lewis's comments indicate that the cultural context in which this name was adopted would have been significant. In the next section I shall argue that the name was adopted by English-speakers in the mid-eleventh century, at the interface between the cultures of Strathclyde and Northumbria.

The popularity of the name Gwas-Patric

The nature of the evidence available for the study of Northumbrian personal names before and during the eleventh century renders it impossible to establish with certainty when a particular family adopted a specific personal name. Little is known of some of the areas that are of interest for the current study because they were sparsely recorded, or not recorded at all, in the Domesday survey.[23] Nevertheless, it is possible to gauge the nature of pre-Conquest English names as a whole by examining the *Prosopography of Anglo-Saxon England* database [*PASE*] (which currently lists names up to c.1000), and the older corpus of names assembled by Searle.[24] As to the house of Bamburgh, the names of tenth-century high-reeves of Bamburgh and their descendants are recorded in the *Anglo-Saxon Chronicle* and charter witness-lists,[25] and a more detailed record of eleventh-century family members is found in twelfth-century texts from Durham.[26]

It is notable that *PASE* currently lists no *gwas-* names, and Searle's *Onomasticon* only lists Gospatrics who lived during the mid-eleventh century or

[22] C. P. Lewis, 'Joining the Dots: A Methodology for Identifying the English in Domesday Book', in *Family Trees and the Roots of Politics: The Prosopography of Britain and France from the Tenth to the Twelfth Century*, ed. K. S. B. Keats-Rohan (Woodbridge, 1997), 69–87, at 78.

[23] For lists of Domesday personal names, see Olof von Feilitzen, *The Pre-Conquest Personal Names of Domesday Book*, Nomina Germanica – Arkiv för Germansk Namnforskning utgivet av Jöran Sahlgren 3 (Uppsala, 1937); K. S. B. Keats-Rohan and David Thornton, *Domesday Names: An Index of Latin Personal and Place-Names in Domesday Book* (Woodbridge, 1997).

[24] https://www.pase.ac.uk, consulted 22 Nov. 2006; William George Searle, *Onomasticon Anglo-Saxonicum: A List of Anglo-Saxon Proper Names from the Time of Beda to that of King John* (Cambridge, 1897).

[25] Richard Fletcher, *Bloodfeud: Murder and Revenge in Anglo-Saxon England* (London, 2002), 38–42, 44; Rollason, *Northumbria*, 266–7.

[26] See below.

later.[27] It is possible that *gwas-* names were used before this time by the echelons of Northumbrian society who are not represented in the documentary record but, on the whole, borrowings of Brittonic personal names into the English naming-stock were not common.[28] Only one *Gwas-Patric* appears in a text that may pre-date the eleventh century, a manumission record in the Durham *Liber Vitae*:[29]

> 7 eac heo hafað gefreod þa men þe heo þigede æt Cwæs-patrike.[30]
>
> [And she has also freed the men whom she received from Cwæs-patrik.[31]]

Whitelock stated that the text was copied into the Durham *Liber Vitae* manuscript in a late tenth-century hand.[32] Nevertheless, Ker cited several palaeographical reasons for dating the hand to the mid-eleventh century, and this dating has been followed by recent commentators.[33] Thus, there is little reason to suspect that the

27 Searle, *Onomasticon*, 143–4, 267.

28 For examples of Brittonic names used or recorded in English-speaking milieux, see Max Förster, 'Keltisches Wortgut im Englischen, eine sprachliche Untersuchung', in *Texte und Forschungen zur englischen Kulturgeschichte, Festgabe für Felix Liebermann*, ed. *idem* and Karl Wildhagen (Halle, 1921), 119–242, at 174–97. However, many of Förster's examples are not relevant for current purposes because they postdate the twelfth century. Of those which are earlier, some are likely to have been borne by Britons, and so need not constitute evidence of borrowing of a Brittonic name into the Anglo-Saxon naming-stock. Some of the other names that Förster cites contain an ultimately Brittonic element but were formed on an English hypocoristic pattern. For the assimilation of Brittonic names into the English naming system, see J. Insley, 'Pre-Conquest Personal Names', in *Reallexikon der germanischen Altertumskunde*, Band 23 (Berlin and New York, 2003), 367–96, at 372–5. For the methodological problems surrounding the investigation of Celtic names in English contexts, see Paul Russell, 'Ye Shall Know them by their Names: Names and Identity among the Irish and the English', in *Anglo-Saxon/ Irish Relations before the Vikings*, ed. James Graham-Campbell and Michael Ryan (forthcoming).

29 *Liber vitae ecclesiae Dunelmensis: A Collotype Facsimile of the Original Manuscript, with Introductory Essay and Notes*, ed. A. Hamilton Thompson, Surtees Society 136 (London, 1923), 43; John Earle, *A Hand-book to the Land-charters, and other Saxonic Documents* (Oxford, 1888), 275, 469.

30 For the name-form, see below.

31 *EHD* 1, 610–11, at 610. An alternative translation: 'whom she interceded for with Cwæs-patrik', was offered by J. M. Kemble, *The Saxons in England: A History of the English Commonwealth till the period of the Norman Conquest*, 2 vols (London, 1849), I.197, but this requires altering the text's *þigede* to *þingede*. I am grateful to Dr Richard Dance for discussing this phrase with me.

32 *EHD* 1, 610–11, at 610; cf. Walter de Gray Birch, *Cartularium Saxonicum: A Collection of Charters Relating to Anglo-Saxon History*, 3 vols (London, 1885–93; repr. 1964), III.538–9.

33 N. R. Ker, *Catalogue of Manuscripts containing Anglo-Saxon* (Oxford, 1957), 186–7; David A. E. Pelteret, *Slavery in Early Medieval England*, Studies in Anglo-Saxon History 7 (Woodbridge, 1995), xv, 161–2. Dr Peter Stokes has told me that the hand is likely to belong to the mid-eleventh century, on the basis of a parallel with a contemporary section of *Anglo-Saxon Chronicle* D. This chapter was written before the publication

Brittonic name *Gwas-Patric* entered the Northumbrian naming-stock before the mid-eleventh century.

Next it is necessary to place this name in the context of the naming practices of Brittonic-speaking territories. It is hard to ascertain the relative popularity of names in Wales, Cornwall and Brittany before 1100, but Meredith Cane has produced numerous ranking-tables for Welsh names c.1100–1400.[34] No *gwas*-names appear in Cane's overall top-twenties and top-forties for any period within that time bracket.[35] Thus, *gwas-* names in general appear to have been rare; clusters of specific *gwas-* names developed in areas where the relevant saints were venerated.[36]

Gwas- names were also uncommon in Brittany and Cornwall. No examples are known from pre-Norman Cornwall, but few texts pertaining to the area survive. Names or patronymics in *Gwas-Dewi*[37] occur twice, and in *Gwas-Peder* three times,[38] in thirteenth- and early fourteenth-century administrative records. As Oliver Padel has pointed out to me, the bearers of the *Gwas-Dewi* names might have come to Cornwall from South Wales. However, it is likely that the *Gwas-Peder* patronymics originated locally because they were found within the sphere of influence of St Petrock's priory.[39] The Breton name *Guos-Cadoc* appears in a charter that is found in the eleventh-century Redon Cartulary, but which relates to the 830s.[40] Interestingly, *Guos-Cadoc* and a number of other witnesses seem to have been based *in plebe Catoc*.[41] Assuming that this charter contains genuine ninth-century material, it indicates that *gwas-* names were part of the Brittonic naming-stock during the early medieval period.

Thus, one would expect *gwas-* names to have been present, but rare, in the

of *Durham Liber Vitae: The Complete Edition*, ed. David and Lynda Rollason (3 vols, London, 2007).

34 Meredith Cane, 'Personal Names of Men in Wales, Cornwall and Brittany 400–1400 AD' (Unpublished PhD thesis, Aberystwyth, 2003).

35 *ibid.*, 99, 101–8, 120.

36 Francis Jones, 'The Subsidy of 1292', *Bulletin of the Board of Celtic Studies* 13 (1948–50), 210–30, at 213.

37 '(Rogerus et Willelmus essoniant) Thomam filium Wastdeui', in *Pleas before the King or his Justices, 1198–1202*, ed. Doris Mary Stenton, Selden Society 67–8, 2 vols (London, 1952–3 for 1948–9), II.43; '(de) Wastdewy de Karwarri', *The Beauchamp Cartulary Charters 1100–1268*, ed. Emma Mason, Pipe Roll Society 81 (London, 1980 for 1971–3), 212. For a relevant place-name, see O. J. Padel, *Cornish Place-Name Elements*, English Place-Name Society 56–7 (Nottingham, 1985), 115.

38 'Nicholas Waspeder', 'Reginaldum Waspeder' and 'Walterus Guaspeder', from unpublished documents brought to my attention by Oliver Padel. For the last two, see Padel, *Cornish Place-Name Elements*, 115.

39 I am extremely grateful to Oliver Padel for supplying me with information about the Cornish and Breton *gwas-* names.

40 *Cartulaire de l'abbaye de Saint-Sauveur de Redon*, ed. Hubert Guillotel *et al.* (Rennes, 1998), fol. 7v; 54, 72; *Cartulaire de l'abbaye de Redon en Bretagne*, ed. M. Aurélien de Courson (Paris, 1863), 13; Léon Fleuriot, *Dictionnaire des gloses en vieux Breton* (Paris, 1964), 199–200.

41 Joseph Loth, 'Étymologiques et lexicographiques', *Revue celtique* 29 (1908), 68–71, at 69.

Brittonic kingdom of Strathclyde.[42] Various commentators have argued that Strathclyde was dominated by the dynasty of Alba,[43] but more recently Hudson, Macquarrie and Broun have suggested that native kings ruled the kingdom into the eleventh century.[44] Therefore, Brittonic language and culture could have remained significant in the heartlands of the kingdom of Strathclyde. This also seems to have been true of the south of the kingdom, although it is unclear whether the language had endured throughout the period of Anglian political domination there, or whether it had been reinvigorated in the formerly Northumbrian territory that came into Strathclyde's political remit during the tenth century.[45]

In order to investigate the naming practices of Strathclyde it is necessary to refer to twelfth-century material because few texts pertain to the kingdom before its demise. The witness-list of a record of the perambulation of Stobo, Peeblesshire, included a *Cosouold* (*Gwas-Oswald*), three sons of *Cosmungho* (*Gwas-Mungho*), *Gillemihhel queschutbrit*, 'servant of Cuthbert', and several people called *Cospatricius*, *Patricius* or *Padinus*.[46] *Queschutbrit* also appears as the given-name of a man who held lands in Corby, Cumberland, according to records of the enfeoffment of Hubert de Vaux there.[47] Another such name, *Wes-Escop*,

42 The Old English text known as 'Gospatric's writ', which concerns land in Cumberland, includes a term deriving from the word *gwas-*, namely *wassenas*. See Andrew Breeze, 'Old English *wassenas* "retainers" in Gospatrick's writ', *Notes and Queries* 237 (1992), 272–5.

43 Kirby, 'Strathclyde', 84–94; Alfred P. Smyth, *Warlords and Holy Men: Scotland AD 80–1000* (London, 1984), 220–31.

44 B. T. Hudson, '*Elech* and the Scots in Strathclyde', *Scottish Gaelic Studies* 15 (1988), 145–9; Alan Macquarrie, 'The Kings of Strathclyde, c.400–1018', in *Medieval Scotland: Crown, Lordship and Community. Essays Presented to G. W. S. Barrow*, ed. Alexander Grant and Keith J. Stringer (Edinburgh, 1993), 1–19, at 6, 12–15; Broun, 'Welsh Identity', 125–35.

45 Phythian-Adams, *Cumbrians*, 79–87, 105. Kenneth Jackson, 'Angles and Britons in Northumbria and Cumbria', in *Angles and Britons: O'Donnell Lectures*, ed. H. Lewis (Cardiff, 1963), 60–84, at 77, 80–4. For recent discussions of this matter, see John M. Todd, 'British (Cumbric) Place-Names in the Barony of Gilsland, Cumbria', *TCWAAS* 3rd series 5 (2005), 89–102; Andrew Breeze, 'Britons in the Barony of Gilsland, Cumbria', *Northern History* 43 (2006), 327–32.

46 *Registrum Episcopatus Glasguensis: munimenta ecclesie metropolitane Glasguensis, a sede restaurata seculo ineunte XII, ad reformatam religionem*, ed. Cosmo Innes, Bannatyne Club 75, 2 vols (Edinburgh, 1843), I.89. For comments on the names in the witness-list, see G. W. S. Barrow, *The Anglo-Norman Era in Scottish History* (Oxford, 1980), 34–5; Thomas Owen Clancy, 'Scottish Saints and National Identities in the Early Middle Ages', in *Local Saints and Local Churches in the Early Medieval West*, ed. Alan Thacker and Richard Sharpe (Oxford, 2002), 397–421, at 406, note 37; Broun, 'Welsh Identity', 121. This record tends to be dated to c.1200 but James Wilson placed it several decades earlier: 'Divise de Stobbo', *The Scottish Antiquary* 17 (1902–3), 105–11. Cf. William J. Watson, *History of the Celtic Place-Names of Scotland* (Edinburgh, 1926), 134, 150; George F. Black, *The Surnames of Scotland: their Origin, Meaning and History* (New York, 1946), 174.

47 Wilson, 'Divise', 107–9; Barrow, 'Northern English Society', 7. Records of the enfeoffment and two confirmations to Hubert's son are found on roll 28, *Cartae Antiquae* rolls, facsimiles of which appear in James Wilson, 'Domesday Book, Pipe Rolls, and Testa de Nevill', *VCH Cumberland*, ed. H. Arthur Doubleday, 2 vols

'devotee of the bishop', appeared in late twelfth-century Tynedale.[48] This name may lie behind the forms *Wescop* and *Wesecop*, which were borne by the son of the man who held Gilsland before the arrival of de Vaux.[49] It is likely that the *gwas* names originated among the Brittonic-speaking strata in Strathclyde's population before the twelfth century. Indeed, some of the recorded forms resemble the *gwas*-names familiar from the other Brittonic-speaking territories, although the sound /*gw*/- was rendered either /*w*/- or /*kw*/- by English-speakers.[50] Hence the forms *Queschutbricht*, *Cwæs-patrik* and *Waspatricwath*, 'Waspatric's ford' (see Appendix). In northern British contexts, *gwas*- was also rendered *gos*- or *cos*-. A full study of the relationship between these forms remains to be undertaken.[51] The idea that *gwas*- names were used in Strathclyde before the twelfth century is supported by the patronal dedications found in the names. The mixture of Northumbrian and native saints reflects the cultural influences present in the Cumbrian kingdom during its heyday.[52]

The Stobo perambulation gives the impression that *gwas*- names were much more popular in Strathclyde than they were in Wales, Brittany and Cornwall. It is difficult to substantiate this point because the sample of names from Strathclyde is so small. Nevertheless, the popularity of *gille*- names among Gaelic-speaking peoples from c.950 onwards may have promoted the use of the *gwas*- names in Strathclyde, as Clancy has suggested.[53] During the tenth and eleventh centuries, Strathclyde's population was exposed to the Gaelic naming practices of Gaelic–Scandinavian settlers and dignitaries from the neighbouring kingdom of Alba.[54]

(London, 1901–5), I.295–335, plates facing 306, 320. A record of *exclusagium* relating to Wetheral priory was witnessed by *Wescubrict*. In a confirmation, this transaction is dated *tempore Westutbricd*: *The Register of the Priory of Wetherhal*, ed. J. E. Prescott, CWAAS Chartulary Series 1 (London, 1897), 6–12, 25. For the problematic nature of this edition, see below 55.

48 Barrow, 'Northern English Society', 8.

49 For these forms, see two transcripts of deeds printed in the appendix to *The Lanercost Cartulary (Cumbria County Record Office MS DZ/1)*, ed. John M. Todd, Surtees Society 203 (1997), 404, 406.

50 Kenneth Jackson, *Language and History in Early Britain: A Chronological Survey of the Brittonic Languages First to Twelfth Century A.D.* (Edinburgh, 1953), 387, 390; Eilert Ekwall, *Scandinavians and Celts in the North-West of England*, Lunds Universitets Årsskrift (Lund, 1918), 79, 110; Breeze, 'Old English *wassenas*', 273.

51 Jackson, *Language*, 707. Paul Russell has work in progress on this matter; I am grateful to him, and to Simon Taylor and John Koch, for discussing the subject with me. For forms of this element in various Celtic languages, see John T. Koch, ' "Gallo-Brittonic" vs. "Insular Celtic": The Inter-relationships of the Celtic Languages Reconsidered', in *Bretagne et pays celtiques: langues, histoire, civilisation: mélanges offerts à la mémoire de Léon Fleuriot*, ed. Gwennolé Le Menn and Jean-Yves Le Moing (Rennes and Saint-Brieuc, 1992), 471–95, at 478–9.

52 Thomas Owen Clancy, 'The Real St Ninian', *IR* 52 (2001), 1–28, at 21; *idem*, 'Scottish Saints', 411.

53 Clancy, 'St Ninian', 12; O'Brien, 'Old Irish Personal Names', 229–30; Brian Ó Cuív, 'Borrowed Elements in the Corpus of Irish Personal Names', *Nomina* 3 (1979), 40–51, at 47; *idem*, 'Aspects of Irish Personal Names', *Celtica* 18 (1986), 151–84, at 167–8; see below 59.

54 Although Alba's political influence seems to have had little long-term impact on the

It is also apparent that the name *Gwas-Patric* was more popular in northern Britain than it was in the other Brittonic-speaking territories. The name is not attested at all in Brittany and Cornwall. The lay subsidy rolls for Wales, 1292–3, have several instances: *Was Patrik* and *Wir ap Was Patrik* appear in the Merioneth roll;[55] *Was patric* in the Montgomery record;[56] *David ap Waspateric* in the Radnor roll.[57] Other medieval records mention divisions of family land (*gwely* and *gafael*) belonging to men bearing this name: *wele Gwas Padryk* in Caernarvonshire and *gavel Was Patryk* in Denbighshire.[58] Yet on the whole, *Gwas-Patric* appears far less frequently in the Welsh records than do *Gwas-Mair*, *Gwas-Dewi* and other such names.[59] The relative popularity of *Gwas-Patric* in northern Britain is explained by the strength of Patrick's cult there and the adoption of the name by the Bamburgh dynasty.

Gospatric, son of Uhtred

In order to ascertain the circumstances under which the name *Gwas-Patric* was adopted by the house of Bamburgh, it is necessary to investigate the first two generations of Northumbrians to bear the name (fl. c.1020–86). The history of the house of Bamburgh is elucidated by texts produced at Durham during the twelfth century. These include the *Historia regum* attributed to Simeon of Durham, the latter's *Libellus de exordio*, and two anonymous tracts, *De primo Saxonum adventu* and *De obsessione Dunelmi*.[60] The dangers of relying on this twelfth-century material are revealed by a brief discussion of *De obsessione Dunelmi*. The work is found in a section of Cambridge Corpus Christi MS 139 that is thought to

kingdom of Strathclyde until the eleventh century: see note 44, above. For the Gaelic–Scandinavian impact on Strathclyde see Downham, *Viking Kings*, 162–70. For Gaelic–Scandinavian settlement to the south of Strathclyde see *ibid.*, 84–5; N. J. Higham, *The Kingdom of Northumbria AD 350–1100* (Stroud, 1993), 184–8; Dumville, *Churches*, 25–6.

55 *The Merioneth Lay Subsidy Roll 1292–3*, ed. Keith Williams-Jones (Cardiff, 1976), 26, 34.

56 'A Powys Lay Subsidy Roll', ed. R. Morgan, *The Montgomeryshire Collections: Journal of the Powysland Club* 71 (1983), 91–112, at 94.

57 'The Assessment of the Fifteenth of 1293 on Radnor and other Marcher Lordships', ed. M. A. Faraday, *Transactions of the Radnorshire Society* 44 (1974), 62–8, at 67.

58 *Registrum vulgariter nuncupatum 'the Record of Caernarvon'*, ed. Henry Ellis (London, 1838), 17. *Survey of the Honour of Denbigh 1334*, ed. Paul Vinogradoff and Frank Morgan, British Academy Records of the Social and Economic History of England and Wales 1 (London, 1914), 53.

59 Jones, 'The Subsidy', 213; Cane, 'Names', 106–8, 120.

60 'Historia regum', *Symeonis opera*, II.3–283, especially the account of the earls' family history s.a. 1072, at 196–9. *Libellus de exordio atque procursu istius, hoc est Dunhelmensis, ecclesie*, ed. and trans. David Rollason (Oxford, 2000); also known as 'Historia Dunelmensis ecclesiae', *Symeonis opera*, I.17–135. 'De primo Saxonum adventu', *Symeonis opera*, II.365–84. 'De obsessione Dunelmi', *Symeonis opera*, I.215–20; trans. C. J. Morris, *Marriage and Murder in Eleventh-Century Northumbria: A Study of 'De obsessione Dunelmi'*, Borthwick Papers 82 (York, 1992), 1–5.

have been written and compiled in the 1160s.[61] However, the date of the tract's composition is uncertain: Meehan suggested that the bulk of the material derived from the 1070s, although some additions were made in the twelfth century, but Anderson placed the tract's composition c.1100 × 1140.[62] Some of the material was selected in order to illustrate a dispute that continued to have repercussions in the twelfth century: the controversy over the fate of six vills that had formed the dowry of Bishop Aldhun's daughter on her marriage to Earl Uhtred.[63] Nevertheless, the genealogical material contained in the tract has inspired some confidence,[64] although the information is far from comprehensive (see table).

The earliest known Northumbrian bearer of the name *Gwas-Patric* was Gospatric, the son of Earl Uhtred and Uhtred's second wife, Sigen.[65] Uhtred's eldest sons, Ealdred and Eadwulf, became earls of Northumbria, but Gospatric never attained this office, which fell instead to Earl Siward of York.[66] This development might have marginalised Gospatric, but Siward attempted to appease the house of Bamburgh by marrying Gospatric's niece.[67] Indeed, Gospatric seems to have remained an important part of the Northumbrian scene until Tostig's earldom (1055–65), when a 'nobilis Northymbrensis minister' called Gospatric was killed at court at the behest of Tostig's sister, Queen Ealdgyth.[68] It is impossible to prove that the victim was Gospatric, son of Uhtred,[69] but this man is the only known candidate: the two other Gospatrics who are known to have been alive at the time (the sons of Arkil and Maldred) died many years after 1064.[70] Fletcher has suggested that Gospatric, son of Uhtred, was murdered because he represented the

61 Peter Hunter Blair, 'Some Observations on the "Historia regum" Attributed to Symeon of Durham', in *Celt and Saxon: Studies in the Early British Border*, ed. Kenneth Hurlstone Jackson and Nora K. Chadwick (Cambridge, 1963), 63–118, at 69–70; Derek Baker, 'Scissors and Paste: Corpus Christi, Cambridge, MS 139 Again', in *The Materials, Sources and Methods of Ecclesiastical History*, ed. *idem*, Studies in Church History 11 (Oxford, 1975), 83–123, at 95–8.

62 Bernard Meehan, 'The Siege of Durham, the Battle of Carham and the Cession of Lothian', *SHR* 55 (1976), 1–19, at 18; Marjorie O. Anderson, 'Lothian and the Early Scottish Kings', *SHR* 39 (1960), 98–112, at 111; cf. Morris, *Marriage*, 7–10.

63 Morris, *Marriage*, 12–18; Fletcher, *Bloodfeud*, 4–5, 75, 123–41.

64 Morris, *Marriage*, 11–12.

65 'De obsessione', *Symeonis opera*, I.215–16; 'De primo', *Symeonis opera III*, II. 383.

66 'Historia regum', *Symeonis opera*, II.197–8; *ASC*, Part 6: *MS D*, ed. G. P. Cubbin (Woodbridge, 1996), 66; *ASC* Part 5, *MS C*, ed. Katherine O'Brien O'Keeffe (Woodbridge, 2000), 107; Fletcher, *Bloodfeud*, 137–8; William E. Kapelle, *The Norman Conquest of the North. The Region and its Transformation, 1000–1135* (London, 1979), 25–6, 245, note 7. Siward killed Eadwulf according to 'Historia regum'; cf. 'De primo', *Symeonis opera*, II.383 and *Libellus*, ed. Rollason, 170–1.

67 'Historia regum', *Symeonis opera*, II.199, 209; 'De obsessione', *Symeonis opera*, I.219; Kapelle, *Norman Conquest*, 29; Fletcher, *Bloodfeud*, 146; Higham, *Kingdom of Northumbria*, 232.

68 'noble Northumbrian thegn'; *The Chronicle of John of Worcester*, ed. and trans. R. R. Darlington, P. McGurk *et al.* 3 vols (1995–in progress), II.596–9; 'Historia regum', *Symeonis opera*, II.178; Higham, *Kingdom of Northumbria*, 235–6.

69 Alex Woolf urges caution on this point: *From Pictland to Alba, 789–1070*, New Edinburgh History of Scotland 2 (Edinburgh, 2007), 249–52.

70 See below, 55–8.

old Northumbrian regime, which had become disenchanted with Tostig's tax-heavy and militarily deficient rule.[71] Gospatric's grandson, Eadwulf Rus, continued to represent Northumbrian interests during the post-Norman period.[72]

Thus, Gospatric remained influential during the 1040s–60s although he did not become earl. Fletcher has argued that Siward granted Gospatric 'an alternative command in newly conquered Cumbria' in order to retain Gospatric's support.[73] There is some evidence to support the notion that Siward's influence extended into Strathclyde. First, Siward appears to have been the patron of the Cumbrian dynasty. After defeating Mac Bethad in 1054, Siward installed Máel Coluim, 'regis Cumbrorum filius' 'son of the king of the Cumbrians', as king.[74] It used to be thought that this Máel Coluim was Máel Coluim III, and therefore that his father, Donnchad I, must have held the kingship of Cumbria before he became the king of Scots.[75] A. A. M. Duncan has pointed out, however, that Máel Coluim III did not become king in the aftermath of Siward's victory in 1054 and that there are no other indications that Donnchad I was a king of Cumbria. Duncan suggests instead that Siward raised a different Máel Coluim, most probably the son of Owain the Bald, king of Strathclyde, to kingship.[76]

Second, two predecessors of the bishops of Glasgow were consecrated by an archbishop of York during Siward's earldom. This information appears in a twelfth-century text that promoted York's claims to suffragan bishops, so its accuracy is questionable.[77] The location of the bishops' base and sphere of operations is also unclear; there are few indications that Glasgow sustained a major ecclesiastical centre during the eleventh century.[78] Nevertheless, some credence is lent to the tradition by the eleventh-century Northumbrian-style cross-heads that have been unearthed at Glasgow Cathedral and Hoddom, Dumfriesshire, as Alex Woolf has pointed out.[79] A more explicit confirmation of Siward's power in the west is

71 Fletcher, *Bloodfeud*, 157–8; cf. Kapelle, *Norman Conquest*, 88–100.

72 'De primo', *Symeonis opera*, II.383; 'Historia regum', *Symeonis opera*, II.197; Kapelle, *Norman Conquest*, 139–40 (although Kapelle incorrectly states that Eadwulf was Gospatric's son).

73 Fletcher, *Bloodfeud*, 147; cf. H. W. C. Davis, 'Cumberland before the Norman Conquest', *EHR* 20 (1905), 61–5, at 64; Kapelle, *Norman Conquest*, 29.

74 *Chronicle*, ed. Darlington and McGurk, II.574–5; William of Malmesbury, *Gesta regum anglorum: The History of the English Kings*, ed. and trans. R. A. B. Mynors *et al.*, 2 vols (Oxford, 1998), I.348–9.

75 Skene, *Celtic Scotland*, I.410–11.

76 Duncan, *Kingship*, 37–41. This argument is accepted by Broun, 'Welsh Identity', 133–4; Clancy, 'Ystrad Clud', 1820; Woolf, *Pictland to Alba*, 238, 262.

77 Hugh the Chantor, *The History of the Church of York*, ed. and trans. Charles Johnson (London, 1961), 32; cf. Kapelle, *Norman Conquest*, 44; Broun, 'Welsh Identity', 138, 156. The information was derived, however, from oral tradition rather than a forged document: Norman F. Shead, 'The Origins of the Medieval Diocese of Glasgow', *SHR* 48 (1969), 220–5, at 220; John Durkan, 'Glasgow Diocese and the Claims of York', *IR* 50 (1999), 89–101, at 89, 100–1.

78 Shead, 'Origins', 220–5; cf. Stephen T. Driscoll, 'The Historical Background', in *Excavations at Glasgow Cathedral, 1988–1997*, ed. *idem* (Leeds, 2002), 1–3, at 1.

79 Woolf, *Pictland to Alba*, 263. For the date, see *ibid.*, 263 n.65, which is a slight modification of K. Forsyth, 'Cross-head', in *Excavations*, ed. Driscoll, 86–7.

found in the text known as 'Gospatric's writ', which states that Siward granted the *gyrth*, 'peace', in formerly Cumbrian lands to the south of the Solway.[80] Thus, Siward exerted power in the south of Strathclyde and it is possible that he had influence over the kingdom's ecclesiastical and dynastic institutions, which were located further north.

The interaction between the earls of Northumbria and the kingdom of Strathclyde in the early to mid-eleventh century explains the adoption of the name *Gwas-Patric* by the house of Bamburgh. The mechanics of the naming process can only be conjectured, but two scenarios deserve consideration. First, it is possible that Earl Uhtred selected the name because he hoped that his third son would establish influence in Cumbria. A parallel is found in the Frankish world: when Chlodomer of Orléans was seeking to expand into Burgundy he gave his son Gunthar a distinctively Burgundian name.[81] The Northumbrians wished to expand westwards in order to neutralise the risk of combined military action by the kings of Alba and Strathclyde.[82] That alliance had wrought a heavy defeat on the Northumbrians at the Battle of Carham (1018) and it apparently underpinned Donnchad I's raid on Durham c.1040.[83] In the second scenario, Gospatric acquired *Gwas-Patric* as an epithet during his sojourn in Strathclyde in the 1040s–60s. The soubriquet was subsequently interpreted as a personal name by the chroniclers and Durham writers (whose works all postdated Gospatric's death).

Gospatric, son of Uhtred, has sometimes been identified with the Gospatric who is mentioned in 'Gospatric's writ'.[84] According to the 'writ', Gospatric had control of formerly Cumbrian territory to the south of the Solway. However, several commentators have identified this dignitary with Gospatric's nephew, Gospatric, son of Maldred.[85] Phythian-Adams has recently made two points in favour of the nephew. First, the writ only survives in an inaccurate thirteenth-century copy, and so it is impossible to determine whether Gospatric was operating under the aegis of a live Siward, or as Siward's successor. In the second

80 F. E. Harmer, *Anglo-Saxon Writs* (Manchester, 1952), 419–24; also trans. in Phythian-Adams, *Cumbrians*, 173; cf. Higham, *Kingdom of Northumbria*, 231.

81 Eugen Ewig, 'Die Namengebung bei den ältesten Frankenkönigen und im merowingischen Königshaus', *Francia* 18 (1991), 21–69, at 27–8, 30–1.

82 Kapelle, *Norman Conquest*, 34–9, 43; Henry Summerson, *Medieval Carlisle: The City and the Borders from the Late Eleventh to the Mid-Sixteenth Century*, CWAAS Extra Series 25, 2 vols (Kendal, 1993), I.14.

83 *Libellus*, ed. Rollason, 154–7, 168–9; 'Historia regum', *Symeonis opera*, II.155–6, 198. For a survey of views about the date of the battle of Carham, see Kapelle, *Norman Conquest*, 21–2, 243, note 48. For the 1040 raid, see *Early Sources of Scottish History: A.D. 500 to 1286*, ed. Alan Orr Anderson, 2 vols (Edinburgh, 1922), I.583; Fletcher, *Bloodfeud*, 134.

84 Davis, 'Cumberland', 61–5; A. M. Armstrong *et al.*, *The Place-Names of Cumberland*, English Place-Name Society 20–2, 3 vols (Cambridge, 1950–2), III.xxvii, xxx; Harmer, *Writs*, 420, 526; Kapelle, *Norman Conquest*, 44, 249–50; Fletcher, *Bloodfeud*, 147.

85 James Wilson, 'An English Letter of Gospatric', *SHR* 1 (1904), 62–9, at 63; *idem* and R. A. Allison, 'Political History', in *VCH Cumberland*, II.221–330, at 231–5; Greenwell, 'Gospatric', 24–5; Anderson, *Early Sources*, II.36–9; Kirby, 'Strathclyde', 93; Duncan, *Scotland*, 98, 120.

circumstance, the individual in question would be Gospatric, son of Maldred, who was earl of Northumbria 1067–8 and 1070–2.[86] Secondly, Phythian-Adams argues that men mentioned in Gospatric's writ, or their immediate descendants, attested the foundation deed for Wetheral priory, which can probably be dated to the first two decades of the twelfth century.[87] These family sequences indicate that the 'writ' belongs to the later eleventh century, rather than the earlier period during which Gospatric, son of Uhtred, flourished.[88] Phythian-Adams's argument is compelling, but, as he has noted, the date of the Wetheral charter is not secure.[89] The published edition of the cartulary was made from transcripts rather than the original manuscript, and in the manuscript the foundation charter appears in two late additions.[90] This raises suspicions about the authenticity of the foundation charter, although some of its details ring true, as Sharpe has noted.[91]

The sons of Maldred and Arkil

The adoption of the name *Gwas-Patric* for, or by, Earl Uhtred's third son is explained by the house of Bamburgh's involvement in Strathclyde. Did this factor underpin the naming of subsequent Gospatrics, or were these men simply named after Gospatric, son of Uhtred? Cecily Clark has demonstrated that kings, local gentry and priests provided name-models during the eleventh and twelfth centuries.[92] The name of a member of the house of Bamburgh would have been equally influential, especially within the family: Gospatric, son of Maldred, and Gospatric, son of Arkil, were tied to Gospatric, son of Uhtred, by blood and marriage. Nevertheless, it can be shown that the Bamburgh dynasty's territorial links to Strathclyde also influenced the selection of the name *Gwas-Patric* for the sons of Maldred and Arkil.

The idea that Gospatric, son of Maldred, was influential in the west is supported by the careers of his children.[93] In 1212 it was noted that Gospatric's son Waltheof had been enfeoffed in Allerdale, Cumberland, by Henry I; this action is perhaps to be associated with Henry's visit to Carlisle in 1122.[94] However, Sharpe has noted that the grants ascribed to Henry can in some cases (including Waltheof's) be interpreted as confirmations of holdings that existed when Ranulf Meschin had

86 Phythian-Adams, *Cumbrians*, 175; cf. Harmer, *Writs*, 420, 531, 534.

87 *Wetherhal*, ed. Prescott, 1–5.

88 Phythian-Adams, *Cumbrians*, 30–1, 174–81.

89 *ibid.*, 177.

90 Richard Sharpe, *Norman Rule in Cumbria 1092–1136*, CWAAS Tract Series 21 (Kendal, 2006), 22–3. I am grateful to Hugh Doherty for pointing out the problematic nature of Prescott's edition.

91 Sharpe, *Norman Rule*, 47, note 119, suggesting the date-range 1101 × 1112.

92 Cecily Clark, 'Willelmus rex? vel alius Willelmus?', *Nomina* 11 (1987), 7–33; repr. in *Words, Names*, ed. Jackson, 280–98.

93 Phythian-Adams, *Cumbrians*, 136–7, 181, 155; cf. Greenwell, 'Gospatric', 26–9.

94 *Liber Feodorum. The Book of Fees Commonly Called Testa de Nevill*, ed. H. C. Maxwell Lyte, 3 vols (London, 1920–31), I.198; Wilson, 'Domesday Book', 308; *idem*, 'Political', II.241; Sharpe, *Norman Rule*, 34, note 80, 52–4.

power in the region, before Henry took personal responsibility for it.[95] It is less clear whether Waltheof's association with Allerdale predates the Norman era, but it is notable that the Gospatric of the writ had control in Allerdale. Another son of Gospatric, Dolfin,[96] is likely to be the lord of Carlisle who was removed by William Rufus in 1092.[97]

In order to understand how Gospatric, son of Maldred, came by his Brittonic name, it is worth asking whether these family links with Cumbrian territory dated back to his childhood. Phythian-Adams has suggested that Gospatric inherited his interest in formerly Cumbrian territory from his father, Maldred. The latter supposedly held authority in the south of the Cumbrian kingdom on behalf of his young nephew, Máel Coluim, 'son of the king of the Cumbrians'.[98] This scenario, however, is problematic in two respects: first, Maldred's family background is obscure. In the Durham material Maldred's father is described as *Crinan tein*, but the conventional identification of this man with Crínán of Dunkeld, father of Donnchad I, rests on shaky foundations, as Barrow has noted.[99] Secondly, even if Maldred was Donnchad's brother, it is now thought that the latter was not 'king of the Cumbrians', and so Maldred's link with Cumbria has to be otherwise explained.[100]

Maldred's name may provide a clue to his origins. The name does not seem to be English: no Anglo-Saxon Maldreds are listed in *PASE* or Searle's *Onomasticon*.[101] Woolf has argued that the name originated as Gaelic *Máel Doraid*, but the extant forms offer little support for this identification (see Appendix).[102] Oliver Padel has compared the first element of *Maldred* with that of the Brittonic name *Maelgwn*.[103] The possibility that the name originated in a Brittonic-speaking milieu has implications for Maldred's links with Strathclyde.

The northern British tales *Lailoken A* and *B* hint that the name *Maldred* was native to Strathclyde.[104] According to tale *A*, Lailoken was a madman who begged St Kentigern for the last sacrament. Having received it, Lailoken was killed by three shepherds employed by King *Meldred*. *Lailoken B* provides the background to the murder, which took place near Meldred's *oppidum* at *Dunmeller* (Drumelzier, Peeblesshire). The tales appear in a fifteenth-century manuscript, BL

95 Sharpe, *Norman Rule*, 53–5; cf. Phythian-Adams, *Cumbrians*, 30; G. W. S. Barrow, 'The Pattern of Lordship and Feudal Settlement in Cumbria', *Journal of Medieval History* 1 (1975), 117–38, at 121.

96 'De obsessione', *Symeonis opera*, I.216; 'De primo', *Symeonis opera*, II.383; 'Historia regum', *Symeonis opera*, II.199.

97 *ASC*, Part 7, MSE, ed. Susan Irvine (Woodbridge, 2004), s.a. 1092, 103; *Chronicle*, ed. McGurk, III.62–3; Summerson, *Carlisle*, I.11, 47–9; Sharpe, *Norman Cumbria*, 34–5, n 80.

98 Phythian-Adams, *Cumbrians*, 132, 136–7, 152, 153, 181.

99 'De obsessione', *Symeonis opera*, I.216; 'De primo', *Symeonis opera*, II.383; 'Historia regum', *Symeonis opera*, II.199. Geoffrey W. S. Barrow, 'Some Problems in Twelfth- and Thirteenth-century Scottish History – A Genealogical Approach', *The Scottish Genealogist* 25 (1978), 97–112, at 98.

100 See above, 53.

101 Cf. Barrow, 'Some Problems', 98; see note 24, above.

102 Woolf, *Pictland to Alba*, 249–50.

103 Pers. comm. For other names in *Maglo-*, see Jackson, *Language and History*, 463–6.

104 I owe this reference to Oliver Padel.

Cotton Titus A XIX,[105] but a version of *Lailoken B* must have been extant by the mid-twelfth century because it inspired an episode of the *Vita Merlini* by Geoffrey of Monmouth (d. 1155).[106] If *Lailoken B* reached its current form in the twelfth century, it is possible that Maldred, father of Gospatric, inspired the character *Meldred.*[107] In this case, the texts have no bearing on the possible Brittonic origin of the name *Maldred.* Jarman argued that a version of the *Lailoken* tales had migrated to Wales by the tenth century, but it cannot be proved that this version contained references to *Meldred.*[108]

Even if Gospatric did not derive his Cumbrian connections from his father, his maternal line would have provided an opening to formerly Cumbrian territory. Gospatric was linked to the house of Bamburgh through his mother, Ealdgyth, daughter of Earl Uhtred.[109] Moreover, Gospatric's name made reference to the maternal uncle whose activities also had a Strathclyde dimension, as has been argued above.

A third Gospatric who had links with the house of Bamburgh flourished in the eleventh century. He was the son of the Yorkshire dignitary Arkil, *potentissimus Nordanhimbrorum.*[110] In the maternal line this Gospatric was descended from Ecgfrida, the first wife of Earl Uhtred. Gospatric's mother, Sigrida, was also connected to the Bamburgh dynasty by her second marriage to Earl Eadwulf, son of Earl Uhtred.[111] Gospatric son of Arkil's links with the Bamburgh dynasty had a political dimension: in 1068 and 1069 his father allied with Gospatric, son of Maldred, in northern rebellions against William the Conqueror.[112]

Several commentators have suggested that Gospatric, son of Arkil, was the major Yorkshire landholder called Gospatric who appears in the Domesday survey.[113] Since the Domesday landholder is only represented by his forename he cannot be conclusively identified with this Gospatric.[114] However, the fact that the

105 For editions, see H. L. D. Ward, 'Lailoken (or Merlin Silvester)', *Romania* 22 (1893), 504–26, at 514–25; Winifred and John MacQueen, 'Vita Merlini Silvestris', *Scottish Studies* 29 (1989), 77–93, at 77–82.

106 Geoffrey of Monmouth, *Vita Merlini*, ed. and trans. Basil Clarke, *Life of Merlin* (Cardiff, 1973), 64–73 (text), viii, 42, 192–4.

107 *ibid.*, 202–3.

108 A. O. H. Jarman, *The Legend of Merlin* (Cardiff, 1960), 18–23; *idem*, 'Early Stages in the Development of the Myrddin Legend', in *Astudiaethau ar yr Hengerdd*, ed. Rachel Bromwich and R. Brinley Jones (Cardiff, 1978), 326–49, at 341–5.

109 'De obsessione', *Symeonis opera*, II.383.

110 'the most powerful of the Northumbrian nobles', *The Ecclesiastical History of Orderic Vitalis*, ed. and trans. Margaret Chibnall, 6 vols (Oxford, 1969–80), II.218–19.

111 'De obsessione', *Symeonis opera*, I.217, 220; Fletcher, *Bloodfeud*, 130–1.

112 *Ecclesiastical History*, ed. Chibnall, II.218–19, 222–3, 226–9, 232–3; Fletcher, *Bloodfeud*, 172–3, 177–8; Kapelle, *Norman Conquest*, 112, 115. The rebellions are also mentioned in *Chronicle*, ed. McGurk, III.6–11; *ASC* D s.aa. 1067–9, 83–4; *ASC* E s.aa. 1068–9, 87–8; 'Historia regum', *Symeonis opera*, II.186–8.

113 Greenwell, 'Gospatric', 23; William Farrer, 'Introduction to the Yorkshire Domesday', in *VCH Yorkshire*, ed. William Page, 3 vols (London, 1907–13), II.133–90, at 158, 183–4; K. S. B. Keats-Rohan, *Domesday People* (Woodbridge, 1999), 234–5; Fletcher, *Bloodfeud*, 172.

114 This difficulty applies to many Domesday landowners, see Lewis, 'Joining the Dots', 70–1, 79–87; Keats-Rohan, *People*, 14–24.

Domesday Gospatric held some lands in 1086 that had belonged to Arkil in 1066, and that the lands in question mostly lay in central Yorkshire, tell against identification with Earl Gospatric.[115] In 1066, the core of Gospatric and Arkil's lands lay between the Rivers Swale and Ure, although Gospatric was also associated with a smaller cluster in Ryedale. Gospatric had lost some of these lands by the time of the survey, but he held others under various tenants-in-chief, and he also held lands in chief between the Rivers Ure and Nidd.[116] The core lands had access to trans-Pennine routes through Wensleydale and a number of outlying landholdings lay further west, in Wharfedale and Airedale.

Gospatric, son of Arkil, married a daughter of *Dolfin* son of *Thorfinn*, according to *De obsessione*.[117] Kapelle argued that Dolfin was a Cumbrian dignitary whose father, Thorfinn, appeared in Gospatric's writ.[118] It is impossible to identify Thorfinn with such confidence since the name *Þorfinnr* was used throughout the north of England and Scotland.[119] Neither can the name *Dolgfinnr* be localised, but it was clearly popular west of the Pennines. Thus it is possible, but not provable, that Gospatric married the daughter of a Cumbrian dignitary. Such an alliance would have been sensible given the westward orientation of Gospatric's core lands.

The three individuals described above are the only Gospatrics who are known to have flourished in mid- to late-eleventh-century Northumbria. The few unidentified Gospatrics who occur in eleventh-century contexts can plausibly be associated with one or other of these three men (see Appendix). The early bearers of the name all belonged to branches of the house of Bamburgh, which had an interest in Strathclyde and its environs. This point helps to explain why these men bore a Brittonic personal name, but it remains to consider why they favoured a name that commemorated St Patrick.

The cult of St Patrick

Patrick's cult was widespread in Strathclyde; it appealed to the native Britons, but also to Gaelic-Scandinavian incomers who settled in the kingdom. The Gaelic–

115 *Domesday Book: Yorkshire* ed. Margaret L. Faull and Marie Stinson, Domesday Book 30, 1 vol. in 2 (Chichester, 1986), 6N 61–2, 72, 79, 117, 139, 149–50; 28W 33, 37, 38; Alfred S. Ellis, 'Bibliographical Notes on the Yorkshire Tenants named in Domesday Book: XXIX Gospatric', *Yorkshire Archaeological Journal* 4 (1877), 384–7; Keats-Rohan, *People*, 234; William M. Aird, 'Gospatric, Earl of Northumbria (d. 1073x5)', *ODNB*, XXII.1033–4, at 1033, contra *Wetherhal*, ed. Prescott, 4, note 11; Freeman, *Norman Conquest*, IV.524.

116 *Domesday*, ed. Faull and Stinson, C11, 13, 18, 1N42, 46, 48–51, 53–6, 93–6, 104–7; 1W42, 54; 5N 28–9, 6N 31–2, 47–8, 61–2, 65, 67, 70, 72, 79, 89, 112–13, 116–18, 135, 139, 149–50; 9W15, 24W1–2, 4–7, 12–16; 28W1–41, 29E22, 22W47, 49; 30W22–3, 30, SWSk3, SWAn17, SWBu2, 4–6, 11–12, 14–15, 20–6, 30, 32, 34, 37, 49; SWH6, SNBi2–3, SEDr6; cf. von Feilitzen, *Domesday Names*, 274.

117 *Symeonis opera*, I.217.

118 Kapelle, *Norman Conquest*, 95, 151.

119 For instances of *Þorfinnr*, see Insley, 'Aspects', 191–2; cf. Sharpe, *Norman Rule*, 35, note 80.

Scandinavians who settled further south and east, in Lancashire and Yorkshire, shared an interest in Patrick's cult with their counterparts in Strathclyde. The interest in Patrick shown by the Northumbrian dignitaries who attained influence in Strathclyde merely added another layer to the cult's diverse constituency.[120]

The popularity of St Patrick's cult among the Scandinavian settlers in Ireland is revealed by a twelfth-century poem that relates Patrick's conversion of the Scandinavians of Dublin;[121] this tale also occurs in Jocelin of Furness's Life of St Patrick.[122] Ó Cuív has pointed out that veneration of Patrick in Dublin coincided with the adoption of the name *Gille Pátraic* by the Scandinavian community there.[123] It is therefore no surprise that this name occurred in an area of Yorkshire that attracted Gaelic–Scandinavian settlers. According to the Domesday Survey, a *Ghilepatric* held lands in several places around Wensleydale in 1066.[124] It is notable that these lands lay in the vicinity of some of the core holdings of Gospatric and Arkil.

It is tempting to associate the incidence of *Gille Pátraic* and *Gwas-Patric* names in this area with the Patrician dedication of the church at Patrick Brompton. Not only did Gospatric's father, Arkil, hold lands at this place in 1066, a certain *Ghile* had a hall there.[125] The proximity of *Ghile*'s landholdings to those of *Ghilepatric* renders it likely that these men were identical, and that *Ghilepatric*'s unusual name had been shortened in this entry.[126] Indeed, another local place-name that commemorated Patrick, the now-lost *Patrik Keld* (Patrick's well), was located in *Ghilepatric*'s landholding at Spennithorne.[127] It is possible that the Patrick affixes on these place-names gave rise to the Patrician dedications of the church and well. Patrick Brompton came to be known as such, however, during the

120 For an example of a saint's cult that flourished under specific political circumstances during the early eleventh century, see Barbara E. Crawford, 'The Dedication to St Clement at Rodil, Harris', in *Church, Chronicle and Learning in Medieval and Early Renaissance Scotland*, ed. *eadem* (Edinburgh, 1999), 109–22.

121 *Lebor na Cert. The Book of Rights*, ed. M. Dillon, Irish Texts Society 46 (Dublin, 1962), 114–19; D. N. Dumville, 'St. Patrick and the Scandinavians of Dublin', in *idem et al.*, *Saint Patrick, A.D. 493–1993* (Woodbridge, 1993), 259–64. I am grateful to Colmán Etchingham for bringing this poem to my attention. Cf. Howard B. Clarke, 'Christian Cults and Cult Centres in Hiberno-Norse Dublin and its Hinterland', in *The Island of St. Patrick: Church and Ruling Dynasties in Fingal and Meath, 400–1148*, ed. Ailbhe MacShamhráin (Dublin, 2004), 152–4; Benjamin Hudson, *Viking Pirates and Christian Princes: Dynasty, Religion and Empire in the North Atlantic* (Oxford, 2005), 114.

122 Jocelin of Furness, *Vita sancti Patricii*, in *Acta sanctorum quotquot toto orbe coluntur*, ed. J. Bolland *et al.* (Antwerp, Tongerloo, Paris, Brussels, 1643–in progress), March II, 555.

123 Ó Cuív, 'Borrowed Elements', 47; cf. *idem*, 'Personal Names as an Indicator of Relations between Native Irish and Settlers in the Viking Period', in *Settlement and Society in Medieval Ireland: Studies Presented to Francis Xavier Martin*, ed. John Bradley (Kilkenny, 1988), 79–88, at 81.

124 *Domesday*, ed. Faull and Stinson, 6–28, 87, 90, 94, 99, 102; Keats-Rohan and Thornton, *Domesday Names*, 87; von Feilitzen, *Personal Names*, 261; A. H. Smith, 'Some Aspects of Irish Influence on Yorkshire', *Revue celtique* 44 (1927), 34–58, at 43.

125 *Domesday*, ed. Faull and Stinson, 6–137.

126 As in 6–29; however, *Gille* occurred on its own as a name: O'Brien, 'Names', 229.

127 Smith, 'Irish Influence', 50; *Domesday*, ed. Faull and Stinson, 6–102.

twelfth century, by which time the church was well established.[128] The church's dedication to Patrick is first attested explicitly c.1230, but the likelihood remains that the Patrician cult in Wensleydale dates back to the time of *Ghilepatric*, or to the settlement of his Gaelic–Scandinavian ancestors in the area.[129] This notion is supported by the fact that Patrick was venerated in other Gaelic–Scandinavian colonies, such as Heysham in Lancashire.[130]

The Patrician churches that lay in coastal areas within the bounds of Strathclyde may have also arisen through Gaelic–Scandinavian enthusiasm for Patrick's cult. One factor in favour of this interpretation is the existence of *Kirkpatrick* place-names in these areas (see map). These place-names are inversion compounds that feature the Norse generic *kirkja* and the specific *Patrick* in the genitive. Ekwall suggested that inversion compounds were coined during the era of Scandinavian settlement, but Brooke demonstrated that they continued to be coined during the thirteenth century.[131] Nevertheless, it is possible that some, if not all, of the *kirk*-names can be attributed to Gaelic–Scandinavian influence.[132] Kirkpatrick (-Fleming), Dumfriesshire, may be a candidate, since its place-name first appears in 1179, shortly after detailed written records start to become available for this region.[133] The expansion of Strathclyde into this area no doubt also promoted the popularity of Patrick's cult, as Clancy suggests elsewhere in this volume.[134]

Further north, in Lanarkshire and north of the Clyde, more place-names or church dedications that betoken an interest in the saint can be found (see map). These may not all relate to the early medieval period, but the coining of the place-name (Old) Kilpatrick may be associated with Gaelic-speakers who settled in the north of the former kingdom of Dumbarton in the late ninth century.[135] It is also possible to glimpse devotion to Patrick among the Brittonic-speaking populace of the kingdoms of Dumbarton and Strathclyde, as Clancy notes.[136] Thus, we

128 Smith, 'Irish Influence', 50. The church was granted to St Mary's, York, before c.1130: see the confirmation by Henry II in *Early Yorkshire Charters, being a Collection of Documents Anterior to the Thirteenth Century*, ed. William Farrer and Charles Travis Clay, 13 vols (Edinburgh and Wakefield, 1914–65), I.271.

129 *Yorkshire Deeds*, ed. William Brown, Yorkshire Archaeological Society Record Series 39 (1909), 124; H. B. McCall, *Richmondshire Churches* (London, 1910), 118; H. A. Cosgrave, 'Patrick Brompton Church', *Journal of the Royal Society of Antiquaries of Ireland* 41 (1911), 63–4.

130 Fiona Edmonds, 'Saints' Cults and Gaelic–Scandinavian Influence in Cumberland and south-western Scotland' (forthcoming).

131 Ekwall, *Scandinavians*, 28. D. Brooke, 'Kirk-Compound Place-Names in Galloway and Carrick', *Transactions of the Dumfriesshire and Galloway Natural History and Antiquarian Society* 3rd series 58 (1983), 56–71.

132 Alison Grant, 'A Reconsideration of the *Kirk*-names in South-western Scotland', *Northern Studies* 38 (2004), 97–121.

133 *ibid.*, 115; Edward Johnson-Ferguson, *The Place-Names of Dumfriesshire* (Dumfries, 1935), 79; Gillian Fellows-Jensen, *Scandinavian Settlement Names in the North-West* (Copenhagen, 1985), 54.

134 Thomas Clancy, 'Patrick and Palladius', above 28–9.

135 Taylor, 'West Dunbartonshire', 20; Alan Macquarrie, 'Early Christian Govan: The Historical Context', *RSCHS* 24 (1992), 1–17, at 10, 15.

136 Clancy, 'Patrick and Palladius', above 26–31; for a discussion of the hagiographical traditions, cf. Taylor, 'West Dunbartonshire', 17–22.

can say with confidence that Patrick's cult was well-established in Strathclyde by the time that Northumbrians had begun to base themselves there in the mid-eleventh century. Adherence to Patrick's cult cut across the disparate strands of Strathclyde's population.

The importance of the Patrician cult to the adoption of the *Gwas-Patric* names is evident; the spread of these personal names in turn contributed to veneration of Patrick. For example, the Patrick suffixes of Preston Patrick and Bampton Patrick (both located in Westmorland) derived from the names of medieval landholders. The Patrick dedications of the local churches were most probably extrapolated from these place-names in more recent times.[137] Even so, the evidence gathered above suggests that Patrick's cult was present in Strathclyde and in nearby areas that experienced Gaelic–Scandinavian settlement during the early medieval period. The cult might have been invigorated by the spread of the name *Gwas-Patric* and its derivatives, but veneration of St Patrick was the reason why those names existed in the first place.

Conclusion

I have argued in this chapter that members of the house of Bamburgh adopted the Brittonic epithet or name *Gwas-Patric* as a result of their interest in western territory, notably the kingdom of Strathclyde. It is likely that the personal names *Gwas-Patric* and *Gille Pátraic* were already being used in Strathclyde among the Gaelic–Scandinavian and Brittonic-speaking communities that venerated Patrick. The fact that Patrick's cult had such a diverse constituency meant that it was accessible to the Northumbrians. The name *Gwas-Patric* seems to have been relatively rare before the late eleventh century, but during the twelfth century the name achieved a more general popularity as a result of its association with the comital dynasties.[138] By this time, the name was no longer associated closely with devotion to Patrick. However, Patrick's cult retained its vibrancy in the areas where the first Northumbrians to bear the name *Gwas-Patric* had put down roots: formerly Cumbrian territory and the neighbouring areas of Yorkshire and Lancashire that had experienced Gaelic–Scandinavian influence.[139]

137 Frances Arnold-Forster, *Studies in Church Dedications, or England's Patron Saints*, 3 vols (London, 1899), II.134; W. G. Collingwood and T. H. B. Graham, 'Patron Saints of the Diocese of Carlisle', *TCWAAS* 2nd series 25 (1925), 1–27, at 12, 17, 25.

138 See note 18, above.

139 For Patrick's cult in twelfth-century Copeland and Furness, see Seán Duffy, 'The First Ulster Plantation: John de Courcy and the Men of Cumbria', in *Colony and Frontier in Medieval Ireland: Essays Presented to J. F. Lydon*, ed. Terry Barry *et al.* (London, 1995), 1–27, at 8–9.

Notes on the map

The dates of the first attestations of church dedications, if not discussed in this volume, are drawn from Collingwood and Graham, 'Patron Saints' and Steve Boardman *et al.*, 'Survey of Dedications to Saints in Medieval Scotland', http://www.shc.ed.ac.uk/Research/saints/index.htm, consulted 11 Sept. 2007. The Patrick dedication at Heysham is attested in *Furness*, II.281.

The coastlines are based on data provided with the support of the ESRC and JISC, using boundary material that is copyright of the Crown, the ED-Line Consortium and the Post Office. Source: 1991 Census: Digitised Boundary Data (England and Wales; Scotland). The rivers and lakes derive from 'ArcWorld' © Environmental Systems Research Institute, Inc.

APPENDIX

List of forms

For forms that decline, and appear in the texts in cases other than the nominative, the case is specified in the middle column.

Nominative	Form in the text	Reference
Gospatric, son of Uhtred		
Cospatricus	Cospatricum (accusative)	'De primo', *Symeonis opera,* II.383.
	" "	'Historia regum', *Symeonis opera,* II.197.
	Cospatrici (genitive)	'De primo', *Symeonis opera,* II.383.
Gospatricus	Gospatricus	'Historia regum', *Symeonis opera,* II.178.
	Gospatrici (genitive)	John of Worcester, s.a. 1065.[1]
Gospatric, son of Maldred		
Cospatricus	Cospatricius	'Historia regum', *Symeonis opera,* II.187, 191, 195, 199.
	" "	'De primo', *Symeonis opera,* II.384.
	" "	Roger de Houeden.[2]
	Cospatricum (accusative)	'De obsessione', *Symeonis opera,* I.216.
	Cospatrice (vocative)	*Libellus*, ed. Rollason, 190–3.
Cospatricius	Cospatricius	Durham tombstone.[3]
Gospatric	Gospatric	John of Worcester, s.a.1068.[4]
	" "	*ASC D*, 83, 84 (1067, 9).

1 ed. McGurk *et al.*, II.596–9.

2 *Chronica Magistri Rogeri de Houedene*, ed. William Stubbs, 4 vols, RS 51 (London, 1868–71), I.59. In general Roger of Howden's chronicle replicates entries in the Durham material and John of Worcester's chronicle. However, this entry, which describes the burial of Gospatric at Norham, is unique.

3 This could be Gospatric, son of Maldred, or one of his descendants: Geoffrey Barrow, 'Scots in the Durham *Liber Vitae*', in *Durham* Liber Vitae, ed. Rollason, 109–25, at 111; Andew McDonald, 'Gospatric, Second Earl of Lothian (d. 1166)', *ODNB*, XXII.1035.

4 ed. McGurk *et al.*, III.6–7.

Nominative	Form in the text	Reference
Cospatric	Cospatricleye	*Place-Names*, ed. Armstrong *et al.*, I.115.[5]
Gaius Patricius	Gaius Patricius	Orderic Vitalis.[6]
Gaius Patricius	Gaius Patricius	*Vita Ædwardi Regis*.[7]
Quaspatricius	Quaspatricius	Inquisitiones post mortem, 31 Henry III.[8]
Waspatric	Waspatricwath	*Place-Names*, ed. Armstrong *et al.*, I.154.[9]
Cwæs-patrik	Cwæs-patrike (dative)	Durham manumission, see n. 29, above.
Gospatric, son of Arkil		
Cospatricus	Cospatricus	'De obsessione', *Symeonis opera*, I.217.
Gospatric	Gospatric	*Domesday*, see n. 116 above.
Maldred, father of Gospatric		
Maldredus	Maldredus	'De obsessione', *Symeonis opera*, I.216.
	Maldredi (genitive)	'Historia regum', *Symeonis opera*, II.199.
Other forms of Maldred		
Meldredus	Meldredus	*Lailoken B.*
	Meldredi (genitive)	*Lailoken A & B.*
	" "	*Furness Coucher*, c.1160–89.[10]

5 This field name was located in Walton parish. Cf. *Lanercost*, ed. Todd, 52, 54.

6 ed. Chibnall, 222–3 (IV.ii.188).

7 ed. Frank Barlow (London, 1962), 35. This text contains a tale about a noble, well-dressed, youth who protected Tostig from robbers while they were on a pilgrimage. Gospatric, son of Maldred fits this description best. Cf. Fletcher, *Bloodfeud*, 153–4, 171.

8 *Calendar of Documents relating to Scotland*, ed. Joseph Bain, 4 vols (Edinburgh, 1881–8), I.316. This inquisition concerned lands located in Northumberland that belonged to Earl Patric of Dunbar; 'Quaspatricius' was Patric's ancestor. Cf. Greenwell, 'Gospatric', 55–7.

9 This lost place-name was located on the bounds of Allerdale Forest. The text in which the place-name occurs dates from c.1300: Phythian-Adams, *Cumbrians*, 39, 138, 148.

10 *The Coucher Book of Furness Abbey*, ed. J. Atkinson and J. Brownbill, 2 vols in 6,

Nominative	Form in the text	Reference
Meldredus (cont.)	Meldredi (genitive)	*Early Yorkshire Charters*, II.122, c.1227–8.[11]
	Meldredo (ablative)	*Lailoken B.*
Meldrid	Meldrid	*Cockersand.*[12]
Meldordus	Meldordi (genitive)	*Cockersand*, c.1250.[13]

Chetham Society, new series 9, 11, 14, 74, 76, 78 (Manchester, 1886–1919), II.318–19: a grant of land at Giggleswick (North Yorkshire) made by Adam filius Meldredi.

11 A quitclaim in which the name 'Robert filius Meldredi' appears.

12 *The Chartulary of Cockersand Abbey of the Premonstratensian Order*, ed. William Farrer, 3 vols in 7, Chetham Society, new series 38–40, 43, 56–7, 64 (Manchester, 1898–1909), III.1059. 'Ricardus f. Meldrid' dwelt in Burrow-with-Burrow, Lancashire. His name occurs in a list of donors of natives.

13 *ibid.*, III.904–5. The phrase 'usque ad croftum Meldordi' appears in a charter concerning land at Overkellet, Lancashire.

4

BISHOP KENTIGERN AMONG THE BRITONS

John Reuben Davies

Saint Kentigern, Bishop and Confessor, also known as Mungo, is patron of Glasgow.[1] He is co-patron too, with Saint Asaph, of Llanelwy in North Wales. And in common with so many of Britain's earliest saints we have no sure knowledge of him from his own time.

Weariness may set in as one repeats a commonplace topos, reminding the reader of the meagre sources for this period. But a stock theme though it may be, the near absence of written evidence, and the troublesome nature of what survives, conditions the task in hand. For where there is a gap there is always a temptation to fill it. Like neo-gothic architects of the nineteenth century, historians from all eras have either rebuilt ruined edifices or pulled down old ones, reconstructing them according to particular ideals and contemporary needs. For the student of the sixth and seventh centuries, whether one reads Bede from the eighth century, or the authors of the twelfth, the exercise is like examining Barry and Pugin's Palace of Westminster for an impression of the earlier building. If we are lucky there might be a Westminster Hall or a St Stephen's Cloister from the medieval complex, but the largest part is mere (architectural) propaganda. That magnificent late overlay of a medieval ideal has, besides, a tendency to embed itself in the popular imagination, so it becomes difficult to envisage the largely plain, unimpressive, higgledy-piggledy 'assemblage of combustible materials' that stood there before.[2]

In the case of Kentigern, we have nothing so certain as a Westminster Hall at the heart of the late structure. The root of the popular and tenacious picture of the saint

1 Mungo is Kentigern's Brittonic pet-name; see Kenneth Hurlstone Jackson, 'The Sources for the Life of St Kentigern', in *Studies in the Early British Church*, by Nora K. Chadwick *et al.* (Cambridge, 1958), 273–357, at 300–1.

2 Sir John Soane, quoted in Rosemary Hill, *God's Architect: Pugin and the Building of Romantic Britain* (London, 2007), 128. The perils and misuses of early medieval sources have famously been described by David Dumville, 'Sub-Roman Britain: History and Legend', *History* 62 (1977), 173–92; Karen Jankulak, 'Adjacent Saints' Dedications', below, shows how medieval evidence is often seen where there is none.

is twelfth-century legendary biography. And that picture is pervasive and influential, contaminating even the scholarly literature on the subject.[3]

Several works in the genre of hagiography deal with Glasgow's patron.[4] The earliest of these Lives of St Kentigern to have come down to us is a fragmentary one, written at the request of Bishop Herbert during his episcopate at Glasgow, 1147–64.[5] The apparently anonymous author tells us it was composed in emulation of Simeon of Durham's Life of St Cuthbert, and gives an account of the conception and birth of Kentigern, but the surviving text breaks off early on in the story. A recent analyst of the text has reasonably proposed that the author was a cleric of Glasgow Cathedral called Simeon, archdeacon of Teviotdale, who may also have indited the Life of St Serf, perhaps even the same Simeon who addressed dedicatory verses for a copy of Adomnán's Life of St Columba to King Alexander I.[6] Also composed during the episcopate of Bishop Herbert, by a certain William, was a poem on the death of Somerled that imputes the defeat of the Hebridean king in 1164 to St Kentigern's heavenly intervention.[7]

The second *uita* in chronological sequence is a complete and full-length Life of St Kentigern by a Cistercian author, Jocelin of Furness, a well-known practitioner of the hagiographer's art in his time.[8] The work is addressed to Jocelin's Cistercian namesake, who was bishop of Glasgow and formerly abbot of Melrose. Bishop Jocelin's episcopate, from 1175 to 1199, is the only certain limit we have for the date of the text.

On a smaller scale, the office of St Kentigern in the Sprouston Breviary, a service-book that dates from around 1300, contains short liturgical readings on the life of the saint.[9] The Breviary of Aberdeen, published in 1509/1510, also has an office with readings on Kentigern's life.[10] A Life by John of Tynemouth, a mid-

3 For example, Alan Macquarrie, 'The Career of St Kentigern of Glasgow: *uitae, lectiones* and glimpses of fact', *IR* 37 (1986), 3–24, although he is less credulous in *The Saints of Scotland. Essays in Scottish Church History AD 450–1093* (Edinburgh, 1997), 117–44.

4 Jackson, 'The Sources', provided the most detailed examination of the Kentigern dossier.

5 *Vita S. Kentigerni*, BL, MS Cotton Titus A.xix, fols 76r–80v: in *Lives of S. Ninian and S. Kentigern*, ed. Alexander Penrose Forbes, Historians of Scotland 5 (Edinburgh, 1874) 123–33 (trans.), 242–52 (text).

6 David Howlett, *Caledonian Craftsmanship: The Scottish Latin Tradition* (Dublin, 2000), 96–7; for Simeon (or Simon), archdeacon of Glasgow and/or Teviotdale, see *Fasti Ecclesiae Scoticanae Medii Aevi Ad Annum 1638*, ed. D. E. R. Watt and A. L. Murray (Edinburgh, 2003), 221. For Simeon's potential authorship of the Life of St Serf (*Vita S. Seruani*), and the verses on St Columba (*Sancte Columbe pater*), see Howlett, *Caledonian Craftsmanship*, 19–23, 86–97, 190–1.

7 *Carmen de morte Somerledi*, ed. and trans. by Howlett in *Caledonian Craftsmanship*, 24–8.

8 Jocelin of Furness OCist (d. c.1210), *Vita S. Kentigerni*, in *Lives*, ed. Forbes, 159–242; for the other works of Jocelin, see Richard Sharpe, *A Handlist of the Latin Writers of Great Britain and Ireland before 1540* (Turnhout, Belgium, 1997; rev. impr. 2001), no. 555.

9 NLS, MS Adv. 18.2.13b: see *Lives*, ed. Forbes, xciv–c, for the text.

10 *Breviarium Aberdonense*, ed. David Laing, 2 vols (Edinburgh, 1854), II, *pars hiemalis*, fols *xxvii* v–*xxx* r. Compiled by William Elphinstone (1431–1514), bishop of Aberdeen 1483–1514, founder of the University of Aberdeen.

fourteenth-century hagiographer, is an epitome of Jocelin of Furness's work, but only now survives in a version published by Wynkyn de Worde in 1516.[11]

Finally, from North Wales, there is a charter in the Red Book of St Asaph, *Llyfr Coch Asaph*, collated early in the fourteenth century, which contains an episode from the life of St Kentigern; the original charter was supposedly discovered in the mid-thirteenth century but probably dates from the twelfth.[12]

The cult of St Kentigern in the early middle ages

The only reference to Kentigern in a source earlier than the twelfth century concerns his death, and comes from a text originally written at the heart of the southern Welsh kingdom of Dyfed. A clerk at St Davids, in compiling the earliest version of *Annales Cambriae*, composed an entry for the year 612 or 613 that records 'The death of Kentigern and of Bishop Dyfrig': *Conthigirni obitus et Dibric episcopi.*[13] This annal was probably entered in the last decade of the eighth century, nearly two hundred years after the deaths of the *Conthigirn* and *Dibric* to whom it refers.[14]

11 *Sanctilogium Angliae Walliae Scotiae et Hiberniae*, rearranged and augmented by Wynkyn de Worde as *Noua legenda Anglie* (London, 1516), fols *ccvii* r–*ccxii* v, ed. C. Horstman (Oxford, 1901), 114–28; see Sharpe, *Handlist*, no. 949, for the surviving manuscripts.

12 Aberystwyth, National Library of Wales, MS NLW 7011D (*saec.* xvii[med.]); the charter was printed by Forbes in *Lives*, lxxix–lxxxi; the only full study and edition of *Llyfr Coch Asaph* is O. E. Jones, '*Llyfr Coch Asaph*: A Textual and Historical Study', unpublished M.A. dissertation, University of Wales, Aberystwyth, 2 vols (1968).

13 *AC* (A) s.a. 169 or 170 [= AD 612 or 613]. The date in *AC* (A) may be up to two years out, putting the real date of Kentigern's death in 614: see Dauvit Broun, 'Kentigern (d.612×14)', *ODNB* [http://www.oxforddnb.com/view/article/15426, accessed 30 Nov. 2007]. The idea that the entry can be interpreted, 'The death of Kentigern and Dyfrig, bishops', is simply wrong: such a meaning would require *episcopus* to be in the genitive plural, *episcoporum* (cf. Henry Gough-Cooper, 'Kentigern and Gonothigernus: A Scottish Saint and a Gaulish Bishop Identified', *The Heroic Age* 6 (Spring 2003) [online journal. Available at http://www.mun.ca/mst/heroicage/issues/6/ gough-cooper.html]). *AC* (A) survives in an eleventh-century copy, BL MS Harley 3859. On the genesis of *AC* (A), see Kathleen Hughes, 'The Welsh Latin Chronicles: *Annales Cambriae* and Related Texts', *Proceedings of the British Academy* 59 (1973), 233–58; reprinted in *Celtic Britain in the Early Middle Ages: Studies in Welsh and Scottish Sources by the Late Kathleen Hughes*, ed. David Dumville (Woodbridge, 1980), 67–85; 'The A-text of *Annales Cambriae*', *ibid.*, 86–100.

14 The name we know as 'Kentigern' is first encountered in that generic form in the twelfth-century Lives as *Kentegernus*. Its origin is a Brittonic compound-name, **Cuno-tigernos*, 'Hound-like Lord' (Jackson, 'The Sources', 298). *Conthigirn*[*us*] of *AC* (A) is an Old-Welsh development which also appears in ninth-century Northumbria as the name of a Welsh or Cumbric monk at Lindisfarne, *Cundigeorn* (Durham *Liber Vitae*, c.840, cited by Kenneth Jackson in *Language and History in Early Britain* (Edinburgh, 1953), 676). *Cundigeorn* is a partly anglicised version of what would have been written regularly in Old Welsh as **Cintigern*; *Conthigirn* in *AC* (A) is just a variant spelling of what would have been pronounced in the same way as **Cintigern* (*ibid.*, 59); the spelling, *Kentegernus*, represents this stage of development. We may therefore

The annalist at St Davids was mainly concerned to record events relating to saints, bishops and kings. There are only three exceptions: the death of 'Bede the priest' in 735, the death of 'Cuthbert the abbot' of Monkwearmouth in 777, and the death of Jonathan, abbot of Abergele, in 856.[15] In each case the status of the person is explicitly defined because he is not a saint, bishop or king. As history has no record of a king called Kentigern, we may assume that *Conthigirn* was at least a bishop, if not a saint. Only two bishops with British names outside the episcopal succession at St Davids are mentioned in *Annales Cambriae*; one is Dyfrig, whose jurisdiction probably lay in south-east Wales; the other is Elfoddw, explicitly called 'archbishop of the Venedotian kingdom', that is, Gwynedd.[16] A bishop named Kentigern was never claimed for St Davids; *Conthigirn*'s name could therefore have entered the annals from the notional body of annalistic notices of north-Welsh or north-British origin that is thought to have been incorporated by the original compiler of *Annales Cambriae*.[17]

In the late eighth century, therefore, a British bishop named Kentigern, probably from North Wales or North Britain, was a figure of sufficient importance in church history for his death-date to be recorded by the annalists of South Wales.

Is this, however, evidence of cult? Let us examine the earliest section of *Annales Cambriae* more closely. The entries are not contemporary until at least AD 777. Before that, the sections AD 445 to 613, and AD 613 to 777, show signs of scholarly construction ultimately from scattered notes. From AD 516 to 613 the main interest is in North Britain and North Wales, and there is a particular focus on church matters; after AD 613 (the death of *Conthigirn* and *Dibric*), down to AD 777, the annals are concerned with secular events and take their backbone from a north-British chronicle. I have set out the entries relating to ecclesiastical affairs in the British section from AD 516 to AD 612/613 as follows.[18]

521	Sanctus Columcille nascitur. Quies sanctae Brigidę.	Saint Colum Cille is born. The repose of Saint Brigid.
544	Dormitatio Ciarani.	The sleep of Ciarán.[19]

dismiss the idea that there was an intermediate Gaelic form, *Ceanntigearn* (cf. Macquarrie, *Saints of Scotland*, 117).

15 *AC* (A), s.a. 291 [= AD 735], *Beda presbiter dormit*; s.a. 333 [= AD 777], *Cudberth abbas moritur*; s.a. 412 [= AD 856] *Ionathan princeps Opergelei moritur*.

16 *AC* (A) s.a. 365 [= AD 809], 'Elbodug archiepiscopus Guenedotae regione migrauit ad Dominum'. On the cult of St Dyfrig, see John Reuben Davies, 'The Saints of South Wales and the Welsh Church', in *Local Saints and Local Churches in the Early Medieval West*, ed. Alan Thacker and Richard Sharpe (Oxford, 2002), 361–95, at 370–6; on his likely episcopal jurisdiction, *idem*, *The Book of Llandaf and the Norman Church in Wales* (Woodbridge, 2003), 10–11.

17 Hughes, 'The A-text', 91–9; for the episcopal succession at St Davids, see John Reuben Davies, 'The Archbishopric of St Davids and the Bishops of *Clas Cynidr*', in *St David of Wales: Cult, Church and Nation*, ed. J. Wyn Evans and Jonathan M. Wooding (Woodbridge, 2007), 296–304.

18 The annalist's year 1 is AD 445; the dates I have supplied here are the unrectified AD dates, calculated by adding 444 to the annalist's year; in some cases the dates are historically incorrect, for example, St Columba died in 597 not 595.

19 Ciarán is the founder of Clonmacnoise, and was regarded as a saint by Adomnán at the

562	Columcillę in brittannia exiit.	Collum Cille departed to Britain.
570	Gildas obíít.	Gildas died.[20]
584	Bellum contra Euboniam et <dispositio> Danielis bancorum.	War against Eubonia [the Isle of Man] and the burial of Daniel of the Bangors.[21]
595	Columcille moritur. Dunaut rex moritur. Augustinus Mellitus anglos ad christum conuertit.	Colum Cille dies. King Dunod dies. Augustine [and] Mellitus convert the English to Christ.[22]
601	Sinodus urbis legion. Gregorius obíít in christo. David episcopus moni iudeorum.[23]	Synod of the City of the Legion. Gregory died in Christ.[24] The death of David, bishop of Mynyw.[25]
606	Depositio Cinauc episcopi.	The burial of Bishop Cynog.[26]

end of the seventh century: *in Clonoensi sancti Cerani cenubio*: *Vita S. Columbae*, i.3, *Adomnán's Life of Columba*, ed. and trans. A. O. and M. O. Anderson, rev. edn (Oxford, 1991), 214.

20 Gildas is commemorated in the *Memento etiam* (the prayer for the faithful departed in the Canon of the Mass) in the Stowe Missal, a manuscript written in Ireland in 792: Dublin, Royal Irish Academy, MS D.II.3, fol. 33r; *The Stowe Missal: MS. D. II. 3 in the Library of the Royal Irish Academy, Dublin*, ed. George F. Warner, Henry Bradshaw Society 31–2, 2 vols (London, 1906–15) [facsimile and printed text].

21 'Daniel of the Bangors' is Deiniol, first bishop of Bangor, who is commemorated in the early Irish martyrologies. Deiniol's feast day, 11 September, is first recorded in the Martyrology of Tallaght (early ninth century); *The Martyrology of Tallaght: from the Book of Leinster and MS. 5100–4 in the Royal Library, Brussels*, ed. and trans. Richard Irvine Best and Hugh Jackson Lawlor, Henry Bradshaw Society 68 (London, 1931).

22 Augustine and Mellitus, who converted the English, were the subject of veneration by Bede's time, and had miracles attributed to them: Bede, *HE*, i.26, 31, ii.7. Mellitus was commemorated in the Mass of the Stowe Missal: Stowe Missal, fol. 32v.

23 *David episcopus moni iudeorum*: one may conjecture that the exemplar in front of the Anglo-Norman scribe who copied this annal originally read *Dauid episcopus Moniu dorm'*, or *Moniu De<is>orum*, 'Mynyw of the Déisi'. For the latter emendation, see Molly Miller, 'Date-guessing and Dyfed', *Studia Celtica* 12/13 (1977/8), 33–61, at 47, n. 6; it has been admitted by David Dumville (*Saint David of Wales*, Kathleen Hughes Memorial Lectures 1 (Cambridge, 2001), 4, n. 9, and J. Wyn Evans, 'Transition and survival: St Davids and St Davids Cathedral', in *St David of Wales*, ed. Evans and Wooding, 20–40, at 39); the idea was originally that of Joseph Loth, *Les Mabinogion*, 2 vols, 2nd edn (Paris, 1913), II.373.

24 The Gregory who died in 601 (actually 604) is Pope St Gregory the Great, also treated as a saint by Bede: Bede, *HE*, ii.3.

25 St David of Wales, whose cult can be traced back to at least the ninth century, and probably earlier: see John Reuben Davies, 'The Saints of South Wales', 376–8; Dumville, *Saint David.*

26 *Cinauc episcopus* is Cynog, a saint of Brycheiniog in mid-Wales. Early references are difficult to pin down, but the place-name Merthyr Cynog, in Brycheiniog, points to an early cult: Welsh *merthyr* < Lat. *martyrium* is one of the few place-name elements that leads fairly securely to early cult with relics. See Richard Sharpe, 'Martyrs and Local Saints in Late Antique Britain', in *Local Saints and Local Churches in the Early*

612	Conthigirni obitus et Dibric episcopi.	The death of Kentigern and of Bishop Dyfrig.[27]

Every ecclesiastical person mentioned is either explicitly a saint or was venerated as a holy bishop at the time these annals were compiled, towards the end of the eighth century. In the light of *Annales Cambriae* alone, therefore, one might reasonably assume that *Conthigirn* was a bishop regarded as a local saint and probably – like the others in the section examined – as a church founder. The question of the nature, location, and extent of his cult, however, remains open.[28]

Bishop Kentigern in Brittany

Sixty-five years before the recorded date of *Conthigirn*'s death in *Annales Cambriae*, a bishop called *Gonotiernus* attended a Church council in Gaul. *Gonotiernus*, bishop of Senlis (Oise, Picardie) in the ecclesiastical province of Reims, subscribed to the canons issued by the Council of Orléans in 549. Several years later, at a Council of Paris, the same bishop was still in post.[29] This time we find his name spelt *Gonothigernus*. *Gonotiernus* and *Gonothigernus* are different spellings of the same name, which is again the same as that of the bishop whose death is noticed in *Annales Cambriae*; in other words, it is the 'Kentigern' name.[30]

There is nothing remarkable, however, about finding a bishop with a British

Medieval West, ed. Thacker and Sharpe, 75–154, esp. 142–4; see also Davies, 'The Archbishopric of St Davids', 298.

27 Bishop Dyfrig was regarded as a saint in the earliest Life of St Samson; see n. 15, above. *Vita I S. Samsonis* (*La Vie ancienne de Saint Samson de Dol*, ed. and trans. P. Flobert (Paris, 1997)) was written in Brittany sometime before the end of the eighth century, and probably earlier.

28 One should also mention the Dunkeld Litany, which looks like a product of the reign of Giric mac Dúngal (d. c.890), and includes the petition, 'S. Kentiyern uere Deo Mungo ora pro nobis' (J. G. F. Gordon, 'Processional Litany of the Monastery of Dunkeld in Scotland', *Notes and Queries* 9, 3rd series (1886), 406–9, at 407; Alexander Penrose Forbes, *Kalendars of Scottish Saints* (Edinburgh, 1872), Appendix III, lvi–lxv; A. W. Haddan and W. Stubbs, *Councils and Ecclesiastical Documents relating to Great Britain and Ireland*, 3 vols (Oxford, 1869–78), II.278–85). This liturgical text, however, survives only in an eighteenth-century transcript by the Scottish Benedictine, Marianus Brockie (1687–1755), prior of the Scots abbey at Regensburg, a notorious forger of historical texts (Edinburgh, Scottish Catholic Archives, SK/12 *Monasticum Scoticanum*: Brockie's notes and transcripts, vol. 4, pp. 4685–700). Brockie in turn supposedly transcribed the text from a copy made by Servanus Thomson at Dunfermline in the sixteenth century (Clancy has discussed all this in 'Scottish Saints', 416–20). The spelling of Kentiyern with initial K, as well as the inclusion of a petition to 'St David the King', means that any exemplar must have been no older than twelfth century; this rules out the appearance of St Kentigern in the Litany as corroborative early evidence of cult.

29 *Concilia Galliae*, ed. C. de Clerq, Corpus Christianorum, Series Latina 148–148A (Turnhout, Belgium, 1963), 205–10, at 210. This Council of Paris can only be dated 556 × 573.

30 Compare *Gonothigernus* and **Cunotigernos*; the initial *g* of the former is just a softening of initial *c* in the latter.

name in sixth-century Gaul. With migrants from Britain, the British church had successfully transplanted itself in Brittany by the early sixth century.[31] At the same Council of Paris, just mentioned, we also find Samson, the British bishop of Dol in Brittany, and Ferrocinctus, the Breton bishop of Évreux.[32]

Although *Gonotiern*, bishop of Senlis, shared his name and ethnic background with Bishop Kentigern of Glasgow, I think the balance of probability weighs against them being the same person. Whereas we must allow that medieval people could hold office at a great age – one thinks of Pope Celestine III (1191–8), who was elected to the Holy See at 85 and lived for a further seven years – it would nevertheless be curious if Kentigern had been a bishop in the Frankish kingdom for at least seven years – perhaps for quarter of a century – and for the shared historical memory not to have held on to that knowledge.[33]

Bishop Kentigern in North Britain

In Jocelin of Furness's legendary Life of St Kentigern, our saint has been given a number of roles to play, among them, founder of the church of Glasgow, and rescuer of the Christian faith in the kingdom of *Cambria*. The kingdom described by Jocelin, however, was not quite the same as that which flourished when

31 Léon Fleuriot, *Les origines de la Bretagne: l'émigration* (Paris, 1980); D. Fahy, 'When did Britons become Bretons?', *Welsh History Review* 2 (1964–5), 111–24.

32 Ferrocinctus was likely a Breton who had Latinised his name from Old Breton *Iarnuuiscid* – both names mean 'girded with iron'; Fleuriot, *Les origines*, 148–9.

33 Gough-Cooper has made a similar point in, 'Kentigern and Gonothigernus'. One more link with Kentigern across the Channel has been seen in a place-name near Saint Pol-de-Léon in Finistère, at a small village called Trégondern. It has been thought that this place-name is composed of the Breton word for a settlement, *treb*, plus the notional eponym *Condern* (supposedly from the older form of Kentigern, *Cunotigernos*) (see Gough-Cooper, 'Kentigern and Gonothigernus'). But one would be uncertain whether a name-form that has become a notional *Condern* in the spelling *Trefgondern* by 1386 can contain the original Brittonic element *tigernos*. (I rely for the attestation on Henry Gough-Cooper's note of his communication with Bernard Tanguy in 'On the Trail of Kentigern: Addendum', in *Placename Notes from the Newsletters*, Spring 2000 [online newsletter of the Scottish Place-Name Society. Available at http://www.st-andrews.ac.uk/institutes/sassi/spns/oldnotes2.htm#kentadd].) In Welsh, Brittonic **tigernos* gives Primitive Welsh **tiʒern*, which in turn gives Middle Welsh *teyrn*, so **Cunotigernos* eventually becomes Cyndeyrn; in Old Breton, lenition occurred, so that ʒ was lost, giving *-tiern*, as in *Gonotiernus*; other examples include *Gurtiern*, *Gurdiern*, *Ritiern* (Jackson, *Language and History*, 69, 446–7). Jackson (*ibid.*, 446–7) showed that **te|ern* is possible in Old Cornish, as in *Wende|ern*; but here, **te|ern* is from Brittonic **tegernos*, a variant spelling of **tigernos*; there are no examples of this last development in Breton. Even if this place-name were indeed to contain the 'Kentigern' name, then it would still not be a sign of cult. First, it is a secular place-name; secondly, there appears to be no evidence of an early church, and certainly not of a dedication. Jankulak (below) describes the hazards of trying to identify the cult of the same saint across several Celtic regions, especially when the saint seems to appear as the eponym in a place-name. Another example of a potential 'Kentigern' toponym, in Carmarthenshire, is discussed below, 87.

Kentigern was alive, around the second half of the sixth century and beginning of the seventh. The sixth-century realm had its headquarters in the seemingly impregnable fortress on the rock of Dumbarton, high above the north bank of the Clyde; and its territories encompassed the Clyde Valley and Ayrshire, perhaps reaching as far west as southern Argyll at times.[34] In 870, the fortress of Clyde Rock was besieged and sacked by Irish-based Scandinavians, led by two kings, Olaf and Ivar.[35] Almost straight away the terms used in the sources change: in 872 the Annals of Ulster record the death of the 'king of the Britons of Strathclyde' – not of 'Dumbarton' or 'Clyde Rock' – and in 875 the Anglo-Saxon Chronicle speaks of the 'Strathclyde Welsh'.[36] These are the first times we hear of 'Strathclyde', and the change of usage tells of a political change too.

The political shift meant a move much further upstream, to Govan on the south bank of the Clyde. By the late ninth century Govan had the trappings of a major ecclesiastical centre, and by the eleventh century possessed enough monumental sculpture to rival Iona. The church was dedicated to St Constantine, a royal saint with an impressive sarcophagus-shrine; this was surely a royal church, and a royal *caput* must have sat close by.[37] If we take into account an apparent reference to Govan in Simeon of Durham's *Historia regum*, then we can point to a politically important settlement there over a hundred years before the sacking of Dumbarton.[38]

Perhaps a shift to the south bank of the Clyde also indicates a more southerly focused outlook for the refigured Strathclyde polity.[39] Contemporary sources next begin referring to the kingdom of Strathclyde as *Cumbra land* in Old English, and *Cumbria* in Latin; and circumstances strongly suggest that it stretched much further south than its predecessor, from the Clyde Valley to modern Cumberland, reaching as far as the River Eamont near Penrith.[40] British kings continued to rule

34 See James E. Fraser, 'Strangers on the Clyde: Cenél Comgaill, Clyde Rock and the bishops of Kingarth', *IR* 56 (2005), 102–20.

35 *AU* 870.6, 'Obsesio Ailech Cluathe a Norddmannis, .i. Amlaiph et Imhar, duo reges Norddmannorum obsederunt arcem illum et distruxerunt in fine .iiii. mensium arcem et predauerunt'; *AC* (A), s.a. 426 [= AD 870], 'Arx alt clut a gentilibus fracta est'.

36 *AU* 872.5, 'Artghal, rex Britanorum Sratha Cluade'; ASC A, s.a. 875, *Stræcled Walas*; ASC D, *Strætled Wealas*; ASC E, s.a. 875, *Strætlædwealas*.

37 John Reuben Davies, *The Cult of St Constantine and the Ecclesiastical History of Strathclyde*, Friends of Govan Old, Lecture Series 6 (Glasgow, 2008).

38 s.a. 756, *Symeonis opera*, II.40; Thomas Owen Clancy, 'Govan, the Name, Again', in *Annual Report of the Society of Friends of Govan Old* 8 (Glasgow, 1998), 8–13.

39 Fiona Edmonds takes the same view, 'Personal Names', above, 44.

40 F. M. Stenton's argument for the extent of Strathclyde in the early tenth century is convincing (*Anglo-Saxon England*, 3rd edn (Oxford, 1971), 332). In 926, King Athelstan chose to meet the king of Scots and his ally, the king of Strathclyde, at Eamont Bridge; it was a well-established custom for kings to negotiate on the boundary between their territories. The evidence for terminology applied to the kingdom has been set out and discussed by P. A. Wilson, 'On the Use of the Terms "Strathclyde" and "Cumbria" ', *TCWAAS*, 2nd series 66 (1966), 57–92. Further aspects of the Brittonic identity of the Strathclyders have been enlightened by Dauvit Broun, 'The Welsh Identity of the Kingdom of Strathclyde c.900–c.1200', *IR* 55 (2004), 111–80, at 111–12; Thomas Owen Clancy, 'Ystrad Clud', in *Celtic Culture: A Historical Encyclopedia*, ed. John T. Koch, 5 vols (Santa Barbara CA and Oxford, 2006), V.1818–21; Simon Taylor,

Strathclyde into the eleventh century, and the Brittonic dialect of the region, closely related to Welsh and known as Cumbric, together with its accompanying culture, survived in the heartlands of the kingdom at least as long.[41] The last reference to the kingdom of 'Strathclyde' is in Simeon of Durham's *Historia regum*, referring to the Battle of Carham in 1018, although the polity appears to have continued for at least another generation.[42]

The relation of Kentigern and Glasgow to each other and to the historical picture just outlined, however, remains to be defined. In Jocelin's Life of the saint, Bishop Kentigern's episcopal authority runs throughout the *regnum Cambrinum*, that is, the kingdom of Strathclyde.[43] The king whom Jocelin makes St Kentigern's contemporary is *Rederech*, or Rhydderch, the Rhydderch ap Tudwal, king of 'Clyde Rock', mentioned by Adomnán as a contemporary of St Columba, and therefore of Kentigern.[44] Jocelin describes how Rhydderch transferred the lordship and sovereignty of his kingdom to St Kentigern.[45] By this literary device, Jocelin has the kingdom of Strathclyde live on in the contemporary bishopric of Glasgow: the diocese is represented as the kingdom, and the bishop is the source of royal power.

Jocelin next relates how Kentigern sought and received a solemn privilege from the pope, granting that 'he should be subject to no bishop, but rather should be

'The Early History and Languages of West Dunbartonshire', in *Changing Identities, Ancient Roots: The History of West Dunbartonshire from Earliest Times*, ed. Ian Brown (Edinburgh, 2006), 12–41, at 25–6; Alex Woolf, *From Pictland to Alba, 789–1070*, New Edinburgh History of Scotland 2 (Edinburgh, 2007), 152–7. A twelfth-century view of the extent of Cumbria is given in King David I's enquiry into the possessions of the bishopric of Glasgow: *The Charters of King David I. The Written Acts of David I King of Scots, 1124–53 and of his son Henry Earl of Northumberland, 1139–52*, ed. G. W. S. Barrow (Woodbridge, 1999), 60, no. 15; *Registrum Episcopatus Glasguensis. Munimenta Ecclesie Metropolitane Glasguensis a sede restaurata seculo ineunte XII ad reformatam religionem*, ed. Cosmo Innes, 2 vols (Edinburgh, 1843), 5–9, no. 1 (includes the preamble).

41 B. T. Hudson, '*Elech* and the Scots in Strathclyde', *Scottish Gaelic Studies* 15 (1988), 145–9; Alan Macquarrie, 'The Kings of Strathclyde, c.400–1018', in *Medieval Scotland: Crown, Lordship and Community. Essays Presented to G. W. S. Barrow*, ed. Alexander Grant and Keith J. Stringer (Edinburgh, 1993), 1–19, at 6, 12–15; Broun, 'Welsh Identity', 125–35. Cf. Kirby, 'Strathclyde', 84–94; Alfred P. Smyth, *Warlords and Holy Men: Scotland AD 80–1000* (London, 1984), 220–31. Elsewhere in this volume, Fiona Edmonds makes the observation that the Cumbric language and culture held a significant position in the south of the kingdom too, as well as in the Clydesdale heartlands, but that we may not be sure whether the language had survived throughout the period of Northumbrian political domination, or whether it had been reinvigorated as a result of Strathclyde's renewed ascendancy in the tenth century. See above, 'Personal names', 49, and n. 44.

42 *Symeonis opera*, II.155–6; A. A. M. Duncan, 'The Battle of Carham, 1018', *SHR* 55 (1976), 20–8; see below, 78–9.

43 Jocelin, *Vita S. Kentigerni*, § 33: *Lives*, ed. Forbes, 94, 218.

44 *Vita S. Columbae*, I.15: 'De rege Roderco filio Tothail qui in petra Cloithe regnauit' (*Adomnán's Life*, ed. Anderson and Anderson, 238).

45 *Vita S. Kentigerni*, § 33: 'eique dominium et principatum super uniuersum regnum suum tradidit'; *Lives*, ed. Forbes, 218.

styled and actually be the vicar and chaplain of the pope'.[46] In this way, Jocelin was explaining Glasgow's recently acquired status as 'special daughter of Rome', exempt from submission to a metropolitan. For Glasgow had been defending its independence from the archbishops of York after the 'great rebellion' of 1174, when William the Lion, having been captured, had submitted to Henry II in the 'treaty of Falaise' and agreed to the ecclesiastical subjection of Scotland to England.[47] In the immediately preceding chapters St Kentigern has founded the bishopric of Llanelwy in North Wales: the legend is a heavy allusion to the bishop of Glasgow's case for an archiepiscopal pallium, as Kentigern goes about founding bishoprics in other parts of Britain and performing episcopal consecrations. Some years earlier – and subsequently – similar arguments had been presented to the pope by bishops of St Davids in their campaign for metropolitan status.[48]

Related, perhaps, to this idea of church-founding in Jocelin of Furness's writing is the string of church dedications to St Kentigern found in Cumberland, Dumfriesshire, Roxburghshire, Lanarkshire and Lothian. Of particular interest is a group of churches north of the Cumbrian Mountains, in Allerdale, all of which have dedications to St Kentigern, either by that name or as St Mungo. None of the dedications is attested before the twelfth century, but Aspatria, Bromfield and Dearham have evidence that they were ecclesiastical sites in or before the eleventh century.[49] Meanwhile, churches at Caldbeck, Castle Sowerby, Grinsdale, Irthington and Great Crosthwaite can be dated to the twelfth century; of these,

46 *Vita S. Kentigerni*, § 33: 'ut nulli episcopo esset subiectus; sed pocius uocaretur et esset domini pape uicarius, et capellanus'; *Lives*, ed. Forbes, 95, 219.

47 Broun, 'The Welsh Identity', 167–8; A. A. M. Duncan, *Scotland: The Making of the Kingdom* (Edinburgh, 1975), 262–4.

48 Gerald of Wales, *Libellus inuectionum*, ed. W. S. Davies, *Y Cymmrodor* 30 (1920), 77–237, at 139–41 and 143–6; for a full account of the campaign for metropolitan status at St Davids, see James Conway Davies, *Episcopal Acts and Cognate Documents Relating to Welsh Dioceses 1066–1272*, 2 vols (Cardiff, 1946–8), I.190–232. From probably some point in the 1130s until 1174, there was a direct link between the Scottish crown and the see of St Davids: the stewardship of the lands of the bishopric of St Davids was given by Bishop Bernard (1115–48) to Earl Henry, son of David I, and probably remained in the control of the Scottish kings, who would have been forced to relinquish it in 1174 because of William the Lion's support for the 'great rebellion' of 1173–4. Bishop Bernard, moreover, had previously been the chaplain of Henry I's consort, Queen Matilda, daughter of Malcolm III and Margaret, and must have known Turgot, author of the Life of Margaret the Queen. Bernard had also appointed as one of his archdeacons Jordan, who had been chaplain to Earl Henry, and chancellor to David I. See *St Davids Episcopal Acta 1085–1280*, ed. Julia Barrow (Cardiff, 1998), 5, and 59, no. 33.

49 These churches were have been listed in Forbes, *Lives*, lxxxiii–v, and *VCH Cumberland*, II.1–3. At Aspatria, the church of St Kentigern has fragments of a tenth- or eleventh-century cross, and a tenth-century hogback stone: Richard N. Bailey and Rosemary Cramp, *Corpus of Anglo-Saxon Stone Sculpture. Volume II. Cumberland, Westmorland and Lancashire North-of-the-Sands* (Oxford, 1988), 50–4. St Mungo's church, Bromfield contains fragments of late tenth- or early eleventh-century crosses and a hogback stone: *ibid.*, 80–2. St Mungo's church at Dearham has a late tenth-century cross: *ibid.*, 94–6. Driscoll's statement that 'the Kentigern dedications along the south shore of the Solway can be dated to the early tenth century' is reckless: Stephen T.

Grinsdale and Great Crosthwaite had certainly received a dedication to St Kentigern by the 1180s.[50] A common explanation for this cluster in Cumberland is that it may reflect the 'recovery' of the area by the kingdom of Strathclyde in the tenth century.[51]

The Cumbrian church dedications to St Kentigern all crop up in an area of modern Cumberland, north of the Derwent, where British village-names are notably frequent: this is the area apparently 'reoccupied' in the tenth century by Strathclyders.[52] The theory that the dedications reflect a recovery of the area by the kings of Strathclyde in the tenth century, however, begs several questions. First, the kind of concentration of church dedications to one local saint that we find in Allerdale would be remarkable even in urbanised Italy or Gaul, and we should not expect to see it in the remoter regions of early medieval northern Britain – at least not in the sense of full cult with altars and relics. Secondly, there is little to suggest that the cult of St Kentigern was powerful much before the twelfth century. Thirdly, there is a presumption that Glasgow was the centre of Kentigern's cult in the tenth century, and that Kentigern was closely associated either with the Strathclyde kings or with the kingdom's (principal) bishopric. The archaeological evidence, however, tells against Glasgow as a powerful political or ecclesiastical centre in the tenth century, or even as the home of a cult identified with the old kingdom of Strathclyde. The archaeological investigations of Stephen Driscoll show that prior to the twelfth century, Glasgow was a place of limited consequence. The near absence of early medieval sculpture or other evidence from the ninth to eleventh centuries suggests that, when the reformed diocese was set up in the early twelfth century, Glasgow had only a modest church, probably built of timber, serving a small rural population. That this church was dedicated to the

Driscoll, 'Church Archaeology in Glasgow and the Kingdom of Srathclyde', *IR* 49 (1998), 95–114, at 107.

50 At Caldbeck, Gospatric granted the church (and hospital) to Carlisle Cathedral Priory sometime before 1170: David Knowles and R. N. Hadcock, *Medieval Religious Houses: England and Wales*, 2nd edn (Cambridge, 1971), 261. Castle Sowerby has a church whose architectural features point to a twelfth-century structure: *Pastscape* [online resource from English Heritage's National Monuments Record, available at http://pastscape.english-heritageorg.uk/hob.aspx?hob_id=510861, accessed 30 Nov. 2007]. At Grinsdale, *ecclesia sancti Kentegerni* was granted to Lanercost Priory by Richard de Newton and Robert le Sor in 1175 × c.1180: *The Lanercost Cartulary (Cumbria County Record Office MS D2/1)*, ed. John M. Todd, Surtees Society 203 ([Durham] 1997), nos 39, 93, 94. Irthington's church is twelfth-century in origin, and was granted to Lanercost Priory by Robert de Vaux in 1165 × 74, although the dedication is not mentioned: *Lanercost Cartulary*, ed. Todd, no. 1. At Great Crosthwaite the church is mentioned by Jocelin in the Life of St Kentigern, § 23 (see below).

51 For example, Jackson, 'The Sources', 316. Thomas Clancy ('Scottish Saints and National Identities in the Early Middle Ages', in *Local Saints*, ed. Thacker and Sharpe, 397–421, at 407) has mentioned that the distribution of sculptured crosses in a style centring on Govan and Inchinnan to some extent matches the spread of Kentigern's cult. See also T. O. Clancy and B. E. Crawford, 'The Formation of the Scottish Kingdom', in *The New Penguin History of Scotland from the Earliest Times to the Present Day*, ed. R. A. Houston and W. W. J. Knox (London, 2001), 28–95, at 66.

52 Kenneth Jackson, 'Angles and Britons in Northumbria and Cumbria', in *Angles and Britons: O'Donnell Lectures*, ed. H. Lewis (Cardiff, 1963), 60–84.

British episcopal saint, Kentigern, is an assumption, though perhaps a reasonable one. A stone cross from the site of the present cathedral in the 'Northumbrian' style, of mid- to late eleventh-century date, does point, however, to the increasing importance of the earlier church in the half-century before the construction of David I's building, consecrated in 1136; and it is from the middle of the eleventh century that we have the first hints that bishops were being consecrated for Strathclyde.[53]

The contrast between Glasgow and nearby Govan in the ninth to eleventh centuries was nevertheless sharp. Govan church was the centre of a rich cult, probably sponsored by the royal house of Strathclyde, and had an impressive cemetery: it was 'one axis of a ceremonial and administrative complex at the heart of the kingdom'.[54] The only trace of a dedication to Constantine in modern Cumberland, however, is at Wetheral, where the priory appears to have been dedicated to St Constantine as early as 1101.[55] Dedications to Patrick in Cumberland – another potential signifier of Strathclyde influence – are relatively numerous, but the earliest evidence of a dedication is from 1170, at Bampton; all the other churches dedicated to Patrick appear to be late.[56] The dedication at Bampton might reflect the piety of a twelfth-century founder, Gospatric of Workington (died after 1179), whose progeny included several Patricks, the earliest being Sir Patrick de Culwen (died c.1258), who were proprietors of the church of Bampton.[57]

At this point in the argument one is drawn to look at the influence of the house of Bamburgh – the dynasty of Northumbrian rulers – in the kingdom of Strathclyde–Cumbria during the eleventh century. Fiona Edmonds makes the connection between personal names of the type *Gwas-Patric* (or Gospatric) adopted by members of the Northumbrian dynasty from the eleventh century, and their influence in Strathclyde at that period. An interest in the veneration of St Patrick, as Clancy also shows, had become one of the features of Strathclyde's ecclesiastical life by 1000, and the use of the *Gwas-Patric* name appears to signify adoption of a

53 K. S. Forsyth, 'Late 12th Century Cross-head', in *Excavations at Glasgow Cathedral, 1988–1997* (Leeds, 2002), 85–7; for the dating of the cross, see Woolf, *From Pictland to Alba*, 263, n. 65; also Edmonds, 'Personal Names', above, 53.

54 Driscoll, 'Church Archaeology in Glasgow', 114; see also Stephen T. Driscoll, *Govan from Cradle to Grave*, Friends of Govan Old Lectures Series 2 (Glasgow, 2004); *idem*, *Govan and its Early Medieval Sculpture*, ed. Anna Ritchie (Stroud, 1994); Alex Woolf, *Where was Govan in the Early Middle Ages?*, Friends of Govan Old Lecture Series 5 (Glasgow, 2007), and Davies, *Cult of St Constantine*.

55 Foundation charter in *The Register of the Priory of Wetherhal*, ed. J. E. Prescott, CWAAS, Chartulary Series 1 (London, 1897), 1–5, no. 1; for dating, see Richard Sharpe, *Norman Rule in Cumbria 1092–1136*, CWAAS Tract Series 21 (Kendal, 2006), 47, n. 119; Edmonds, 'Personal Names', above, 55.

56 Alex Woolf (*From Pictland to Alba*, 154) seems to hold with the view that dedications in the Carlisle area to Constantine, Kentigern and Patrick are part of the evidence for 'British reoccupation'.

57 John Flavel Curwen, *A History of the Ancient House of Curwen of Workington in Cumberland* (Kendal, 1928); *idem*, *The Later Records relating to North Westmorland or the Barony of Appleby*, CWAAS, Record series 8 (Kendal, 1932), 245. See also Edmonds, 'Personal Names', above, 61.

local cultural characteristic.[58] Likewise, Northumbrian political power in the eleventh and twelfth centuries, and the cult of St Kentigern, appear to have some kind of correlation.

In Jocelin of Furness's Life of St Kentigern, he tells how the 'holy bishop … building churches in Holdelm, ordaining priests and clerics, placed his see there for a certain reason for a time; afterwards, warned by Divine revelation, justice demanding it, he transferred it to his own city Glasgu'.[59] 'Holdelm' is Hoddom in Dumfriesshire, the site of an Anglian minster-church that may be dated to the eighth century on archaeological grounds; which has stone sculpture comparable to the cross at Glasgow; and which has signs of episcopal status too, an eleventh-century crozier having been found on the site.[60] Apart from taking Jocelin at absolute face-value, there are two other possible explanations for this passage. First, Jocelin seems to be justifying Hoddom as a possession of the bishops of Glasgow, the church having been confirmed in King David's enquiry of c.1124, and to Bishop Engelram (1164–74) by Pope Alexander III in 1170.[61] Additionally, the story might be close to the truth, acknowledging that an earlier episcopal seat had been established at Hoddom and had been moved to Glasgow.

I have already alluded to the possibility that two predecessors of the bishops of Glasgow were consecrated in the middle of the eleventh century: the consecration was claimed for the archbishops of York and would have taken place under the auspices of Siward, earl of Northumbria (d. 1055).[62] Edmonds argues that Siward became a patron of the Cumbrian dynasty, installing Malcolm, 'son of the king of the Cumbrians', as king after the defeat of Macbeth in 1054.[63] This Malcolm was probably the son of Owen 'the Bald', the last certainly recorded king of Strathclyde, who died at Carham in 1018.[64] Siward may also have granted the peace in formerly Cumbrian territory south of the Solway.[65] In this way, Siward brought his power to bear in the southern parts of Strathclyde–Cumbria, and may also have

58 Edmonds, 'Personal Names', above, esp. 58–61; Clancy, 'The Cult of Saints Patrick and Palladius', above.

59 *Vita S. Kentigerni*, § 33: 'Sanctus presul Kentegernus in Holdelmo ecclesias construens, presbiterum et clerum ordinans, sedem episcopalem aliquanto tempore, certa de causa, ibi constituit. Postea diuina reuelatione commonitus, illam ad ciuitatem suam Glasgu, equitate exigente transtulit'; *Lives*, ed. Forbes, 219.

60 C. A. R. Radford, 'Hoddom', *Antiquity* 27 (1953), 153–60; *idem*, 'Hoddom', *Transactions of the Dumfriesshire and Galloway Natural History and Antiquarian Society*, 3rd series, 31 (1954 for 1952–3), 174–97; J. G. Scott, 'Bishop John of Glasgow and the Status of Hoddom', *ibid.*, 66 (1991), 37–45; Christopher E. Lowe, Derek Craig, Dianne Dixon, 'New Light on the Anglian "minster" at Hoddom', 11–35; Perette E. Michelli, 'Four Scottish Crosiers and their Relation to the Irish Tradition', *PSAS* 116 (1986), 375–92.

61 *Charters of King David I*, ed. Barrow, 60, no. 15; *Registrum*, ed. Innes, I.23, no. 26.

62 The evidence is laid out in *Fasti*, ed. Watt and Murray, 187.

63 John of Worcester, *Chronicle*, ed. Darlington and McGurk, II.574–5; William of Malmesbury, *Gesta regum anglorum – The History of the English Kings*, ed. and trans. R. A. B. Mynors *et al.*, 2 vols (Oxford, 1998), I.348–9. For the full argument, see Edmonds, 'Personal Names', above, 53.

64 *ibid.*, n. 76.

65 *ibid.*, 54.

exercised personal authority over church and dynasty in the kingdom's more northerly heartlands.

In the reign of Henry I, another descendant of the Bamburgh dynasty, Waldeve, son of Gospatric, earl of Northumbria (d. 1073 × 5), had been granted the lordship of Allerdale in Cumberland, and it is possible that the lordship had been held since pre-Norman times.[66] This Waldeve witnessed the foundation-deed of Wetheral Priory, Cumberland, in 1101 × 12.[67] The group of Cumberland churches dedicated to St Kentigern is to be found, as we have already seen, in Allerdale. In particular, St Kentigern's churches at Aspatria and Bromfield, which both have stone sculpture comparable with that found at Govan and Glasgow; Aspatria was granted by Waldeve, son of Gospatric, to Carlisle Priory; and he granted Bromfield church to the abbey of St Mary's, York.[68] St Kentigern's church at Caldbeck, also in the lordship of Allerdale, was granted by Gospatric of Workington, maternal grandson of Gospatric, earl of Northumbria, to Carlisle Priory in 1170.[69]

Kentigern dedications, moreover, are to be found in Lothian too, where sometime in the period 1072 × 1093, Gospatric (d. 1138), son of Gospatric earl of Northumbria (d. 1073 × 5), was granted lands in Lothian by Malcolm III, later acquiring the title of Earl of Lothian.[70] There are two plausibly early dedications, one at Borthwick, the other at the nearby Crichton, the former attested in the reign of David I, the latter not until the fifteenth century. Any direct connection between the earls of Lothian and this or any other church, though, is not forthcoming.[71]

66 See *ibid.*, 95, and Sharpe, *Norman Rule*, 53–5. Waldeve was also the brother of Dolfin, lord of Carlisle, who was driven out by William Rufus in 1092; his sister, Etheldreda, was wife of Duncan II, king of Scots (1093–4); see Sharpe, *Norman Rule*, 34–5, n. 80; William M. Aird, 'Gospatric, Earl of Northumbria (d. 10735)', *ODNB* [http://www.oxforddnb.com/view/article/11110, accessed 5 Dec. 2007]. Waldeve did not become abbot of Crowland: that is an error in Orderic, who is no doubt confused with Waltheof, earl of Northumberland and Huntingdon (d. 1076), who was buried at Crowland in the eleventh century ('Vita et passio Waldevi comitis', *Vita quorundum Anglo-Saxonum: Original Lives of Anglo-Saxons and Others who Lived before the Conquest*, ed. J. A. Giles, Caxton Society, 16 (1854), 1–30): I owe this opinion to Richard Sharpe and Hugh Doherty, to whom I am grateful. Cf. Aird, 'Gospatric'.

67 See n. 55, above.

68 See Sharpe, *Norman Rule*, 59; William Dugdale, *Monasticon Anglicanum: A History of the Abbies and other Monasteries, Hospitals, Frieries, and Cathedral and Collegiate Churches, with their Dependencies, in England and Wales*, ed. J. Caley and H. Ellis, 6 vols (London, 1846), VI (i).144.

69 See nn. 50 and 57, above.

70 Andrew McDonald, 'Gospatric, First Earl of Lothian (d. 1138)', *ODNB* [http:// www.oxforddnb.com/view/article/50322, accessed 4 Dec. 2007].

71 Borthwick: *The Charters of King David I. The Written Acts of David I King of Scots, 1124–53 and of His Son Henry Earl of Northumberland, 1139–52*, ed. G. W. S. Barrow (Woodbridge, 1999), 164, no. 232. Crichton: the parish church of St Kentigern was made a collegiate church in 1449, by William, lord Crichton, chancellor of Scotland, which is the first time we know of its dedication; but there was an old church of St Kentigern, which formed a prebend, as did the nearby Borthwick; see Ian B. Cowan and David E. Easson, *Medieval Religious Houses. Scotland*, 2nd edn (London, 1976), 217–18. Other dedications may be found at Currie, on the outskirts of Edinburgh, and at Garleton Castle, East Lothian, but they are late. Currie: the earliest reference to a

Culross in Fife is the reputed home of St Serf, where a Cistercian abbey was founded in 1217 dedicated to him. Jocelin's Life of St Kentigern (§ 4) makes Serf Kentigern's teacher and leads us to expect a cult of St Kentigern there. The earliest such reference, however, does not turn up until 1503, when James IV confirmed in mortmain a charter of Robert Blackadder, archbishop of Glasgow (1483–1508), by which he founded 'a chaplainry for perpetual ministry in the church of the most blessed Kentigern, confessor, built by him near the monastery of Culross'.[72] The Life of St Serf, perhaps written by the author of the fragmentary Life of St Kentigern in the late twelfth century, makes no mention of the Kentigern connection.

Other potentially early dedications to St Kentigern in Scotland are to be found firmly within the diocesan jurisdiction of Glasgow. The parish church of Lanark was dedicated to St Kentigern and was granted in 1150 by David I to the Premonstratensian abbey at Dryburgh.[73] At Kirkmahoe (Dumfriesshire), in the next valley to Hoddom, the place-name preserves a Brittonic diminutive of Kentigern's name, *Mochoe*, equivalent to the Gaelic *Mungo*; yet the earliest firm reference to the dedication is in a charter of Robert I, 1321.[74] Finally, at Hassendean, Roxburghshire, archdeaconry of Teviotdale, diocese of Glasgow, we find the church dedicated to St Kentigern; but an early reference to this dedication is elusive. The earliest record of the church itself is apparently in 1193 in a confirmation by William I to Melrose abbey of the church for the reception and maintenance of paupers and pilgrims.[75]

Whereas one should not, on the one hand, dismiss the possibility of early dedications merely on the grounds that the historical record does not furnish the evidence for them; one should not, on the other hand, make assumptions. We may also look to circumstances that might explain the late appearance of such dedications; and here the creation of the reformed diocese of Glasgow after 1107 by Earl David, heir to the Scottish throne, later David I, is important.[76]

The first bishop of Glasgow proper, a Cumbrian called Michael, was consecrated by Archbishop Thomas II of York (1108–14); he dedicated churches within

Kentigern dedication is from 1296; Alan Reid, 'Notes of the Churchyards of Currie, Kirknewton, and the Calders', *PSAS* 40 (1905–6), 217–45, at 217. Garleton: a chaplainry in the reign of James V; *RMS*, III, 146. There are other possible sites, none of which looks early, at Penicuik and Cockpen, both near Edinburgh: James Murray Mackinlay, *Ancient Church Dedications in Scotland. Non-Scriptural Dedications* (Edinburgh, 1914), 180–1.

72 *RMS*, II, 578.

73 The earliest reference to the dedication is from a judgment of 1220, when mention is made of the 'mother church of St Kentigern of Lanark': *Liber S. Marie de Dryburgh. Registrum Cartarum Abbacie Premonstratensis de Dryburgh*, ed. William Fraser, Bannatyne Club 83 (Edinburgh, 1847), 168–9. See also John M. Davidson, 'St Kentigern's Church, Lanark', *PSAS* 46 (1911–12), 133–9.

74 *The Acts of Robert I King of Scots 1306–1329*, ed. A. A. M. Duncan, Regesta Regum Scottorum 5 (Edinburgh, 1988), 467. See Clancy, 'Scottish Saints', 405–6.

75 *The Acts of William I, King of Scots, 1165–1214*, ed. G. W. S. Barrow, Regesta Regum Scottorum 2 (Edinburgh, 1971), 359–61.

76 N. F. Shead, 'The Origins of the Medieval Diocese of Glasgow', *SHR* 48 (1969), 220–5.

the diocese of York and held ordinations in the church at Morland, Westmorland, where he was eventually to be buried.[77] His successor, Bishop John, was consecrated about 1117 by a reforming pope, Paschal II.[78] The first cathedral was consecrated during his episcopate in 1136, and it is from the time of Bishop John (supported by King David) that we see the systematic promotion of St Kentigern's cult.[79]

We need not be concerned that St Kentigern's cult appears to have been dormant, or even forgotten, down to the twelfth century. New churches generally need new saints to launch successful cults. The introduction in 1120, for example, of the cults of St Dyfrig and St Teilo at Llandaf, Glamorgan, is instructive in this respect.[80] A new see would benefit from an episcopal patron saint to launch the new diocese. At Glasgow, again as at Llandaf, an episcopal saint was found to do the job. For this reason too, the cult of St Constantine had to be eclipsed: just as the ecclesiastical diocese replaced the former kingdom, so the episcopal saint had to replace the royal one. Jocelin of Furness dealt with the situation deftly: St Constantine had been 'always subject to the bishop, like his father [Rhydderch] before him'.[81]

Despite the evidence for the existence of earlier churches at several of the sites later known to be dedicated to St Kentigern, one is nevertheless strongly led to infer that as late as 1133 St Kentigern's cult was still either weak or absent in Cumberland. When in that year Henry I founded the bishopric of Carlisle, we should notice that King David made no objection.[82] In fact, ten years earlier, David had carried out an enquiry to find out what properties properly belonged to Glasgow, and had come across no ancient endowments of Glasgow in Cumberland.[83] Geoffrey Barrow has shown how, in this process of enquiry, church dedications must have been taken as evidence that a church or parish formed part of the possessions of Glasgow.[84] He thought it more likely that a dedication to Kentigern would have come first, and that claims on behalf of Glasgow followed, rather than once Glasgow's ownership was established, the Kentigern dedication was quickly

77 Hugh the Chanter, *The History of the Church of York 1066–1127*, ed. and trans. Charles Johnson, rev. edn by M. Brett *et al.* (Oxford, 1990), 52; *Fasti*, ed. Watt and Murray, 187–8.

78 *Fasti*, ed. Watt and Murray, 188.

79 For an account of the cult of St Kentigern at Glasgow cathedral in the twelfth century, see A. A. M. Duncan, 'St Kentigern at Glasgow Cathedral in the Twelfth Century', in *Medieval Art and Architecture in the Diocese of Glasgow*, ed. Richard Fawcett, British Archaeological Association Conference Transactions 23 (London, 1998), 9–24.

80 John Reuben Davies, *The Book of Llandaf and the Norman Church in Wales* (Woodbridge, 2003), esp. 63–97.

81 *Vita S. Kentigerni*, § 33: *Lives*, ed. Forbes, 95/219. St Constantine's church at Govan became a prebend of Glasgow Cathedral, *Registrum episcopatus Glasguensis*, ed. Cosmo Innes, Bannatyne and Maitland Clubs, 2 vols (Edinburgh, 1843), I.10–11, 23, 26, 30, nos 6, 26, 28, 32.

82 John of Hexham, *Historia XXV annorum*, a continuation of *Historia regum: Symeonis opera*, II.285. For a discussion of the chronology, see Sharpe, *Norman Rule*, 60–1.

83 *The Charters of David I*, ed. Barrow, 60, no. 15; preamble in *Registrum*, ed. Innes, 5–9.

84 G. W. S. Barrow, *King David I and the Church of Glasgow*, Glasgow Cathedral Lecture Series 4 (Glasgow, 1996).

applied as a species of name-tag. A similar process can again be seen happening in South Wales with the bishopric of Llandaf as it sought to establish possession of estates and churches under the patronage of St Teilo.[85] In support of his judgement, Barrow drew our attention to a grant by the bishop of St Andrews to Herbert, bishop of Glasgow (John's successor, 1164–74), of the parish church of *Lochwharret* (Borthwick in Midlothian, under the diocese of St Andrews).[86] This church had already been inadvertently given by David I to the Augustinians of Scone. Now, prompted by the king after he had reconsidered the situation, Lochwarret was 'restored' to Glasgow and the anomaly was regularised when Bishop Herbert presented the prior of Scone to Bishop Robert as parson of the church. It cannot be down to chance that Lochwarret was dedicated to Kentigern or Mungo, and that it figures in Jocelin's Life of the saint.[87]

At the end of 1135, in response to Stephen's assumption of the English crown, King David had taken control of Carlisle and Newcastle, so effecting a restoration of Scottish power, which had been unthinkable during the reign of Henry I.[88] David came to terms with King Stephen in February 1136, and formalised his possession of Cumbria, but relinquished Northumberland. A second treaty between the Scottish and the English kings was reached at Durham in April 1139, Stephen yielding rule between the Tees and the Tweed to David, where the Scottish king remained in control until his death in May 1153 at Carlisle Castle.[89]

It is, I think, during this period of Scottish control in Cumberland that we should place the flourishing of Kentigern's cult. The promotion of the cult at Glasgow was especially vigorous from this point on. The *Scotichronicon*, written in the fifteenth century, records a story of how King Henry I was angry at seeing that John, bishop of Glasgow, 'was dedicating churches throughout Cumberland'.[90] Although the story is without authority, and appears to be chronologically misleading, it nevertheless allows us to imagine a situation in which the bishop of Glasgow acted in such a way, to Anglo-Norman dismay, during the period of Scottish ascendancy in the area.[91] Another strong hint that this kind of thing had been going on is provided by Jocelin of Furness. Crosthwaite Church, on the outskirts of Keswick – Crosthwaite meaning 'the cross in the clearing' – is dedicated to St Kentigern, and

85 Davies, 'The Saints of South Wales', 365–76.

86 *Registrum,* ed. Innes, I.13, no. 11; granted to Scone Priory by David I: *The Acts of Malcolm IV, King of Scots, 1153–1165, together with the Scottish Royal Acts Prior to 1153 not included in Sir Archibald Lawrie's 'Early Scottish Charters'*, ed. G. W. S. Barrow, Regesta Regum Scottorum 1 (Edinburgh, 1960), 164–5, 263–5, nos 57, 243; *Liber Ecclesie de Scon: munimenta vetustiora Monasterii Sancte Trinitatis et Sancti Michaelis de Scon*, ed. Cosmo Innes, Maitland Club 62 (Edinburgh, 1843), 33. The name survives as Loquhariot (NT 370608), and is British in origin: Andrew Breeze, 'St Kentigern and Loquhariot, Lothian', *IR* 54 (2002), 103–7.

87 Jocelin, *Vita S. Kentigerni*, § 41: *Lives*, ed. Forbes, 110/234. In this episode, the saint constructs a cross out of sandstone at Loquhariot and remains in the place for eight years.

88 Henry of Huntingdon, *Historia Anglorum*, x.4, ed. Diana Greenway (Oxford, 1996), 706.

89 For all this, see G. W. S. Barrow, 'King David I, Earl Henry, and Cumbria', *TCWAAS*, 2nd series, 99 (1999), 117–27.

90 *Chron. Bower*, viii.3 (IV.254–7).

91 For the chronology of the story, see Sharpe, *Norman Rule*, 61.

this appears to be the church mentioned in *Vita S. Kentigerni*, § 23, as having been 'recently built':

> [Kentigern] stayed some time in a wood to strengthen and reassure the men who were living there in their faith; he also set up a cross there, as a sign of their salvation. From this episode the place gained the name Crosfeld in English, that is, *Crucis Nouale* ['the field of the cross']. Indeed, in this very place there is a basilica, recently built, dedicated to the name of Blessed Kentigern.

So the evidence from North Britain points towards a cult of St Kentigern that may have existed in Glasgow before the twelfth century, but which probably existed in the Lothian area too, as well as at Dumfriesshire. With the foundation of the diocese of Glasgow, the cult of Kentigern was relaunched and promoted; as the saint came to embody the diocese of Glasgow, and Scottish royal power together with Glaswegian episcopal pretensions stretched southwards once more, his cult spread into Scottish-controlled Cumberland during the twelfth century.

Kentigern among the Welsh

The resurgence and renewed popularity of Kentigern's cult in North Britain may also be the key to his association with North Wales, and the Welsh saint, Asaph.

The diocese of Llanelwy occupies the north-eastern quarter of Wales, encompassing the old counties of Denbighshire, Flintshire and Montgomeryshire. Whatever its earlier history, there had been no bishops in the area for some considerable time before the foundation or re-foundation of the bishopric in 1141.[92] Llanelwy was certainly an ancient ecclesiastical site, on the eastern bank of the River Elwy, a tributary of the Clwyd. The place was soon to be known as St Asaph. The position of the cathedral, in the border territory between the Welsh and the English, had been, until this point, unfavourable for the growth of the see. Llanelwy was within the English sphere of influence, being included in the domains of the Earl of Chester, while the greater portion of the diocese was in the possession of the Welsh. When in 1125 attempts were afoot to settle the ongoing quarrel between the archbishops of Canterbury and York, it was proposed to transfer from Canterbury to York the bishoprics of Chester, Bangor and 'a third which lies between these two, but is now vacant, owing to the desolation of the country and the rudeness of the inhabitants'.[93] In the early 1140s, Owain ap Gruffudd ap Cynan, ruler of Gwynedd (and more commonly known as Owain Gwynedd), had defeated the armies of the Earl of Chester east of the River Conwy.[94] Owain's intention may

92 Matthew J. Pearson, 'The Creation and Development of the St Asaph Cathedral Chapter, 1141–1293', *Cambrian Medieval Celtic Studies* 40 (2000), 35–56.

93 Hugh the Chanter, *History of the Church of York*, ed. Johnson, 122–3.

94 *Brut y Tywysogion or the Chronicle of the Princes, Peniarth MS 20 Version*, trans. Thomas Jones (Cardiff, 1952), s.aa. [1145=1146], [1148=1149], and [1149=1150]. John Edward Lloyd, *A History of Wales from the Earliest Times to the Edwardian Conquest*, 2 vols, 3rd edn (London, 1939), II.487–95; R. R. Davies, *Conquest, Coexistence and Change. Wales 1063–1415* (Oxford, 1987); reprinted in paperback as *The Age of Conquest. Wales 1063–1415* (Oxford, 1991), 46.

have been to annex the whole of the north-east to the bishopric of Bangor; in the end, he retained the enclaves of the deaneries of Arwystli and Dyffryn Clwyd as detached portions of the diocese of Bangor. Owain's military campaign may have been what finally impelled the Earl of Chester and the archbishop of Canterbury, Theobald of Bec, to provide north-east Wales with a Norman bishop dependent on the ecclesiastical jurisdiction of Canterbury, and located near the military and political base of Rhuddlan. The first bishop of Llanelwy, a shadowy figure by the name of Richard and – given his name – presumably of Anglo-Norman extraction, was consecrated in 1141.[95]

The earliest known mention of Kentigern's connection with Llanelwy and St Asaph is made by Jocelin in the Life of St Kentigern. In the portion of that work (§§ 23–31) that deals with the exile of Kentigern and the founding of St Asaph, Kentigern escapes from the avenging relatives of *Morken*, king of Cumbria, who dies of gout after kicking Kentigern.[96] Kentigern makes for St Davids in South Wales, where he meets and lives with St David. King Cadwallon befriends him and gives him a site called *Nant Carvan*, where he founds a monastery. Then a white boar leads him to a place on the banks of the River Elwy.[97] He and his followers begin to build a monastery, but they are stopped by a heathen prince called *Melconde Galganu*, apparently a subject of King Cadwallon; he orders the monastery to be pulled down, but is struck blind. He then repents, and when Kentigern is recalled to the North, Asaph becomes his successor as abbot and bishop.

This story of St Kentigern and St Asaph must be taken in conjunction with another document. What appears to be a foundation charter was said to have been discovered in London by Bishop Einion (*Anianus*) ap Maredudd in 1256, in a then old book relating to the liberties and rights and endowments of the bishop and chapter, which enumerates the rights and endowments made by Maelgwn to Kentigern.[98] The language and form of the document resemble other charter material from twelfth-century Wales, especially the hagiographical charters found in the Book of Llandaf.[99] It says that Kentigern came from the east to Llanelwy with 300 priests, knights and servants, and was ordained bishop by *Maye*, king of Powys (who is unknown), and *Malginus* gave him Llanelwy, with various estates, which are listed. Later, a quarrel arose between *Malginus* and one *Kedicus*, who took sanctuary at Llanelwy. *Malginus* came in pursuit and was blinded; he begged pardon of Kentigern, who restored his sight; and in gratitude he granted the church extensive rights of sanctuary and further estates. This is typical of the kind of hagiographical charter that was being written elsewhere in late eleventh- and early twelfth-century Wales, at Llancarfan and at Llandaf most notably.

As it stands, the charter is later than Jocelin's time, yet it seems to bear witness to the existence of a story at Llanelwy, not wholly derived from Jocelin, that the

95 See Pearson, 'The Creation', 38–9.

96 *Lives*, ed. Forbes, 73–92/199–216.

97 The Elwy flows into the Clwyd just beyond Llanelwy; the story of the boar may be a play on Old Welsh *aper*, 'confluence' (modern Welsh, *aber*), and Latin *aper*, 'boar'.

98 The text is printed in *Lives*, ed. Forbes, lxxix–lxxxi; see n. 12, above.

99 Compare the narrative charters in the Book of Llandaf, especially *Book of Llan Dâv*, 193–7. See also K. L. Maund, 'Fact and Narrative Fiction in the Llandaff Charters', *Studia Celtica* 31 (1997), 173–93.

church was founded by St Kentigern, and that it received benefactions from Maelgwn Gwynedd after that king had been blinded as the result of a quarrel with Kentigern, and then cured. This account does not seem to derive from Jocelin, but bears independent witness to the existence of the legend at Llanelwy.[100]

The key to this material might lie in an unsuspected place. Oliver Padel has recently returned to the theme of Geoffrey of Monmouth and the Merlin legend.[101] Padel directs us towards a body of textual evidence: three Latin compositions about St Kentigern of Glasgow, two of which we have already encountered. First, the fragment of a Life of St Kentigern written for Bishop Herbert at Glasgow; second, Jocelin of Furness's Life of the saint; and finally, two free-standing episodes about the northern prophetic wild-man Lailoken, one of them telling how he was befriended by St Kentigern. A most notable fact is that the only known copies of the earlier Life of St Kentigern and of the Lailoken episodes occur together in the same manuscript, London, British Library, MS Titus A.xix (*saec.* xv), which also contains an abridgement of Geoffrey of Monmouth's *Vita Merlini*. Now, Geoffrey's *Vita Merlini* shares some themes with this Latin material about the wild-man. The fragment of the Life of St Kentigern does not contain the Lailoken material, because it breaks off after the birth of St Kentigern (here a virgin birth, vaguely analogous to that of Ambrosius in the *Historia Brittonum*, and hence to that of Geoffrey's Merlin in his *Historia Regum Britanniae*). The most significant overlap for the purpose of my argument, however, is that found between the Lailoken material, Geoffrey's *Vita Merlini*, and Jocelin's *Vita S. Kentigerni*. Jocelin's Life contains a truncated form of the material, saying only that a fool or jester (*homo fatuus*; not a wild-man, therefore) called *Laloecen*, at the court of King Rhydderch (*Rederech*), was inconsolable after Kentigern's death, and prophesied the death of two others – Rhydderch himself and a nobleman (§ 45). In Geoffrey's *Vita Merlini*, Merlin reveals the adultery of the queen by means of a leaf in her hair; she discredits his vision by asking him to prophesy the death of a boy in three guises; although the story draws on a different thread of the Lailoken material, the king in both instances is Rhydderch, and so there is overlap between Jocelin's material and Geoffrey's.

We also find overlap with Geoffrey elsewhere in Jocelin's *Vita S. Kentigerni*. Some phrases and words in Jocelin's Preface suggest knowledge of Geoffrey's addresses to his prospective patrons: one to Robert, earl of Gloucester, and Waleran, count of Meulan, the other to Alexander, bishop of Lincoln.[102] In addition to this, however, one should also recognise another tell-tale sign of Geoffrey's influence on Jocelin: a peculiar display of one-upmanship. This may be discerned in the episode at the end of § 23 of the *uita*: Dewi grants to Kentigern a place called *Nantcarvan*, where the saint proceeds to found a monastery. Jocelin's choice of Nantcarfan (Llancarfan, Glamorgan) is as intriguing as his designation of Dewi as presiding bishop in the area. Dewi, or St David, is of course the founder and patron of the diocese of St Davids, but Nant- or Llancarfan was one of the most important

100 Jackson, 'The Sources'.

101 O. J. Padel, 'Geoffrey of Monmouth and the Development of the Merlin Legend,' *Cambrian Medieval Celtic Studies* 51 (2006), 37–65.

102 See D. R. Howlett, *The English Origins of Old French Literature* (Dublin, 1996), 36–48.

churches and centres of learning in the neighbouring diocese of Llandaf. In fact, there had been, during Geoffrey's lifetime, a great dispute over boundaries and property between the bishops of St Davids and Llandaf, and the episcopal *familia* of Llandaf was almost exclusively drawn from Llancarfan. One by-product of Llandaf's dispute with St Davids was the Book of Llandaf, a history of the bishops of Llandaf through seven centuries, probably written by the bishop of Llandaf's brother, the hagiographer Caradog, *magister* at the school of Llancarfan. Caradog and his work was certainly known to Geoffrey, for he mentions him in an epilogue to *Historia Regum Britanniae* as his 'contemporary', to whom he was leaving the writing of the subsequent history of the Welsh kings from where he had left off. Now, Geoffrey, in his *Historia*, had been sniping at Caradog's version of Llandaf's history. Geoffrey belittled Llandaf, first by depriving it of Dubricius (St Dyfrig), one of the church's patron saints, making him archbishop of Caerleon; he then went to work on another of Llandaf's patrons, St Teilo – a supposed archbishop of Llandaf – and demoted him to the status of 'illustrious priest of Llandaf', sending him instead to become archbishop of Dol in Brittany. This, in particular, is an inside joke, because much of the Book of Llandaf is – in the words of Christopher Brooke – the Life of St Samson of Dol plus water.[103] The idea put forward in Jocelin's *Vita S. Kentigerni* that Llancarfan, the ecclesiastical community where Caradog was *magister*, should have been founded by Kentigern and granted to him by St David smells strongly of Geoffrey. This, and the apparent Merlin connection, arouses the suspicion that Jocelin had access to material composed by Geoffrey. Another further link with Geoffrey may be visible in Jocelin's work, for it is in *Vita S. Kentigerni* that we find our earliest record of the connection of St Kentigern with the see of Llanelwy.

There are, I think, some strong grounds for the idea that Geoffrey of Monmouth first linked the persons of St Asaph and St Kentigern, and so associated St Kentigern with Llanelwy. We might even suppose that he was responsible for associating St Asaph with Llanelwy. In order to understand this notion, however, we ought briefly to consider in more detail Llanelwy's counterpart in south-east Wales, the see of Llandaf.

At early twelfth-century Llandaf, we encounter some striking parallels with Llanelwy. In both places a diocese was refounded, based at an ancient *llan* that takes its name from a river.[104] Both churches are roughly two miles upstream of a Norman castle, the *capita* of recently founded Marcher lordships. The parallels go further, if the hypothesis is correct. Llandaf claimed St Dyfrig as its founding father – the founder of the Church among the *Britannos dextralis partis Britanniae*, 'the Britons of South Wales'. At Llanelwy, by comparison, there is St Kentigern, the patriarch of the Church among the Britons of the North. At Llandaf, the founding bishop is succeeded by a famous local bishop-saint with a Hebrew name, Eliud (St Teilo's real name); the parallel at Llanelwy is found in Bishop Asaph.[105] In both cases the cult of a once-powerful but now withering episcopal cult is transferred to the new see: Dyfrig and Teilo are co-patrons of Llandaf, while

103 Christopher N. L. Brooke, *The Church and the Welsh Border in the Central Middle Ages* (Woodbridge, 1986), 31.

104 Llanelwy < *llan* + *Elwy*; Llandaf < *llan* + *Taf*.

105 Eliud is a form of Elihu and is found in Mt 1.14–15; see John Reuben Davies, 'Old

Kentigern and Asaph are honoured at Llanelwy. Both were bishoprics on the Anglo-Welsh border under the control of Marcher lords.

Whereas scholars of an earlier age argued that the author of the Book of Llandaf was Geoffrey of Monmouth, it seems to me, on the other hand, that Geoffrey put his ingenious talent to work elsewhere; for whom should we find consecrated as bishop of St Asaph in 1152, but Geoffrey himself. It is with Geoffrey that the name of St Asaph is first applied to the see.[106] With his customary disregard for historical fact, Geoffrey appears to have looked about for a patron of his new see to rival Llandaf, for whose official history he had displayed contemptuous disregard. In his research, he must have alighted on a version of *Annales Cambriae*, where, as we have already seen, the death-notice recorded beside that of Llandaf's St Dyfrig is of none other than St Kentigern.[107]

One further perplexing and potentially early trace of Kentigern appears, however, in south Carmarthenshire, at Llangyndeyrn. The evidence of commemoration lies in the place-name, which is a compound of Welsh *llan* ('church' or 'ecclesiastical enclosure') + *Cyndeyrn* (i.e. Kentigern), so 'Cyndeyrn's church'. Usually, one would expect this type of name to have been generated quite early, probably some time between the ninth and the end of the tenth century, but possibly as early as the seventh.[108] The shape of the churchyard conforms to a type of early medieval subdivided curvilinear site found in Ireland, and in Wales at Llandyfaelog, Rhoscrowdder and Llanilar.[109] The earliest attestation of the place-name is in 1540, with the dedication of the church to St Cyndeyrn attested in 1656.[110] The church dedication is of limited value, as its first attestation is too late; but it is interesting that the Welsh form 'Cyndeyrn' is used, and not 'Kentigern', as at St Asaph parish church. One is tempted to follow Baring-Gould and Fisher in their postulation of the existence of another local figure called Cyndeyrn, rather than with Yates, who thought (one would say wrongly) that the place-name need not be earlier than the twelfth century.[111] Llangyndeyrn is the only example of the full 'Kentigern' name appearing in a toponym anywhere: it is this fact, above all, which makes one suspicious of any relation with St Kentigern of Glasgow.

Testament Names among the Britons', forthcoming. The Asaph of the Old Testament was appointed by King David as principal musician for singing the Lord's praises.

106 But see H. E. Salter, 'Geoffrey of Monmouth and Oxford', *EHR* 34 (1919), 382–5, at 384–5.

107 See above, 68.

108 See Davies, 'The Saints of South Wales', for a suggested chronology of the evolution of *llan*- place-names.

109 Terrence A. James, 'Air Photography of Ecclesiastical Sites in South Wales', in *The Early Church in Wales and the West*, ed. Nancy Edwards and Alan Lane (Oxford, 1992), 62–76, at 73.

110 Graham Jones, 'Wales and the English Marches', *Transnational Database and Atlas of Saints' Cults* [electronic resource. Available online at http://www.le.ac.uk/elh/grj1/database/dedwales.xls (accessed 9 Oct. 2007)].

111 *LBS*, II.83 (note). Cf. W. N. Yates, 'The "Age of the Saints" in Carmarthenshire: A Study of Church Dedications', *Carmarthenshire Antiquary* 9 (1973), 53–81, at 65–6.

Bishop Kentigern among the Britons

We may now conclude that the dedications to St Kentigern, bishop and confessor, in Cumberland and Wales, appear to be a product of the twelfth century. In those areas controlled by the king of Scots, they represent the power of that king, and of the new bishops of Glasgow. In north-east Wales, the Kentigern-connection may be viewed as invention. The *Gonotiernus* who was a bishop in sixth-century West Frankia must have been of Brittonic ethnicity; he could conceivably have been the *Conthigirn* of *Annales Cambriae*; but there is little reason outside the chronological proximity and matching name to identify him with the St Kentigern venerated at Glasgow. A bishop with a Frankish career has not been remembered in North Britain.

The spread of dedications one sees in Cumberland, southern Scotland and the Forth–Clyde belt would normally be the result of royal and high-powered aristocratic patronage. It is not until the twelfth century that we can see any sign that Kenitgern's cult was likely to have been promoted systematically in the Strathclyde area. The churches in Cumberland dedicated to Kentigern appear to have received their designation in the twelfth century. The Lothian connection in Jocelin's Life was probably designed to encourage and justify pre-existing dedications to Kentigern in that area.

In the end I think we should see the spread of Kentigern's cult as closely bound up with the rise of Glasgow as a powerful episcopal see in the twelfth century. Thomas Clancy has shown how Cumbric-speaking inhabitants of Cumbria and Lothian may have looked on Kentigern as a national saint: he is one of only four saints who appear in patronal personal names with Cumbric *gos*- or *cos*- ('servant') from the late twelfth century onwards, the type of name that Fiona Edmonds discusses in this volume.[112] The only other names that occur in such compounds are Patrick, Oswald, and Cuthbert, which might leads us to conclude, as Clancy has, that this class of personal name indicates ethnic identity rather than a purely religious or local allegiance. We should also note, in this respect, that the cult of Kentigern had been adopted among Gaels too by the twelfth century.[113] This no doubt explains in part the encounter between Kentigern and Columba in Jocelin's Life (§§ 39–40). Just as Clancy and Edmonds have shown how the ethnically British Patrick and his cult had become increasingly linked with Strathclyde–Cumbria during the eleventh century, so the ethnically British Gildas was being associated with Strathclyde in the eleventh and twelfth centuries too. The Life of St Gildas by the monk of the Breton monastery of Saint-Gildas-de-Rhuys, Morbihan, written in the first half of the eleventh century, makes the saint a native of the kingdom of Clyde Rock, and the Life of St Gildas, written about a century later by Caradog of Llancarfan, makes him the son of a king of Scotland.[114]

112 Clancy, 'Scottish Saints', 406; see also Fiona Edmonds, 'Personal Names', above.

113 Clancy, 'Scottish Saints', 405–6; Jackson, 'Sources', 302; C. Ó Baoill, 'St Machar – Some Linguistic Light?', *IR* 44 (1993), 1–13, at 9–10. The Gaelic cult of Kentigern/ Mungo, however, leads us down another path, which would divert us for too long on this occasion, and so needs to be treated separately.

114 *Vita I S. Gildae*, in *Gildae De Excidio Britanniae*, ed. H. Williams, Cymmrodorion

'Association of Patrick and Gildas with Strathclyde', David Howlett has written, 'may be part of an imaginative attempt to enrich the historic antiquity of Scotland by including in it the very founders of the traditions of the British and the Irish.'[115]

The rise of St Kentigern's cult should also be seen in the context of twelfth-century historical writing; and for Scotland, historical writing is of the first importance, because little exists before the twelfth century.[116] The body of historical material that documents the early medieval territories and peoples that were to become the Kingdom of Scots was pulled together by English writers working in Scotland in the twelfth century. A current trend in scholarship has been emphasising the idea that writers were deliberately supplying the new Kingdom of Scots with a defined range of literary compositions like those that existed already among neighbouring peoples. In artistic terms (it has been argued) we may see the creation of a Scottish Latin literature; in political terms, it amounts to the literary definition of the Kingdom of Scots – in both respects, a response by Englishmen to the Norman Conquest of England. Englishmen successfully defined Scotland as a place in which to preserve their Englishness, and Jocelin of Furness helped and encouraged them.[117] These authors created a body of material that encompassed the Pictish, British, Gaelic and English cultural traditions of the kingdom, providing a historical dignity and an air of antiquity that could be compared with the traditions of the Welsh, the Irish and the English.[118] On a larger scale, it is parallel with the literary enterprises of eleventh- and twelfth-century Welsh clerics who, facing a new political settlement with an historical lacuna, had been busy collecting charters, producing ecclesiastical histories, and creating the Lives of their rehabilitated saints.[119]

The re-emergence, the promotion, and the growth of St Kentigern's cult during the twelfth century were an outcome of changes in the Scottish kingdom, the reorganisation of the bishoprics of Scotland, and the ongoing reform of the western

Record Series 3–4 (London, 1899–1901), 322–88; Caradog of Llancarfan, *Vita S. Gildae*, in *ibid*., 390–413.

115 *Caledonian Craftsmanship*, 198.

116 The classic statement of this problem is Kathleen Hughes, 'Where are the Writings of Early Scotland?', in *Celtic Britain in the Early Middle Ages: Studies in Welsh and Scottish Sources by the Late Kathleen Hughes*, ed. David Dumville (Woodbridge, 1980), 1–22.

117 The prologue to *Vita S. Waldeui* by Jocelin of Furness provides a striking example of the importance of Anglo-Saxon heritage to the Scottish royal dynasty in the late twelfth century. The Life of St Waldef is edited by W. Cooper in *Acta Sanctorum quotquot toto orbe coluntur*, August I (1733), 248–76; a text and translation of the prologue may be had in David Howlett, *Caledonian Craftsmanship: The Scottish Latin Tradition* (Dublin, 2000), 124–9; an edition of the *uita*, based on the Bollandists' text, was done with emendations and translated in full in an unpublished Columbia University PhD dissertation by George McFadden, 'An Edition and Translation of The Life of Waldef, Abbot of Melrose, by Jocelin of Furness' (1952), where he makes unwarranted emendations to the text. I have in hand an edition of the text from the only extant manuscript source (of which McFadden was unaware), Madrid, Real Biblioteca, MS II/2097, fols 41vb–68rb.

118 See Howlett, *Caledonian Craftsmanship*.

119 See Davies, *The Book of Llandaf*.

Church as a whole at that time.[120] These changes came about partly as a result of Anglo-Norman political ambitions in northern Britain, partly in the wake of a reordering of the English episcopate after the Norman Conquest, and partly as a response to the swelling metropolitical claims of York. Kentigern was made into a figure who could represent the history of a kingdom and its Christian community in a new way; he became a bridge between the dignified past of a refashioned historical memory and the confident, aspirant reality of the present. Kentigern's story interpreted the contemporary state of affairs for a twelfth-century audience – a developing Scottish realm of diverse cultural, linguistic and ecclesiastical constituents. St Kentigern, as he appears in the sources, is really a later re-creation of an earlier artefact. In the same way that Barry and Pugin in the mid-nineteenth century built a Palace of Westminster to house and embody a reformed parliament, the seat of a government that ruled over an expanding empire, so the twelfth-century bishops of Glasgow built a cathedral for the heart of their reformed and expanding diocese, and commissioned histories of its founding bishop, whose newly constructed shrine stood at its heart. Embedded in the core of these histories may lie an original edifice of sixth-century historical reality, but it has been lost to modern view: we are only able to observe the embellished reconstruction, which was raised for a contemporary purpose and to serve contemporary needs. Such figures as Glasgow's Bishop Jocelin, and his namesake, Jocelin of Furness – not to mention Llanelwy's Geoffrey – were the Charles Barry and Augustus Pugin of their day, the one building the grand structure, the other decorating it with a pseudo-historical flourish. Just as our view of the Gothic has been influenced by the nineteenth century, we should also recognise the extent to which our view of the 'Age of Saints' has been conditioned by the twelfth.

120 Aspects of the reforming ideals of Scottish monarchs may be seen in the correspondence of Queen Margaret (d. 1093), and her son, King Alexander I (d. 1124), with the archbishops of Canterbury; Margaret with Lanfranc (*The Letters of Lanfranc Archbishop of Canterbury*, ed. and trans. Helen Clover and Margaret Gibson (Oxford, 1979), no. 50), and Alexander with Anselm and Ralph d'Escures (*Eadmeri Historia Novorum in Anglia*, ed. Martin Rule (London, 1884), 279–82, 286–8.

5

ADJACENT SAINTS' DEDICATIONS AND EARLY CELTIC HISTORY

Karen Jankulak

In 1986, Oliver Padel coined the phrase 'recurrent adjacency' to describe

> a feature of Brittonic church dedications which has often been noted but never fully explained ... Two saints with adjacent dedications in one country may often turn up, again adjacent, in another part of the Brittonic world ... it is ... a geographical dimension to the dedications of Brittonic saints, and one which has struck antiquarian writers from the Middle Ages to the twelfth century.[1]

This 'geographical dimension to the dedications of Brittonic saints' was of particular interest to Gilbert Hunter Doble (1880–1945) and Emrys George Bowen (1900–1983), as well as, earlier on, to a range of Breton and Welsh scholars.[2] The greatest nexus of clusters of 'adjacent' dedications is between Cornwall and Brittany (with some found also in Wales as well as in Devon). These two regions in particular are replete with notably obscure 'saints', often known only as church dedications or from place-names. Cults found across both regions are therefore all the more striking. Some of these shared cults may arise from early medieval emigration from Britain to Brittany. This is difficult to prove in specific cases while being a broadly reasonable assumption. Close contact between Cornwall

1 B. Lynette Olson and O. J. Padel, 'A Tenth-Century List of Cornish Parochial Saints', *Cambridge Medieval Celtic Studies* 12 (1986), 33–71, at 67.

2 See Jonathan Wooding, 'The Figure of David', in *St David of Wales: Cult, Church and Nation*, ed. J. Wyn Evans and Jonathan Wooding (Woodbridge, 2007), 1–19, at 8, for his discussion of historiographical implications of the geographical approach to cults of saints, which he terms a 'British (in the wider sense) school of interpretation'. For another recent critique of the methods of Doble, Bowen and others, see John Reuben Davies, 'The Saints of South Wales and the Welsh Church', in *Local Saints and Local Churches in the Early Medieval West*, ed. Alan Thacker and Richard Sharpe (Oxford, 2002), 361–95, esp. 361–5.

and Brittany persisted, of course, through the medieval into the modern periods and may be responsible for later installations and conflations of saints' cults.[3]

The investigation of the geographical patterns of dedications to saints has changed considerably since the inspiring but perhaps somewhat naive work of Doble and Bowen. Their approach to patterns of dedications to saints as showing for the most part the movements of the saint himself or herself has been abandoned for more critical approaches. First, the dedications themselves are now somewhat more critically established according to linguistic and historical criteria. Second, they are viewed as a geographically and chronologically sensitive map of a cult over time. Only within this critical context are dedications related, if possible, to the actions of the saint in question, or to those of his immediate followers.

Place-names are a valuable category of evidence – and for Cornwall and Brittany invaluable, given the relative paucity of other types of evidence – especially for the cults of saints; but their primary, early character can be overstated. The very density of ecclesiastical place-names in Celtic regions, and in particular in Cornwall and Brittany, arguably shows a real change in society and the landscape with the coming of Christianity, accomplished mainly through the actions of the numerous obscure but remembered eponyms of ecclesiastical place-names (whether founders, donors, or early inhabitants of church-sites).[4] But the individual place-names, and in particular the geographical patterns of dedications, should be subject to the same sort of caution as other types of evidence. While philology can provide a guide to the evolution of names and words, the accommodations and changes to which place-names are subject are not all purely linguistic: philological concerns should not blind us to the historical dimension. By the twelfth century or so, when our knowledge of the ecclesiastical landscape of Cornwall, and to a lesser degree, Brittany, increases notably, the creation and rationalisation of perceived patterns of saintly activity were probably well under way, in an exercise perhaps comparable to the work of the great synthesising historians of Ireland (and to a lesser extent Wales), which produced texts such as *Historia Brittonum* and *Lebor Gabála Érenn*. Dumville's description of this genre – which he calls 'synchronising history' – is worth quoting in full:

> the point about synchronising history is that it attempts, though rarely with complete success, to provide a smooth account of a period of history by combining all the available, and often wildly contradictory, witnesses into a slick, coherent, and "official" whole. The "harmonisation" … is the important process.[5]

The sort of intellectual milieu that produced this synchronising or synthesising history can also be seen in the work of genealogists. Much of this had to do with political relations or aspirations at the time of the composition or re-edition of the texts concerned. Such interrelations also expressed, one might argue, a wider concern to locate each local item within a larger framework. Nor was this process

3 K. Jankulak, *The Medieval Cult of St Petroc* (Woodbridge, 2000), 111–14.

4 O. J. Padel, 'Local Saints and Place-Names in Cornwall', in *Local Saints*, ed. Thacker and Sharpe (Oxford, 2002), 303–60, at 306.

5 David Dumville, 'The Historical Value of the *Historia Brittonum*', *Arthurian Literature* 6 (1986), 1–26, at 5.

confined to 'secular' history and literature: in Lives of saints and related texts, saints were associated with each other, through descent, through the place of their work, or through various earthly or heavenly covenants.[6] Hagiographical fashion, which affected the perception of individual local saints, also played its part – one thinks, for example, of the attribution of an Irish background to many Brittonic and English saints.[7] Cults of saints are potentially as subject to these external forces as other types of cultural artefacts. This is not purely, or even mainly, a manifestation of political forces, although recent scholarly attention tends to focus on those instances where cults of saints can be seen as part of a larger political machination. The devotional element is of significant, even primary, importance.[8]

The foregoing is relatively uncontroversial. What has perhaps not been explicitly appreciated, however, is the significance of church and place-name dedications, especially those commemorating otherwise entirely obscure saints, to the overall picture of a cult. Rather than taking such dedications as relatively stable anchors with which one might moor a more amorphous collection of evidence, one might do well to regard dedications as one more potentially shifting piece of evidence. In a world of obscure dedications, we welcome patterns as much as the synthesising historians of the middle ages. A reconsideration of the 'recurrent adjacency' phenomenon, therefore, is in order. This particular investigation should be located, as well, within the larger question of the adjacency of saints' cults (recurrent or otherwise), keeping in mind the striking examples of the lack of adjacency, where it might otherwise be expected, of some cults.

The legacy of Bowen and Doble

We should perhaps separate the putative adjacencies into three categories. First, we can perceive adjacencies of dedications to numerous saints, often spanning several of the Celtic regions (including Wales, Cornwall, Somerset and Brittany). These perceived groupings informed the geographically deterministic models advanced by Doble and Bowen, whose main purpose was to illuminate otherwise obscure periods of history. Secondly, we have a category that we might consider as recurrent adjacency *proper*, in which adjacent dedications can be discerned between not groups but pairs of saints, often for no obvious reason. Thirdly, we

6 Jankulak, *The Medieval Cult of St Petroc*, 114; J. F. Kenney, *The Sources for the Early History of Ireland: Ecclesiastical* (New York, 1929), 299; P. Grosjean, 'S. Fintan Máeldub', *Analecta Bollandiana* 69 (1951), 77–88, at 86–7; P. Ó Riain, 'The Composition of the Irish Section of the Calendar of Saints', *Dinnscheanchas* 6 (1974–7), 63–82, at 78; *idem*, 'Irish Saints' Genealogies', *Nomina* 7 (1983), 23–9, at 23; *idem*, *Corpus Genealogiarum Sanctorum Hiberniae* (Dublin, 1985), xiii, xv–xvi.

7 Gwenaël Le Duc, 'Irish Saints in Brittany: Myth or Reality?', in *Studies in Irish Hagiography: Saints and Scholars*, ed. John Carey *et al.* (Dublin, 2001), 93–119; Karen Jankulak, 'Fingar/Gwinear/Guigner: An "Irish" Saint in Medieval Cornwall and Brittany', in *Studies in Irish Hagiography*, ed. Carey *et al.*, 120–39; Robert Bartlett, 'Cults of Irish, Scottish and Welsh Saints in Twelfth-century England', in *Britain and Ireland 900–1300*, ed. Brendan Smith (Cambridge, 1999), 67–86, at 68–77.

8 Such as I have argued for St Petroc in Basse Bretagne (Jankulak, *The Medieval Cult of St Petroc*, 101–5).

have non-recurrent adjacencies, which reproduce relationships expressed in hagiographical traditions. The first category seems to be the result of modern, often overenthusiastic, positivism; the second, by its very obscurity, seems more possibly to represent much earlier connections; the third sits somewhere in between. All are susceptible to interpretation.

Surprisingly few students of the cults of Brittonic saints have commented explicitly on the significance either of clusters or pairs of saints appearing in more than one Celtic region. Whereas this deficiency may often be put down to enquiries which, in concentrating on just one region, leave this sort of question to one side, on the other hand, even Sabine Baring-Gould and John Fisher, in their wide-ranging *Lives of the British Saints*, seem not to have remarked on the phenomenon (although see below with respect to SS Nectan and Winnoc).[9] Rice Rees, however, in his book on Welsh saints, noticed that cults of SS David and Non seemed to come in pairs, viewing dedications to St Non as additional proof of 'the tradition of [David's] presence' in Devon and Cornwall, and so indirectly arguing for the perception of recurrent adjacency as a tool to illuminate the history of cult.[10]

Doble, as we have already seen, was an especially enthusiastic discerner of recurrent adjacency. His search for patterns in dedications that showed, he argued, the movements of groups of saints from Cornwall to Brittany, enthusiastically endorsed by Bowen, may be found in his accounts of the many Cornish saints who have Breton cults, and whose dedications are perceived as adjacent in both regions. The perception of Breton clusters led Doble to conclude, in one instance,

> that the parishes of the Newquay district [in Cornwall] form a group. They are called after a band of monks from Cardigan and Pembrokeshire (and perhaps from North Wales) who settled here and afterwards founded a fresh settlement in the N.W. of Brittany.[11]

While Bowen often came to similar conclusions using Doble's 'evidence', he was, especially in his book, *Saints, Seaways and Settlements* (although not consistently), more cautious:

> No claim is made for the argument that these saints and others associated with them were contemporaries, or that they necessarily moved in the same direction. All that is stressed is that most of the churches that carry the names of these wandering monks are located within easy access of the coast, and it is obvious that either these saints themselves, or some of their immediate followers (desirous of honouring their names) did use the sea routes, linking Ireland, Wales, Cornwall and Brittany to propagate their cults.[12]

9 *LBS*.

10 Rice Rees, *An Essay on the Welsh Saints* (London, 1836), 200.

11 G. H. Doble, *S. Carantoc, Abbot and Confessor*, 2nd edn (Long Compton, 1932), 27. For an account of Doble's many pamphlets, see R. M. Catling and J. P. Rogers, *G. H. Doble. A Memoir and a Bibliography*, 2nd edn (Exeter [1949]). While Doble's material has been reprinted in *The Saints of Cornwall,* 6 vols (Truro, 1967–97), the reprints omit valuable material, in particular Charles Henderson's notes, which contain information valuable not only in its own right, but also as having clearly informed Doble's own conclusions (see below, n. 104).

12 E. G. Bowen, *Saints, Seaways and Settlements in the Celtic Lands* (Cardiff, 1969), 72.

For all his enthusiasm for discerning patterns, however, Bowen did frequently introduce a note of entirely reasonable caution (even if it was in response to periodic criticism).[13] He thought it worth noting, in time, that

> geographical proximity of dedications is enough to suggest to the professional hagiographer, and possibly to local tradition, that there must have been some connection between these persons, although, of course, there is no evidence from the dedications themselves that these individuals were, in fact, contemporaries.[14]

But Bowen's caution did not extend to considering whether this process might have worked in the other direction, with legends and perceived associations affecting dedications. His belief in the primacy and transparency of the dedication and place-name evidence led him to the conclusion that,

> Whatever the facts may be, there does seem to be a close relationship between the topographical and the hagiological evidence in the *Lives* of the saints, and the inference is once more that the topographical evidence is the older.[15]

In Bowen's scheme, moreover, this 'older' topographical evidence appearing in Lives of saints was, by definition, 'certainly pre-medieval and probably survives in most instances directly from the Age of the Saints'; there was no room for medieval rearrangements between the earliest implantation of Christianity and the much later writing of Lives.[16] His reasoning was that the geographical associations between saints would have betrayed their origin as 'the arbitrary creation of the medieval mind', had they been the product, not the source, of connections in the Lives; but as 'the area over which a particular saint's cult spread is always … distinctive', a more meaningful and coherent impetus must have created it.[17]

Both Doble and Bowen were particularly interested in the idea that dedications to groups of saints might fill in some of the huge gaps in our knowledge of early British history. After a complicated discussion of SS Petroc, Cadoc, Maugan, Hernin, Congar, Nectan, John, Mabon, Tedda, Cleder and Ké, Doble concluded,

> The study of the cult of the eponym of Congresbury [i.e. Congar] promises therefore to provide a most valuable clue to the early history of Somerset, linking the information afforded us of its condition in prehistoric times by the excavation of its lake-villages with its first mention in documents as part of the West Saxon kingdom, and shows how important is the scientific pursuit of hagiography, combined with that of toponymy, in the work of re-constructing the lost history of the making of England.[18]

13 Wooding, 'The Figure of David', 10. For criticisms, see Owen Chadwick, 'The Evidence of Dedications in the Early History of the Welsh Church', in N. K. Chadwick *et al.*, *Studies in Early British History* (Cambridge, 1959), 173–88, at 175–6.

14 Bowen, *Saints, Seaways*, 96.

15 *ibid.*, 98.

16 Bowen, *The Settlements*, 9.

17 *ibid.*, 8–9; *idem*, 'The Travels of the Celtic Saints', *Antiquity* 18 (1944), 16–28, at 17–18.

18 G. H. Doble, 'Saint Congar', *Antiquity* 19 (1945), 32–43, 89–95, at 94. Doble (*St. Cadoc*

Bowen too believed that the movements of large groups of saints or their disciples were valuable historical data. Writing of a different group, he commented,

> It is obvious that by plotting the distribution of churches bearing the names of these saints [*peregrini*] we can get some idea of their respective 'spheres of influence' ... But ... it would be absurd to think that the present-day dedications to Celtic saints are all originally associated with the saint concerned ... However ... maps showing the distribution of ancient churches dedicated to the *peregrini* ... are likely to produce the best indication of how the seaways were, in fact, actually used in the Dark Ages.[19]

The main difference between Doble and Bowen is the latter's lack of interest in individual pairings. This lack of interest is understandable, given that Bowen was looking to examine large, connected movements of people in a very broad historical setting, rather than cults of individual saints.

An example of a perceived cluster of saints' dedications

One particularly striking example of the first category outlined above – clusters of saints in several regions showing movements of groups of saints or their disciples – is that grouped around St Carantoc, the patron saint and eponym of Crantock, Cornwall.[20] St Carantoc is widely considered as a pan-Celtic saint, with cults in Wales, Cornwall and Brittany, although the cult in each area is unusually obscure, despite a relatively ample supply of hagiographical material, and there is no way to establish that we are dealing with the same saint in each case.[21] Looking at other parishes near Crantock, Doble identified the eponym and patron saint of two of them, St Columb Major and St Columb Minor, as a Cornish monk rather than as St Columba of Sens, their 'traditional' patron saint, because of a perceived adjacency in Brittany of a cult site of St Carantoc to evidence of a saint whom Doble identified as a Cornish/Breton local saint, Columb.[22] This Columb, Doble argued, is

in Cornwall and Brittany [Truro, 1937], 3) also wrote that, 'In this way we might eventually be able to throw some light on the Christian origins of this part of the country', and, 'Our researches have thus led us to an important discovery, which promises to throw new light on the history of the Celtic peoples in the 5th and 6th centuries' (*ibid.*, 27). In his *S. Carantoc*, 27, Doble said, 'No doubt much remains to be explained, but I think our researches have given us a glimpse into a forgotten piece of the history of Mid-Cornwall, which may lead to further discoveries'.

19 See, for example, Bowen, *Saints, Seaways*, 69; see also *The Settlements of the Celtic Saints in Wales*, 2nd edn (Cardiff, 1956), 4.

20 Doble, *S. Carantoc*, 24–8; *idem*, *Saint Brioc, Bishop and Confessor* (Exeter, 1928), 50–2. Another large perceived cluster often cited by Doble surrounded SS Petroc and Cadoc in the Oust valley in eastern Brittany: *idem*, *St. Cadoc*, 26–7; *idem*, *Saint Petrock, Abbot and Confessor*, 3rd edn (Long Compton, 1938), 44; *idem*, 'Saint Congar', 93.

21 Karen Jankulak, 'Carantoc *alias* Cairnech?: British Saints, Irish Saints, and the Irish in Wales', in *Ireland and Wales in the Middle Ages*, ed. Karen Jankulak and Jonathan M. Wooding (Dublin, 2007), 116–48.

22 Doble, *S. Carantoc*, 24.

discernible in a place-name Plougoulm, with its church dedicated to a St Coulm, or Columba, partway between two sites named from a Breton version of Carantoc, St Carantec. Thus, a relatively obscure Cornish dedication (Padel argues that the eponym of St Columb Major and Minor was probably an obscure local saint) was given an identity by Doble with respect to perceived adjacencies in Brittany.[23] Our ability to endorse these patterns depends in part on the authority of Doble's identifications, and difficulties arise in the relative obscurity of SS Columb of Cornwall and Coulm of Brittany. St Columb of Cornwall was evidently thought of as female, although we have several sixteenth-century examples of local baptisms of boys under the name Columb; the church of St Coulm of Brittany is now dedicated to a male St Columban, either the St Columba of Iona or St Columbanus of Luxeuil and Bobbio.[24] Difficulties also arise in the identification of the Breton saints lying behind Carantec and Trégarantec, the two Breton sites that Doble argued were evidence of the cult of St Carantoc. The former takes its name from its church's patron saint, St Carantec (who also has a holy well nearby), usually identified with the Cornish St Carantoc but who seems to have a different feast day; the latter place-name is made up of a normally secular place-name element *tref*, and its church is dedicated to St Théarnec, whose cult is attested from the ninth century.[25] Trégarantec's relevance to the cult of St Carantec is debatable, and it is a comment on the strength of the geographical determinism of the period that Doble included Trégarantec in the equation based on

> the rule laid down by M. Largillière that the saints who evangelised Brittany first lived as hermits on the shore, where they landed, and where there is now usually a chapel bearing their name, and afterwards moved inland to minister to the colonists there, who had recently left the mother country to found a home in Armorica.[26]

Leaving Trégarantec aside, one could still argue for a recurrent adjacency between SS Carantoc/Carantec and Columb(a)/Coulm in Cornwall and Brittany (though not Wales for Columb), but the connections are tenuous.[27]

23 Padel, *A Popular Dictionary*, 71.

24 Nicholas Orme, *The Saints of Cornwall* (Oxford, 2000), 91–3; Bernard Tanguy, *Dictionnaire des noms de communes, trèves, et paroisses du Finistère: origine et signification* (Douarnenez, 1990), 163–4 (as St Columba); *idem*, *Dictionnaire des noms de communes, trèves, et paroisses des Côtes d'Armor: origine et signification* (Douarnenez, 1992), 32, 347 (as St Columbanus).

25 Tanguy, *Dictionnaire ... Finistère*, 222.

26 Doble, *S. Carantoc*, 26. In 1925, René Largillière had written, 'une règle existe pour les établissements du culte des saints anciens: plusieurs de ces saints ont une sanctuaire sur le rivage et un autre à l'intérieur, dans l'arrière pays ... L'établissement côtier peut être donné comme marquant l'emplacement où le saint a pris terre en venant de l'île de Bretagne; l'établissement dans l'arrière pays marquerait l'emplacement où le saint aurait résidé, après s'être enfoncé dans les terres.' (*Les saints et l'organisation chrétienne primitive dans l'armorique bretonne* [Rennes, 1925], 149). Bowen repeated the same 'rule' in *Saints, Seaways*, 164. See also Jonathan M. Wooding, 'Island and Coastal Churches in Medieval Wales and Ireland', in *Ireland and Wales*, ed. Jankulak and Wooding, 214–18.

27 Doble (*S. Carantoc*, 26) added that the Lives of St Carantoc contain stories of doves

Doble suggested other connections in this area, based on perceived recurrent adjacency. He saw in the entirely obscure St Enoder, eponym and patron saint of the church of St Enoder (Cornwall), a counterpart of an equally obscure Breton saint, St Tinidor (who is without an existing dedication but who was mentioned in a dubious Life known from a seventeenth-century compilation).[28] Moving north from St Columb Major, in Cornwall, Doble noted several parishes taking their names and church dedications from saints who also have Breton counterparts, 'all honoured on the north coast of Brittany': SS Ervan, Merryn, Breock and Eval.[29] St Ervan's name occurs in Breton place-names but there are no medieval records for these and in effect his cult is difficult to localise there.[30] The patron saint and eponym of St Merryn, a putative St *Merin*, again has a counterpart or counterparts in Brittany, including at least one on Brittany's north coast (Lanmérin in Côtes d'Armor), but none of these cult sites are near Carantec and Plougoulm.[31] St Breock has a Breton counterpart in the very well-known St Brieuc, the subject of a medieval Life (of Breton provenance and eleventh-century date) that locates him initially in Ceredigion, but then moves him to Brittany, not mentioning Cornwall.[32] None of his many churches are near Trégarantec. Finally, St Eval, originally St *Uvel*: Doble (following Joseph Loth's *Les noms des saints bretons*) gives a Breton saint of this name a dedication at Langolen in Finistère, and through this connects him to St Collen of Llangollen in north Wales, and finally to a Cornish St Colan whose parish is near Crantock, St Columb Major and Minor, and St Enoder.[33] The dedication to St Huel/Uvel at Langolen, however, is questionable and, what is more, Langolen, with the suggestive Collen/Colan connection, is not near Trégarantec. Ultimately, Doble cast his net too widely in geographical terms, and, more importantly, made identifications on the basis of perceived adjacencies in order to prove these adjacencies.

Doble's enthusiasm for recurrent adjacency reached its apogee in one final piece of this particular puzzle, concerning the patron saint of the Cornish church of Cubert, which is located near Crantock. As a logical outcome of his search for a Welsh counterpart to St Cubert (and no doubt as a by-product of Doble's insistence that the 'true patron' of Cubert was a local Cornish saint rather than the more probable English saint Cuthbert) Doble invented a Welsh saint, Gwbert, based on the existence of a place-name, Gwbert, located near Llangrannog, St Carantoc's apparent Welsh dedication.[34] Unfortunately there is not and never has been a

guiding the saint: 'May it not be that both stories owe their origin to some dim remembrance that a Columb was a close companion of Carantoc?'

28 Jankulak, 'Carantoc *alias* Cairnech?', 130.

29 Doble, *S. Carantoc*, 26.

30 Orme, *Saints*, 117–18; O. J. Padel, *A Popular Dictionary of Cornish Place-Names*, 82. I am unable to locate the source of Doble's contention that St Ervan was honoured at Tréguier.

31 Orme, *Saints*, 174–5; Padel, *A Popular Dictionary*, 120.

32 Orme, *Saints*, 75–6.

33 Cf. J. Loth, 'Les noms des saints bretons', *Revue celtique* 29 (1908), 222–48; 29 (1908), 271–311; 30 (1909), 121–55, 283–320, 395–403, at 30 (1909), 306 under *Uuel*.

34 Doble, *S. Carantoc*, 26–7. Doble (*Saint Winnoc, Abbot and Confessor* [Long Compton, 1940], 17–18) also seems to have made a saint out of the eponym of Boconnoc, which is

church at Gwbert, and there is no trace of a St Gwbert in any form, there or elsewhere.[35] Nevertheless, such is Doble's influence, and such is the power of geographical models in popular historiography, that St Gwbert has had an unquestioned existence for several decades.[36] As there is a dedication to St Petroc near Llangrannog and Gwbert, at Y Ferwig (in whose parish Gwbert lay, before a chapel at Mwnt was given parochial status), Doble was able to also connect the Carantoc complex with St Petroc, whose churches in Cornwall are also located on the north Cornish coast, near the others discussed by Doble.[37]

Doble's conclusion, that the story of St Carantoc and his band, from origins in Wales, a stop in Cornwall, and further travels to Brittany, could be traced from these apparent patterns of dedications, is less a work of critical deduction than an active creation of a pattern of adjacency, the sort of creation that arguably lies behind many if not all of our examples of multiple 'recurrent adjacency' from medieval to modern periods. It is salutary to keep in mind that our attempts to see patterns can actively contribute to further extensions, changes, diminutions and manipulations of cults of saints themselves.[38]

Examples of individual pairs of saints with recurrent adjacency

Bowen, as we have seen, showed almost no interest in our second category of recurrent adjacency, in which adjacent dedications can be perceived between individual pairs of saints, often for no obvious reason.[39] Their very obscurity made them less interesting to a historical geographer such as Bowen, who was interested in large overall patterns; this obscurity therefore seems to have protected them from being set into the patterns that Doble and Bowen described so persuasively. The same caution that we might apply to interpreting adjacency of better-documented saints needs to be applied to these far more obscure saints: all

far more understandable although probably misguided; see Padel, *A Popular Dictionary*, 55, 205.

35 P. Ó Riain, 'The Saints of Cardiganshire', in *Cardiganshire County History, Volume 1: from Earliest Times to the Coming of the Normans*, ed. J. L. Davies and D. P. Kirby (Cardiff, 1994), 378–96, at 390; Iwan Wmffre, *The Place-Names of Cardiganshire* (Oxford, 2004), 23–4. The place-name is better explained as a secular personal name, although its exact derivation is ambiguous.

36 Bowen, *The Settlements*, 87, 89–90; *idem*, *Saints, Seaways*, 70; Catherine Rachel John, *The Saints of Cornwall* (Redruth, 1981), 33; T. D. Breverton, *The Book of Welsh Saints* (Cowbridge, 2000), 280–1.

37 Doble, *S. Carantoc*, 27.

38 Compare the role played by seventeenth-century editors of Lives of saints in the establishment of St 'Fingar' as an Irish saint: Jankulak, 'Fingar', 137.

39 See, for example, his discussion of the cults of SS David and Non, in which he has grouped dedications to Non in with those to David as an undifferentiated group, one whose geographical dimension he is primarily interested in for its supposed halt at the Ystwyth–Wyre line: E. G. Bowen, 'The Celtic Saints in Cardiganshire', *Ceredigion* 1 (1950–1), 3–17, at 15–17. Iwan Wmffre ('Post-Roman Irish Settlement in Wales: New Insights from a Recent Study of Cardiganshire Place-names', in *Ireland and Wales*, ed. Jankulak and Wooding, 46–61, at 55) has recently cast doubt on the usefulness of this boundary.

dedications should not be viewed as self-evidently stable, unaffected by Lives and local legends, unchanging over a vast period of time. Those without obvious factors to trigger change, that is those without Lives or legends, should not be automatically assumed to have therefore not changed. Nevertheless, those adjacencies whose surviving history shows no factors that might tend to lead to reinterpretation are striking for this very reason.

Doble noted the phenomenon of recurrent adjacency (although not under that name) as early as 1925, and invoked it frequently thereafter.[40] On two occasions he listed pairs of saints showing this adjacency (leaving aside for now individual comments on adjacencies of pairs or groups). The first list occurs in a footnote to a discussion of the adjacencies of SS Gwinear and Meriadoc:

> There are numerous cases of dedications to Celtic saints being found in pairs. Thus dedications to S. David adjoin those to S. Nonna, while S. Winnow and S. Nectan, S. Mewan and S. Austol, S. Kea and S. Fili, S. Brioc and S. Marcan, seem to be always associated with each other.[41]

A slightly different list occurs in his pamphlet on SS Mewan and Austol:

> A remarkable fact, of which no explanation has yet been offered, is the existence in Cornwall and Brittany of traces of the close association of one saint with another, the cult of two saints being constantly found side by side in different places. Thus churches dedicated to S. Gwinear and S. Meriadoc are found in adjacent parishes in Cornwall and in the same parish in Brittany, and the same is true of S. Ké and S. Fili, S. Brioc and S. Marcan, S. Cadoc and S. Mawgan, S. David and S. Nonna. The joint cult of SS. Mewan and Austol is a particularly striking example of this phenomenon.[42]

Some of these pairs are well-known, and some are obscure, either in terms of one or both saints. In the case of the better-known saints, there is usually more information about dedications as well as hagiographic traditions. One assumes that there is therefore more scope for the perception of adjacencies either in the medieval or modern period, as a well-known saint will perhaps bring the expectation of companionship with other saints. The difficulty with the apparent adjacency between more obscure saints, of course, is a fundamental lack of information.

40 G. H. Doble, *Saint Winwaloe: Patron of Landewednack, Gunwallre, Tremaine and Portlemouth* (Shipston-on-Stour, 1925 [2nd edn, 1940]), 4: 'Now the names of the two Lizard parishes of Cury and Gunwalloe are of quite extraordinary interest to the historian. They … take their names from the two chief saints of Cornouaille, SS Corentin and Winwaloe, honoured respectively at Quimper and Landevennec.'

41 G. H. Doble, *Saint Meriadoc, Bishop and Confessor* (Truro, 1935), 43 n. 4.

42 G. H. Doble, *Saint Mewan and Saint Austol*, 2nd edn (Long Compton, 1939), 16 n. 29. This is a revised version of an earlier pamphlet published in 1927 (Catling and Rogers, *G. H. Doble*, 8); the earlier version does not contain this statement.

SS David and Non

SS David and Non are the best-known pairing of adjacent saints. St David, the patron saint of Wales, is relatively secure in his historicity, and has many dedications in south Wales, although he is notably absent from north Wales. In Cornwall he is the eponym of Davidstow, and is the dedicatee of its church. His cult in Brittany is more difficult to establish. St Non, David's reputed mother, is an entirely more complicated figure. Her historicity is relatively insecure: there are place-names and church dedications that do not self-evidently refer to the same figure, and they often have slight variations on the name itself. The striking examples of adjacency of the two cults therefore have the potential to be based on the widespread knowledge of St David's legend, and this possibly affects dedications to both David and Non.[43]

There are three significant examples of adjacency between the cults of SS David and Non: in Wales there is a chapel dedicated to St Non, along with a holy well, in the parish of St Davids (Pembrokeshire); in Cornwall the parish of Altarnun adjoins that of Davidstow; in Brittany the parish of Saint-Divy is near to, although not adjoining, that of Dirinon.[44] The earliest account of David's origins, Rhygyfarch's Life of St David, introduces us to his mother and father, whose generic names give one pause: Nonita ('little nun') and Sanctus ('saint'), Non and Sant in the Welsh version of the Life.[45] The Life includes an unusual, although not unprecedented, account of how David was conceived as the result of rape of Non by Sanctus.[46] Rhygyfarch does nothing to identify Non except to locate David's conception in Dyfed. It is clear that there is a strong tradition, of uncertain date, in favour of setting these events in Ceredigion, partly owing to a perceived dedication to Non at Llanon (Cardiganshire), and partly due to the identification of Henfynyw (also Cardiganshire) with the *Vetus Rubus* of Rhygyfarch's Life, the location of St David's youthful education; the two are probably connected.[47] The earliest textual tradition localising David's birth is found in the revision of Rhyygfarch's Life by

43 G. H. Doble, *Saint Nonna, Patron of Altarnon and Pelynt* (Liskeard, 1928), 3–4: 'I want you to notice that where you find a church of S. Nonna, you very often find S. Dewi, or David, honoured close by … It is clear that S. Non and S. David have always been associated with each other.'

44 See Heather James, 'The Geography of the Cult of St David: A Study of Dedication Patterns in the Medieval Diocese', in *St David of Wales*, ed. Evans and Wooding, 41–83, at 70, for Cil-Ddewi uchaf and Cil-Ddewi fawr.

45 Rhygyfarch, *Vita S. Dauid*, § 4: ed. and trans. Richard Sharpe and John Reuben Davies in *St David of Wales*, ed. Evans and Wooding, 107–54, at 112–13; *Hystoria o Uuched Dewi: The Welsh Life of St David*, ed. D. Simon Evans (Cardiff, 1988), 2.

46 Cf. Jane Cartwright, 'The Cult of St Non: Rape, Sanctity and Motherhood in Welsh and Breton Hagiography', in *St David of Wales*, ed. Evans and Wooding, 182–206, at 203–6, to which one might add the example of St Cadog, conceived after a somewhat bizarre violent abduction of his mother by his father: *Vitae Sanctorum Britanniae et Genealogiae*, ed. and trans. A. W. Wade-Evans (Cardiff, 1944), 24–8. See also a strikingly similar example in the tale, *The Voyage of Máel Dúin*, ed. H. P. A. Oskamp (Groningen, 1970), 100–1.

47 Rhygyfarch, *Vita S. Dauid*, § 7: ed. and trans. Sharpe and Davies, 116–17, and n. 35.

Gerald of Wales, who located several events before and after the birth near, although not explicitly at, St Non's chapel in Pembrokeshire.[48] The chapel itself is of late medieval date, but is probably located in an earlier site, arguably datable to the sixth to eighth centuries, based on the presence of a cross-inscribed stone and 'probable long-cist graves' (neither of which is conclusive evidence of this date, however).[49] The dedication of the chapel is not attested until 1335,[50] and one can only concur with Heather James's suggestion that 'the linkage [between St Non's chapel and David's birth] may have been firmly fixed when the chapel was built and dedicated'.[51] Were the names of David's parents not so 'transparently manufactured'[52] one might suspect Rhygyfarch of the entirely respectable practice of inserting into a hagiographical narrative local toponymic and topographical features, themselves at least possibly taking their identities from older tradition.[53] As it is, one strongly suspects that the dedication to St Non at St Non's chapel post-dated and followed from the nearby dedication to St David, almost certainly based on the desire to localise a story that originally had no specific location, with a *terminus ad quem* of 1335 for the whole process.

Pádraig Ó Riain has voiced entirely reasonable doubts about Non's existence as the eponym of Llanon in Ceredigion, citing the difficulty in distinguishing in the place-names *Llanon* a personal name Non from a place-name element *-onn*, 'ash trees' as well as the fact that Non's feast day (3 March) is very close to that of David (1 March).[54] Iwan Wmffre argues that there is no reason not to see Non as a personal name in these and other place-names, but the identity of Non herself (or less probably himself) remains obscure; he suggests that the cult of St David might have given rise to many of these apparent dedications.[55] It is equally possible, however, to see the process operating in the opposite direction, at least as regards Llanon in Ceredigion, and to suspect that Rhygyfarch, with his strongly felt family connections in Ceredigion,[56] did his best to give St David an indirect link with Ceredigion through his father Sanctus, through *Vetus Rubus*, and through Non, perhaps having Llanon in mind.

48 A. W. Wade-Evans, *Life of St David* (London, 1923), 71; *Giraldi Cambrensis Opera*, ed. J. S. Brewer *et al.*, 8 vols (London, 1861–91), III.379, 381, 383.

49 Heather James, 'The Geography of the Cult', 49; Nancy Edwards, 'Monuments in a Landscape: the Early Medieval Sculpture of St Davids', in *Image and Power in the Archaeology of Early Medieval Britain*, ed. Helena Hamerow and Arthur MacGregor (Oxford, 2001), 53–77, at 57–8.

50 B. G. Charles, *The Place-Names of Pembrokeshire* (Aberystwyth, 1992), 300.

51 Heather James, 'The Cult of St. David in the Middle Ages', in *In Search of Cult: Archaeological Investigations in Honour of Philip Rahtz*, ed. Martin Carver (Woodbridge, 1993), 105–12, at 108.

52 James, 'The Geography of the Cult', 76.

53 Cf. Hippolyte Delehaye, *The Legends of the Saints: An Introduction to Hagiography*, trans. V. M. Crawford (London, 1907), 224–5: 'All that scientific criticism [of hagiographical narratives] may assume from a narrative topographically correct, is that the author had familiarised himself with the places in which his personages reside.'

54 Ó Riain, 'The Saints of Cardiganshire', 390, 394.

55 Wmffre, *Place-Names of Cardiganshire*, 729–30.

56 Michael Lapidge, 'The Welsh-Latin Poetry of Sulien's Family', *Studia Celtica* 8/9 (1973/4), 68–106, at 71.

The only connection between David and Non in Brittany is found at Dirinon and the nearby Saint-Divy. The place-name Dirinon, first attested in 1173, is made up of the elements Breton *diri* ('oaks') and apparently a personal name Non, and the church has been dedicated to St Non at least since 1218 (as *Sancta Nonnita*).[57] This is the only dedication to a saint of this name in Brittany.[58] As in Pembrokeshire, the date of the dedication to St Non, as well as the date of the identification of this figure with St David's mother, is unclear, and it seems possible that the name Non resulted from a reinterpretation of a pre-Christian place-name. Bernard Tanguy has argued that it is Non, not David, who is the earlier dedication (or perceived dedication), citing the fact that although the Latin Life of St David was in part rendered quite closely into Breton in the fifteenth or sixteenth centuries as a play, it was presented as a Life of Non rather than of the otherwise better-known David and is associated with the church of St Non at Dirinon. Whether or not the perceived dedication to David's mother Non was due to knowledge of Rhygyfarch's text is arguable, although it is surely suggestive that the earliest record of the dedication of the church of Dirinon, in the records of the abbey of Daoulas, shows the form of the name to be *Nonnita*, the form that the name takes in Rhygyfarch's work, rather than the local form of Nonn or the Welsh form Nonn.[59] A further complication in terms of assessing recurrent adjacency is that the cult of St David in Brittany is difficult to establish, dedications to St David having replaced probably several Breton saints of similar names, in particular St Ivi, who seems to have been the original eponym at Saint-Divy.[60] By the seventeenth century St David of Wales was understood as the patron saint of the church (*eccl. Sancti Davidis* in 1637), and in 1676 a series of episodes from Rhygyfarch's Life of St David (not, it should be noted from *Buez Santez Nonn*) were painted on the ceiling of the church at Saint-Divy.[61] While Jane Cartwright has suggested that the content of the paintings might relate to the availability of two *epitomae* of Rhygyfarch's Life of St David from 1668, this explanation will not serve for the dedication itself, as the earliest attestation of it is several decades earlier.[62] Nevertheless, one suspects that the identification of the patron saint of the church of Saint-Divy with St David of Wales arose from knowledge in Brittany of Rhygyfarch's Life coupled with the proximity of Dirinon. It is interesting to speculate, with Tanguy, on how *Buez Santez Nonn* might have contributed to the spread of St David's cult (at the expense of that of St Ivi), but apparently it did not serve to spread the cult of St Non beyond Dirinon.[63] At any rate, the proximity of the cults of SS David and Non in Brittany is best explained as the result of perceived

57 Tanguy, *Dictionnaire ... Finistère*, 61.

58 Bernard Tanguy, 'The Cults of SS. Nonne and Divi in Brittany', in *St David of Wales*, ed. Evans and Wooding, 207–19, at 207; originally published as 'Les cultes de sainte Nonne et de saint Divi en Bretagne', in *Buez santez Nonn. Vie de sainte Nonne. Mystère Breton*, ed. Yves Le Berre *et al.* (Tré'flé'vé'nez, Brest, 1999), 10–31.

59 Tanguy, 'The Cults of SS. Nonne and Divi', 208.

60 *ibid.* 217; Tanguy, *Dictionnaire ... Finistère*, 196.

61 Yves-Pascal Castel, 'L'inconographie des sainte Nonne et de saint Divi', in *Buez santez Nonn*, ed. Le Berre *et al.*, 33–70 at 49–70.

62 Cartwright, 'The Cult of St Non', 198.

63 Tanguy, 'The Cults of SS. Nonne and Divi', 219.

connections leading to the replacement of at least one earlier dedication, with the process having been accomplished by 1637, before the publishing of the *epitomae*.

This leaves the adjacent cults in Cornwall to be examined. The name of Altarnun, in north-east Cornwall, is relatively well-attested from at least c.1100. It is the sole example of the Cornish place-name element *alter* 'altar', in this case followed by the name of a saint.[64] As Oliver Padel has explained, the name

> clearly implies a very special altar, no doubt incorporating a shrine for St Nonn's body, which must have been a prominent object of veneration in the church significantly before 1100 to have given rise to the name.[65]

As early as 1281 Altarnun was arguably considered to be dedicated to the mother of St David, as shown by the reference on that date to the possession by the parish church of a Life of Nonnita and David.[66] In 1478 William Worcestre affirmed the claims of Altarnun to possess the body of St Non, here as *Sancta Nonnita*, using the form in Rhygyfarch's Life of St David, and specifically identifying her with St David's mother, adding that David was born at Altarnun, a statement that has no parallel elsewhere.[67]

An apparent dedication at Pelynt, now dedicated to St Nonn, the mother of St David, has served to confuse matters: the forms of this place-name, from Domesday Book onwards, suggest the personal name Nynnid, a name borne by a male saint in Glamorgan.[68] Moreover, in 1442 the patron saint of Pelynt was described as *sanctus*, that is, as a male, and in 1478 William Worcestre, who garbled the name of the saint, clearly also described him as *sanctus*.[69] By the eighteenth century the patron saint of Pelynt was considered to be St David's mother.[70] There is no reason to view Pelynt's medieval dedication as relevant to that of Altarnun. Pelynt was useful to Doble as a Nonn dedication for an additional purpose: in his search for adjacencies, Doble noted that the parish of Duloe (whose patron saint is St Cuby) adjoins Pelynt, a fact made significant by the presence at another Cuby dedication, Tregony (nowhere near Duloe or Pelynt, and even farther from Altarnun), of a stone bearing the inscription NONNITA ERCILI[V]I

64 O. J. Padel, *Cornish Place-Name Elements* (Nottingham, 1985), 4; *idem*, *A Popular Dictionary*, 50.

65 Padel, 'Local Saints', 315–16.

66 Orme, *Saints*, 205 (referring to an Exeter Cathedral Inventory: Exeter, Cathedral Archives, D&C, MS 3672, fol. 7r).

67 William Worcestre, *Itineraries*, ed. and trans. John H. Harvey (Oxford, 1969), 62–3; cf. Padel, 'Local Saints', 354.

68 The place-name also contains the only British example of *plu* as a generic place-name element, which is extremely common in Brittany: Padel, *A Popular Dictionary*, 132; *idem*, *Cornish Place-Name Elements*, 187.

69 Padel, 'Local Saints', 358; William Worcestre, *Itineraries*, ed. and trans. Harvey, 106–7. A male St Nonna at Penmarch in Brittany may or may not have resulted from a confusion of the name of St Onna: Tanguy, 'The Cults of SS. Nonne and Divi', 212.

70 Nicholas Orme, *English Church Dedications with a Survey of Cornwall and Devon* (Exeter, 1996), 109–10. There seems to have been a chapel dedicated to a female saint of a similar name in the parish, according to the thirteenth-century Taxation of Pope Nicholas.

RICATI TRIS FILI ERCILINGI, '[the stone of] Nonnita, of Ercili[v]us [and] of Ricatus, three children of Ercilingus'.[71] This circuit of perceived adjacencies must lie behind Alan Thacker's otherwise obscure comment that,

> The cult of St Nonn at Alternunn in east Cornwall perhaps originates in the stone, inscribed with the name Nonnita and dating from the sixth to eighth century, at St Cuby's church, Tregony.[72]

It is probably safer to say that, in common with other Cornish parishes, the origins of the cult at Altarnun are obscure, although the undoubted antiquity and strength of the claim to have the relics of its patron saint (whoever this might be) are worth noting.

Davidstow, the only parish in Cornwall having David as a patron saint, partially adjoins Altarnun. The dedication is known from the first half of the thirteenth century (1224 × 1244) and the place-name from the second half (1269), with forms in Dewy, the Cornish form of the name, predominating.[73] The place-name shows a construction with Old English *stow*, common in Devon and Cornwall, in its general meaning of 'church' or 'monastic house', probably dating from after the ninth century.[74] There is no obvious sign that this dedication replaced that of another, perhaps more obscure Celtic saint, and it is perhaps worth noting the relative popularity of his cult in medieval Devon.[75] Thus the chronology of known dedications to SS David and Non in Cornwall shows a dedication to St Non being the first attested, then slightly over 100 years later a dedication to St David being attested, and a link between the two strongly argued by the record some 50 years later of the presence of a Life of both (related somehow to the predecessor – Latin? – of *Buez Santez Nonn*?) at Altarnun, all this having been accomplished by the late thirteenth century. There is no sense, as there seems to be at Dirinon, that any original dedications have been changed, although it does seem possible that, as at Dirinon, the presence of a written Life had cemented these perceived links – our earliest evidence of this at Dirinon dates, however, from the seventeenth century. The evidence of the Pembrokeshire adjacency dates from the fourteenth century, slightly later than the evidence for the Cornish adjacency; the Breton evidence stands out as distinctively later, perhaps as a result of the flurry of activity in hagiographical research in the seventeenth century.[76] Such a pattern of documentation is not unexpected, given the relative paucity of the Breton evidence.

71 G. H. Doble, *S. Cuby (Cybi), a Celtic Saint* (Long Compton, 1929), 31; Elizabeth Okasha, *Corpus of Early Christian Inscribed Stones of South-West Britain* (Leicester, 1993), 299–301.

72 Alan Thacker, '*Loca sanctorum*: The Significance of Place in the Study of the Saints', in *Local Saints*, ed. Thacker and Sharpe, 1–43, at 33.

73 Padel, *A Popular Dictionary*, 77; Orme, *Saints*, 102.

74 Margaret Gelling, 'Some Meanings of Stow', in *The Early Church in Western Britain and Ireland*, ed. Susan M. Pearce (Oxford, 1982), 187–96, at 191–2.

75 Orme, *Saints*, 103.

76 See Bernard Tanguy's discussion of a Life of St Non that the great seventeenth-century hagiographer Albert Le Grand may have consulted; David does not figure among Le Grand's Breton saints (Tanguy, 'The Cults of SS. Nonne and Divi', 211).

Other pairs of saints

The other pairs of adjacencies listed by Doble are far more obscure, but here we encounter the other side of this problem: where there isn't much information, in particular medieval hagiographical tradition, we have no context in which to assess the dedications. The case of Nectan and Winnoc, for example,[77] rests not on recurrent adjacency as such, but on the fact that the parish of St Winnow in Cornwall, dedicated to a saint of uncertain identity (Winnoc? Winnow? Winwaloe?), contained a chapel of St Nectan at least from 1281, with no corresponding link in any potentially relevant hagiographical legend to explain this.[78] Doble argued that this adjacency was mirrored in Brittany, where the parish of Plouhinec (which he argued was dedicated to St Winnoc) is located close but not adjacent to another, Plonéour-Lanvern, itself containing two place-names (*Lan-neizant*, *Ker-neizan*), which, according to Joseph Loth, include the name Neizan, a Breton version of Nectan.[79] Whatever the merits of Doble's etymologies of these place-names, they are not dedications to 'saint' Neizan/Nectan; moreover Tanguy has disputed the identification of the original dedicatee of Plouhinec.[80] As with the clusters discussed above, one suspects that Doble sought too enthusiastically for a pattern and used Loth's long list of names of Breton saints to find an equivalent to Nectan, although not one represented in dedications as such.[81] A further complication arises if one considers that the Welsh saint Gwynog, a name phonologically equivalent to Winnoc (although we must keep in mind the considerable obscurity of Winnoc's identity), is said in the genealogical tract *Bonedd y Saint* to have had a brother, *Noethon*, both being sons of St Gildas.[82] The name Noethon could well be the equivalent of Nectan, although it presents a problem in Brythonic philology that has yet to be worked out.[83] SS Gwynog and Noethon were the dedicatees of chapels in the parish of Llwngwm Dinmael, Denbighshire, and the two share a festival in several Welsh calendars. The remarks on this by Baring-Gould and Fischer are as close as these exhaustive scholars came to commenting, even indirectly, on recurrent adjacency.[84] Baring-Gould and Fischer

77 G. H. Doble, *S. Nectan, S. Keyne and the Children of Brychan in Cornwall* (Exeter, 1930), 18–20; *idem*, *Saint Winnoc, Abbot and Confessor* (Long Compton, 1940), 30.

78 Orme, *Saints*, 197; Padel, *A Popular Dictionary*, 180.

79 Loth, 'Les noms', at 150; Doble, *S. Nectan*, 18–20. See also Doble, *Saint Winnoc*, 30, n. 5: 'In Renfrewshire in Scotland, Mr. M. H. N. C. Atchley tells me, there is a *Lochwinnoc* not far from *Cambusneithan* [sic].'

80 Tanguy, *Dictionnaire ... Finistère*, 166–7.

81 Note that Tanguy does suggest that the eponym of Nizon, near Quimperlé, might be a place-name made up of the name of a saint alone (supported by a village name Cleu-Nizon, which includes the Breton *kleuz*, 'ditch', perhaps indicating an early church boundary), but that there is no hint of the 'saint' in the church dedication, which seems to have commemorated first a local Breton saint and then a French saint (*Dictionnaire ... Finistère*, 137–8).

82 *Bonedd y Saint*, no. 59: *Early Welsh Genealogical Tracts*, ed. P. C. Bartrum (Cardiff, 1966), 63.

83 Oliver Padel, pers. comm. Cf. *Canu Aneirin*, ed. Ifor Williams (Cardiff, 1961), xli–xlii.

84 'In Wales Gwynog is generally found coupled with his brother, Noethan or Nwython': *LBS*, III.246–7; IV.21.

did not connect St Nectan with St Noethon, giving each separate entries. While Doble commented on the name Nectan and Neithon or Nwython, he did not make any connection to a saint Noethon.[85] P. C. Bartrum commented on the possible connection between Noethon and the Cornish Nectan, as did Orme, although the latter noted that their feast day is not similar to that of Nectan in the south-west, commenting 'this suggests that, if the saints had a common origin, their cults diverged'.[86] Most surprisingly, however, no one, including Doble, has commented on the possible case of recurrent adjacency if we were to equate (in fact or perception) SS Nectan and Winnoc and Noethon and Gwynog. This seems to be owing to the fact that none of these scholars have considered a possible equation (again either in fact or perception) of Winnoc with Gwynog, despite this being an obvious conclusion in phonological terms, one reinforced by the recurrent adjacency (itself supported by calendar and genealogical evidence).[87] Why this should have been the case, when all other potential adjacencies have been noted by Doble, is entirely unclear.

In the case of Gwinear and Meriadec, the Breton parish of Pluvigner, from the mid-thirteenth century, had as its patron saint and eponym St Guigner, who bears the same name as, and is often identified with, St Gwinear; among the parish's numerous chapels is one dedicated to St Meriadoc (sixteenth-century?), who is arguably the same as the Cornish St Meriadec. In Cornwall, the parish of Camborne is dedicated to St Meriadec (attested since the fourteenth century) among others, and the adjacent parish of Gwinear is dedicated to St Gwinear (attested since the thirteenth century).[88] Doble's suggestion that the proximity of these Breton dedications and the adjacency of the Cornish parishes 'must surely be more than a coincidence' is entirely reasonable.[89] Doble's further inclusion of dedications to St Éguiner is probably misguided, for this saint is visibly separate from Gwinear/Guigner (although the identification of Gwinear with Guigner is also uncertain).[90] Leaving St Éguiner aside, however, one is struck by the recurrent adjacency, the more so as both saints have Lives (Gwinear being arguably the same as the Fingar of the Life of St Fingar), and neither Life mentions the other saint. There is one character common to both sets of Lives, King Theodoric or Teudar, but he is a relatively generic figure, appearing in several other Lives from Cornwall and, in the case of the Fingar material, what is probably Cornish tradition occurring in a Breton source.[91] Brian Murdoch did point out that King Macence, who appears in one of the Lives of St Fingar, has a similar name to King Massen, who appears not in St Meriadoc's Latin Life (which is set exclusively in Brittany)

85 Doble, *S. Nectan*, 23, n. 1.

86 P .C. Bartrum, *A Welsh Classical Dictionary* (Aberystwyth, 1993), 508; Orme, *Saints*, 198.

87 I owe this example to Oliver Padel, who should thus be credited with the discovery of a further example of recurrent adjacency.

88 Orme, *Saints*, 136, 188.

89 G. H. Doble, *Saint Meriadoc, Bishop and Confessor* (Truro, 1935), 36.

90 Doble, *Saint Meriadoc*, 43; Jankulak, 'Fingar', 130–1.

91 Jankulak, 'Fingar', 128–9; O. J. Padel, 'Oral and Literary Culture in Medieval Cornwall', in *Medieval Celtic Literature and Society*, ed. Helen Fulton (Dublin, 2005), 95–116, at 103–8.

but in the Cornish drama of St Meriadec's Life, *Beunans Meriasek*.[92] Murdoch's interest in these apparent links was strengthened by the fact that, as he said, 'Gwinear is sometimes seen as a companion of Meriasek', but in fact the only 'evidence' of this is Doble's comments on the proximity of their dedications and his interpretation of these as indicating that the two travelled together.[93] Again, we can see not only the lure of the idea of recurrent adjacency, but the influence of Doble, an overwhelmingly powerful figure in the study of Brittonic hagiography.

In the case of SS Cadoc and Mawgan, while the adjacency of the cults is sufficiently visible in Cornwall, the difficulty with establishing the recurrence of the adjacency lies to a large extent in the obscurity of St Cadoc's cult in Brittany.[94] St Cadoc appears to have been conflated with a Breton saint, St Cado, by Lifris of Llancarfan in his Life of St Cadoc, who included episodes relating to the island of Saint-Cado (Morbihan).[95] There is another site in Morbihan whose place-name, Pleucadeuc, in its early forms, shows its eponym to have been Cadoc, although this is not necessarily the same Cadoc as the subject of Lifris's Life.[96] As regards Saint-Maugan, while Doble argued that there was a seigneurie in Pleucadeuc called Saint-Maugan, Loth pointedly states that the name in question, which he gave as *Mogon,* 'doit être différent de *Maugan*'.[97] In the miscellaneous material probably added to Lifris of Llancarfan's Life of St Cadoc before its incorporation into the manuscript in which it is found (London, British Library, MS Cotton Vespasian A.xiv, c.1200) is an episode (§ 69) duplicating an existing episode (§ 23), but adding various details, including the participation of St David.[98] Among the additions are a holy man (*uir sanctus*) named *Moucan* and a messenger (apparently a different person?) named *Maucan*, but Doble's conclusion, 'I think we may accept it in this case as proof that Welsh tradition connected S. Maugan with S. Cadoc', puts too great a weight on very slender evidence.[99] In passing, the case of St Cadoc brings up the interesting fact that although SS Cadoc and Petroc have adjacent cults in Cornwall, and although both their Lives as well as genealogical texts connect them intimately, there is no recurrence of this adjacency in Wales

92 Brian Murdoch, *Cornish Literature* (Cambridge, 1993), 102; see also Jankulak, 'Fingar', 129–30.

93 Murdoch, *Cornish Literature*, 102; Doble, *Saint Meriadoc*, 43.

94 G. H. Doble, *Saint Mawgan, with some Notes on the Parish of Mawgan in Pydar and Lanherne* (Long Compton, 1936), 6: another version, also published in 1936, includes a note giving further information: 'In Scotland "S. Machan, who is commemorated as *Ecclesmachan*, in Linlithgowshire, is said to have been a disciple of S. Cadog" while "Cambuslang is dedicated to S. Cadoc of Llancarfvan" (Watson, *Celtic Place-Names of Scotland*, 1926, pp. 195, 151)': Doble, *Saint Mawgan, with the History of the Parishes of Mawgan in Kerrier and St Martin in Martin in Meneage* (Long Compton, 1936), 6; see also Doble, *Saint Cadoc*, 3.

95 Bernard Tanguy, 'De la Vie de saint Cadoc à celle de saint Gurtiern', *Études celtiques* 26 (1989), 159–85, at 165–7.

96 *ibid.*, 165.

97 Loth, 'Les noms', 148; Doble, *Saint Mawgan ... Pyder and Lanherne*, 6; cf. Orme, *Saints*, 183.

98 Hywel Emanuel, 'An Analysis of the Composition of the "Vita Cadoci" ', *National Library of Wales Journal* 7 (1951–2), 217–27, at 221–3.

99 *Vita S. Cadoci*, § 69: *Vitae Sanctorum*, ed. and trans. Wade-Evans, 136–40; Doble, *Saint Mawgan ... Pyder and Lanherne*, 9–10; *idem*, *Saint Cadoc*, 15.

where cult sites honouring a saint by the name of Petroc are nowhere near cult sites of Cadoc, and absent entirely in Glywysing, where their hagiographical traditions locate their ruling family.[100]

Moving down Doble's list of recurrent adjacencies, it is not immediately clear why he included SS Brioc and Marcan. The only comment Doble made on the subject implied that he saw an adjacency between the cults of SS Briac, Marcan and Columb, but not between Briac (or Brioc) and Marcan as such.[101] Indeed, there are no dedications in Cornwall to a St Marcan. Charles Henderson's additional notes to Doble's pamphlet on St Brioc provide us with our elusive, and mistaken, Cornish St Marcan. Mr Picken has shown that what is now Morgan Wood in St Breock parish, and what was known (including to Henderson) as 'Saynt Morgan' in the sixteenth century, originated as the place-name *Stymwoythegan* (att. 1296), that is, **stum*, 'bend of a stream, wood, etc', + personal name.[102] Thus we have a saint created from a place-name.[103] Henderson thought this to be St Marcan, which then led to Doble's inclusion of SS Brioc and Marcan in his list.[104]

Apart from the cases of SS Kea and Fili and SS Mewan and Austol (which are considered below), this completes Doble's list. Several other cases arise in his comments elsewhere on individual saints: Euny and Ia, Corentin and Winwaloe, Decuman and Petroc, Cadoc and Keyne. In the case of SS Euny and Ia, Doble discerned dedications to patron saints of the adjacent Lelant and St Ives replicated in the nearby (but by no means adjacent) parishes of Plouyé (Finistère) and Plévin (Côtes d'Armor).[105] Despite the attraction of the notion of recurrent adjacency, however, Tanguy has disputed the identification of the eponym of Plévin with Euny, arguing that here we have instead St Ethbin or Ediunet; there is no evidence that anyone apart from Doble thought differently.[106] In the case of SS Corentin and Winwaloe, while the churches of Cury (Corentin) and Gunwalloe (Winwaloe) are

100 Jankulak, *The Medieval Cult of St Petroc*, 10–13.

101 G. H. Doble, *Saint Brioc, Bishop and Confessor* (Exeter, 1928), as reproduced in his, *Saints of Cornwall*, IV.94. Elsewhere, St Branwaladr is brought into the group as well: G. H. Doble, 'Saint Branwaladr', *Laudate* 23 (1945), 22–33; reprinted as *Saint Branwaladr* (Guildford and Esher, nd [1946?]) and in his *Saints of Cornwall*, IV.116–27, at 117.

102 W. M. M. Picken, 'Stumwoedgan in Cornwall', *Devon and Cornwall Notes and Queries* 37 (1992–6), 172–4, at 174; Padel, *Cornish Place-Name Elements*, 213. I would like to thank Oliver Padel for this reference.

103 See Karen Jankulak, 'The Many-Layered Cult of St Caron of Tregaron', *Studia Celtica* 41 (2007), 101–4, at 103–4. To the list of saints invented from place-names I would now add St Coose, from Stencoose: Picken, 'Stumwoedgan', 174; Charles Henderson, *Essays in Cornish History* (Oxford, 1935), 146.

104 Charles Henderson, 'Notes on the Parish of St Breoke, Cornwall', in Doble, *St Brioc*, 62; Charles Henderson, *The Ecclesiastical Antiquities of the Four Western Hundreds of Cornwall* (Journal of the Royal Institution of Cornwall, Truro, 1955–60), pt. I, 45. I would like to thank Dr Padel for this and other references from Doble's pamphlets.

105 G. H. Doble, *Saint Euny, Abbot and Confessor, with S. Ya and S. Erc*, 2nd edn (Long Compton [?1932]), 12. This information has been added to the second edition, which is a greatly expanded version of the first edition of 1924.

106 Tanguy, *Dictionnaire ... Côtes d'Armor*, 198. This is evidently a reconsideration of his statement in *Dictionnaire ... Finistère*, 174, that St Euny was indeed the eponym of Plévin, and thus the two presented a telling proximity.

near each other, their churches in Brittany dedicated to saints of these names, Quimper (Corentin) and Landévennec (Winwaloe), are not.[107] In the case of SS Decuman and Petroc, while the proximity of dedications in Pembrokeshire is interesting, the lack of other information throws up a problem that can be addressed in two opposing fashions.[108] On the one hand, as there is no information about St Petroc's church (attested since the late thirteenth century), might the recurrent proximity to St Decuman's church (attested as early as the ninth century?) provide a context for this otherwise obscure dedication?[109] But in the absence of more information, do we accept the suggested recurrent adjacency of these saints who are otherwise separate in their legends and dedications? The same difficulties present themselves with respect to the suggestive adjacencies of SS Keyne and Cadoc in Wales and Cornwall.[110]

Doble's identification of a recurrent adjacency between the cults of SS Budoc and Mawes (Maudez) in Cornwall and Brittany is slightly better documented, but the documentary evidence provides individual pieces of the puzzle, not the connections between them (which are purely geographical).[111] The Life of St Guénolé, written c.880 by Wrdisten, abbot of Landévennec, has its subject educated by St Budoc at the latter's school on the island of *Laurea*, which from the seventeenth century onwards has been identified with the Île Lavret in the Brehat archipelago, although the identification is not without its problems.[112] This island shows traces of a Carolingian structure, probably an oratory or chapel, but its exact purpose, let alone its dedication, is unknown. Lavret's connection with Budoc rests solely on its identification as Budoc's school *Laurea*.[113] None of the other medieval texts that speak of Budoc mention an island.[114] Nevertheless, Doble noted that Lavret was in the same island archipelago as another much smaller island that takes its name from another saint, Maudez. St Maudez is extremely well-attested and the island is mentioned in the saint's eleventh- or twelfth-century Life as the site of a church built by Maudez and two disciples, including one bearing a form of the name Budoc, Bothmael.[115] This served, not surprisingly, to

107 Doble, *Saint Winwaloe*, 4; Padel, *A Popular Dictionary*, 77, 92.

108 G. H. Doble, *Saint Decuman, patron of Watchet (Somerset) and of Rhoscrowther (Pembroke)* (Williton and Minehead, 1932), 12. The dedication to St Petroc in Somerset is more easily explained as an outlier of a large cult in Devonshire.

109 Charles, *Place-Names*, 712, 732; Thomas Charles-Edwards, 'The Seven Bishop-Houses of Dyfed', *Bulletin of the Board of Celtic Studies* 24 (1971), 247–62, at 262.

110 Doble, *St Cadoc*, 13.

111 G. H. Doble, *Saint Budock*, 2nd edn (Long Compton, 1937), 16; see also Doble, *Saint Winwaloe*, 2nd edn, 38.

112 *Vita S. Winwaloei*, I.4–22: 'Vita S. Winwaloei', ed. C. De Smedt, *Analecta Bollandiana* 7 (1888), 167–264, at 178–210); Tanguy, *Dictionnaire ... Côtes d'Armor*, 31, who notes that 'la forme *Laurea* ne s'accorde pas cependant avec la forme Lavret'.

113 Pierre-Roland Giot, 'Bréhat, Lavret', in Nathalie Molines and Philippe Guigon, *Les églies des îles de Bretagne* (Rennes, 1997), 25–35, at 35. A later chapel (seventeenth century) was dedicated to SS Simon and Jude (*ibid.*, 28).

114 Budoc's various mentions in other medieval texts are conveniently collected by Doble, *Saint Budock*.

115 Molines and Guigon, *Les églises*, 35–6; cf. Tanguy, *Dictionnaire ... Côtes d'Armor*, 117.

strengthen the identification of *Laurea* with nearby Lavret. Thus in Brittany we have an apparent proximity; in Cornwall, across the estuary of the River Fal we find on one side the parish of Budock (the dedication to St Budoc is attested since the early thirteenth century) and on the other, in the parish of St Just-in-Roseland, a chapel of St Mawes (Maudez, attested since the late thirteenth century). This proximity, and that between the Île Maudez and Lavret (perhaps Budoc), reinforce each other. The matter is complicated by the fact that the Breton legends of St Maudez were well-known in Cornwall in the mid-sixteenth and seventeenth centuries, as the writings of John Leland and Nicholas Roscarrock show, each mentioning the saint's stone chair, which is also mentioned in the saint's earliest Life.[116] Each individual connection is tenuous, but put together they make a (too-) tidy whole, with proximity from the medieval period in Cornwall used in the modern period to identify a proximity in Brittany.

SS Kea and Fili

Finally, we come to SS Kea and Fili, which is probably the strongest case for a discernibly early recurrent adjacency, in which the strength of the expectation of recurrent adjacency may have eased the insertion of an entirely new saint into a site in Brittany from a relatively early date and with immediate and lasting effect. The church of St Kea in Cornwall is mentioned in Domesday, and had significant wealth and status.[117] In Brittany there are several parishes having a saint of this name (as St Quay) as patron saint and eponym, and the seventeenth-century hagiographer Albert Le Grand produced a French version of a Latin Life that he claimed was written by Maurice, a vicar of Cléder (Finistère), a church founded by the saint according to the Life. Gwenaël Le Duc was dismissive of Le Grand's account of St Kea, noting on the one hand that, 'the author of the Latin work on which [Le Grand] drew knew Cornwall well', but on the other that Le Grand is known to have taken a creative approach to his saints, in this case claiming dubious sources.[118] It seems arguable that Le Grand's involvement has further confused an already muddy situation, with doubtless conflations already in progress between saints of similar names and nicknames (Arthur's steward Kay creeps in, as well as the reputed SS Colodoc and Kerian).[119] Nevertheless, it is striking that St Kea's epithet, *Coledoc*, which appears in what is arguably a Latin Life lying behind Le Grand's version, also appears in three references to St Kea's church in Cornwall from the fourteenth to the sixteenth centuries.[120] St Kea's story must have been well known in medieval Cornwall and Brittany, and the discovery of portions of a

116 Orme, *Saints*, 81–2; Doble, *St Mawes*, 5.

117 W. M. M. Picken, 'The Manor of Tremaruustel and the Honour of St. Keus', *Journal of the Royal Institution of Cornwall*, new series 7 (1975/6), 220–30.

118 Le Duc, 'Irish Saints in Brittany', 101, 103: 'Le Grand's source is a breviary, but his text is longer than any breviary's version. He also quotes a manuscript, now lost, written by his great-uncle, which would be nice if he had such a great-uncle.'

119 Cf. Linda Gowans, 'St Ké: a Reluctant Arthurian?', *Folklore* 101 (1990), 185–97, at 186–7.

120 Orme, *Saints*, 156–7; *Bewnans Ke: The Life of St Kea*, ed. and trans. Graham Thomas and Nicholas Williams (Exeter, 2007), xxiii.

Cornish Life of the saint, *Bewnans Ke* (which owes a considerable debt to Geoffrey of Monmouth's *Historia Regum Britanniae*), offers further proof of this.[121]

St Fili, on the other hand, is far more obscure. He is understood as the patron saint of the parish of Philleigh, adjacent to that of Kea, and it is surely in this connection that he appears in a tenth-century list of Cornish saints as *Filii*.[122] The list itself is geographically ordered, to the extent that Olson and Padel wondered if it was produced in a context of 'a tenth-century scribe's musings on this phenomenon [of recurrent adjacency]', although they point out that, 'few if any of the adjacent dedications involved in the list reappear, also adjacent, in Wales or Brittany', and in the case of Fili it is notable that he is grouped with several saints of adjacent parishes (SS Just, Entenin, Gerent and Rumon) but *not* St Kea, who does not appear in the list. Nor is anyone of this or a similar name mentioned in the texts about St Kea.

Possible dedications in Devon present further complications. The parish of Landkey, whose name is attested from 1166, presents what Orme describes as 'a rare example of a Devon dedication that is pre-Saxon' to a saint of the same name as Kea. Doble commented on the proximity (although not adjacency) of the parishes of Landkey and Filleigh, the latter representing, he implied, a dedication to St Fili. However the most likely explanation of this place-name, which appears in Domesday Book as *Fileleia*, is 'clearing used for hay'; this coupled with the fact that the original patron of the parish is unknown (it has been dedicated to the Virgin Mary from the fifteenth century onwards), renders the possibility that we might have a dedication to St Fili remote.[123]

The situation in Brittany is tantalisingly suggestive: the church of Saint-Quay-Portrieux (Côtes d'Armor) has now as its patron and eponym St Ke, who is attested as the patron saint of the church from 1163, often with the epithet *Coledoc* (*eccl. S. Kecoledoci*, 1163; *eccl. S Coledoci*, 1181; *eccl. S. Kecoledoci*, 1197; *S. Ke*, 1237, 1240; *par. S. Gue*, 1270; *par. S. Kequoledoci*, 1278, etc.). However the two earliest references to the church name its patron saint as Scophili (*eccl. S. Scophili*, 1138; *eccl. S. Cophili desuper mare*, 1158).[124] François Duine was the first to suggest that the name might have consisted of *Sco* + *Fili*, that is St Fili, and cited St Fili's apparent cult elsewhere in Wales and Cornwall in support of his identification. He did not mention recurrent adjacency or St Kea.[125] This was left to Doble who, with

121 Padel, 'Oral and Literary Culture', 108–15; *Bewnans Ke*, ed. Thomas and Williams, xxi–xxxiv.

122 Olson and Padel, 'A Tenth-Century List', 45–6.

123 Orme, *English Church Dedications*, 177, 164; Orme, *Saints*, 123; J. E. B. Gover, A. Mawer and F. M. Stenton, *The Place-Names of Devon*, 2 vols (Cambridge, 1931–2), 42–3. A further dedication to St Rumon (who is represented by the church of Ruan Lanihorne, near but not adjacent to the parish of St Kea in Cornwall) at Romansleigh is also doubtful: Gover *et al.*, *The Place-Names of Devon*, 391; Orme, *English Church Dedications*, 195.

124 Tanguy, *Dictionnaire ... Côtes d'Armor*, 307.

125 See F. Duine, *Memento des sources hagiographiques de l'histoire de Bretagne. Première partie, les fondateurs et let primitifs* (Rennes, 1918), 161 n. 2. Cf. Olson and Padel, 'A Tenth-Century List', 46. Joseph Loth noted the appearance of the name *Fily* in Brittany but stated, 'Cependant rien n'indique qu'il y ait eu un saint Fily', before

reason, endorsed Duine's suggestion, and identified the posited St Fili lying behind Scofili with St Fili of Cornwall, with specific reference to the idea of recurrent adjacency with the cult of St Kea in Cornwall and Devon.[126] More recently, Bernard Tanguy adopted Doble's view of the importance of dedications in Cornwall and Devon in establishing St Fili's identity, but argued that rather than discovering in St Scofili an original dedication to St Fili that was replaced by one to his companion St Kea (as Doble did), we should view the identification of St Scofili with St Fili as a later reinterpretation, with the original St Scophili probably either a local saint or a doublet of an entirely separate saint, St Scubilion.[127] Tanguy does not specify how much later he believes this reinterpretation to have been made, but the implication seems to be that he has in mind Duine and Doble.

The complicating factor, one that it is difficult to explain, is that there was clearly a significant change in patron saint and eponym at Saint-Quay-Portrieux: from 1163 references to the church dedications and place-name concern exclusively St Kea (here St Ke/Colodec). The fact that St Kea's Life has nothing to do with Saint-Quay-Portrieux, but has him founding a monastery and being buried at Cléder (Finistère),[128] strongly suggests that something has intervened to insert St Kea firmly at a site with which he had no previous connection. On the one hand, it seems farfetched to believe that St Kea would have replaced St Scofili in Brittany in the twelfth century owing to knowledge in Brittany of adjacency in Cornwall (and perhaps Devon?), without this knowledge percolating into or being reflected by the saint's hagiographic traditions.[129] On the other hand, it is striking that the suggestively named St Scofili was replaced by St Kea so completely for no obvious reason.

SS Mewan and Austol

While Doble included SS Mewan and Austol in his list of saints whose cults showed recurrent adjacency, what we have here is arguably a separate category, that of saints showing a single adjacency with echoes of this in their hagiographical traditions. In this case, the adjacency is in Cornwall, and the hagiographical traditions arguably emanate from Brittany, so we do have significant attestations of cult in more than one Celtic region, although not adjacent dedications as such. Beginning in Cornwall, St Austol is the patron saint and eponym

going on to mention the existence of Philleigh in Cornwall: 'Les noms des saints Bretons'. No mention was made of St Ké in this connection.

126 G. H. Doble, *Four Saints of the Fal: St Gluvias, St Kea, St Fili, St Rumon* (Exeter, 1929), 26–7.

127 Tanguy, *Dictionnaire ... Côtes d'Armor*, 307: 'Inconnu par ailleurs, ce saint [Scophili] a été, du fait du voisinage des paroisses de Kea et de Phileig, en Cornwall, de Landkey et de Filleigh, en Devon, ayant respectivement pour éponymes saint Ke et saint Fili, identifié avec ce dernier, mais sans prendre en compte l'élément *Sco-*.'

128 Tanguy, *Dictionnaire ... Finistère*, 52. St Kea is not the eponym, and seems not to have been the original patron saint of this parish, who is attested at least until the fourteenth century as St Cleder.

129 Compare the situation of SS Gwinear and Meriadoc, above: neither saint's Life mentions the other, despite suggestive dedications in Cornwall and Brittany.

of the parish of St Austell, and St Mewan is the patron saint and eponym of the adjacent parish of St Mewan. Both saints appear in the above-mentioned tenth-century list, one after the other.[130] The dedication at St Austell, implied by the tenth-century list, is known from the mid-twelfth century onwards, and that at St Mewan, also implied by the tenth-century list, is attested from the late thirteenth century onwards.[131] In the early seventeenth century, Nicholas Roscarrock repeated a local story that, 'this St Austells and St Muen were great freindes, whose parishes ioyne and enioye some priuiledges togeather, and that they liued there togeather'.[132] It is a mark of the relative insignificance of St Mewan in Cornwall that Roscarrock only added this remark to his account of St Austol, as well as inserting a heading for 'St Muen', with a cross-reference to St Austol, at a later date, apparently knowing little of both saints but slightly more about St Austol. The parish of St Austell was, as Doble noted, 'one of the largest in Cornwall', and its church is suitably magnificent, especially its fifteenth-century additions.[133] It was a possession of Tywardreath Priory, and in the twelfth century that church was said to be dedicated to St Austol as well as St Andrew, perhaps indicating possession of relics.[134]

While in terms of size and importance of church St Austol outstrips St Mewan in Cornwall, in Brittany the situation is entirely the opposite: St Méen (as he is known in Brittany) is extremely well-known and attested, while St Austol is almost entirely unknown, except at Saint-Méen (Ille-et-Vilaine) where he was commemorated liturgically. An eleventh-century Latin Life of St Méen describes how the saint came to Brittany from his native Gwent, and founded his monastery at or near the present Saint-Méen.[135] It does not mention relics, but implies that that saint was buried where he was accustomed to spend his days.[136] The Life also, in its account of Meén's death, introduces a certain *presbyter* named *Austolus*, his godson (*filiolus*), who is comforted by Méen's prediction that Austol will join him in death within seven days. This indeed happens, and when Austol is taken for burial beside Méen, the monks find that

> the saint's body, which diffused a fragrant odour instead of the odour of corruption, had moved and was lying on the right of the grave facing the vacant space on the left, as if waiting for his disciple. They believed that this had happened by God's appointment, and they buried the blessed godson by his blessed godfather. And thus the dead

130 Olson and Padel, 'A Tenth-Century List', 59–60.

131 Orme, *Saints*, 67, 191.

132 *Nicholas Roscarrock's Lives of the Saints: Devon and Cornwall*, ed. Nicholas Orme (Exeter, 1992), 56.

133 G. H. Doble, *Saint Mewan and Saint Austol*, 2nd edn (Long Compton, 1939), 36, 39.

134 Orme, *Saints*, 67.

135 Composed according to François Duine by Ingomar, a monk of Saint-Méen: Duine, *Memento*, 98. See for a recent discussion of its date and authorship, Bernard Merdrignac, 'Introduction', in Christophe Poulin, Bernard Merderignac and Herve Le Bihan, *La vie de saint Méen; Buhez Mewen* ([Lesneven] 1999), 9–26 at 11–13.

136 *Vita S. Mevenni*, §§ 19, 20: 'Vita S. Mevenni: abbatis et confessoris in Britannia armoricana', ed. F. B. Plaine, *Analecta Bollandiana* 3 (1884), 141–58, at 155–6.

> bones of the two saints declared the love which had ever united them ...[137]

By the seventeenth century the abbey of Saint-Méen claimed to have relics of SS Méen and Austol, as well as those of Judicaël and Petroc.[138] The claim to possess relics of St Petroc is due to the presence of these at Saint-Méen in 1177; presumably the claim to have relics of Austol and Judicaël resulted from the links made by the Life of St Méen between its subject and these saints.[139] St Judicaël, a Breton ruler and saint in his own right, is mentioned in the Life of St Méen as a benefactor and finally as a monk in St Méen's monastery.[140] St Judicaël's cult, such as it is, seems to have been concentrated in the area around Saint-Méen, apart from some wanderings of his relics, alongside those of St Méen, with whom he appears in liturgical documents.[141] There is no sign of a cult of Judicaël in Cornwall, except that he is listed (as *Iodechall*) along with Mewan and Austol in the tenth-century list: this can be explained either as a reflex of an originally lost double dedication to Mewan and Judicaël in Cornwall, or as an inclusion on the basis of association rather than dedication as such.[142]

St Austol plays a notably minor role in the Life of St Méen: he is not mentioned at all in it until the account of St Méen' death, at which point he is accorded great importance. His cult in Brittany is limited to liturgical commemoration at Saint-Méen.[143] He is indeed, as Olson and Padel conclude, 'thus distinctively Cornish as the patron saint of a church'.[144]

There is no documented reason for SS Mewan and Austol to be adjacent in Cornwall, apart from their connection in Brittany, and this connection in Brittany does not seem to owe anything to Cornish traditions, unless one views Nicholas Roscarrock's statement in the seventeenth century, that the two were friends, as an echo of long-held local tradition rather than a percolation to Cornwall from Brittany of our medieval material.[145] Were it not for these strong associations in the hagiographical material, we would have good reason to wonder if Mewan and Austol were actually the same as their Breton counterparts: the feast day of St

137 *Vita S. Mevenni*, § 20: ed. Plaine, 156. Doble, *Saint Mewan*, 11.

138 Jankulak, *The Medieval Cult of St Petroc*, 155.

139 *ibid.*, passim.

140 *Vita S. Mevenni*, § 11: ed. Plaine, 149. Judicaël's hagiographic dossier is extremely complicated; for our purposes it is worth noting that St Méen is also mentioned in it. See *Vita S. Iudicaeli*: 'Excerpta ex uita inedita S. Judicaeli S. Mevenni discipuli', ed. F. B. Plaine, *Analecta Bollandiana* 3 (1884), 157–8; André-Yves Bourgès, 'Le dossier littéraire des saints Judicaël, Méen, et Léri', in *Corona monastica. Moines bretons de Landévennec: histoire et mémoire celtiques. Mélanges offerts au père Marc Simon*, ed. Louis Lemoine and Bernard Merdrignac (Rennes, 2004), 91–101, at 91–5.

141 Jankulak, *The Medieval Cult of St Petroc*, 153–60; L'abbé Le Claire, 'Saint Judicaël au pays de Gaël', *Association bretonne. Comptes-rendus, procès verbaux, mémoires* 3rd series 36 (1925), 1–19; Olson and Padel, 'A Tenth-Century List', 60.

142 Olson and Padel, 'A Tenth-Century List', 60.

143 Doble, *Saint Mewan*, 16, 22.

144 Olson and Padel, 'A Tenth-Century List', 59.

145 There is no sign of the 'shared privileges' that Roscarrock mentions, although had Charles Henderson been alive to contribute an account of the histories of these parishes to Doble's pamphlet, we would probably have more information.

Mewan/Méen is consistent inasmuch as St Méen's feast day was 21 June, and this date was also observed at Exeter from the twelfth to the fourteenth centuries, but the feast day of the parish church of St Mewan in Cornwall was apparently quite different from at least the seventeenth century; St Austol is less well-attested, and his Breton feast day (enshrined in the Life of St Méen, in which he dies seven days after his master) is not replicated in Cornwall.[146] While evidence of multiple feast days does not disprove identifications, strong evidence of consistent feast days would have done much to support it.

In this category of single adjacency (or at times perceived single adjacency) supported by apparent connections in hagiographical material we should also locate Doble's references to SS Carantoc and Tyssilio,[147] and to SS Melor and Samson.[148] The former case is merely a passing comment. In the latter case, in comparing two competing sites for St Samson's main Cornish monastery, either Golant or Southill, Doble opted for what is arguably the weaker case, Southill, on the basis that a parish adjacent to it, Linkinhorne, is dedicated to St Melor.[149] St Melor's complicated cult, spanning Cornwall and Brittany and probably conflating several saints, shows no connection to St Samson. Inasmuch as one can separate saints with essentially the same name, the connections to St Samson seem to belong to St Magloire, supposed hermit of the island of Serk, claimed as Samson's cousin.[150] For Doble, however, the overall decision in favour of Southill seems to have been finally decided by the proximity of Linkinhorne (and thus St Melor) to Southill on the one hand, and François Duine's somewhat inexplicable attribution of a relic label naming *Sanctus Meloirus, consobrinus Sancti Samsonis* to Meloir (as he spelled it) rather than Magloire as it probably properly should be.[151]

Conclusion

If we look at recurrent adjacency in reverse, and ask whether there are cases where we would expect to see it but do not, the answer is yes. There are many cases where we might imagine there would be saints' dedications in proximity but where there

146 Orme, *Saints*, 67, 192.

147 'S. Tyssilio is described as the brother of S. Carantoc. See Stanton's Menology [Richard Stanton, *A Menology of England and Wales* (London, 1887)], pp. 531, 532. It is interesting to find the two parishes dedicated to the two brothers side by side' (Doble, *S. Carantoc*, 12n).

148 'It is to be noted that the church of Linkinhorne is only a very short distance from that of Southill, where the patron is S. Samson. Now the S. Melor, Abbot, was "consobrinus Sancti Samsonis" ': G. H. Doble, *Saint Melor* (Long Compton, 1927), 26n; see also 50.

149 G. H. Doble, *Saint Samson in Cornwall* (London, 1935), 18–19.

150 André-Yves Bourgès, *Le dossier hagiographique de saint Melar* (Landévennec, [1997]), 132; Lynette Olson, *Early Monasteries in Cornwall* (Woodbridge, 1989), 14. I would like to thank John Hereward for bringing this example to my attention.

151 Duine, *Memento*, 100. Perhaps also worth a mention is the recurrent proximity of the communes of Elliant and Tourc'h in Finistère, taking their names from probably a saint in the former and the word for boar in the latter, whose proximity is apparently replicated in Denbighshire, which contains Llanelian and the River Twrch: Tanguy, ... *Finistère*, 66, 218. I would like to thank Oliver Padel for this reference.

are not. We have already noticed the adjacency between dedications to St Petroc and St Cadoc in Cornwall, at Padstow. In Wales, on the other hand, where the one saint is intimately connected with the other (as uncle and nephew) in the literary traditions of both, we do not find any adjacency of dedications. Whereas the cults of St Petroc in Cornwall and Brittany show many similarities, one arguably being the outgrowth of the other, the cult of St Petroc in Wales, on the other hand, seems to be drawing on one or more specifically Welsh literary traditions, related to Arthurian material, which may have nothing to do with Cornwall.[152] The explanation for a lack of adjacent dedications of St Petroc and St Cadoc in Wales may therefore be that we are dealing with different saints with the same name. This explanation could no doubt be extended to other instances.

Links between saints, then, were a fertile theme in the medieval Celtic regions, and the desire to create such links has long been recognised as an important driving force behind the production of various types of hagiographical, pseudo-historical texts – genealogies of the saints in particular. John Carey has described genealogy as 'the most important component of Irish legendary history … the anchoring of kindreds in a coherent framework of relationships which stretched back to their forefathers' first arrival in the island'.[153] The literary outgrowths of this genealogical schema sought 'partly to provide it with greater authority, partly to gratify less pragmatic instincts of curiosity and creativity'.[154] The cults of saints have been subject to similar pressures: both the forceful pull of a 'framework of relationships' and the 'instincts of curiosity and creativity'.

The geographical proximity of dedications, we may now see, has served these same ends, so that the phenomenon of recurrent adjacency seems as potentially malleable as any other manifestation of historical or pseudo-historical activity. Our inevitable reliance, moreover, on written evidence to trace the manifestation of recurrent adjacency means that we see its greatest activity corresponding with periods of greater literary activity; so in many cases we may simply be mapping the trail of the sources rather than the phenomenon itself. Where the 'sources', that is documentary evidence, is lacking, do we attribute the establishment of the cults to an early date in order to explain their obscurity? And so the consideration of the work of Doble and Bowen that has been undertaken in this chapter leaves us with a deep uncertainty – a seemingly unanswerable question. Are there any cases of recurrent adjacency that are not, in fact, the result of later reinterpretation, either medieval or modern? Is it possible to discover cases of recurrent adjacency that can be attributed to events in the early medieval period, at the implantation of Christianity – in particular, when Breton society was being shaped?[155] In the end,

152 Jankulak, *The Medieval Cult of St Petroc*, 13–14. The question of whether or not one had in Wales a local Petroc or the universal saint, Peter (see Ó Riain, 'The Saints of Cardiganshire', 394–5), is unanswerable, but for our purposes is irrelevant.

153 John Carey, '*Lebor Gabála* and the Legendary History of Ireland', in *Medieval Celtic Literature*, ed. Fulton, 32–48, at 32–3.

154 *ibid.*, 33.

155 See, for example, Gwenaël Le Duc, 'The Colonisation of Brittany from Britain. New Approaches and Questions', in *Celtic Connections: Proceedings of the 10th International Congress of Celtic Studies. Volume One: Language, Literature, History, Culture*, ed. Ronald Black *et al.* (East Linton, 1999), 133–51.

perhaps we can at least say this much: although specific comment on the recurrent adjacency of saints' dedications was notably limited before G. H. Doble set to work, as an idea it had a considerable impact on both medieval and modern expectations of the Celtic saints.[156]

[156] Versions of this chapter were presented at the International Medieval Congress, Leeds, in July 1999, and the annual *Tionól*, School of Celtic Studies, Dublin Institute for Advanced Studies, in November 2006. I would like to thank the participants in these sessions for helpful suggestions. In addition, I would like to thank Dr Oliver Padel for reading successive drafts and making valuable suggestions, although he should not be held responsible for its arguments.

6

CUTHBERT THE CROSS-BORDER SAINT IN THE TWELFTH CENTURY

Sally Crumplin

In the mid-twelfth century, a Durham monk named Alan was sent by Bishop Hugh du Puiset on a tour of southern Scotland. He travelled throughout East Lothian, across the Forth to St Andrews and Dunfermline, and ventured as far as Perth, carrying with him a small bag of St Cuthbert's relics, which were used in ceremonial processions and to perform a number of miracles during his perambulations.[1] St Cuthbert is often seen as an Anglo-Saxon saint, and certainly his life and cult were integral to the great Anglo-Saxon golden age of the seventh century,[2] but he sits far more comfortably in a northern insular world, where saints' cults transcended the political border between England and Scotland. This is particularly true of the twelfth century, a time when Anglo-Scottish conflicts resulted in the drawing of political borders but when, paradoxically, Anglo-Scottish saintly connections were particularly prominent.[3] St Cuthbert's cult was indeed flourishing in the twelfth century, predominantly across northern England and southern Scotland, with veneration also extending to southern England and Scandinavia. Cuthbert is thus a very fitting inclusion in a volume on insular saints and his cult

1 Reginald of Durham, *Libellus de admirandis beati Cuthberti virtutibus*, ch. 97: *Reginaldi monachi dunelmensis Libellus de admirandis beati Cuthberti virtutibus quae novellis patratae sunt temporibus*, ed. James Raine, Surtees Society 1 (London, 1835), 215–17.

2 There were two early *vitae* of St Cuthbert, dating from the late seventh and early eighth centuries: *Two Lives of St Cuthbert*, ed. and trans. Bertram Colgrave (Cambridge, 1940). For discussion of Cuthbert's cult in the Anglo-Saxon period, see also *St Cuthbert, his Cult and his Community to A.D. 1200*, ed. Gerald Bonner, David Rollason and Clare Stancliffe (Woodbridge, 1989).

3 On these connections see, for example, cross-border dedications in James Murray Mackinlay, *Ancient Church Dedications in Scotland: Non-Scriptural Dedications* (Edinburgh, 1914) and Robert Bartlett, 'Cults of Irish, Scottish and Welsh Saints in Twelfth-century England', in *Britain and Ireland 900–1300*, ed. Brendan Smith (Cambridge, 1999), 67–86. See also Alan Macquarrie, *The Saints of Scotland. Essays in Scottish Church History AD 450–1093* (Edinburgh, 1997).

suggests the further ties that sainthood represented, between the insular world and the continent.

Much scholarship has been produced on this political border between England and Scotland, and on the importance of Cuthbert's church in Durham to it, on the role of the powerful Durham bishops and their community in this frontier zone. I do not wish to discuss this in detail here, but should briefly summarise.[4] First, it is important to note the great influence and political autonomy of the Durham church, its monastic community and in particular its bishops. G. Scammell's evocative image, in his biography of the long-serving bishop of Durham, Hugh du Puiset (1154–95), encapsulates this most effectively, referring to the long fingers of Angevin power that never pressed too heavily on the Durham episcopate.[5] Thus, while many have emphasised the Norman infiltration of the Durham church, through implantation of bishops and monks from the later eleventh century, it seems that these newcomers operated largely independently of the English power centre in the distant southern reaches of Britain.[6]

It is with this independence borne in mind that one should consider the embroilment of the Durham church in the pervasive cross-border machinations of the twelfth century. William Aird ended his book on the great power of the Cuthbertine church in the Norman period by demonstrating that Durham was able to seek alliances in Scotland just as much as in England, the decision depending on the potential benefits that such allegiance might offer to Durham.[7] It is therefore unsurprising that there was an inherent ambiguity in political relations between Durham and Scotland in the period. Geoffrey Barrow provides a comprehensive description of these relations, beginning with the attacks by Malcolm III (in 1061, 1070 and 1091) followed by the king's veneration of St Cuthbert, possibly due to the ecclesiastical interests of his wife Margaret and her confessor Turgot who was prior of Durham. Indeed, Malcolm III laid the foundation stone of Durham Cathedral in 1093, and the bishop of Durham at that time, William de St Calais,

4 See William E. Kappelle, *The Norman Conquest of the North: The Region and its Transformation 1000–1135* (London, 1979); Richard Lomas, *North-East England in the Middle Ages* (Edinburgh, 1992); G. W. S. Barrow, 'The Scots and the North of England', in *The Anarchy of King Stephen's Reign*, ed. Edmund King (Oxford, 1994), 231–53; W. M. Aird, 'Northern England or Southern Scotland? The Anglo-Scottish Border in the Eleventh and Twelfth Centuries and the Problem of Perspective', in *Government, Religion and Society in Northern England, 1000–1700*, ed. John C. Appleby and Paul Dalton (Stroud, 1997), 27–39. On Durham specifically, see for example G. W. S. Barrow, 'The Kings of Scotland and Durham' and Paul Dalton, 'Scottish Influence on Durham, 1066–1214', both in *Anglo-Norman Durham*, ed. David Rollason, Margaret Harvey and Michael Prestwich (Woodbridge, 1994), 311–23 and 339–52, and William M. Aird, *St Cuthbert and the Normans* (Woodbridge, 1998).

5 G. V. Scammell, *Hugh du Puiset, Bishop of Durham* (Cambridge, 1956), 184.

6 David Rollason, *Northumbria 500–1100: Creation and Destruction of a Kingdom* (Cambridge, 2003); Donald Matthew, 'Durham and the Anglo-Norman World', in *Anglo-Norman Durham*, ed. Rollason, Harvey and Prestwich, 1–22. Cf. Aird, *Cuthbert and the Normans*, esp. 268–75.

7 Aird, *Cuthbert and the Normans*, chapter on 'St Cuthbert and the Scots', 227–67. See also William M. Aird, 'St Cuthbert, the Scots and the Normans', *Anglo-Norman Studies* 16 (1993), 1–20.

fostered close relations with Malcolm's successors, Duncan II (1094) and Edgar (1093/7–1107).[8] Just one result of this was that when Edgar refounded Coldingham Priory in 1098 he named as its patrons Cuthbert along with Aebbe and the Virgin Mary; he colonised this priory on Scottish territory with Durham monks and granted the church to the Durham canons.[9] Such actions seem to indicate that this was the height of political accord between the Cuthbertine church and the Scottish dynasty.[10]

Differing attitudes and actions of bishops, the monastic community and kings of Scots could greatly affect the relations between the Scottish royal dynasty and Durham. To provide just a few examples: after the relatively harmonious episcopate of William de St Calais, his more aggressive successor, Ranulf Flambard (1099–1128), caused relations to deteriorate, exemplified and exacerbated by his defensive border activity, such as the construction of a castle at Norham. King Edgar responded by retracting much of his earlier, vast grant of Coldinghamshire and Berwickshire. Meanwhile though, the monks of Durham under Prior Turgot, operating largely separately from Bishop Flambard, maintained far more cordial and supportive relations with the Scottish kings. Notably, the future king Alexander I was the only layman present at the great opening of Cuthbert's coffin in 1104 – a formative moment that underpinned the holy power of the Church by demonstrating Cuthbert's saintly incorrupt state, not least by the flexibility of his ears.[11] Most importantly, the kings of Scots from Malcolm III to William the Lion featured prominently in the Durham *Liber Vitae*.[12] However, Scottish dynastic relations with Durham continued to be marked by fluctuation. David I's reign shows probably the greatest level of Scottish royal involvement in Durham affairs: David attempted to place his chancellor, William Cumin, as bishop of Durham, and he installed his son Henry as earl of Northumberland; there was also increased aggression, with David's violent attacks on Northumbria in 1136 and 1138.[13] Relations finally seem to have reached their lowest point during the lengthy episcopate of Hugh du Puiset spanning the reigns of Malcolm IV and William the Lion.[14] Perhaps most telling are the events of 1189, when Richard I of England gave the earldom of Northumbria to Bishop Hugh, taking the title from Scottish hands despite William the Lion's vain efforts to reverse the action.[15]

The key features, then, of the Durham church's association with the Scottish

8 Barrow, 'Kings of Scotland'; Valerie Wall, 'Malcolm III and the Foundation of Durham Cathedral', in *Anglo-Norman Durham*, ed. Rollason, Harvey and Prestwich, 325–37.

9 James Murray Mackinlay, *Ancient Church Dedications in Scotland: Scriptural Dedications* (Edinburgh, 1910), 156.

10 Cf. Donald Matthew's depiction of Durham in crisis, with a waning cult of Cuthbert and at the mercy of the Scottish and English politics: Matthew, 'Durham', 12–21.

11 *Capitula de miraculis et translationibus sancti Cuthberti*, § 18: *Symeonis opera*, I.247–61.

12 By contrast, there is little or no representation of later kings. Geoffrey Barrow, 'Scots in the Durham *Liber Vitae*', in *The Durham* Liber Vitae *and its Context*, ed. David Rollason, A. J. Piper, Margaret Harvey and Lynda Rollason (Woodbridge, 2004), 109–16.

13 Aird, *Cuthbert and the Normans*, 257–60.

14 Barrow, 'Kings of Scotland', 319–21.

15 Scammell, *Hugh du Puiset*, 48–50.

dynasty were of constant – but constantly shifting – relations through the late eleventh and twelfth centuries, ranging from mutual support and veneration to aggression and retaliation. Durham was part of England, but this was by no means an intractable certainty for the kings of Scotland; indeed, the Durham church was largely independent of any central royal authority. Most significantly, Cuthbert was never threatened in these machinations. Although contemporary narrative sources of the Scottish attacks on Cuthbertine land by Malcolm III and David I attribute the Scots' failure to take Durham to Cuthbert's miraculous protection, it nevertheless seems that the Scottish forces may have chosen not to attack Durham itself because of their deep-seated reverence for Cuthbert.[16]

This underlying veneration for Cuthbert, transcending society on the Anglo-Scottish border, is the subject of this chapter: it is a subject rather less tangible than the well-documented political events of the time, but it was nonetheless a phenomenon deeply rooted throughout the area from the Tees to the Tay, despite the cross-border machinations of the time in which the Durham church was undoubtedly involved. Cuthbert's cult transcended the fickle oscillations of political allegiance, illustrating the great influence of saints' cults, and demonstrating the common cultural ground that existed between those who dwelt in this area between England and Scotland. It should be noted that, from its inception in the 690s, Cuthbert's cult was present in what is now Scotland. The earliest *vitae* of Cuthbert, from the late seventh and early eighth centuries, refer to the *in vita* activities of the saint in Pictish lands, with mention of a missionary journey to the land of the Niduari, as well as deep associations with Carlisle, which was at various times claimed by Scottish as well as Anglo-Saxon kings.[17] The *Historia de sancto Cuthberto*, dating from the tenth to eleventh centuries, records Cuthbert's church possessing land as far north as the Firth of Forth from its foundation in the seventh century; and Simeon's twelfth-century tract on the church of Durham shows Cuthbert's community fleeing from Viking threats in the ninth century as far as Whithorn in Galloway, suggesting that they were protected there.[18] The *Historia* does, however, also record a miracle in which the Scots are punished for disrespecting Cuthbertine lands, reflecting that relations between political entities in the north of Britain had long been inconsistent.[19] Here though, the focus will be on later twelfth-century sources for two reasons: first, because this is where we find a rich vein of evidence for the *veneration* of Cuthbert in Scotland; and secondly, because this was a period during which many ecclesiastical connections were being formed that spanned the Anglo-Scottish border.

Our most detailed written source is Reginald of Durham's *Libellus de admirandis beati Cuthberti virtutibus*, a lengthy miracle collection produced between the 1160s and 1170s, through which we may chart the diaspora of

16 Dalton, 'Scottish Influence', 339.

17 Bede, *Vita sancti Cuthberti*, §§ 11 and 28: *Two Lives*, ed. Colgrave, 192–5 and 248–51.

18 *Historia de sancto Cuthberto*, § 4: *Historia de Sancto Cuthberto: a History of Saint Cuthbert and a Record of his Patrimony*, ed. and trans. Ted Johnson South (Cambridge, 2002), 46; Simeon of Durham, *Libellus de Exordio atque Procursu istius, hoc est Dunhelmensis Ecclesie*, ii.12: ed. and trans. David Rollason (Oxford, 2000), 116–20.

19 *Historia de sancto Cuthberto*, § 33: ed. South, 68–70.

Cuthbert's cult in the twelfth century. It incorporates a rare profusion of social detail, including the provenance of Cuthbert's pilgrims, locations of miracles and Cuthbertine churches, and associations with other saints from the region. Reginald's *Libellus* forms the focus of this study, augmented by a diverse range of other evidence – liturgical calendars, church dedications, architectural evidence and other hagiography – to show the veneration of Cuthbert at all levels of society in this region of northern Britain.

Reginald's miracle collection yields a wealth of information about the diaspora of Cuthbert's cult. Location was essential to the organisation of his *Libellus*: the miracles are recorded in groups, usually of three or four chapters, almost always from a single location or region.[20] This is revealing of the process by which the miracle collection was first recorded, and indeed further light is shed on this process by the autograph manuscript of the *Libellus*.[21] The manuscript is the work of a single scribe but the *ductus* varies between groups of miracles. It seems that a number of miracles were reported at Durham by a reliable source from the place in which they occurred, and that they were recorded at that time.[22] They were thus written down group by group, over the course of the decade or so that the *Libellus* spans. Most of these groups of miracles are from the Durham locale, with a further concentration from Lindisfarne and Farne Island. But there are many groups that pertain to the broader Anglo-Scottish region stretching from the Tees in the south to the Tay in the north. If the miracles were indeed collected locally for later conveyance to the cult centre in Durham, this would suggest that Cuthbert's cult was being actively venerated and recorded across southern Scotland as well as northern England.

Here I will focus on three groups of miracles that exemplify key aspects of Cuthbert's cult in this Anglo-Scottish context, and raise questions concerning the nature of cross-border cult veneration. The first group (chs 136–40), based in and around Slitrig, Teviotdale, and reported by a local man named Dolfin, is typical of the type of local veneration afforded to St Cuthbert.[23] The group contains a standard range of miracles: Cuthbert shelters devotees from a storm on his feast day in his church in Slitrig (one of many dedicated to Cuthbert, according to Reginald), he miraculously produces a candle on another of his feast days, cures Dolfin's mother of an intestinal ailment, saves sheep from wolves, cures a crippled woman, and saves a man from William the Lion's ravages by rendering him invisible through the use of moss. These miracles reflect Cuthbertine patronage in the lowest strata of society, through parish church dedications and observation of his feasts in this area. While this should perhaps be expected in lands that had been held by Cuthbert's church from its earliest times, it also exemplifies the enduring veneration for Cuthbert in a region beset by Anglo-Scottish political struggles.

The second group of miracles from the *Libellus* is more pertinent to these political issues. It centres on the perambulations of Alan, the monk sent to southern Scotland by Bishop Hugh du Puiset. The group comprises five chapters (97–101)

20 See map, Sally Crumplin, 'The Cult of St Cuthbert', in *Atlas of Medieval Europe*, ed. David Ditchburn, Simon MacLean and Angus MacKay (London, 2007), 74–6.

21 Durham, Cathedral Library, MS Hunter 101.

22 Reginald, *Libellus*, chs 68–72: ed. Raine, 138–48.

23 Reginald, *Libellus*, ed. Raine, 284–90.

in which Cuthbert performs miraculous cures via a small piece of the cloth used for wrapping his incorrupt body, which was carried by Alan.[24] Cuthbert cures a merchant in Perth of headaches and a local demoniac in Dunfermline, notably on the feast of St Margaret. He then twice heals Countess Ada, mother of William the Lion and Malcolm IV, who, Reginald tells us, had given generous landed gifts to St Cuthbert, including Haddington in Lothian, where she is cured. Finally, he heals a poor boy with an intestinal tumour, also at Haddington. In the *Libellus*, Cuthbert's miracles are dominated by minor nobles, poor people and the odd monk, and such diverse patronage is reflected in this group, but it also has a marked emphasis on Scottish royal veneration.

The second miracle of this group (ch. 98) presents further avenues for enquiry: Cuthbert's relics are carried in a procession at Dunfermline for St Margaret's feast, and on that day a number of gifts are given to St Cuthbert. Such emphasis of Cuthbert's cult on the feast day of Dunfermline's patron is not surprising in a Durham source, and may suggest that there was competition between the cults of Cuthbert and Margaret. Indeed, one could postulate that Alan's tour was conceived to assert Cuthbert's power in areas where the relatively new cult of Margaret was flourishing. Nonetheless, there was undoubtedly respect between these cults, demonstrated by the gifts exchanged between Dunfermline and the Durham monk Alan. Perhaps the perceived ambiguity of Scottish royal relations with Cuthbert's cult can be broken down into a Scottish distrust of Durham combined with a constant reverence for the saint.

This balance of established, but perhaps uneasy, relations may also be behind the single cursory mention of St Andrews in the *Libellus*, also in chapter 98. The reference is fleeting, precluding any association, at least in the *Libellus*, between Durham and this powerful Scottish ecclesiastical centre. This may be explained in the light of the banishment of Durham's influential prior, Turgot, to St Andrews in the early twelfth century, as a response to his increasing power, which threatened Durham's bishops. Perhaps St Andrews was thenceforth seen by Durham as an institution that could undermine its unity. There may certainly have been tensions between the two churches, as Durham ceded control of Lothian to St Andrews in the twelfth century, at the latest by 1150.[25] Whatever the reason, Reginald avoided expressing – and conspicuously in this example – any ties that may have existed between these two powerful churches.

The final group of miracles transports us to the west coast of Britain: chapters 55 and 56 pertain to Furness.[26] During the reign of Henry II, land has been wrongfully taken from the abbot and brothers of the abbey there, and their case is refused at the king's court and in Rome. When Abbot John suggests invoking Cuthbert, an altar is built to him in the abbey, and miraculously the next hearing at the king's court finds in favour of the Furness monks. There follows a related miracle in which a thief tries to steal the horse that the abbot was preparing for a journey to give thanks to Cuthbert at Durham, but the horse cannot be moved. This Cuthbertine patronage in Furness provides evidence of devotion in the west which is all the more significant when seen as part of a string of Cuthbertine dedications

24 *ibid.*, 215–25.

25 Matthew, 'Durham', 4–12.

26 Reginald, *Libellus*, ed. Raine, 112–15.

mentioned by Reginald. His *Libellus* refers to churches dedicated to Cuthbert in Plumbland, Cumbria (ch. 129), Lixtune in Cheshire (chs 68–72), Lytham (now St Anne's) in Lancashire (chs 132–5) and Kirkcudbright on the Galloway peninsula, whose town was also named after Cuthbert (chs 84 and 85).[27] This coastal concentration of Cuthbertine dedications adds to the early associations of his church with western Britain, in particular Carlisle and Whithorn.

The prominence of St Cuthbert dedications on the British western seaboard also hints tantalisingly at the further extent of his cult. Although there is no conclusive evidence of Cuthbertine veneration in Ireland, the Furness dedication is nevertheless especially interesting in the context of the Cistercian network that extended over this same region of northern England and southern Scotland, and into Ireland and the Continent. The Cistercian abbey at Furness was home to Jocelin, author of several saints' lives: of St Kentigern, patron saint of Glasgow; of St Waltheof, abbot of Melrose, stepson of David I of Scotland; and St Patrick and St Helen.[28] Jocelin, a monk in a northern English abbey, was evidently well-acquainted with saints' cults from across Scotland and Ireland, and indeed culled his Life of Kentigern from Scottish and Irish sources.[29] He was also active in bringing the Cistercian order to Ireland, where he helped to found the abbey at Down.[30] Jocelin provides just one example of the Cistercian cross-border connections between England and Scotland;[31] Aelred of Rievaulx was another key player, and it is he who forms the most obvious link between the Cistercians and the cult of St Cuthbert. This abbot of a Yorkshire abbey was educated with the same Waltheof of Melrose and he wrote extensively about Waltheof's stepfather, David I. Aelred was also a dedicated patron of Cuthbert's cult: he recounted a Cuthbert miracle in his *Genealogia regum Anglorum*;[32] moreover, it was he who suggested that Reginald write the *Libellus*, and reported a group of six miracles (§§ 83–8), including those from Kirkcudbright.[33] Aelred was, crucially, descended from the esteemed Alfred Westou, the early eleventh-century sacrist at Durham who tenderly ministered to the incorrupt body of Cuthbert, brushing his fire-retardant hair and banishing weasels from his tomb.[34] Durham may not have been Cistercian, but it certainly played an important role in the ecclesiastical–political cross-border network that was built around that order. This was, of course, a network that extended beyond the Anglo-Scottish and Irish context, and

27 *ibid.*, 275–8; 138–41; 280–4; 177–9.

28 For the *vitae* written by Jocelin, see Richard Sharpe, *A Handlist of the Latin Writers of Great Britain and Ireland before 1540* (Turnhout, Belgium, 1997; rev. impr. 2001), no. 555.

29 Cf. Davies, 'Bishop Kentigern', above.

30 Madeleine Hope Dodds, 'The Little Book of the Birth of St Cuthbert', *Archaeologia Aeliana*, 4th series 6 (1929), 52–94, at 61–2; see also Macquarrie, *Saints of Scotland*, 117–44.

31 On this, see Bartlett, 'Cults', 67–86; Anne Lawrence-Mathers, *Manuscripts in Northumbria in the Eleventh and Twelfth Centuries* (Woodbridge, 2003), 236–51.

32 Aelred of Rievaulx, *Genealogia regum Anglorum*, ed. R. Twysden in *PL*, CXCV.719–20. I am grateful to Joanna Huntington for bringing this to my attention.

33 Reginald, *Libellus*, ed. Raine, 175–88.

34 Simeon, *Libellus de Exordio*, iii.7: ed. Rollason, 160–6; Reginald, *Libellus*, chs 16 and 26: ed. Raine, 28–32 and 57–60.

Cuthbert's cult should be seen in this light. The connections within the British Isles were the basis for much wider cult dissemination, and this can be seen in particular through the number of Cuthbertine manuscripts produced by, or for, Cistercian houses on the Continent in the twelfth century. In particular, Dijon, Bibliothèque Publique MS 574 and Laon, Bibliothèque Publique MS 163 contain extensive selections of Cuthbertine hagiography and were produced for the Cistercian houses of Citeaux and Vauclair respectively. Reginald's *Libellus* does not appear in these manuscripts – its immense detail implies that it was intended for a more local audience – but through its allusions to various Cistercian influences, it does imply Durham's involvement in this ecclesiastical network.

Reginald's *Libellus* provides abundant evidence for the dissemination of Cuthbert's cult across northern Britain, for the veneration of this saint from east to west across this Anglo-Scottish area, through church dedications, observation of feast days and active collection of miracles. The text also raises issues that may be extrapolated beyond the cult of Cuthbert: that the veneration of this saint transcended political borders, in spite of the inherent border instability of the twelfth century; and that this veneration was not confined to a northern British context, but extended overseas as part of a complex and sophisticated network of ecclesiastical institutions.

These conclusions extrapolated from Reginald's text are well supported by evidence from outwith Durham: the *Libellus de nativitate sancti Cuthberti*, and liturgical calendars, church dedications, and architecture. The *Libellus de nativitate*,[35] written in the 1190s, uniquely describes the purported Irish origins of Cuthbert, depicting his birth in Ireland, his baptism and childhood there, his voyage to Britain where he landed in Galloway, travelled to Dunkeld, and then settled in Lothian. We are also told that Cuthbert travelled further north, becoming a hermit in Dull and then Weem (Perthshire). This text, often referred to as the 'Irish Life' of Cuthbert, could be seen to open our twelfth-century view of Cuthbert westwards, and this is tempting in the light of the Anglo-Scottish and Irish ecclesiastical network outlined above. However, as Thomas Clancy has shown, this is not an Irish text, but rather a composite of several Scottish sources, almost entirely unrelated to St Cuthbert: the author states his use of Scottish sources himself, and is elsewhere careful to distinguish between the Irish and Scots, precluding any confusion between the two.[36] This text is, then, a fabrication of Cuthbert's origins, but this is rather less important here than the fact that it seems to have been written in Scotland; exactly where is unclear, though tentative suggestions of Melrose or another southern abbey would be especially plausible

[35] Reginald, *Libellus*, ed. Raine, 63–87; trans. in part in Dodds, 'Little Book'.

[36] Reginald, *Libellus*, ch. 29. Thomas Owen Clancy, 'Magpie Hagiography in Twelfth-Century Scotland: The Case of *Libellus de nativitate sancti Cuthberti*', in *Celtic Hagiography and Saints' Cults*, ed. Jane Cartwright (Cardiff, 2003), 216–31. The attribution of the text to Reginald of Durham, discussed most recently by Richard Sharpe, 'Were the Irish annals known to a twelfth-century Northumbrian writer?', *Peritia* 2 (1983), 137–9, is countered by Clancy, who argues most compellingly that the Reginald attribution is stylistically improbable: 'Magpie Hagiography', 227–8. Interestingly, the *Libellus de nativitate* was compiled in a very similar fashion to that of Jocelin's Life of Kentigern, although without the smooth transitions of Jocelin's text: Dodds, 'Little Book', 58.

within the framework of Cistercian connections.[37] The *Libellus de nativitate* provides rather nebulous evidence, with which one may speculate only over the details behind its production; the significant point to note is that Cuthbert's written cult did not emanate exclusively from Durham in the twelfth century, but was simultaneously stimulating hagiographic production in Scotland.

The inclusion of Cuthbert in liturgical calendars and church dedications is far more difficult to date precisely, but they do provide more widespread and indeed solid evidence for the active veneration of Cuthbert in medieval Scotland. He is listed in all but two of eleven cases in the great edition of *Kalendars of Scottish Saints*, and most of these record both his main feast on 20 March and his translation feast of 4 September.[38] As a note of comparison, I should mention another vibrant cult from later twelfth-century England, that of Thomas Becket, who appears in seven of the eleven calendars. His cult seems not quite as widespread in calendars as that of our northern saint, Cuthbert, but popular nonetheless, although this was possibly a patronage that developed after the twelfth century.[39] The frequency of Cuthbert's appearance in calendars is therefore not especially striking *per se*. However, it is notable that in these liturgical documents, which rarely provide extra detail on their saintly subjects, *Menologium Scoticum* is careful to mention Cuthbert's Scottish background: it states that he was a monk of Melrose, again underlining the importance of this border abbey in the cult of our saint.[40] Together, these calendars show the importance of Cuthbert in the liturgical tradition throughout Scotland, north of the region covered in Reginald's *Libellus* as far as Aberdeen.

Church dedications show Cuthbert's cult extending even further beyond the region covered in Reginald's *Libellus*, and they reflect a more committed veneration of this saint. As Reginald suggests, there were numerous Cuthbertine dedications throughout northern England and southern Scotland, including the string along the west coast and the apparent plethora in Lothian.[41] Mackinlay's list of church dedications in Scotland does suggest a number of Cuthbert dedications, many of which may date from the twelfth century or earlier.[42] He adds to Reginald's locations in Lothian, and suggests that Cuthbertine veneration went further north to Strathtay and even Wick.

Local church dedication provided the means for all levels of society, in many different locations, to connect with a particular saint. We finish by returning to Durham, the most prominent Cuthbertine dedication, to exemplify the dominant and tangible impact of our saint on the highest levels of society. The architectural influence of Durham demonstrates the power of Cuthbert's cult, and by extension of the Durham church itself. This grand and innovative cathedral, built between

37 Dodds, 'Little Book', 63; Clancy, 'Magpie Hagiography', 228–9.

38 Alexander Penrose Forbes, *Kalendars of Scottish Saints* (Edinburgh, 1872).

39 This would be supported by the lack of Scottish Becket miracles in his earliest miracle collections: Ronald C. Finucane, *Miracles and Pilgrims: Popular Beliefs in Medieval England* (London, 1977), 165. Michael Penman discusses the later development of Becket's cult in Scotland in 'The Bruce Dynasty, Becket and Scottish Pilgrimage to Canterbury, *c.*1178–*c.*1404', *Journal of Medieval History* 32 (2006), 346–70.

40 Forbes, *Kalendars*, 210.

41 Reginald, *Libellus*, ch. 136: ed. Raine, 284–5.

42 Mackinlay, *Ancient Dedications. Non-Scriptural*, 243–58.

1093 and 1133, would inevitably be a model for other churches seeking to associate with Durham and to echo its power. There are several prominent examples of its architectural influence: Durham's daughter house on Lindisfarne, Waltham in southern England, Selby in Yorkshire, Dunfermline abbey in Fife, and St Magnus's cathedral in Kirkwall. The latter two examples are particularly instructive. At Dunfermline, where St Margaret was buried, building began in 1128 with the support of King David I. The close similarities between the surviving nave there and the layout and detail of Durham imply that, very soon after Durham was built, the Scottish royal dynasty was seeking to align the final resting place of St Margaret with that of St Cuthbert.[43] This should be considered alongside the veneration of Cuthbert by Margaret and her husband Malcolm during their lifetimes, most evident in the covenant included in the Durham *Liber Vitae*, which, having been confirmed, ensured the continuation of Scottish royal patronage of Cuthbert's cult.[44]

St Magnus's cathedral was, like Dunfermline, built very soon after Durham, from 1137 under Ronald, Norse earl of Orkney; its design seems to denote that builders were using both Durham and Dunfermline as models.[45] This Orkney cathedral reflects Durham's significance in the North Sea world, which can be readily supported by a Trondheim liturgical document, and by a miracle from Reginald's *Libellus* in which a Norwegian boy seeks aid from saints throughout the North Sea world, and is eventually cured by Cuthbert at Durham.[46]

I end on the architectural echoes of Durham for two reasons. First, it again broadens the wide area over which Cuthbert's cult spread in the twelfth century: St Magnus's cathedral, bolstered by the *Libellus*'s Norwegian miracle, shows the influence of Durham in a North Sea world, adding to the Irish and Continental connections identified earlier. Secondly, having tried to distinguish here between the political conflict of the Anglo-Scottish border and the cross-border popularity of Cuthbert's cult, the influence of Durham and Cuthbert through grand architectural echoes poses the question of where the line should be drawn. How far could a saint's cult unite this region? At what levels of society?

This returns us to the ambiguity of cross-border relations in the twelfth century.

43 E. C. Fernie, 'The Architectural Influence of Durham Cathedral', in *Anglo-Norman Durham*, ed. Rollason, Harvey and Prestwich, 269–79, at 271–2.

44 *Liber Vitae Ecclesiae Dunelmensis*, ed. A. Hamilton Thompson, Surtees Society 126 (London, 1923) (Collotype facsimile), fol. 48v; trans. Barrow, 'Scotland and Durham', 314.

45 Fernie, 'Architectural Influence', 272–3.

46 On the Trondheim liturgical reference, see C. Hohler, 'The Durham Services in Honour of St Cuthbert', in *The Relics of St Cuthbert*, ed. C. F. Battiscombe (Oxford, 1956), 155–91, at 161–2, and Matthew, 'Durham', 10. On the *Libellus*'s Norwegian miracle (ch. 112: ed. Raine, 248–54), see Haki Antonsson, Sally Crumplin and Aidan Conti, 'A Norwegian in Durham: An Anatomy of a Miracle in Reginald of Durham's *Libellus de admirandis beati Cuthberti*', in *West Over Sea: Studies in Scandinavian Sea-Borne Expansion and Settlement Before 1300*, ed. Beverley Ballin Smith, Simon Taylor and Gareth Williams (Leiden, 2007), 195–226. The autograph manuscript of Reginald's *Libellus* contains a note to numerous Scandinavian sites and Scottish islands alongside this chapter. There are two further *Libellus* miracles that mention Norwegian connections: chs 32 and 52: ed. Raine, 72–4 and 108–9.

Cuthbert seems to have held a special significance in both northern England and southern Scotland, reflecting the social and cultural unity of the region.[47] What also emerges from the case of Cuthbert is that his cult appears to have transcended the border-imposed divisions between higher echelons of society. This contrasts somewhat with the later situation, when the Wars of Independence saw Cuthbert being depicted in a far more overtly partisan role, as defender of the northern English border, not least through the use of his banner in battle.[48] Nonetheless, veneration of Cuthbert continued north of the border: the example of David II encapsulates this coexistence, of Scottish royal patronage alongside the English partisan Cuthbert. Walter Bower's *Scotichronicon* recounts how St Cuthbert appears to King David II, warning him not to invade Durham's lands; the king of Scots ignores the advice 'just as a snake foolishly closes his ears in response to a charmer' and the result is his disastrous defeat at the battle of Neville's Cross (17 October 1346). Bower does not stint in his further criticism of David II: 'Note how disastrously David king of Scotland was defeated and captured along with his army on account of his attack on the lands of the church of St Cuthbert.'[49] Yet, we learn elsewhere that on 5 May 1346, only five months prior to Neville's Cross, David had granted lands in Carrick in return for an annual payment of a penny on the feast of St Cuthbert.[50] Cuthbert continued to represent a powerful, semi-independent political force, which may have been harnessed, but was never owned, by England. In the crucible of border conflict and fluctuating Anglo-Scottish relations of the twelfth century, Cuthbert had become firmly established as a cross-border saint. His cult became simultaneously intrinsic to, and transcendent of, these political machinations.

47 Robert Bartlett, *England under the Norman and Angevin Kings 1075–1225* (Oxford, 2000), 77–85.

48 John R. E. Bliese, 'Saint Cuthbert and War', *Journal of Medieval History* 24 (1998), 215–41, at 235–41; Lynda Rollason, 'Spoils of War? Durham Cathedral and the Black Rood of Scotland', in *The Battle of Neville's Cross, 1346*, ed. David Rollason and Michael Prestwich (Stamford, 1998), 57–65.

49 *Chron. Bower*, VII.109–11.

50 Michael Penman, *David II* (East Linton, 2004), 131.

7

DAVID OF SCOTLAND: 'VIR TAM NECESSARIUS MUNDO'[1]

Joanna Huntington

Famously, James I of Scotland allegedly said that David I's extreme generosity towards the church had rendered him 'ane sair sanct for the Croune'.[2] David was also explicitly a saint for Walter Bower,[3] who was reliant for material on John of Fordun,[4] who in turn borrowed heavily from a eulogy written shortly after David's death by Aelred of Rievaulx. David's sanctity in these later sources does not, however, simply reproduce the twelfth-century depiction; it is instead adapted to suit the *mores* and requirements of the later authors.[5] Aelred's David is virtuous and explicitly to be emulated, but he is not a saint. The later medieval reworkings of Aelred's David suggest, however, that he was, as it were, an embryonic saint – that is, that there was sufficient hagiographical 'raw material' for him

1 This is based on aspects of my doctoral research at the Centre for Medieval Studies, University of York, which was undertaken with the financial assistance of the A.H.R.B. and the support and encouragement of my supervisors, Peter Biller, Felicity Riddy and Elizabeth Tyler. The final revisions were undertaken during my Leverhulme Early Career Fellowship, and I am most grateful for the Leverhulme Trust's support. I should like to thank Steve Boardman, for his advice and encouragement, and the audience at Leeds IMC 2006, at which a version of this chapter was presented, for their helpful questions and comments. I am also most grateful to my viva voce examiners, Mark Ormrod and David Bates, for their continued support, and to the anonymous reader for their invaluable feedback and for generously allowing me to consult their copy of Oxford, Bodleian Library, MS Laud Misc 668.

2 An early sixteenth-century account put these words into the mouth of the early fifteenth-century king: Boece, *Chronicles*, II.185.

3 *Chron. Bower*. See, for example, III.290, IV.2, 251, 284, where David is clearly *sanctus* in the sense of saint.

4 *Chron. Fordun.*

5 On these later sources and their contexts, see, for example, Steve Boardman, 'Late Medieval Scotland and the Matter of Britain', in *Scottish History: The Power of the Past*, eds Edward J. Cowan and Richard J. Finlay (Edinburgh, 2002), 47–72. On David in them, see Richard Oram, *David I: The King who Made Scotland* (Stroud, 2004), 209–16.

to be subsequently seen as saintly. It is now widely accepted that saints' *vitae* can provide valuable insights into the concerns of the cultural and political landscape from which they emanate, and were often written with didactic intent. The eulogy was presented as an exemplar to Henry of Anjou, shortly before he was to become Henry II of England. What kingship was Aelred recommending to the king-in-waiting? What were the pitfalls of which he believed Henry needed to beware? By examining Aelred's virtuous, but – crucially – flawed David, this study points to the wider application of quasi-hagiographical ideas in relation to non-saintly subjects, and suggests that subjects who were not saintly could be equally (and perhaps still more) valuable tools in attempts to shape the behaviour of others.

David I of Scotland (1124–53), youngest son of Malcolm III and Margaret of Scotland, had been reared in the English court, and knighted by Henry I.[6] Shortly after Henry's death in 1135, David embarked on a campaign (ostensibly at least) in support of his niece Matilda's claim to the throne, and to claim Cumberland, Westmorland and Northumberland on his son's behalf. In January 1138, David again invaded Northumberland, in what was generally seen as an unnecessarily brutal campaign, which culminated in the Battle of the Standard.[7] Thereafter, David's reign was relatively peaceful, and he furthered the institutionalisation of government, law and church reform on which much of his subsequent good reputation centred. He died at Carlisle, having designated his grandson heir to the throne.

Walter Daniel stated that Aelred of Rievaulx 'published a life of David, King of Scotland, in the form of a lamentation, and added to it a genealogy of the King of England, the younger Henry, uniting them in one book'.[8] Subsequent manuscript transmission, editions, and studies have been uncertain whether to treat what Aelred allegedly wrote as two works, but circulated as one, as a single whole or separate texts. In those manuscripts where both works are included, the *Eulogium* stands as the first chapter of *Genealogia regum Anglorum*, addressed to Henry Plantagenet. The works may therefore be dated to 1153 × 1154, that is, between David's death and Stephen's, after which Henry would have been addressed as king. It does seem that they were written separately, as David's qualities in the *Genealogia* are rather different from those in the *Eulogium*. Regrettably, as yet

6 For a general introduction to the period, see, for example, R. L. Graeme Ritchie, *The Normans in Scotland* (Edinburgh, 1954); G. W. S. Barrow, *The Kingdom of the Scots: Government, Church and Society from the Eleventh to the Fourteenth Century* (London, 1973); A. A. M. Duncan, *Scotland: The Making of a Kingdom* (Edinburgh, 1975); Marjorie Chibnall, *Anglo-Norman England, 1066–1166* (Oxford, 1986); G. W. S. Barrow, *Scotland and its Neighbours in the Middle Ages* (London, 1992); Judith A. Green, 'David I and Henry I', *SHR* 75 (1996), 1–19; Robert Bartlett, *England under the Norman and Angevin Kings, 1075–1225* (Oxford, 2000); Richard Oram, 'Malcolm III or Máel Coluim Mac Donnchada (1058–1093)', in *The Kings and Queens of Scotland*, ed. *idem* (Stroud, 2001), 51–6; *idem*, *David I*.

7 On the Battle of the Standard, see John Beeler, *Warfare in England, 1066–1189* (Ithaca NY, 1966), 85–95.

8 Walter Daniel, *Vita Ailredi* (London etc., 1950), 41: 'uitam Dauid Regis Scocie sub specie lamentandi edidit cui genealogiam Regis Anglie Henrici iunioris uno libro comprehendens adiunxit'.

there is no single edition of the *vita*/lament and genealogy,[9] and modern scholarship has tended to consider the texts separately. I suggest, however, that as Aelred himself apparently disseminated the works together, it seems logical to study them together.[10] Most commentators on the *Genealogia regum Anglorum* have noted that it was intended as a *speculum*.[11] That peacemaking was a key theme has also been noted.[12] I want to interrogate the text a little further, to identify *what* Aelred privileged as a route towards national reconciliation. This chapter therefore has

9 According to Hoste, the genealogy is extant in nineteen manuscripts, Anselm Hoste, *Bibliotheca Aelrediana: A Survey of the Manuscripts, Old Catalogues, Editions and Studies concerning St. Aelred of Rievaulx*, Instrumenta Patristica 2 (Steenbruge, 1962), 111–12. He is less clear, however, on the transmission of the *vita*/lament, citing just four manuscripts, *ibid.*, 113–14. Marsha L. Dutton's current research, however, suggests that the *vita*/lament exists in far more manuscripts than Hoste identified. I am most grateful to Professor Dutton for generously sharing her thoughts on this and many other aspects of Aelred's works. Twysden published a drastically abridged edition of the two texts together, allegedly based on two manuscripts, Roger Twysden, *Historiae Anglicanae Decem Scriptores* (London, 1652). Although the resultant text of the genealogy is similar to extant manuscripts, Twysden's *vita*/lament bears little resemblance to any known manuscript version, Marsha Dutton, personal communication. Migne used Twysden's edition for the *Patrologia Latina* edition, *PL* 195:711–38, the abridged version of the *vita*/lament is at cc. 713–16. The full version of the vita/lament, as known in extant manuscripts [Marsha Dutton, personal communication; see also *eadem*, 'Ælred of Rievaulx on Friendship, Chastity, and Sex: The Sources', *Cistercian Studies Quarterly* 29 (1994), 121–96, at 124, n. 11, where she notes that it is Pinkerton's version that is in 'all manuscripts containing the Genealogy that [... she has] examined in the British and Bodleian libraries'], was published as *Eulogium Davidis regis Scotorum*, in John Pinkerton, *Vitae antiquae sanctorum qui habitaverunt in ea parte Britanniae nunc vocata Scotia vel in ejus insulis* (London, 1789), which was revised and enlarged by W. M. Metcalfe, as *Pinkerton's Lives of the Scottish Saints*, 2 vols (Paisley, 1889), II.269–85. Professor Dutton's critical edition is eagerly awaited, and Jane Patricia Freeland's most welcome translation has made the works available to an Anglophone audience, in *Aelred of Rievaulx: The Historical Works*, Cistercian Fathers Series 56 (Kalamazoo, 2005), 39–122. I am extremely grateful to Professor Dutton for generously sending an early copy of the translation of the *Genealogia*.

10 For ease of reference, this chapter will refer to the relevant part of Freeland's translation, even where my given translation differs from the published one. Citations of the *vita*/lament are from Metcalfe's edition of Pinkerton's text, as *Eulogium*, and Aelred's prefatory letter to Henry and the *Genealogia* will be cited from *PL*. For the most part, the relevant passages from these editions correspond to the text in Bodleian, MS Laud Misc 668, one of the oldest manuscripts, on which Dutton's edition will be based. I have silently amended the very few, very slight variations, but have retained the printed editions' editorial principles. The *Eulogium* and *Genealogia* together will be referred to as *Genealogia regum Anglorum*.

11 See, for example, Marsha L. Dutton, 'Introduction. Aelred's Historical Works: A Mirror for Twelfth-century England', in *Aelred of Rievaulx: The Historical Works*, 1–37, at 10–12.

12 See, for example, Aelred Squire, *Aelred of Rievaulx: A Study* (London, 1969; repr. 1981), 88; Martha G. Newman, *The Boundaries of Charity: Cistercian Culture and Ecclesiastical Reform, 1098–1180* (Stanford CA, 1996), 178–81; Paul Dalton, 'Churchmen and the Promotion of Peace in King Stephen's Reign', *Viator: Medieval and*

two aims: to refine our understanding of Aelred's message to Henry by looking at the two works together, and to consider this message as a register of non-saintly exemplary virtue.

Aelred's prefatory letter opens with a typically Cistercian exposition of the soul's natural inclination towards virtue.[13] The practical application of this for Henry was that striving towards good morals wins the favour of others – an attractive prospect to a king-in-waiting.[14] Aelred praised Henry's rulership, attributing to him 'at such an age so much wisdom, in the midst of so many pleasures so much continence, in such great affairs such foresight, in so high a station such austerity, and in such austerity so much kindness'.[15] Henry had avoided the pitfalls of achieving temporal power,[16] but Aelred urged him to ensure that he had that power in perspective: 'This alone remains, that you acknowledge Jesus Christ as the bestower of these gifts.'[17] Henry's capacity for such virtues was borne of a dual transmission: blood and knighthood.[18] The conferral of knighthood created a special relationship, which Aelred further glossed as transmitting David's spiritual qualities of chastity, humility and piety, so that Henry was 'the heir of his [David's] piety'.[19] Aelred concluded, 'when you read of his praiseworthy life and valuable death, may you imitate the former that you may deserve the latter'.[20] The *incipit*, therefore, establishes Henry's position as heir to the virtues of David and his ancestors, and promises to set down a template for Henry. What, then, was *laudabilis* about David's life?

Squire placed Aelred's lament for David in the tradition of laments that stretched back, through Ambrose for Satyrus, to those of David for Saul and Jonathan, of Jeremiah for Jerusalem.[21] More recent examples included Aelred's lament for his friend Simon and Bernard of Clairvaux's for his brother Gerard.[22] Squire

Renaissance Studies 31 (2000), 79–119, at 116–17; Elizabeth Freeman, *Narratives of a New Order: Cistercian Historical Writing in England, 1150–1220*, Medieval Church Studies 2 (Turnhout, 2002), 65. I am grateful to Dr Freeman for generously sharing her thoughts and sending me a copy of her very valuable chapter on the *Genealogia*.

13 Freeland, 41–2; *PL* 195:712. See Freeman, *Narratives*, 63.

14 Freeland, 42; *PL* 195:712–13, 'Quoniam igitur animae rationali naturaliter inest amor virtutum, odium vitiorum, quicunque bonis moribus virtutique studuerit, facile sibi omnium illicit et inclinat affectum.'

15 Freeland, 42; *PL* 195:713, 'in tali aetate tanta sapientia, in tantis deliciis tanta continentia, in tantis negotiis tanta providentia, in tali sublimitate talis severitas, in tali severitate talis benignitas'.

16 Freeland, 42; *PL* 195:713, 'Quis enim non obstupeat juvenem pro regno certantem abstinere rapinis, caedibus parcere, cavere incendia, nullum gravamen inferre pauperibus, pacem et reverentiam ecclesiis et sacerdotibus conservare?'

17 Freeland, 42; *PL* 195:713, 'Hoc tantum superest, ut Jesum Christum horum munerum largitorem agnoscas.'

18 Freeland, 42–3; *PL* 195:713.

19 Freeland, 43; *PL* 195:713, 'pietatis illius haeredem'.

20 Freeland, 43; *PL* 195:713, 'cum laudabilem ejus vitam et pretiosam legeris mortem, illam imiteris ut ista consequi merearis'.

21 Squire, *Aelred*, 82–3; *idem*, 'Aelred and King David', *Collectanea ordinis Cisterciensum Reformatorum* 22 (1960), 356–77, at 360.

22 Aelred, *Speculum caritatis*, *PL* 195:539–46; Bernard of Clairvaux, *Sermones super*

summarised the form thus: 'first the exordium, then an encomium and lament with its development of *τόποι* dealing with the manner of life, moral qualities and achievements of the subject, and in conclusion an exhortation and prayer'.[23] Significantly, neither Bernard's lament for Gerard nor Aelred's for Simon includes moral flaws.[24] David, however, is flawed, and it is here that we may identify the pitfalls of secular rulership.

The *Eulogium* immediately establishes David's piety: 'Religiosus et pius Rex David.'[25] He is not, however, explicitly saintly, here or at any point in the text. David's kingship was hands-on – 'who would not mourn for a man so necessary [or essential][26] to the world, now freed from human affairs, except one who resents peace and success in human affairs?'[27] Essentially, he was all things to all men, to be mourned by all. The first chapter's conclusion foreshadows the depiction of David throughout the *Eulogium*: 'we have lost a man who lived not for himself but for everyone; caring for everyone, providing for the welfare of everyone; a guide of morals, censor of sins, incitor of virtues; whose life was a model of humility, a mirror of justice, an exemplar of chastity'.[28] Here too, then, David's life is explicitly a didactic tool.

Aelred marvelled that such virtues were still worthier in a king, whose very position creates dangerous opportunities to fall away from virtue: 'He could ... have transgressed, and he did not transgress.'[29] Instead, David's head was not turned by the trappings of power and royal authority,[30] and again we are told of his humility to all people, of his deference to priests.[31] Aelred outlines how David tamed and civilised the Scottish people, with a civilising process grounded in humility, justice and gentleness.[32] His justice was balanced by a natural inclination towards gentleness.[33] Janet L. Nelson has well characterised justice as, 'a two-way

cantica canticorum, sermon 26, in *Sancti Bernardi Opera*, ed. J. Leclercq, C. H. Talbot and H. M. Rochais, 8 vols (Rome, 1957–1977), I.169–81.

23 Squire, 'Aelred and King David', 360.

24 Squire did note this apparent anomaly, but inferred that this frankness renders the Eulogium a trustworthy source as to historical reality, 'Aelred and King David', 362.

25 Freeland, 45; *Eulogium*, 269.

26 The primary definitions, according to *Dictionary of Medieval Latin from British Sources* (Oxford, 1975–), Fasc. VII.N:1897.

27 Freeland, 45; *Eulogium*, 269, 'quis ... non lugeat virum tam necessarium mundo, rebus humanis exemptum, nisi is qui rebus humanis pacem invidet et profectum?'

28 Freeland, 45–6; *Eulogium*, 269, 'qui eum amisimus virum qui non sibi vivebat, sed omnibus; omnium curam agens, omnium saluti prospiciens; rector morum, censor scelerum, virtutum incentor; cujus vita humilitatis fuit forma, justitiæ speculum, castitatis exemplar'.

29 Freeland, 46; *Eulogium*, 270, 'Potuit ... transgredi et non est transgressus.'

30 Freeland, 46; *Eulogium*, 270.

31 Freeland, 46; *Eulogium*, 270.

32 Freeland, 47–8; *Eulogium*, 271.

33 Freeland, 47–8; *Eulogium*, 271, 'Nec mansuetudo illa remissa videbatur aut segnis; cum in puniendis iniquis et justitiæ per omnia cederet, ne videretur gladium sine causa portare; et mansuetudinem in corde teneret, ne videretur non exercere judicium, sed suæ potius impatientiæ satisfacere. Credo eum nunquam sine magna cordis contritione, etiam in eos qui proditionis ipsius rei fuerant, exercuisse vindictam. Vidimus eum sæpe in pœnis latronum, vel proditorum, pectus tundere, lacrimas fundere, ut manifestum

stretch: it combines two very different qualities, severity and mercy. … There was a complementarity in *pax* and *iustitia*, and between severity and equity as twin aspects of justice',[34] and David's balance of leniency and harshness fits this model neatly: 'he observed both justice and mercy in the same measure, so that he was loved by everyone in the severity of his justice and feared by everyone in the leniency of his mercy'.[35] This balance allowed David to bring peace to his realm, uniting disparate factions:

> Not undeservedly then did he, a gentle man, inherit the earth …; and he delighted in an abundance of peace, which he brought about with great foresight among barbaric peoples, hostile to each other through diversities of tongues and manners, deadly enemies because of deaths and injuries on both sides. He preserved the peace with such authority that we have scarcely ever seen such a federation maintained so long, even among related peoples of the same lineage and language.[36]

David had peacefully united disparate races and linguistic cultures through effective kingship. The advantages of emulating such kingship must have been apparent to Henry.

The following chapter deals with David's generosity to the Church, monasticism and the poor.[37] His patronage is glossed as deferential to *clerici*, and both patronage and deference are linked with kingly protection of *pauperes*:

> I know that with me weep priests and clerics, whom he venerated as fathers; holy nuns and monks, whom he embraced as brothers, weep; knights, to whom he held himself not as a lord, but as a companion, weep; widows, whom he protected, weep; orphans whom he consoled; paupers whom he supported; wretched people, whom he cherished.[38]

faceret se in reis puniendis, ut ministrum legum, obedire justitiæ, non sævitiam exercere.'

34 Janet L. Nelson, 'Kings with Justice, Kings without Justice: An Early Medieval Paradox', *La Giustizia Nell'alto Medioevo (Secoli ix–xi): Settimane di Studio del Centro Italiano di Studi Sull' alto Medioevo* 44 (1997), 797–823, at 821.

35 Freeland, 48; *Eulogium*, 271, 'talem servabat modum in utroque, ut in severitate justitiæ ab omnibus amaretur, et in lenitate misericordiæ ab omnibus timeretur'.

36 Freeland, 48–9; *Eulogium*, 271, 'Unde non immerito velut mansuetus hereditabat terram …; et delectabatur in multitudine pacis, quam inter barbaras gentes, et diversitate linguarum et morum sibi contrarias, et propter mutuas mortes et vulnera sibi inimicissimas, tanta cautione composuit, tanta auctoritate servavit, ut inter cognatas gentes, ejusdemque generis et linguæ, homines tale fedus tanto tempore vix aliquando viderimus custodiri.'

37 On the historical David's monastic patronage, see Christopher N. L. Brooke, 'King David I of Scotland as a Connoisseur of the Religious Orders', in *Mediaevalia Christiana: XIe–XIIIe siècles: hommage à Raymonde Foreville de ses amis, ses collèges et ses anciens élèves*, ed. Coloman Etienne Viola (Paris, 1989), 320–34; G. W. S. Barrow, 'The Royal House and the Religious Orders', 'Benedictines, Tironensians and Cistercians', both repr. in *idem*, *Kingdom of the Scots*, 165–211; Oram, *David I*, 159–65.

38 Freeland, 50; *Eulogium*, 272–3, 'Scio … lugent mecum sacerdotes et clerici, quos venerabatur ut patres; lugent sancti moniales et monachi, quos amplectebatur ut fratres; lugent milites, quorum se dominum nesciebat, sed socium; lugent viduæ, quas tuebatur; orphani quos consolabatur; pauperes quos sustentabat; miseri quos fovebat.'

This protection of *pauperes* and widows is expanded upon, thus bringing David's kingship back to diligent enactment of justice.[39] Deference, humility and mildness notwithstanding, David was no pushover when it came to enforcing the law: 'often they argued with him, and he with them, when he was unwilling to take the part of a pauper if it were contrary to justice, and they were unwilling to agree to the reason which he was showing'.[40] His justice is therefore perfectly in keeping with that advocated in Gregory's *Regula pastoralis*: firm and impartial.[41] David's moderation of temperament similarly sits at ease with Gregory's model: he is affable and moderates himself according to his audience.[42]

We eventually learn, however, of David's spiritual Achilles' heel. Aelred turned to the ultimate Old Testament model of repentance, David:

> David ..., as if forgetful of divine goodness, first committed adultery with the wife of his faithful servant; and then did away with him by an astonishing betrayal. I admit that he sinned, and so did our David.[43]

David of Scotland's sin, however, was not, according to Aelred, borne of proactive sinning on his own part. Instead,

> He sinned, not by himself committing some foul crime, but by taking advantage of the violence of the cruelty of others beyond what was appropriate. For after the death of King Henry, when he had led an army into England, that savage people, exceedingly hostile to the English, carried out cruel judgments, raging beyond human custom against the church, against priests, against both sexes, against all ages. All this happened even though he did not wish it – indeed the deeds may even have been forbidden. Yet he could have not led the army; he could, after one experience, have not led them again, he could, perhaps, have restrained them more. With tears, I confess that he sinned.[44]

39 Freeland, 50–1; *Eulogium*, 273.

40 Freeland, 51; *Eulogium*, 273, 'Nam sæpe litigabant cum illo, et ipse cum illis, cum ipse nollet contra justitiam personam pauperis accipere, et ipsi nollent rationi quod ostendebat acquiescere.'

41 On the relevance of the Regula to all who exercised authority, see Matthew Kempshall, 'No Bishop, No King: The Ministerial Ideology of Kingship and Asser's Res Gestae Aelfredi', in *Belief and Culture in the Middle Ages: Studies Presented to Henry Mayr-Harting*, ed. Richard Gameson and Henrietta Leyser (Oxford, 2001), 106–27.

42 Freeland, 51; *Eulogium*, 273, 'Denique si contingeret ut sacerdos, vel miles, vel monachus, vel dives vel pauper, vel civis vel peregrinus, vel negociator vel rusticus cum eo haberet sermonem, ita cum singulis de suis negotiis et officiis convenienter et humiliter disserebat, ut singulus quisque sua eum tantum curare putaret.'

43 Freeland, 53; *Eulogium*, 275, 'David ..., quasi divinæ bonitatis oblitus, primum servi sui fidelis adulteravit uxorem; quem deinde mira proditione peremit. Fateor peccavit, et noster David.'

44 Freeland, 53–4; *Eulogium*, 275, 'Peccavit non se ipsum aliquo fœdando scelere, sed alienæ crudelitati vires plusquam oportuit ministrando. Nam post mortem regis Henrici, cum exercitum egisset in Angliam, gens illa effera, et Anglis inimicissima, supra humanum morem sævientes in ecclesiam, in sacerdotes, in utrumque sexum, in omnem ætatem, crudelia exercuere judicia. Quæ omnia, licet eo nolente, immo etiam

David's 1138 military foray into England, culminating in the Battle of the Standard, was seen as unnecessarily brutal. Richard of Hexham, for example, was appalled at the barbaric behaviour of David's men, and saw the way in which his men were hunted down and killed after their defeat in the Battle of the Standard as divine judgment for their earlier behaviour.[45] Twelfth-century commentators were far from unanimous on David's military activity. Henry of Huntingdon described David as dissembling, impious and cowardly and even made him the progenitor of his army's barbarous behaviour.[46]

The Anglo-Scottish border was far from fixed at this period, and David arguably had a legitimate claim on the region.[47] His 1138 campaign, however, is relevant here for two reasons. First, in the context of the *Genealogia regum Anglorum*, it provided a salutary warning with regard to military action. Whereas, as we will see, military violence is important in the construction of several kings in the *Genealogia*, it had to be pursued appropriately and for the correct reasons. Secondly, it provided Aelred with an opportunity to extol the virtue of sincere penitence:

> Others may excuse him. ... I, however, knowing that it is good to confess to you, have chosen to ask, not to excuse; seeking mercy, not presuming judgement. ... For he himself preferred to accuse, rather than to excuse himself, he preferred to beat his breast rather than to thrust it out.[48]

Aelred approvingly described him atoning for his sin by subjecting himself entirely to the counsel of religious men.[49] This subjection to clerical counsel is one of the leitmotivs of the *Eulogium* and, as we will see, the *Genealogia*, and enabled David to redeem himself.[50] God punished David, first with the trouble stirred up in the realm by a fraudster, and second, by the untimely death of his son and heir.[51]

prohibente, facta sint quia tamen poterat eos non duxisse, poterat eos semel expertos non reduxisse, poterat fortasse eos plus cohibuisse, et ipsum cum lacrimis peccasse confitemur.'

45 Richard of Hexham, *De Gestis Regis Stephani*, in *Chronicles of the Reigns of Stephen, Henry II and Richard I*, ed. Richard Howlett, RS 82, 4 vols (London, 1884–9), III.139–78, at 151–64.

46 Henry of Huntingdon, *Historia Anglorum: The History of the English People*, trans. Diana Greenway (Oxford, 1996), 710–11.

47 See, *inter alia*, Keith Stringer, 'King David I (1124–53): The Scottish Occupation of Northern England', *Medieval History* 4 (1994), 51–61; Green, 'David I and Henry I', 3–4; G. W. S. Barrow, 'King David I, Earl Henry and Cumbria', CWAAS 99 (1999), 117–27; Bartlett, *England under the Norman and Angevin Kings*, 77–85; G. W. S. Barrow, 'The Scots and the North of England', in *The Anarchy of King Stephen's Reign*, ed. Edmund King (Oxford, 1994), 231–53.

48 Freeland, 54; *Eulogium*, 275, 'Excusent eum alii. ... Ego autem sciens quia bonum est confiteri tibi, elegi rogare, non excusare; misericordiam petens, non præsumens de judicio. ... Maluit enim ipse se accusare, quam excusare, maluit pectus tundere, quam exerere.'

49 Freeland, 55; *Eulogium*, 276.

50 Freeland, 55; *Eulogium*, 276.

51 Freeland, 55–7; *Eulogium*, 276–7.

Thus spiritually cleansed, David subjected himself to the counsel of religious men, paid even more alms, confessed weekly, and lived a quasi-monastic existence, until his suitably pious death.[52]

The standard virtues of medieval Christian kingship are all present in Aelred's narrative: protection of *pauperes*, humility in exalted office, establishment of peace and unity, firm but fair patronage of justice, teaching by word and example, patronage of the Church. Nonetheless, David did not avoid sin, and therefore provided Henry with a salutary example of the pitfalls of kingship. David's repentance was absolute, he was extremely pious, and worthy of emulation, but not, at this early point, saintly, and it seems that military violence was a sticking-point. How does this sit with the models presented in the *Genealogia*?

Aelred urged Henry to remember that his earthly kingdom's priorities were subservient to those of the heavenly kingdom:

> when you see that their great glory has perished through death and old age, and that because of the merits of their lives they earned the heavenly reward which will not perish, then may you learn always to prefer justice to riches and worldly glory, so that after temporal life you may come to life eternal.[53]

Kingly office, therefore, is transitory, but it can be a means to salvation. Aelred wrote to enable Henry to live up to his ancestors' examples:

> when you see the integrity of your ancestors, the *virtus* which glittered within them, the piety which shone, you will realize how natural it is for you to abound in riches, to flourish in *virtutes*, to be illustrious with victories, and, more than all this, to glow with Christian religion and the prerogative of justice.[54]

The *Genealogia* too, then, is an exemplary text. The qualities privileged in Aelred's summary of Henry's ancestors are *probitas*, *virtus*, *pietas*, which facilitate *divitiae*, *victoriae*, Christian religion and *justitia*. *Virtus* is often translated as virtue, but also denotes 'manliness, ... strength ...; bravery ...'.[55] As the *virtutes* in which Henry may flourish are immediately followed by the promise of illustrious victories, it seems that *virtus* here suggests manly power.

The *Genealogia* is emphatically English, as suggested by its very title.[56]

52 Freeland, 57–9; *Eulogium*, 277–84.

53 Freeland, 72; *PL* 195:716, 'cum videris tantam eorum gloriam morte ac vetustate perisse, eosque pro vitae meritis coeleste praemium quod perire non poterit meruisse, discas semper divitiis gloriaeque mundiali praeferre justitiam, ut post vitam temporalem pervenias ad aeternam'.

54 Freeland, 71; *PL* 195:716, 'ut cum videris quanta fuerit antecessorum tuorum probitas, qualis in eis virtus innituerit, qualis splenduerit pietas, agnoscas etiam quam naturale tibi sit abundare divitiis, florere virtutibus, victoriis illustrari, et quod his omnibus praestat, Christiana religione et justitiae praerogativa fulgere'.

55 Charlton T. Lewis and Charles Short, *A Latin Dictionary* (Oxford, 1879), 1997.

56 This is also noted, for example, in Squire, *Aelred*, 88; see also Freeman, *Narratives*, 55–87; Rosalind Ransford, 'A Kind of Noah's Ark: Aelred of Rievaulx and National Identity', *Religion and National Identity: Studies in Church History* 18 (1982), 137–46, at 140–2.

William I stands alone in a Norman hinterland, his only explicit (cursory) genealogical link to David's wife, Matilda. No other Norman is discussed in detail, unless they have been explicitly or implicitly associated with the English royal line. This English emphasis is understandable: Henry was the new boy, about to be Norman king of the English.

Having traced Henry's lineage, through Empress Matilda, Edith-Matilda, David, Margaret, Edward the Exile and Edmund Ironside, to the Wessex royal line, Aelred provided a typically West Saxon regnal genealogy, via Woden to Adam.[57] Aelred then travelled back down the ancestral line, dwelling in varying detail on particular ancestors. Thirteen chapters are devoted to specific kings: Ethelwulf, Alfred, Edward the Elder, Athelstan, Edmund, Eadred, Edwin, Edgar (with one chapter also devoted to his sermon to the clergy), Ethelred, Edmund Ironside, Edward the Confessor, and William I. This final chapter, however, concentrates more on the families and characters of David and his siblings.

Aelred was not concerned here with the transmission of sanctity. Those kings traditionally treated as saints – Edward the Martyr and Edward the Confessor – are dealt with cursorily. Of Edward the Martyr, Aelred simply noted that he was saintly by virtue of the *sanctitas* of his life and his martyrdom.[58] Edward the Confessor's reign is described as peaceful, but with little detail.[59] Having designated Edward as a *rex pacificus*, Aelred did not dwell on how he achieved or maintained peace, but instead turned to Edward's kindliness towards Edward the Exile's family, from whom Henry was descended, thereby glossing over the minor detail that Henry was not directly descended from Edward. Edward primarily serves within the narrative to restore the Anglo-Saxon line of kingship after the Danish interregnum, as a bridge between Edgar and Edward the Exile's ancestors.

The kings to whom Aelred afforded most praise are those who bore themselves appropriately in relation to the authority of churchmen (Edmund, Eadred, and especially Alfred and Edgar), and those who fought only in order to protect their people (Alfred, Edward the Elder, Athelstan, Edmund, Eadred, Edmund Ironside).[60] Obedience to *clerici* and appropriate military violence are, I suggest, Aelred's key themes in the *Geneologia*, and provide a thematic link to the depiction of David in the *Eulogium*. Before considering these themes, we will briefly note those who were apparently of less interest to Aelred.

57 Freeland, 72–4; *PL* 195:716–17. See the similar genealogies for Alfred in *Asser's Life of King Alfred together with the Annals of Saint Neots erroneously ascribed to Asser*, ed. William Henry Stevenson (Oxford, 1959; repr. 1998), pp. 1–95, at 2–4 and for Ethelwulf in *The Anglo Saxon Chronicle: A Collaborative Edition*, general eds David Dumville and Simon Keynes, 17 vols, vols 1, 3–8, 10, 17 published to date (Cambridge, 1983–2004), s.a. 855 A, 3.45–6.

58 Freeland, 104; *PL* 195:729–30.

59 Freeland, 113–14; *PL* 195:734.

60 The emphasis in the *Genealogia* on cooperation between kings and *clerici* has been explored by other scholars. See, for example, Newman, *The Boundaries of Charity*; Freeman, *Narratives*, 55–87; Marsha L. Dutton, '*Sancto Dunstano cooperante*: Collaboration between King and Ecclesiastical Advisor in Aelred of Rievaulx's *Genealogy of the Kings of the English*', in *Religious and Laity in Western Europe 1000–1400: Interaction, Negotiation, and Power*, ed. Emilia Jamroziak and Janet Burton (Turnhout, 2006), 183–95.

Ethelwulf was mindful of the proper relationship between the earthly and spiritual realms, and is praised for governing with *caritas*, protecting *pauperes* and being a generous benefactor to the Church[61] – effectively for appropriate use of his wealth and power, and was therefore 'gathered to his fathers in a good old age, not losing a kingdom surely but exchanging one, leaving one that is temporal and obtaining one that is eternal'.[62] Edwin provides a salutary example of inappropriate kingship, despite Dunstan's good advice.[63] Although Edwin eventually repented of his adultery, he still needed Dunstan's intercession to free him from the demons who punished him after his death.[64] During Ethelred's reign, the Danes regained much of England. This, Aelred explained, was foretold by Dunstan, and was God's punishment upon England for Edward the Martyr's death. Aelred noted Ethelred's wives and heirs, before explaining his enforced exile from the realm as a result of others' treachery.[65] Upon Swein of Denmark's death, Ethelred was recalled to England and 'rose up again against the Danes, powerful in his strength', but Cnut, Swein's son, 'ceased not to carry on his father's hatred against him'.[66] Although Ethelred merited his own chapter, he is not a shining example of good kingship, but did exhibit valour in the face of retribution upon the whole realm. The best that could be said of him was that he was *rex strenuissimus*, that he tried, albeit not always successfully, and that he left an heir.[67]

From these kings, we see that Aelred valued protecting *pauperes*, generous patronage of the Church, adhering to the counsel of *clerici*, fighting pagans, converting subjects to Christianity, promoting just laws, and providing an heir – essentially, what one would expect of a good king at this time. Can the more detailed or more praiseworthy portraits shed any further light?

Alfred's importance may be seen in the space devoted to him: more than one-fifth of the length of the thirteen chapters. He was humble in exalted office and adjusted his demeanour according to his company.[68] Moreover, he was aware of his position vis-à-vis the Church and its officials:

> he believed that a king's great dignity had no power at all in the church of Christ. He said, 'The dignity of a ruler must recognize that in Christ's kingdom, which is the church, he is not a king but a citizen. Thus he must not govern priests by his laws but be humbly subject to the laws of Christ that the priests have established'.[69]

61 Freeland, 75–6; *PL* 195:718.

62 Freeland, 76; *PL* 195:718, 'in senectute bona collectus est ad patres suos, regnum certe non amittens sed mutans, temporale deserens et aeternum adipiscens'.

63 Freeland, 94–5; *PL* 195:725–6.

64 Freeland, 95; *PL* 195:726.

65 Freeland, 104–6; *PL* 195:730.

66 Freeland, 105; *PL* 195:730, 'iterum contra Dacos virtute potens erigitur'; 'paternum odium exercere non desiit'.

67 Freeland, 106; *PL* 195:730.

68 Freeland, 78; *PL* 195:719: 'Ita se bonis amabilem, impiis terribilem, ecclesiarum ministris pavidum, amicis et sociis jucundum, pauperibus mitem et largum exhibuit, ut videretur omnium hominum moribus ac naturae congruere, omnibus utilis ac necessarius esse'.

69 Freeland, 78; *PL* 195:719, 'illam maximam regis credidit dignitatem, nullam in ecclesiis Christi habere potestatem. "Illa ...", inquit, "... regnantis dignitas si se in regno Christi

Alfred's careful adherence to suitable royal *exempla* provoked Satan to inflict the Danish invasions upon the realm, trials that Alfred bore with Job-like patience.[70]

He was duly rewarded by a vision of St Cuthbert, in which he assured Alfred of imminent military success and the restoration of kingly authority.[71] Alfred's rousing battle speech includes a justification for battle:

> Remember against whom we are fighting, for what reason, above all for what necessity: we are Christians fighting against pagans, and pious men against wicked men, the contrite in heart and humble in spirit against the proud. … we are not seeking what belongs to others but the return of what is ours. … we fight lest our wives be stolen, lest our sons be captured, lest our virgins be violated, lest the wicked and perverse bring down the whole of the English nobility to base servitude.[72]

This was not, in short, a war motivated by greed; it was to regain what the pagans had taken, and to forestall pagan atrocities.[73] Having achieved victory, Alfred ruled in pious peace, fostering learning and justice, relieving and protecting *pauperes*, repairing monasteries, and bestowing gifts on the Church.[74]

Edward the Elder was not as literate as his father, was almost as holy, but more powerful.[75] Edward's kingship was unashamedly military against the impious:

> He expanded the borders of his kingdom more widely than had his father, founded new cities, and rebuilt devastated ones. As for the utterly ungodly Danes, whom his father had not driven off, those who rebelled against him he either routed thoroughly, worn down as they were by many battles, or reduced them to a wretched servitude.[76]

Gentle and devout, he was a patron of justice, refused to abuse his royal power, and accordingly won the loyalty of Scots, Cumbrians, Welsh, Northumbrians and

quae est ecclesia, non regem sed civem cognoscat, si non in sacerdotes legibus dominetur, sed Christi legibus quas promulgaverunt sacerdotes humiliter subjiciatur." '

70 Freeland, 79; *PL* 195:719–20.

71 Freeland, 79–81; *PL* 195:720–1.

72 Freeland, 83; *PL* 195:721, 'Cogitate, qui adversum quos, qua ratione, qua insuper necessitate pugnamus. … Christiani contra paganos, et pii contra impios, contriti corde et humiles spiritu contra superbos dimicamus. … non aliena petimus, sed nostra repetimus . … ne diripiantur uxores nostrae, ne captiventur filii, ne virgines violentur, ne impii et perversi totam Anglorum nobilitatem ad degenerem transferant servitutem.'

73 On the embodiment of notions of just war within this speech, see John Bliese, 'The Battle Rhetoric of Aelred of Rievaulx', *Haskins Society Journal* 1 (1989), 99–107, at 104–5.

74 Freeland, 84–6; *PL* 195:722.

75 Freeland, 86; *PL* 195:722, 'erat autem in scientia litterarum patre minor, sanctitate vero non multum inferior, sed superior potestate'.

76 Freeland, 86–7; *PL* 195:722–3, 'Multo enim latius quam pater regni sui fines dilatavit, et urbes novas condidit, et dirutas renovavit. Impiissimam Danorum gentem quam pater ejus non expulerat, rebellantem sibi multis contritam praeliis vel fugavit penitus, vel misera servitute compressit.'

Danes.[77] Aelred allowed Edward a sex life, mentioning his children and wives, albeit briefly, before recounting an instance of clairvoyance. Edward, then, was a temporally active king: powerful, territorially expansionist, military, ruling moderately and fostering justice, sexually active, but was still sufficiently devout and just to be rewarded with supernatural knowledge of distant events.

Like Alfred, Athelstan entrusted his military success to a northern saint, John of Beverley, who assured Athelstan of his intercession in a vision.[78] Edmund was ' "a simple, upright, and God-fearing man" '.[79] He defeated the pagans, and consequently converted the local people to Christianity.[80] He 'took special care of monasteries and churches', and, heeding Dunstan's advice, 'established what needed establishing and corrected what needed correcting'.[81] Eadred continued the family tradition of combining military prowess with just rule, assisted by the counsel of Dunstan.[82] Although Eadred takes up little space in the *Genealogia*, his was a laudable kingship: 'A precious death concluded his praiseworthy life.'[83]

Edgar provided a return to good Christian kingship after the blip of Edwin. Edgar's importance in Aelred's scheme is shown by his prominence: at almost one-fifth (including his sermon to the clergy) of the chapters, Edgar takes up less space than Alfred, but more than is devoted to Edward the Elder, Athelstan, Edmund, Eadred and Edwin combined. Unlike his ancestors, he subjugated enemies and rebels without recourse to the sword:

> He united the kingdom of the English in a kind of heavenly peace and joined peoples of many languages in a federation under one law. Hence he was called by the same name as Solomon, so that everyone called him 'the Peaceful', ... He presented such signs of inner sweetness in his words, his appearance, and his manner, that, with God's help, the whole island submitted to him without bloodshed, and Scotland, Cumbria, and Wales hastened freely to subject themselves to him.[84]

77 Freeland, 87; *PL* 195:723, 'vir mansuetus et pius, omnibus amabilis et affabilis, adeo omnium in se provocabat affectum. ... Tanta dehinc modestia regebat subditos, tanta justitia inter proximum et proximum judicabat, ut contra veritatem non dico nihil velle, sed nec posse aliquid videretur.'

78 Freeland, 92; *PL* 195:724–5.

79 Freeland, 92; *PL* 195:725, 'homo "simplex et rectus, et timens Deum" '.

80 Freeland, 92–3; *PL* 195:725.

81 Freeland, 93; *PL* 195:725, 'monasteriorum et ecclesiarum maxime curam habuit', 'statuenda statuit, et corrigenda correxit'.

82 Freeland, 93–4; *PL* 195:725, 'ambulavit in viis fratris sui; beati Dunstani consiliis in omnibus obediens, et justissimis legibus subditos regens. Erat enim tantae probitatis, ut rebellantes sibi Northymbros et Scotos facile vicerit, et in pristinam subjectionem sine magno labore redegerit.'

83 Freeland, 94; *PL* 195:725, 'hujus laudabilem vitam mors pretiosa conclusit'.

84 Freeland, 96; *PL* 195:726, 'Hic enim regnum Anglorum coelesti quadam pace composuit, et multarum linguarum gentes, unius foedere legis conjunxit, unde ei cum Salomone commune vocabulum fuit, ut Pacificus ... communi omnium voce diceretur. ... Tanta enim in verbis, in vultu, in moribus, interioris suavitatis indicia praeferebat, ut, Deo cooperante, tota ei insula sine sanguine manus daret, et ad subdendum se ei Scotia, Cumbria, Wallia libens accurreret.'

Solomonic kingship does not explicitly feature prominently in the *Genealogia* as a whole, but it is important here, producing a symbiotic relationship between good rulership and regnal prosperity: unity and successfully enforced justice were underscored even by nature: 'While he was reigning the sun seemed to be more fair, the waves of the sea more peaceful, the earth more fruitful, and the face of the whole kingdom with its abundant beauty more lovely.'[85] This political and natural concord allowed Edgar to concentrate on being a generous patron of the Church, administering law, protecting *pauperes*, and teaching his people.[86] His patronage of the Church extended to reform, and Aelred presents Edgar's sermon to the clergy, concluding with concord of Church, people, heaven and nature.[87] Edgar's reign was often depicted as a golden age in the twelfth century, and, as in the passage above, he was seen to have united disparate peoples, which rendered him a particularly suitable exemplar for Henry.[88] He balances the emphasis elsewhere in the *Genealogia* on violence, albeit appropriate, defensive, divinely sanctioned violence against pagans.

Edmund Ironside, the nominal subject of the next chapter, provides a model of military kingship tempered by caution and *simplicitas*:

> Against his enemies he had the ferocity of a lion, and toward his own people the *simplicitas* of a dove. No one was braver than he, but no one gentler; no one bolder but no one more cautious; no one more confident in adversity, in prosperity no one more moderate.[89]

Edmund valiantly regained those regions that had defected to Cnut. One of Cnut's elders suggested one-to-one combat, which Cnut and Edmund duly undertook, and their mutual respect for one another led them to agree to dividing the kingdom: 'Words accomplished what swords had not, and one who was not persuaded by arms was persuaded by a speech.'[90] Whereas appropriately motivated and conducted military action is *good*, peace achieved without recourse to violence is *better*. Unfortunately Edmund was treacherously murdered. Cnut avenged him,

85 Freeland, 96; *PL* 195:726, 'eo namque regnante sol videbatur esse serenior, maris unda pacatior, terra fecundior, et totius regni facies habundantiori decore venustior'.

86 Freeland, 96–7; *PL* 195:727.

87 Freeland, 103; *PL* 195:729, 'O vere tunc beata Anglorum ecclesia, quam innumerabilium monachorum et virginum adornabat integritas, quam devotio plebium, moderatio militum, judicum equitas, terrae fecunditas laetificabat! Exsultabat rex beatissimus suis temporibus ordinem suum rerum omnium invenisse naturam, cum homines Deo, terra homini, coelum terrae, justitia, fructu, aerum temperie debitum praestaret officium.'

88 See, for example, Eadmer, *Historia Novorum in Anglia*, ed. Martin Rule, RS 81 (London, 1884), 1–302, which opens, at 3, with a paean to an age in which king, church and realm existed in peaceful Christian harmony. See also William of Malmesbury, *Gesta regum Anglorum: The History of the English Kings*, ed. and trans. R. A. B. Mynors, completed by R. M. Thomson and M. Winterbottom, 2 vols (Oxford, 1998–9), I.238–40, I.262, and Henry of Huntingdon, *Historia Anglorum*, 322.

89 Freeland, 106; *PL* 195:730, 'Contra hostes leoninae feritatis, erga suos columbinae simplicitatis; quo nemo fortior, sed quo nemo suavior; quo nullus audacior, sed quo nemo cautior; quo in adversis nemo securior, quo in prosperis nemo temperantior.'

90 Freeland, 111; *PL* 195:732–3, 'cessit enim verbis qui non cesserat gladiis, et oratione flectitur quia armis flecti non poterat'.

but proceeded, by the counsel of flatterers, to disinherit Edmund's heirs. This chapter is as much about Cnut as Edmund Ironside, and depicts both valiant kingship tempered by *simplicitas*, and potentially valiant kingship corrupted by evil counsel.

The final chapter deals with William I's rightful assumption of the kingdom. Rather than following the line from William through Henry I, or even a regnal line through William Rufus, Henry I and Stephen, Aelred switched to Edgar Ætheling and his sisters, and thence to Margaret's sons. Both the Norman and Anglo-Saxon routes led to Henry II, but the Anglo-Saxon connection is privileged. Aelred focused on the Scottish cadet-line, recounting an anecdote that shows Malcolm of Scotland's *caritas* when confronted by a would-be assassin.[91] Edgar of Scotland's reign is lauded as peaceful,[92] and the curt description of Alexander implies that being deferential to churchmen was not enough on its own to make for good kingship.[93] David's patronage and generosity was extended to all. The brief depiction here of David has a different focus than that in the *Eulogium*: here he is *litteratus*, responsible for the production of books and priestly vestments, and generous to all, especially *pauperes*.[94]

Aelred turned to the piety of David's sister, Edith-Matilda, recounting her penchant for kissing leprous feet.[95] He then briefly mentioned her sister Mary, then Empress Matilda and her marriages, before returning to David of Scotland, and then the respective offspring of David and Matilda. So much 'hopping' from branch to branch of the genealogical tree is confusing for the modern reader, and may not have been much less so for a twelfth-century reader. Whether deliberately or not, it serves to blur the boundaries between familial cadet-lines, and Aelred ended this section by admonishing Henry to be patron and protector to David's grandchildren.[96]

So what inheritance was Aelred writing for Henry? Throughout, two themes are privileged: military activity and obedience to *clerici*. Although fostering peace within the realm was crucial, violence as a means to achieving peace could be a necessary evil.[97] That it would not necessarily jeopardise his chances of salvation is demonstrated by Aelred's inclusion of military violence in his depictions of Alfred, Edward the Elder, Athelstan, Edmund, Eadred, Ethelred and Edmund Ironside, all of whom are Good Kings despite, and even because of, their military action. Six of the kings to whom chapters are devoted are suitably deferential to churchmen.[98] By emulating his illustrious Anglo-Saxon forebears, Henry can forge peaceful unity within the realm, with appropriately motivated warfare if necessary, but ideally with models of peaceful reconciliation at the forefront. It is

91 Freeland, 116–18; *PL* 195:735. On this anecdote, see Freeman, *Narratives*, 66–7.

92 Freeland, 118; *PL* 195:735–6.

93 Freeland, 118; *PL* 195:736.

94 Freeland, 118–19; *PL* 195:736.

95 Freeland, 119–20; *PL* 195:736.

96 Freeland, 122; *PL* 195:737–8.

97 Similarly, as Bliese has pointed out, in the *Genealogia* and the *Relatio de Standardii*, Aelred stressed the 'necessity of battle much more than other [battle] speeches do', 'Battle Rhetoric', 106.

98 Alfred, Athelstan, Edmund, Eadred, Edwin (eventually), and, perhaps most significantly, Edgar.

with this in mind that we may suggest a thematic unity between the *Genealogia* and *Eulogium*, which was perhaps instrumental in Aelred's decision to unite the two works. Aelred's David in the *Eulogium* satisfied all of the criteria but one: ensuring that his wars were conducted appropriately. He was exemplary, but not quite good enough – yet – to be saintly.

In his study of warfare and sanctity in Anglo-Saxon England, Damon has argued that 'by the twelfth century, a hagiographer no longer needed to distance his subject from warfare or even justify a saint's participation in battle', but noted a lingering ambivalence.[99] Aelred's treatment of David suggests that at this point, for Aelred at least, the picture was still ambiguous for non-saintly as well as saintly subjects. By highlighting David's failure to quite live up to the ideal, Aelred presented a *speculum* of kingship as well as a warning of the consequences of falling short of that ideal. In both the *Eulogium* and the *Genealogia*, the main stumbling-block was inappropriately motivated or conducted military violence. In both works, Aelred presented a way to avoid that stumbling-block: respect for clerical counsel. Far from being 'ane sair sanct for the Croune', Aelred's David was indeed 'vir tam necessarius mundo': he was not only a useful tool in Aelred's vision of what the Croune should be, but, moreover, his inappropriately conducted military activity rendered him a far more useful tool than a saint would have been.

99 John Edward Damon, *Soldier Saints and Holy Warriors: Warfare and Sanctity in the Literature of Early England* (Aldershot, 2003), 282.

8

THE CULT OF ST GEORGE IN SCOTLAND

Steve Boardman

On 17 July 1385 the English king Richard II was in Durham, overseeing the assembly of an army to counter a Franco-Scottish force that threatened England's northern counties. King Richard ordered the production of a series of ordinances to govern the conduct of the host that was about to head north towards the Anglo-Scottish border.[1] Among a number of detailed points, the ordinances declared that the English king's troops were to display the arms of St George and that if any of the enemy were found bearing the insignia of the saint they were to be put to death, even after capture.[2] The regulations of 1385 provide one example, among many others, of the fourteenth-century English identification of St George as the special protector of the armies that furthered the ambitions of the English monarchy. By the second half of the fourteenth century the association of St George with the English nation-in-arms was unambiguous. English forces were distinguished by their wearing of George's cross, they marched under banners bearing the same device, and had adopted the saint's name as their characteristic war cry.[3]

The promotion of St George as a particular, indeed *the* distinctive, patron of the English monarchy and nation in the fourteenth century and thereafter has been a

1 For the ordinances, see *Monumenta Juridica. The Black Book of the Admiralty, with an appendix*, ed. Travers Twiss, RS, 4 vols (London, 1871–6), I.453–8. For general analysis, see Maurice Keen, 'Richard II's Ordinances of War of 1385', in *Rulers and Ruled in Late Medieval England*, ed. Rowena E. Archer and Simon Walker (London, 1995), 33–48.

2 Keen, 'Richard II's Ordinances', 40–1. Curiously, the same campaign of 1385 also provided the first unequivocal evidence of the adoption of St Andrew's cross as the identifying symbol to be worn by soldiers in Scottish hosts: *The Acts of the Parliaments of Scotland*, ed. Thomas Thomson and Cosmo Innes, 12 vols (Edinburgh, 1814–75) [hereafter *APS*], I.554–5.

3 Thomas Walsingham, *Historia Anglicana*, ed. H. T. Riley, RS, 2 vols (London, 1862–4), I.273–4 records the early use of George's name (alongside that of St Edward) as a rallying call by Edward III at the siege of Calais.

widely studied phenomenon.[4] A critical development in securing the association between the saint and the English royal line was Edward III's establishment of the Order of the Garter in 1348 as a chivalric order with St George as its principal spiritual focus. Recent historical analysis has brought out the implications of the growing cult of St George in a peculiarly English context, and has explored the way in which the figure of St George promoted certain images of monarchical power, reflected and aided the definition of an 'English' national identity in the late medieval period, and may have encouraged or fostered a greater sense of social coherence within the realm.[5] A slightly different perspective on the George cult has emerged in the work of David Morgan. Morgan has encouraged historians to view the growing popularity of St George within a wider European context, and to place less emphasis on the uniqueness of the English interaction with the cult.[6] A number of points made by Morgan can be noted. First, although St George was celebrated in England prior to the middle of the fourteenth century with an enthusiasm that reflected his general reputation as the protector of crusading knights, he was not at that stage especially associated with the English crown.[7] Secondly, the George cult appealed to the fourteenth-century English monarchs who actively promoted commemoration of the saint precisely because George was a figure of European-wide significance. The English crown's identification with the cult was thus not a commemoration of a longstanding 'special relationship', but an attempt to express English royal power and prestige in a new way in an international setting and one that deliberately invoked a saint with a cosmopolitan following and reputation. Edward III's foundation of the Order of the Garter was not, then, a celebration of 'Englishness' as such, but a statement of the king's ambition to act as a leader among the rulers of western Europe. Thirdly, that St George, despite increasing evidence of popular remembrance of his supposed dragon-slaying, was essentially a saint that appealed to a royal and aristocratic audience, celebrated specifically as a protector of knights and crusaders.

It is useful to bear Morgan's points in mind when examining evidence for the veneration of St George in late medieval Scotland. It might be expected that the

4 Jonathan Bengtson, 'Saint George and the Formation of English Nationalism', *Journal of Medieval and Early Modern Studies* 27 (1997), 317–40; Henry Summerson, 'George', *ODNB*, XXI.775–92; Anthony Goodman, 'The British Isles Imagined', in *The Fifteenth Century VI: Identity and Insurgency in the Late Middle Ages*, ed. Linda Clark (Woodbridge, 2006), 1–14, at 12–13; *idem*, 'Introduction', in *Richard II. The Art of Kingship*, ed. James L. Gillespie and Anthony Goodman (Oxford, 1999), at 10–12.

5 See, for example, the studies in *St George's Chapel, Windsor, in the Fourteenth Century*, ed. Nigel Saul (Woodbridge, 2005).

6 David A. L. Morgan, 'The Cult of St George c.1500: National and International Connotations', in *L'Angleterre et les pays bourguignons: relations et comparaisons (XVe–XVIe s.)*, ed. Jean-Marie Cauchies, Publication du Centre Europeen d'Etudes Bourguignonnes (XIVe–XVIe s.) 35 (Neuchâtel, 1995), 151–62; *idem*, 'The Banner-bearer of Christ and Our Lady's Knight: How God became an Englishman Revisited', in *St George's Chapel*, ed. Saul, 51–62.

7 For the emergence of George as a protector of those involved in the first Crusade of 1098, see *Anonymi Gesta Francorum et aliorum Hierosolymitanorum*, ed. B. A. Lees (Oxford, 1924), 67 (and notes at 133), 101; Carl Erdmann, *The Origin of the Idea of Crusade*, trans. Marshall W. Baldwin and Walter Goffart (Princeton, 1977), 6, 54–5, 87, 134–5, 273–80.

increased identification of the cult with the English monarchy and the English nation-in-arms would act to limit the appeal of the saint to fourteenth- and fifteenth-century Scots.[8] However, while Scottish devotion to George was certainly not comparable in scale or intensity to that found in late medieval England, particularly in the matter of church and altar dedications, there are plenty of indications that the Scots elites were quite happy to commemorate George as a defender of Christian knighthood and that acknowledgement of the saint's role and power in this regard was more or less unaffected by the attempts to portray him as a peculiarly 'English' saint.[9]

One indication of interest in George in fourteenth-century Scotland was the increasingly widespread adoption of the saint's name. Prior to the middle decades of the fourteenth century George was largely unknown as a personal designation in Scotland.[10] By the end of the century, however, the name could be found in a

8 The assumption that medieval Scots must have developed an antipathy towards George's cult remains pervasive. See Colin Thompson and Lorne Campbell, *Hugo van der Goes and the Trinity Panels in Edinburgh* (Edinburgh, 1974), 12–13 for the argument that the saintly figure depicted on the Trinity panels as an intercessor for James III's queen, Margaret of Denmark, might have been St Canute rather than St George partly because 'It is difficult ... to explain why Margaret of Denmark should be presented by St George, who, as patron of England, was never a popular saint in Scotland.'

9 Although by the mid-sixteenth century some Scots, such as David Lindsay of the Mount, certainly thought of St George's cross as a fundamentally 'English' symbol. In Lindsay's *Squire Meldrum*, the eponymous hero jousts with an English knight, easily identified as such in the tale because he bore 'Sanct Georges Croce ... On Hors, Harnes, and all his geir': *The Works of Sir David Lindsay of the Mount 1490–1555*, ed. Douglas Hamer, Scottish Text Society [hereafter STS], 3rd series 1–2, 6, 8, 4 vols (Edinburgh, 1931–6), I.157, lines 424–5. For observations on the disparity between Scotland and England in terms of church and altar dedications to St George, see James Murray Mackinlay, *Ancient Church Dedications in Scotland: Scriptural Dedications* (Edinburgh, 1910), 463: 'St George's popularity in England was such that over a hundred pre-Reformation churches were built in his honour. Compared with these his Scottish dedications were few indeed.'

10 See Virginia Davis, 'The Popularity of Late Medieval Personal Names as Reflected in English Ordination Lists, 1350–1540', in David Postles and Joel T. Rosenthal (eds), *Studies on the Personal Name in Later Medieval England and Wales* (Kalamazoo, 2006), 103–14, at 106–9, for a discussion of the growing use of the personal name George in fourteenth- and fifteenth-century England. Also Morgan, 'The Cult of St George c.1500', 155 (and n. 22) for the observation that it was around this time that the personal name became used more widely in England and elsewhere in Europe. The earliest adoption of the name in Scotland seems to have occurred in the Abernethy of Saltoun family, with the appearance of a George Abernethy who was old enough in 1346 to take part in the Neville's Cross campaign of 1346: *Rotuli Scotiae in Turri Londinensi et in Domo Capitulari Westmonasteriensi Asservati*, ed. David Macpherson *et al.*, 2 vols (London, 1814–19) [hereafter *Rot. Scot.*], I.678; *Foedera, Conventiones, Litterae et Cujuscunque Generis Acta Publica*, ed. Thomas Rymer, 7 vols (London, 1816–69), V.534; *Calendar of Documents Relating to Scotland*, ed. Joseph Bain, 4 vols (Edinburgh, 1881–8), III.1641; *The Acts of David II: King of Scots 1329–1371*, ed. Bruce Webster, *Regesta Regum Scotorum* 6 (Edinburgh, 1982), no. 417. A second George

number of prominent aristocratic lineages, including the Dunbar earls of March and the Douglas earls of Angus, and in the fifteenth century use of the Christian name became even more prevalent. How far this development indicated active engagement with the saint's cult in any deep way is difficult to say (especially where it was not linked to explicit evidence for other devotional activity in the form of altar or church dedications), since personal names could swiftly become commemorative of ancestors and thereafter be carried into other lineages by intermarriage. Nevertheless, it was clearly a contemporary clerical expectation that the choice of Christian name might initiate a 'real' devotional relationship between an infant and his or her saintly namesake.[11] While the use of a saint's name could be due to the birth of a child on a particular feast day, it could also result from a special devotion on the part of the parents to the saint in question.[12] In this regard, it was surely significant that many of the Scottish lineages in which George appeared early as a Christian name were distinguished by their active participation in Anglo-Scottish or continental warfare, or involvement in tournaments, crusades and pilgrimage. The men who chose the name George for their male offspring usually had direct personal experience of social and military contexts in which the saint was regarded and celebrated as an especially appropriate and effective intercessor. The very ubiquity of St George as a figure of veneration for the chivalry of Europe makes it extremely difficult to isolate the most important or principal routes by which attachment to the cult may have spread into Scotland, but it is possible to highlight some of the many possible and probably overlapping influences that might have persuaded parents to adopt what was initially a rather novel name.

As Morgan has stressed, the George cult was enthusiastically embraced by a variety of kingly or noble families during the fourteenth century, but most notably (and competitively) by the royal houses of France and England.[13] Given the political circumstances of the early decades of the fourteenth century the Scots necessarily found themselves involved in intense and prolonged diplomatic and military interaction with both the English and French dynasties. During the reign of David II (1329–71) the Scottish king and many of his nobility came under the influence of the French and English courts in a very direct way at precisely the time that the

Abernethy who appeared at Robert II's coronation in 1371 may have been his son: *APS*, I.545. See also *RMS*, I.nos 280, 289, 850.

11 John Ireland's late fifteenth-century treatise on penance urged the faithful to 'Mak for the[e] Intercessouris: the saull of Ihesu, The blissit moder of god thyne aduocater and of thyne nature and kyn thi patroun, thi gud angel, The **sanct that thow art named efter** and otheris that thow has devocioun to, …': *The Asloan Manuscript: A Miscellany in Prose and Verse written by John Asloan in the reign of James the Fifth*, ed. W. A. Craigie, STS, 2nd series 14, 16, 2 vols (Edinburgh, 1923–5), I.47. See the case of George Brown, bishop of Dunkeld, noted below for an example of an individual who took the relationship with his name saint very seriously.

12 *Saints and their Cults: Studies in Religious Sociology, Folklore and History*, ed. Stephen Wilson (Cambridge, 1983), 'Introduction', 15.

13 Morgan, 'The Banner-bearer of Christ', 58–9. Indeed, Morgan sees the English victories of the early stages of the Hundred Years' War as allowing Edward III to make 'a successful take-over bid from the defeated Valois for the patronage of St George as the supreme exemplar of chivalry'.

two great monarchies were contesting for the leadership of the chivalry of western Europe. In 1334 the young David was forced to flee his realm in the face of the military successes enjoyed by the English-backed rival to the Scottish throne, Edward Balliol, and Edward III's effective annexation of much of southern Scotland. Between 1334 and 1341 David was harboured by the French crown. The Scottish king's court in exile became a regular port of call for those who remained loyal to David within Scotland, and the French crown emerged as a source of military and financial assistance to those noblemen most active in the ongoing Anglo-Scottish struggle. David returned to his kingdom in 1341, but in 1346, while personally leading a raid into the north of England, he was captured by English forces at the Battle of Neville's Cross and spent the next eleven years in the custody of his brother-in-law Edward III.[14] David's spell in English captivity thus coincided exactly with the period in which Edward III embarked on the foundation of the Order of the Garter and St George's Chapel at Windsor.[15]

There is little doubt that many of the Scots taken captive at Neville's Cross, including David II himself, found the high-octane internationalism of Edward's household and court, the commitment to crusade and the ostentatious chivalric display that was bound up with the English manifestation of the cult of St George, highly attractive.[16] The decade after 1346 saw particularly intense diplomatic and social traffic between the two realms as the captured king communicated with his subjects, and many of the links established between David and Edward during this period appear to have survived beyond the Scottish king's release in 1357.[17] As recent studies have emphasised, David attempted to replicate some aspects of the English king's chivalric lifestyle and persona within his own court and affinity after his liberation. Certainly David surrounded himself with a group of retainers and household knights notable for their participation in crusade or their careers as mercenaries on the European stage.[18] Even after David's death, Scottish noblemen and knights came into frequent contact with the cult of St George at the English court as members of diplomatic missions, as prisoners of war, or, during periods of peace between the two kingdoms, as participants in tournaments sponsored by the English crown.[19] The Edwardian and post-Edwardian celebration of George thus did not necessarily alienate Scots noblemen, but rather had the potential to draw them into what must have appeared as an international movement centred on the values of Christian knighthood and crusade. It thus seems likely that the

14 Michael Penman, *David II* (East Linton, 2004), 52–75, 117–93.

15 W. M. Ormrod, 'For Arthur and St George: Edward III, Windsor Castle and the Order of the Garter', in *St George's Chapel*, ed. Saul, 13–34.

16 See Juliet Vale, *Edward III and Chivalry: Chivalric Society and Its Context 1270–1350* (Woodbridge, 1982) for discussion of Edward III's court.

17 For a compelling discussion of the importance of this cordial Anglo-Scottish interaction in the fourteenth century, see Anthony Goodman, 'Anglo-Scottish Relations in the Later Fourteenth Century: Alienation or Acculturation?', in *England and Scotland in the Fourteenth Century: New Perspectives*, ed. Andy King and Michael A. Penman (Woodbridge, 2007), 236–54.

18 Stephen Boardman, *Robert II and Robert III: The Early Stewart Kings* (East Linton, 1996), ch. 1; Penman, *David II*, chs 7–11.

19 Goodman, 'Anglo-Scottish Relations'.

burgeoning interest in George displayed by English monarchs was an important conduit through which the cult was promoted in Scotland.

There were, however, other contexts in which Scottish noblemen would have enjoyed an active relationship with George as a patron relevant to their lives as men of war. Principal among these would have been crusade. In the fourteenth century small numbers of Scottish noblemen were involved in crusading ventures in Iberia, the eastern Mediterranean and, above all, in the Baltic, where the annual summer and winter campaigns against the Lithuanians organised by the Teutonic Order attracted a number of Scottish knights on a regular basis.[20] Many Scots may have been painfully aware of St George's cross in the context of Anglo-Scottish warfare, but those who participated in the northern crusades would also have had experience of fighting in the name of St George, alongside the Virgin Mary the principal spiritual focus for the knights of the Teutonic Order. Thus, an account of the winter Reyse of 1385 described how the crusaders 'entered enemy territory with banners raised: first that of St George, followed by the pilgrims, then the banner of the Blessed Virgin, also that of the order, with the eagle and cross. ... They laid waste the lands to a distance of six miles, wherever they reached, and practised chivalry in honour of St George.'[21] On at least two occasions attempts by English knights to fly the cross of St George during campaigns in the Baltic were resisted by the Teutonic Order as an infringement of its exclusive right to display George's banner.[22] For the Scottish Baltic crusaders, then, St George could hardly have been regarded as an exclusively, or even predominantly, English saint.[23] The great annual gatherings at Königsberg were a celebration and a confirmation of a wider European brotherhood of arms for all of whom St George acted as an exemplary model of Christian knighthood.[24]

While there was no automatic or invariable link, it is striking that many of the Scottish families in which the name George appeared early were noted for involvement in the northern crusade or other chivalric enterprises, close and active ties

20 Alan Macquarrie, *Scotland and the Crusades: 1095–1560* (Edinburgh, 1985), 84–7. See David Ditchburn, *Scotland and Europe: The Medieval Kingdom and its Contacts with Christendom, 1214–1560* (East Linton, 2001), 65–73, for a more sober assessment of the level of Scottish participation in the northern crusade.

21 *Documents on the Later Crusades, 1274–1580* (Basingstoke, 1996), ed. and trans. Norman Housley, 56 (g). See also 57 (i) and (j), 58 (k), 5, 14. For a general review of the use of George's banner on the northern crusade, see Werner Paravicini, *Die Preussenreisen des Europäischen Adels*, 2 vols (Sigmaringen, 1989–95), II.139–50.

22 Paravicini, *Die Preussenreisen*, II.142–3, 145.

23 Indeed, George was the focus or leading patron for a number of crusading/chivalric orders or confraternities across Europe in the fourteenth and fifteenth centuries besides the Order of the Garter. These included the Hungarian Fraternal Society of Knighthood of St George (founded 1325) and the Iberian 'Enterprise of St George' (founded 1371–9): D'Arcy Jonathan Dacre Boulton, *The Knights of the Crown. The Monarchical Orders of Knighthood in Later Medieval Europe 1325–1520*, 2nd edn (Woodbridge, 2000), chs 2 and 10.

24 See Howard Kaminsky, 'Estate, Nobility and the Exhibition of Estate in the Later Middle Ages', *Speculum* 68 (1993), 684–709, at 706–7, for a discussion of the importance of the annual gatherings at Königsberg as occasions that created new ties, and a measure of cohesion, among the European aristocratic elite.

with the French and English monarchies, careers as mercenaries, or a combination of all of these traits.

A few examples may suffice to illuminate the general trend. One of the first and most powerful Scottish lords to bear the saint's name was George Dunbar, earl of March. George's father, Sir Patrick Dunbar, was a man with an illustrious military pedigree. Dunbar seems to have been one of the men associated with the redoubtable Sir Alexander Ramsay in the conduct of war against English forces in the south of Scotland during the 1330s and early 1340s. Ramsay's so-called 'school of chivalry' was remembered by Scottish chroniclers as the most prestigious proving-ground for the kingdom's young warriors, and membership of the group bestowed high renown.[25] In 1346, some four years after Ramsay's death, Dunbar took part in David II's ill-fated campaign into the north of England and was captured alongside his king at the Battle of Neville's Cross.[26] After his release, Sir Patrick resumed his military career and in 1356 he was one of a small group of Scottish lords involved in the battle of Poitiers, fighting on behalf of the French king John II. Surviving the carnage of the bloody French defeat, Dunbar set off on a 'pilgrimage' to Jerusalem, but died on Crete before he reached the Holy Land.[27]

Dunbar's prominent role in Anglo-Scottish warfare, his involvement with the French host in 1356, and his final attempted act of pilgrimage to Jerusalem all suggest that he would have been a man who might naturally regard St George as a saint relevant to his life as a Christian knight. Moreover, despite Dunbar's service against the armies of the English crown over three decades it was not entirely impossible that he chose his son's name because of exposure to George as the emergent patron saint of the English royal house. In the aftermath of Neville's Cross Dunbar had been imprisoned in the southern kingdom until at least early 1348, and it is tempting to see the name Patrick gave to his son as a reflection of this connection, albeit rather involuntary, to the English crown at a critical stage in the development of the George cult.[28] Overall, however, it seems more likely that George Dunbar was born and baptised before, rather than after, his father's capture in 1346.[29]

25 Andrew of Wyntoun, *The Original Chronicle of Andrew of Wyntoun*, ed. F. J. Amours, STS, 1st series 50, 53–4, 56–7, 63, 6 vols (Edinburgh, 1903–14) [hereafter *Chron. Wyntoun*], VI.146–9. Assuming that the Patrick of Dunbar mentioned by Wyntoun was the individual who fathered George Dunbar. See also *Chron. Bower*, VII.151 where only the family name Dunbar is invoked.

26 Penman, *David II*, 136.

27 *Chron. Fordun*, I.377.

28 Although he seems to have been allowed to return to Scotland for a short period late in 1347 to act as an envoy for King David (*Rot. Scot*, i.678), on 20 November 1347 Edward III issued a safe-conduct allowing William Ramsay and Patrick Dunbar to depart to Scotland on David II's business, a concession repeated on 30 January 1348 (*Rot. Scot*, I.709).

29 George first appears on record on 28 June 1363 as the recipient of lands resigned by his uncle Patrick, earl of March: *RMS*, I.no. 149. At first sight the calendared grant would seem to imply that George had already reached his majority (twenty-one years of age) by 1363, giving him a date of birth well before 1346, but there was little to indicate his emergence as an active adult lord until July 1368 when he received more estates formerly held by Earl Patrick. George was knighted, and became earl of March, soon after receiving these lands on a date between 25 July 1368 and 20 July 1369. The

The other great border family of late fourteenth-century Scotland was headed by the earl of Douglas. Like Patrick Dunbar, William, first earl of Douglas, was noted for his prominent role in Anglo-Scottish warfare, his military service alongside French forces and, after 1346, his contacts with the court of Edward III.[30] In the late 1370s Earl William fathered an illegitimate son in an affair with Margaret Stewart, heiress to the earldom of Angus. The infant was named George and went on to become earl of Angus.[31] Although he died young in 1402–3, George Douglas may have been active already in the northern crusade by the time of his death. Certainly an earl of Angus appeared in a list of debtors to the Teutonic Order covering the years 1396–1417.[32]

Aside from the Dunbars and Douglases, many of the lesser families in which the name George appeared at this time also had an obvious interest in crusade. The list of debtors to the Teutonic Order mentioned above included a number of Scots, such as Walter Haliburton, lord of Dirleton, James Douglas, lord of Dalkeith, Sir John Dalziel, and a 'Jors Apristin', perhaps George Preston of Gorton. George Preston's father, Sir Simon Preston of Gorton, had been a Lothian knight greatly favoured by David II whose active career seems to have spanned much of the second half of the fourteenth century. A charter without a year date, but which may belong to early 1370 or 1382, recorded a transaction involving Simon and other Scottish lords at Königsberg.[33] It is tempting to see Sir Simon's involvement in the Baltic crusade as one of the factors influencing the naming of his son, who succeeded to the lordship of Gorton before 1410.[34] The general popularity of Saint

accession to the comital title and knighthood in 1368–9 might indicate that George 'came of age' in that period, but the variability in age at which men accepted the order of knighthood hardly allows for certainty: *RMS*, I.nos 265, 291, 292, 354; Katie Stevenson, *Chivalry and Knighthood in Scotland, 1424–1513* (Woodbridge, 2006), 17–19.

30 Indeed, the first earl was effectively brought up in France: Michael Brown, *The Black Douglases: War and Lordship in Late Medieval Scotland, 1300–1455* (East Linton, 1998), 43–9, 137–41, 147–50, 210–13.

31 See S. I. Boardman, 'Douglas, George, First Earl of Angus (1378×80?–1403?)', *ODNB*, http://www.oxforddnb.com/view/article/7883 (accessed 9 Nov. 2007).

32 Paravicini, *Die Preussenreisen*, I.135–8, table at 137; Th. A. Fischer, *The Scots in Germany* (Edinburgh, 1902), Appendix, 238–9.

33 NAS GD143 Inventory of Whitehill Papers Box 1/No. 2. See Ditchburn, *Scotland and Europe*, 69, for the argument in favour of 1370. It is interesting to note, however, that three of the witnesses to the charter, Sir John Abernethy, Sir John Edmonston and Sir John Tours, received English safe-conducts allowing them to travel abroad on 4 December 1381. 'Jors Apristin' is included in Fischer's table of Scots debtors, but not Paravicini's.

34 George was not the eldest of Simon's sons, but succeeded to the lordship because of the early death of his elder brother Simon: *RMS*, I.no. 885 (for George as a knight by 20 August 1406); NAS GD78 Hunter of Bargany Muniments, no. 1. See Ditchburn, *Scotland and Europe*, 71, for the continuing interest of the Prestons in crusade during the fifteenth century. One of the men named alongside Preston as a debtor to the Teutonic Order, Walter Haliburton, lord of Dirleton, had a younger brother named George: *RMS*, I.nos 900, 934. Walter and George Haliburton likewise came from distinguished martial stock. Their father, Sir John Haliburton, had enjoyed a long and active military career, participating in Franco-Scottish campaigns against England in 1385 and the Otterburn campaign of 1388: *Chron. Bower*, VII.417, 421; Brown, *Black Douglases*, 83, 168–9.

George for the martial class within Scotland was attested in an off-hand way by the inclusion of an account of his martyrdom in the anonymously authored *Legends of the Saints*, a collection of saints lives (largely derived from James de Voragine's thirteenth-century *Legenda Aurea*) produced in Scotland in English c.1400. The compiler of the collection reported that St George was greatly revered, and that in particular:

> ... men of armys ofte se I
> in til his helpe mykil affy
> and namely quhen thai are in ficht.[35]

It is perhaps unsurprising that the individual who displayed the greatest interest in the cult of St George in Scotland in the years around 1400 was the most celebrated Scottish knight of the age, David Lindsay, lord of Glen Esk (from 1398 earl of Crawford). David was the most prominent and successful member of an extended family thoroughly steeped in the culture of crusade and chivalric endeavour. David's father, Alexander, had died on Crete on pilgrimage to the Holy Land in 1382, while his uncle William Lindsay was said to have knighted the son of St Bridget of Sweden in the Holy Sepulchre in c.1372–3. David's half-uncle, Norman Leslie may well have died in the siege of Alexandria in 1365, while another half-uncle, Walter Leslie earned a fearsome reputation as a crusader and a soldier of fortune on the Continent. David himself won fame jousting with English knights at Richard II's Smithfield tournament in 1390 and later in the decade was one of two Scottish knights (the other being his brother Alexander) invited to join Phillipe de Mezieres' crusading order, the Order of the Passion. In 1402 Lindsay entered into an indenture of military service with Louis duke of Orléans and later in the year was one of the commanders of a Franco-Scottish maritime force at work in the Bay of Biscay. It is little wonder, then, that Scottish chroniclers regarded Lindsay as a 'flower of chivalry'.[36] It was entirely appropriate that nearing the end

35 *Legends of the Saints in the Scottish Dialect of the Fourteenth Century*, ed. W. M. Metcalfe, STS, 1st series, 3 vols, STS (Edinburgh, 1888–96), II.176. It is worth noting in passing that books of hours and calendars of saints produced for patrons in late medieval Scotland continued to feature, and occasionally to emphasise, St George: John Higgitt, ' "Imageis maid with mennis hand": Saints, Images, Belief and Identity in Later Medieval Scotland', 9th Whithorn Lecture (Whithorn, 2003), 11 nn. 53, 55; Alexander Penrose Forbes, *Kalendars of Scottish Saints* (Edinburgh, 1872), 39 [Herdmanston], 56 [Culross], 70 [Fearn], 99 [Arbuthnot], 115 [Aberdeen Breviary]; Cambridge, Magdalene College, Pepys Library, MS 1576, fol. 46v. I should like to thank Dr Helen Brown for this reference.

36 For a summary of the Lindsay family's commitment to crusading activity over several generations, see Steve Boardman 'Kingship in Crisis? The Reign of Robert III, 1390–1406', in *Kingship in Late Medieval Scotland, 1306–1542*, ed. Michael Brown and Roland Tanner (forthcoming); *Chron. Bower*, VII.388–9, 374–5; Claes Gejrot, *Diarium Vadstenense: The Memorial Book of Vadstena Abbey* (Stockholm, 1988), 124; *Rot. Scot.*, II.40; Kenneth Fowler, *Medieval Mercenaries: Volume I – the Great Companies* (Oxford, 2001), 36, 73; *Chron. Wyntoun*, VI.359–62; *Chron. Bower*, VIII.13, 15–19, 155, 156; *The Westminster Chronicle: 1381–1394*, ed. and trans. L. C. Hector and Barbara F. Harvey (Oxford, 1982), 435–7; Boardman, *Early Stewart Kings*, 240–1; Macquarrie, *Scotland and the Crusades*, 88; Neculai Jorga, *Philippe de Mézières, 1327–1405 et la Croisade au XIVe siècle* (Paris, 1896), 491.

of his life David Lindsay, who had spent his years earning a reputation as a paragon of chivalric ambition and achievement, should turn at the last to the saint that embodied the virtues of Christian knighthood. On 10 December 1406 Earl David endowed four chaplains who were required to sing a daily mass for his soul at the 'ninth hour of the day' at St George's altar in the parish kirk (St Mary's) of Dundee.[37] By the early sixteenth century the patronage of St George's altar in Dundee was thought to be related to David Lindsay's 1390 joust with Lord Wells on London Bridge:

> Wellis chesit the Brig of Londoun for the place, and Erle David chesitt Sanct Georgis Daye, because he was sum tyme ane wailzeand knycht. ... sic thingis done, Erle David returnit in Scotland with mony nobillis of Ingland; and because he vyncust Lord Wellis apon Sanct Georgis Day, he founditt sevin preistis to syng for him in Oure Lady Kirk of Dunde in the honour of Sanct George.[38]

The tale is mistaken in detail, since the duel, while close to St George's day, actually took place in early May, but is nevertheless interesting for the way in which David's status as a 'valiant knight' was seen in the sixteenth century automatically to explain his interest in St George. David's attachment to George was evidently shared by his son Alexander, second earl of Crawford, who on St George's Day 1429 (23 April) made a grant to God, St Mary, and St George the Martyr and Leonard the confessor which endowed a fifth chaplain to celebrate at the altar of Saints George and Leonard in Dundee.[39] Alexander had been in English captivity as a hostage for James I between 1424 and November 1427, perhaps inspiring the choice of St Leonard (a saint especially associated with obtaining release from imprisonment) alongside George in the 1429 grant. The Lindsay grants to Dundee parish kirk may have stimulated some local emulation in Angus, with Sir Walter Ogilvy of Carcary, also founding a chaplainry that appears to have been focused on an altar of St George in the cathedral church of Brechin (and naming one of his sons after the saint).[40]

37 *RMS*, I.nos 877–80. Lindsay died shortly after the establishment of the chaplainries, apparently on a date between 12 February and 16 March 1407: *RMS*, II.nos 881,882; *The Exchequer Rolls of Scotland*, ed. J. Stuart *et al.* (Edinburgh, 1878–1908), IV.35. See also *Registrum de Panmure*, ed. John Stuart, 2 vols (Edinburgh, 1874), II.186.

38 Boece, *Chronicles*, II.356. In 1419 one of the chaplainries was described as the chaplainry of St George: *Calendar of Scottish Supplications to Rome, 1418–1422*, ed. E. R. Lindsay and A. I. Cameron, Scottish History Society, 3rd series 23 (Edinburgh, 1934), 64–5. The substance of Bellenden's tale was repeated in *Extracta e Variis Cronicis Scocie*, a sixteenth-century collection of material derived from a variety of Scottish chronicles, with the additional observation that the anonymous author of that section of the *Extracta* had actually witnessed this mass in Dundee: *Extracta e Variis Cronicis Scocie*, Abbotsford Club 23 (Edinburgh, 1842), 203–4.

39 *Registrum Episcopatus Brechinensis*, ed. Cosmo Innes, Bannantyne Club 102, 2 vols (Edinburgh, 1856), II.20–3. Alexander had witnessed his father's foundation of the four chaplainries in 1406.

40 *RMS*, I.no. 941. The grant was confirmed by the duke of Albany in January 1408, an act witnessed by Earl David's son and successor Alexander, earl of Crawford; *The Scots Peerage*, ed. James Balfour Paul, 9 vols (Edinburgh, 1904–14), I.112; Walter also had a

The presence of St George's altar in St Mary's of Dundee, and the impressive Lindsay sung mass associated with it, meant that the saint enjoyed a prominent public role in the liturgical cycle of the parish kirk. Whether this encouraged any wider identification with George on the part of the burgh's inhabitants is impossible to say, although the career of George Brown, bishop of Dunkeld, certainly points to an individual Dundee family with a strong attachment to the saint in the fifteenth century. George was said to have been the son of the treasurer of Dundee (also George), was baptised in St Mary's kirk (perhaps at the altar dedicated to his name-saint?), and later in life founded a chaplainry in the same church for the Virgin and the Three Kings.[41] More strikingly, in the first decade of the sixteenth century the bishop founded a hospital dedicated to St George in Dunkeld and provided his cathedral kirk with three new bells, the 'Columba' [the patron of Dunkeld], the 'Mary' and the 'George'.[42]

George Brown's obvious personal fascination with St George may have been rather idiosyncratic, but it was not the only indication of a quickening (or at least better recorded) interest in the saint within late medieval Scottish burghs. In particular, the powerful allegorical tale of George's triumph over the Dragon became part of the public ceremonial of at least two Scottish towns. By 1490 the story of George's encounter with the Dragon had been incorporated into the Corpus Christi procession of the burgh of Lanark, while by c.1510 responsibility for the 'pageant' of George (either his clash with the Dragon or an account of his martyrdom) in the Corpus Christi parade in Aberdeen was assigned to the Baxters' Guild.[43] George also appealed to individual Aberdonian burgesses in terms of their personal devotion, for in 1491 Thomas Prat founded an altar in the burgh's parish kirk of St Nicholas dedicated to Thomas the Apostle (his name-saint) and George the Martyr.[44] After Thomas Prat's death an enhanced cycle of commemorative masses was established at the altar.[45]

Despite the evidence for George attracting individual devotees amongst the aristocracy and burgesses of late medieval Scotland there were few indications that the

nephew named George who was killed at the battle of Harlaw in 1411: *Chron. Bower*, VIII.74–5. The bishop of Brechin had visitation rights over the kirk of St Mary's in Dundee and had been named in the 1406 grants as the official to ensure that the terms of Lindsay's gift were adhered to. For St Leonard's role in securing the release of prisoners, see John Higgitt, 'From Bede to Rabelais – or how St Ninian got his Chain', in *New Offerings, Ancient Treasures. Studies in Medieval Art for George Henderson*, ed. Paul Binski and William Noel (Stroud, 2001), 187–209, at 194–5.

41 Robert Keith, *Catalogue of the Bishops of the several sees within the Kingdom of Scotland down to the year 1688* (Edinburgh, 1755), 56 for the assertion of George's parentage; *Rentale Dunkeldense: being accounts of the Bishopric A.D. 1505–1517, with Myln's 'Lives of the Bishops' A.D. 1483–1517*, trans. and ed. Robert Kerr Hannay, Scottish History Society, 2nd series 10 (Edinburgh, 1915), 311; *RMS*, III.no. 157.

42 *Rentale Dunkeldense*, ed. Hannay, 3, 12–13, 80, 82, 87, 92, 204, 212, 242, 312, 314–15; *RMS*, II.no. 3482. I am grateful to Dr Eila Williamson for this reference.

43 Anna Jean Mill, *Mediaeval Plays in Scotland* (Edinburgh and London, 1927), 60, 70–1, 124–5, 261–2. Again, thanks are due to Dr Williamson for this reference.

44 *St Nich. Cart.*, I. 33–5, 36, 101–3.

45 *ibid.*, 223–4.

cult was actively promoted and exploited by the Scottish royal dynasty.[46] The first suggestion of a specifically royal interest in George came with the foundation of the collegiate church of the Holy Trinity in Edinburgh, a scheme that may have been initiated by James II (1437–60), but which was certainly brought to fruition after James's death by his widow Mary of Guelders.[47] Holy Trinity displayed a double association with George. At some point before 1510 the collegiate church had been provided with an altar dedicated to the saint.[48] More strikingly, c.1473–8, an ornately decorated altarpiece was commissioned by the provost of the collegiate kirk, Edward Bonkill, perhaps with the support of James III (1460–88) and his queen, Margaret of Denmark. The two surviving panels of the Trinity altarpiece, the work of the distinguished Flemish artist Hugo van der Goes, include a depiction of George as the saintly sponsor of James III's wife Margaret of Denmark.[49] Tolley has suggested that the missing central panel of the Trinity triptych portrayed the Coronation of the Virgin. If correct, this may help to clarify the choice of St George as a presenting saint, for by the fifteenth century George was inextricably linked with Marian devotion, to the extent that he was habitually described as 'Our Lady's Knight'.[50] It could be that George's universally acknowledged 'special relationship' with the Virgin, the putative focus of the

46 James I, while a prisoner in England, was knighted at Windsor on St George's Day 1421 by Henry V. Michael Brown, *James I* (East Linton, 1994), 23. There is little to suggest that James retained an active interest in the saint in the period after his return to Scotland in 1424, although George's feast day does appear to have been one of the dates on which no government business was conducted during James's reign, leaving open the possibility that the anniversary was observed by the king. I am grateful to Nicki Scott, PhD student at Stirling University, for the last observation.

47 The first reference to the foundation of a collegiate church came in a papal Bull of 23 October 1460, which allowed the annexation of Soutra Hospital to support the new establishment: A. Theiner, *Vetera Monumenta Hibernorum et Scotorum historiam illustrantia* (Rome, 1864), 439, 442; *Charters and Documents relating to the Collegiate Church and Hospital of the Holy Trinity and the Trinity Hospital, Edinburgh*, ed. J. D. Marwick, Scottish Burgh Records Society (Edinburgh, 1871), 3–15, 15–29, 29–34, 35–9, 39–43.

48 *Registrum Domus de Soltre, necnon Ecclesie Collegiate S. Trinitatis prope Edinburgh ... Charters of the Hospital of Soltre, of Trinity College, Edinburgh, and other collegiate churches in Mid-Lothian*, [ed. David Laing], Bannatyne Club 109, (Edinburgh, 1861), 165, 166, 213, 214. Exactly when the altar was established is impossible to say.

49 Thompson and Campbell, *Hugo van der Goes*, 12–13. As mentioned above, Thompson and Campbell thought it unlikely that any Scots would commission an image of George because of his English associations and suggested that the figure presenting Margaret might be, despite some obvious iconographic difficulties, St Canute, the patron of Denmark. In a more recent study Tolley argues, surely correctly, that the saint depicted as Margaret's patron is unambiguously St George: Thomas Tolley, 'Hugo van der Goes's Altarpiece for Trinity College Church in Edinburgh and Mary of Guelders, Queen of Scotland', in *Medieval Art and Architecture in the Diocese of St Andrews*, ed. John Higgitt, British Archaeological Association Transactions 14 ([Tring], 1994), 213–31, at 216–17.

50 Tolley, 'Altarpiece', 222–5; Morgan, 'Banner-bearer of Christ', 54–5, 59–60, for the development of the idea of George as Mary's knight. The c.1400 Scottish legend of St George noted of the saint that 'men callis hym oure lady knycht': *Legends of the Saints*, ed. Metcalfe, II.176.

devotional iconography of the altarpiece, is enough to explain his appearance on the Trinity panel, without the need to establish, as Tolley attempts, a particular link between the personal or familial piety of the founder of the collegiate church, Mary of Guelders, and George's cult.[51] That Margaret of Denmark, the individual actually associated with the saint in the Trinity panel, might have had a singular interest in St George is a strangely neglected possibility.[52]

Aside from the Trinity panel there is little to suggest that the Stewart dynasty displayed any notable affection for George, beyond the conventional offerings to be made to an illustrious martyr saint. In 1497 and 1512 Margaret of Denmark's son James IV, a monarch who clearly enjoyed the culture of war and tournament and paid due regard to the vision of a renewed crusade that peppered the diplomatic correspondence of the leaders of western Europe in the years around 1500, arranged for masses to be said on St George's day in honour of the saint.[53] Perhaps a more telling indication of James's affinity with George came in 1503 when, according to Somerset Herald, one of the English officers who accompanied Margaret Tudor to Edinburgh for her marriage to the Scottish king, James attended mass wearing 'a saunt George of Gold, apon the Dragon a Ruby'.[54] On the whole,

51 Tolley, 'Altarpiece', 216, where the devotional interests of Mary's mother, Catherine of Cleves, and her extended family, especially the commissioning of books of hours in which George featured prominently, is discussed; John Plummer, *The Hours of Catherine of Cleves* (London, 1966), plate 132.

52 Margaret's father, Christian I, was reputedly the founder of the Confraternity of the Virgin Mary (otherwise known as the Order of the Elephant): Boulton, *The Knights of the Crown*, 399–402. The adoption of the elephant as the distinctive symbol of this confraternity remains mysterious. In medieval texts the elephant was often represented as a particular enemy of serpents or dragons (creatures symbolic of Satan). George Claridge Druce, 'The Elephant in Medieval Legend and Art, *Archaeological Journal* 76 (1919), 1–73; Boulton, *The Knights of the Crown*, 402. In that light it is intriguing to note that in the thirteenth century James de Voragine composed a number of sermons in which George was represented as an elephant in combat with a dragon: Morgan, 'Banner-bearer', 53 n. 14. James III may have been made a member of the Order of the Elephant by his father or brother-in-law; at his death in 1488 the Scottish treasury certainly contained a 'collare of gold maid with eliphantis, and a gret hinger at it': *TA*, I.81. At some point before 1506 the Scottish/Orcadian nobleman David Sinclair of Sumburgh also received a collar from the Danish monarch. In the testament he had drawn up on 10 July in that year Sinclair asked that the golden collar should be given to St George's altar in Roskilde (perhaps, but not certainly, indicating an altar in the cathedral rather than one of the other churches in the town?): *The Bannatyne Miscellany*, ed. W. Scott, D. Laing and T. Thomson, Bannatyne Club 19, 3 vols (Edinburgh, 1827–55), II.109. There is no indication that the George altar in Roskilde was connected to the chapel of the Order of the Elephant founded by Christian I. The order's chapel was dedicated to the Holy Trinity, the Virgin Mary, Saint Anne, the Three Magi and All Saints. The murals decorating the chapel did include an image of St George, although not in a particularly prominent or 'privileged' position. I am grateful to Dr Janus Møller Jensen for this information.

53 *TA*, I.330; IV.187, the latter an offering on St George's day to his light (presumably before an image of the saint) at Linlithgow. The offerings to George are not particularly numerous or regular in comparison to James's patronage of other saints.

54 John Young, Somerset Herald, 'The Fyancells of Margaret, Eldest Daughter of King

however, James seems to have been much more enthusiastic about the cult of St Michael the Archangel, another intercessor with a martial profile who in many ways appealed to the same aristocratic and knightly audience that found George attractive.[55]

Overall, then, and despite the development of a mutual political antipathy between the two realms in the centuries after 1300, it would seem that England's warrior-saint remained a figure widely, if rather sporadically, venerated in late medieval Scotland. George's status as a universal saint revered by the martial classes across Europe meant that his cult retained its relevance for certain groups within the northern kingdom, regardless of English attempts to annexe and monopolise his prestige and iconography for their own royal house.

Henry VIIth to James King of Scotland', in *Joannis Leland Antiquarii de Rebus Britannicis Collectanea*, ed. Thomas Hearne (London, 1770), 296–7.

55 Higgitt, 'Imageis', 5, 11; Norman Macdougall, *James IV* (Edinburgh, 1989), 235–8 (the construction of his warship the 'Great Michael'); Boulton, *The Knights of the Crown*, 427–47 for the French foundation of the Order of St Michael the Archangel in 1469. James III received a collar of St Michael at some point before his death: *TA*, I.81. Given James IV's known interest in the cult of St Michael, a saint often portrayed, like George, in combat with a dragon, it is tempting to speculate that Somerset Herald may have mistaken the identity of the figure celebrated on James IV's badge in 1503.

9

THE CULT OF THE THREE KINGS OF COLOGNE IN SCOTLAND

Eila Williamson

In Cullen Bay, Banffshire, in the north-east of Scotland there can be seen the rocks known as the Three Kings of Cullen. In an article in 1897, W. Cramond related an older belief that these rocks commemorated a conflict or burial place of three kings from Scotland, Denmark and Norway respectively – a legend of such a conflict had also been mentioned in the *New Statistical Account* of the parish in the middle of the same century.[1] Nevertheless, both Cramond and Francis Groome, editor of the *Ordnance Gazetteer of Scotland*, recognised that the rocks were likely to have been named after the Magi or Three Kings of Cologne. Cramond believed that the confusion doubtless occurred owing to 'the similarity of the word Cullen or Culane to that of Cologne, written "Culane" in the mystery plays …',[2] as can be seen in examples from fifteenth- and sixteenth-century Scottish records, such as an entry for Epiphany 1512 in the Treasurer's Accounts: 'offerit to the three Kingis of Culane iij Franch crounis'.[3]

This chapter aims to examine the ways in which medieval and early modern Scots commemorated and expressed devotion to the Three Kings of Cologne – the Magi who visited the infant Christ to present their gifts of gold, frankincense and myrrh. The evidence is diverse, ranging from inscriptions on jewellery to altar

1 W. Cramond, 'Notes on Tumuli in Cullen District; and Notice of the Discovery of Two Urns at Foulford, near Cullen', *PSAS* 31 (1896–7), 216–23, at 217; Rev. George Henderson, 'Parish of Cullen', in *The New Statistical Account of Scotland by the ministers of the respective parishes, under the superintendence of a committee of the Society for the Benefit of the Sons and Daughters of the Clergy*, 15 vols (Edinburgh and London, 1845), XIII.313–55, at 316. Online version is available at http: // www.edina.ac.uk/ stat-acc-scot/

2 *Ordnance Gazetteer of Scotland: A Survey of Scottish Topography, Statistical, Biographical and Historical*, ed. Francis H. Groome, 6 vols (Edinburgh, 1882–5), II.317. An online version of the entry for Cullen is available at http:// www.geo.ed.ac.uk/ scotgaz/towns/townhistory208.html (accessed 27 March 2007); Cramond, 'Notes on Tumuli', 217.

3 *TA*, IV.181.

dedications, and from literature to historical records of pageantry. Since the cult of the Three Kings is a universal saint's cult, it will be pertinent to examine not only the local and national context of the evidence but also how it compares with evidence of the cult outwith Scotland.[4]

According to legend the relics of the Magi had been acquired in Persia by St Helena, who had transported them to Constantinople. From there they had been translated to the church of St Eustorgius in Milan in the fourth century. They were 'rediscovered' during the siege of Milan by the emperor Frederick Barbarossa and then translated to the cathedral of St Peter in Cologne in 1164 by Rainald von Dassel, archbishop of Cologne.[5] A magnificent shrine was made for them between 1190 and 1220 by craftsmen from the workshop of Nicholas of Verdun and other German workshops.[6] It was to this shrine that pilgrims came to offer their devotion, at times stopping there en route to the shrines of SS Peter and Paul at Rome or of St James the Greater at Santiago de Compostela. Cologne was an important pilgrimage site, being defined, along with Canterbury, Santiago and Rome, as one of the four major pilgrimages by the Inquisition of Languedoc in the mid-thirteenth century.[7]

In the middle ages pilgrims to Cologne included kings Edward II and Edward III of England in 1322 and 1338 respectively, Aeneas Sylvius Piccolomini (later to become Pope Pius II) in 1447, and King Christian I of Denmark in 1475.[8] Many of the pilgrims are likely to have returned home with pilgrim badges, which have been found at various locations in Europe and Scandinavia. A thirteenth-century rectangular badge that depicts the Three Kings making their offerings to the Virgin and Child is exhibited in the Nationalmuseet in Copenhagen.[9] Other examples

4 The seminal work on the cult is Hans Hofmann, *Die Heiligen Drei Könige. Zur Heiligenverehrung im kirchlichen gesellschaftlichen und politisehen Lebendas Mittelalters* (Bonn, 1975). For a short overview, see Geoffrey Grigson, 'The Three Kings of Cologne', *History Today* 41 (December 1991), 28–34. See also Richard C. Trexler, *The Journey of the Magi: Meanings in History of a Christian Story* (Princeton, 1997).

5 Sylvia C. Harris, 'The *Historia Trium Regum* and the Mediaeval Legend of the Magi in Germany', *Medium Aevum* 28 (1959), 23–30, at 23–4; Grigson, 'The Three Kings of Cologne', 31. See also *The Three Kings of Cologne: An Early English Translation of the 'Historia Trium Regum' by John of Hildesheim*, ed. C. Horstmann, Early English Text Society 85 (London, 1886), xvii–xxi.

6 The shrine can be seen on the website of Cologne Cathedral at http://www.koelner-dom.de See also Benoît Van den Bossche, 'The Iconography of the Rheno-Mosan Châsses of the Thirteenth Century', in *Art and Architecture of Late Medieval Pilgrimage in Northern Europe and the British Isles*, ed. Sarah Blick and Rita Tekippe, 2 vols (Leiden and Boston, 2005), I.649–67, at 651–3; II.Fig. 308a.

7 Jonathan Sumption, *Pilgrimage* (London, 1975), 104; Diana Webb, *Pilgrims and Pilgrimage in the Medieval West* (London and New York, 1999), 51.

8 Hofmann, *Die Heiligen Drei Könige*, 134–5. The Welshman, Adam of Usk travelled through Cologne in 1402 while en route to Rome, but does not mention visiting the shrine: David Ditchburn, *Scotland and Europe. The Medieval Kingdom and its Contacts with Christendom, 1214–1560* (East Linton, 2001), 22; *The Chronicle of Adam Usk 1377–1421*, ed. and trans. C. Given-Wilson (Oxford, 1997), 152–3.

9 Copenhagen, Nationalmuseet, 'Pilgrim's badge of lead. Brought from Cologne. 13th century. Near Sct. Kathrine Monastery in Ribe', D7744.

include a fifteenth-century pilgrim badge from Cologne (depicting the busts of the Kings) found on the Thames foreshore in London.[10]

Although no Cologne pilgrim badge has been found in Scotland, it is quite likely that Scots visited the shrine itself in a city that had trade links with Scotland prior to 1350.[11] Examples of Scots who would have had the opportunity to do so include the Franciscan philosopher John Duns Scotus, who moved to Cologne to teach in 1307 and died there the following year.[12] From 1419 there is evidence of Scottish students at the university of Cologne, which had been founded in 1388.[13] In the fifteenth century it was a popular destination for Scottish scholars, with an average of between five and six matriculants annually in the period 1428–1500.[14] One of these scholars was Robert Stoddart who matriculated in 1454, became a master in 1457 and dean in 1462, 1472, 1481 and 1485. He was also a canon of the church of St Mariengraden, in close proximity to the cathedral.[15] Archibald Whitelaw, secretary to James III and tutor to James IV, had taught at Cologne, and Bishop Elphinstone visited the city as a diplomat in 1492 and 1495.[16] Aside from clerical figures, two Scots from Irvine served in Cologne's city guard in 1391.[17]

In Scotland knowledge of the cult and the relics could be gained from written material. In John of Fordun's chronicle there is a passage regarding the kings (named as Jasper, Melchior and Balthasar) coming to worship Christ and returning home by a different route to avoid Herod.[18] This passage was used by Bower in his *Scotichronichon*.[19] Bower also records an account of the translation of the relics to Cologne. Referring to 1162:

> Also in that same year, having destroyed the city of Milan, Rainald archbishop of Cologne translated the bodies of the three holy magi to Cologne. They had formerly been translated to Constantinople by the [eastern] emperor, and been miraculously conveyed [to Milan] by St Eustorgius the Milanese [bishop].[20]

10 For this badge and others found in London, see Brian Spencer, *Pilgrim Souvenirs and Secular Badges* (London, 1998), 261–6; *Gothic Art for England 1400–1547*, ed. Richard Marks and Paul Williamson (London, 2003), 434 no. 324j. For an illustration see *ibid.*, 426.

11 *Atlas of Scottish History to 1707*, ed. Peter G. B. McNeill and Hector L. MacQueen (Edinburgh, 1996), 264.

12 Gordon Leff, 'Duns Scotus, John (c.1265–1308)', *ODNB*, http://www.oxforddnb.com/view/article/8285 (accessed 9 Nov. 2006).

13 R. J. Lyall, 'Scottish Students and Masters at the Universities of Cologne and Louvain in the Fifteenth Century', *IR* 36 (1985), 55–73. See also, Ditchburn, *Scotland and Europe*, 39, 233–9.

14 Ditchburn, *Scotland and Europe*, 255.

15 Lyall, 'Scottish Students and Masters', 63–4; Ditchburn, *Scotland and Europe*, 239.

16 Lyall, 'Scottish Students and Masters', 60–1; Norman Macdougall, 'Whitelaw, Archibald (1415/16–1498)', *ODNB*, http://www.oxforddnb.com/view/article/8285 (accessed 26 Nov. 2007); Ditchburn, *Scotland and Europe*, 129; Leslie J. Macfarlane, *William Elphinstone and the Kingdom of Scotland 1431–1514: The Struggle for Order* (Aberdeen, 1995), 308.

17 Ditchburn, *Scotland and Europe*, 223.

18 *Chron. Fordun*, I.54.

19 *Chron. Bower*, I.222–3.

20 *ibid.*, IV.266–9 (Latin text and English translation).

According to Bower's most recent editors the source of the second sentence has not been traced, but there is some similarity with the account given in Jacobus de Voragine's *Golden Legend*, a work that was not unfamiliar to medieval Scots. The *Golden Legend* contains a chapter on the feast of the Epiphany of the Lord that recounts the story of the Magi and their shrine in Cologne.[21] It states that:

> The bodies of the Magi used to be at Milan, in the church of the Friars Preachers, but are now in Cologne. Helena, the mother of Constantine, first brought them to Constantinople, and later they were transferred to Milan by Saint Eustorgius, the bishop of that city. After the emperor Henry took possession of Milan, he moved the bodies to Cologne on the Rhine river, and there they are honored by the people with great veneration and devotion.[22]

There was probably a manuscript copy of the *Golden Legend* in the cathedral library of Elgin or Aberdeen before 1400 and it also appears in the 1432 inventory of Glasgow Cathedral.[23] Furthermore, there are several examples of ownership by Scottish clerics in the fifteenth and sixteenth centuries.[24]

Another important source to consider is that of the *Historia Trium Regum* of John of Hildesheim, a Carmelite friar who died in 1375. It contains *inter alia* an account of the Three Kings' lives, including their visits to Herod and to Christ, their baptism by St Thomas the Apostle, their deaths, burial and subsequent translations of their bodies.[25] The *Historia Trium Regum* was a popular Latin text, existing in over one hundred manuscripts as well as a number of printed versions. In the National Library of Scotland there is a printed copy of the 1478 Cologne edition, which is bound up with other texts including some notes by Archibald Whitelaw.[26] The combination of an edition of the *Historia Trium Regum* and notes by Whitelaw, who had taught at the university of Cologne may support a thesis that Scots returning from Cologne brought home knowledge of the legend of the Kings and their cult. Unfortunately, however, no direct correlation can be made between the edition and Whitelaw as the various texts 'were not necessarily brought together before the sixteenth century'.[27]

21 Jacobus de Voragine, *The Golden Legend. Readings on the Saints*, trans. William Granger Ryan, 2 vols (Princeton, 1993), I.78–84 (ch. 14).

22 *ibid.*, I.84.

23 Ditchburn, *Scotland and Europe*, 123; *Registrum Episcopatus Glasguensis: Munimenta Ecclesie Metropolitane Glasguensis, a sede restaurata seculo ineunte XII, ad reformatam religionem*, ed. Cosmo Innes, Maitland and Bannatyne Clubs, 2 vols (Edinburgh, 1843), II.334, 335.

24 John Durkan and Anthony Ross, *Early Scottish Libraries* (Glasgow, 1961), 63, 67, 70, 71, 84, 96, 105, 126, 135, 138, 139, 147, 158, 162.

25 *Historia Trium Regum* is the standard title for this work, although a variety of titles are used in the manuscript and print versions: *The Three Kings of Cologne*, ed. Horstmann, ix n.1. Attribution of the work to John of Hildesheim has been disputed, however. For discussion of this, see *The Three Kings of Cologne edited from London, Lambeth Palace MS 491*, ed. Frank Schaer, Middle English Texts 31 (Heidelberg, 2000), 17.

26 NLS, Adv. MS 18.4.8; R. J. Lyall, 'Books and Book Owners in Fifteenth-Century Scotland', in *Book Production and Publishing in Britain 1375–1475*, ed. Jeremy Griffiths and Derek Pearsall (Cambridge, 1989), 239–56, at 248.

27 Lyall, 'Books and Book Owners', 248.

The *Historia Trium Regum* was translated into several languages and two English prose translations of the legend have been identified. One of these (composed c.1400) exists in twenty-one manuscripts and in at least four editions printed by Wynkyn de Worde in ?1496, after July 1499, 1511 and 1526.[28] In addition to the two English prose translations, however, there is a verse translation, contained in the mid-fifteenth-century London Thornton manuscript (BL Additional MS 31042). It developed independently from the prose translations as it contains material from the Latin original, which is missing from them.[29] Discussing the language of the verse translation, MacCracken in the introduction to his 1912 edition suggested that the poem may have come from Scotland.[30]

Hildesheim's version of the legend of the Three Kings describes their meeting at the junction of three roads. This description was used in pictorial representations such as Hans Memling's 'Joys of the Virgin', an altarpiece that was completed in 1480 for the Tanners' or Saddlers' Guild chapel (also the Lady chapel) in the Church of Our Lady in Bruges.[31] This church served as the meeting place of the confraternity of Our Lady of the Snow to which several Scots belonged.[32] Therefore it is likely that Scots would have been acquainted with this image, which, according to Vida Hull, 'would have been fully visible from the ambulatory outside the Lady Chapel ...'[33] Hull further comments that the 'decorative harnesses and saddles that adorn the Magi's mounts in the foreground might serve a further purpose of advertising the guild's products'.[34]

28 *The Three Kings of Cologne*, ed. Schaer, 17–18, 26–7; Julia Boffey, ' "Many grete myraclys ... in divers contreys of the eest." The Reading and Circulation of the Middle English Prose *Three Kings of Cologne*', in *Medieval Women: Texts and Contexts in Late Medieval Britain: Essays for Felicity Riddy*, ed. J. Wogan-Browne *et al.* (Turnhout, 2000), 35–47, at 40. The second English prose translation can be dated to c.1425. For an edition of this text, see *The Three Kings of Cologne*, ed. Schaer.

29 *The Three Kings of Cologne*, ed. Schaer, 27 n. 41.

30 H. N. MacCracken, 'Lydgatiana III: The Three Kings of Cologne', *Archiv für das Studium der neueren Sprachen und Literaturen* 129 (1912), 50–68, at 50–1. Frank Schaer, who has recently edited one of the prose versions, accepts this possibility: *The Three Kings of Cologne*, ed. Schaer, 28. I should like to thank Dr Janet Hadley Williams for discussing this with me.

31 Vida J. Hull, 'Spiritual Pilgrimage in the Paintings of Hans Memling', in *Art and Architecture of Late Medieval Pilgrimage*, ed. Blick and Tekippe, I.29–50, at 34. The scene depicting the meeting of the Three Kings is in the upper left of the altarpiece. A similar scene can be seen on fol. 51v of the *Tres Riches Heures du Duc de Berry*: *ibid.*, 40 n. 35.

32 Alexander Stevenson, 'Medieval Scottish Associations with Bruges', in *Freedom and Authority: Scotland c.1050–c.1650. Historical and Historiographical Essays Presented to Grant G. Simpson*, ed. Terry Brotherstone and David Ditchburn (East Linton, 2000), 93–107, at 106. For the confraternity, see also Andrew Brown, 'Bruges and the Burgundian "Theatre-state": Charles the Bold and Our Lady of the Snow', *History* 84 (1999), 573–89, esp. 580–7. Brown states that it 'is not clear when the guild was founded: there was certainly an altar in the church dedicated to Our Lady of the Snow by 1450': *ibid.*, 581. There were two Scottish altars, dedicated to St Ninian and St Andrew respectively, in St Gilliskerk in Bruges: Stevenson, 'Medieval Scottish Associations with Bruges', 98. Memling died in 1494 and was buried in this church as a plaque on the exterior wall of the church still testifies.

33 Hull, 'Spiritual Pilgrimage', 35.

34 *ibid.*, 35.

Urban drama involving guilds was also a means by which a guild could advertise its products as well as demonstrate its integration into salvific history. In medieval urban plays throughout Europe it was often the goldsmiths' or the tailors' guilds that were responsible for pageants featuring the Three Kings of Cologne, presumably because these guilds would be able to supply the requisite precious gifts and regal clothing. For example, in the Corpus Christi procession of Dublin in 1498 the goldsmiths had to provide the pageant of the Three Kings, while in Hereford at Corpus Christi in 1503 the tailors supplied the Three Kings.[35] In Aberdeen it was the smiths and hammermen who were responsible for providing the Three Kings of Cologne at Candlemas in 1442. By 1506 it was the Aberdeen smiths and goldsmiths.[36] A 1507 record from Lanark refers to the purchase of 'gold fuilyie [gold-leaf] and parchment' for the Three Kings of Cologne.[37] It is not clear what time of year it refers to. Other evidence shows that there were Corpus Christi processions there, though.

In addition to these urban events can be mentioned the visit of Margaret Tudor to Aberdeen in 1511. The poet Dunbar recorded the occasion, mentioning the subjects of the pageantry. In stanzas three and four (lines 17–28) he writes:

> Ane fair processioun mett hir at the port,
> In a cap of gold and silk full pleasantlie,
> Syne at hir entrie with many fair disport
> Ressaueit hir on streittis lustilie;
> Quhair first the salutatioun honorabilly
> Of the sweitt Virgin guidlie mycht be seine,
> The sound of menstrallis blawing to the sky:
> Be blyth and blisfull, burgh of Aberdein.
>
> And syne thow gart the orient kingis thrie
> Offer to Chryst with benyng reuerence
> Gold, sence and mir with all humilitie,
> Schawand him king with most magnificence ...[38]

35 Alan J. Fletcher, *Drama and the Performing Arts in Pre-Cromwellian Ireland: Sources and Documents from the earliest times until c.1642* (Cambridge, 2001), 229; Alan J. Fletcher, 'The Civic Pageantry of Corpus Christi in Fifteenth- and Sixteenth-Century Dublin', *Irish Economic and Social History* 23 (1996), 73–96; *Records of Early English Drama: Herefordshire. Worcestershire*, ed. David N. Klausner (Toronto, 1990), 115–16, at 116. Among other examples is Newcastle where the goldsmiths, plumbers, glaziers, pewterers and painters were responsible for the Three Kings: *Records of Early English Drama: Newcastle upon Tyne*, ed. J. J. Anderson (Toronto, 1982), xii, xiii, 20–1, 132. In Freiburg im Breisgau in 1516 and Zerbst in 1507 it was the tailors who were entrusted with organising pageants of the Magi: *The Medieval European Stage, 500–1550*, ed. William Tydeman (Cambridge, 2001), 389, 391–2.

36 Anna Jean Mill, *Mediaeval Plays in Scotland* (Edinburgh and London, 1927), 116, 119–20.

37 *ibid.*, 262.

38 For the full text of the poem and a commentary, see *The Poems of William Dunbar*, ed. Priscilla Bawcutt, The Association for Scottish Literary Studies 27–8, 2 vols (Glasgow, 1998), I.64–6; II.304–6. The poem is also discussed in Priscilla J. Bawcutt, *Dunbar the Makar* (Oxford, 1992), 89–92.

Three Kings featured also in the pageantry for the royal visits of Edward II to Paris in 1313 and Prince Edward to Coventry in 1474.[39]

The records of urban drama in Scotland involving the Three Kings show no evidence of representing the meeting of the Kings at the intersection of three routes or of Caspar being dark-skinned as described by John of Hildesheim.[40] Nor is there evidence of the Kings appearing in the guise of lords of misrule in Scotland, such as King Balthasar at an Oxford college in 1432.[41] The drama may seem fairly low key in comparison to elsewhere in Europe. For instance, at the festival of St John the Baptist in Florence in 1454 the retinue of the Kings included two hundred horses while a fifteenth-century Passion play text from Revello has stage directions for the Magi departing by ship.[42] Nevertheless, it is unclear whether the drama in Aberdeen and Lanark took the form of *tableaux vivants* or more fully developed plays. In a royal context Epiphany celebrations took place at the Scottish royal court, as evidenced by the purchase of cloth for dancing costumes in 1494 and the play coats that are mentioned in 1540, for example, but these do not appear to match more extensive celebrations in other royal courts such as the pageant of 'The Dangerous Fortress' enjoyed by Henry VIII's court in 1512.[43] Furthermore, there is no Scottish equivalent to the Welsh play text *Y tri brenin o Gwlen* ('The three kings of Cologne'), which, according to Lynette Muir, is 'the only Celtic play on the childhood of Christ'.[44] The earliest manuscript of this text is dated c.1552 but the play may date to the end of the fifteenth century.[45]

Guild commemoration of the Three Kings of Cologne in Scotland is limited to urban drama. In contrast, in the Nationalmuseet in Copenhagen are displayed three fifteenth-century drinking horns, two of which are inscribed on their rim mounts with the names of the Three Kings.[46] The third has on its rim mount the inscription

39 *Medieval European Stage*, ed. Tydeman, 200–1; *Records of Early English Drama: Coventry*, ed. R. W. Ingram (Toronto, 1981), 53–5, at 54. St George was also a character in the pageantry for the Coventry royal visit as well as in the 1498 Dublin pageants and in the Corpus Christi procession at Lanark. See Boardman, 'Cult of St George', above.

40 Grigson, 'The Three Kings of Cologne', 32; *The Three Kings of Cologne*, ed. Schaer, 21. See also Trexler's discussion of the black magus: Trexler, *Journey of the Magi*, 102–7.

41 Sandra Billington, *Mock Kings in Medieval Society and Renaissance Drama* (Oxford, 1991), 32. Billington also mentions the misrule figure of Prester John at Canterbury College between 1414 and 1430. See also *Records of Early English Drama: Oxford*, ed. John R. Elliott Jr and Alan H. Nelson / Alexandra F. Johnston and Diana Wyatt, 2 vols (Toronto, 2004), II.797–8.

42 *Medieval European Stage*, ed. Tydeman, 460, 435. For the splendid Florence pageantry, see Rab Hatfield, 'The Compagnia de' Magi', *Journal of the Warburg and Courtauld Institutes* 33 (1970), 107–61, at 108–19. The Magi departing by ship are described in *The Golden Legend*: de Voragine, *The Golden Legend*, ed. Ryan, I.57. For a succinct discussion of the Magi in drama in medieval Europe, see Lynette R. Muir, *The Biblical Drama of Medieval Europe* (Cambridge, 1995), 104–8.

43 *TA*, I.232–3; VII.276–7; Ronald Hutton, *The Stations of the Sun. A History of the Ritual Year in Britain* (Oxford, 1996; repr. 2001), 16.

44 Muir, *Biblical Drama of Medieval Europe*, 228 n. 32.

45 *Records of Early Drama: Wales*, ed. David N. Klausner (Toronto, 2005), lxv. I am grateful to Professor John J. McGavin for providing this reference and for discussing the drama evidence with me.

46 Copenhagen, Nationalmuseet, drinking horns with gilded bronze mounts, 10543, 382.

iaspar fert miram tus melchior ('Jaspar bears myrrh, Melchior incense').[47] They would have been used in the ceremonial drinking rituals of guilds and societies. In Bergen and Arendal there are also horns that bear the names of the Three Kings.[48] The most notable northern European example does not originate with a guild, however, but is the ornamental horn (now known as the Oldenburg horn), which is likely to have been presented by Christian I to the shrine of the Three Kings at Cologne at Epiphany 1475.[49]

The names of the Three Kings were used as charms against epilepsy, headache, fevers, the dangers of travel, sudden death and sorcery.[50] Examples of medieval finger-rings exist that are inscribed with the names of the Magi. For example, a gold finger-ring with the inscription 'Jaspar . Melchior . Baltazar' was found in excavations on the Castle Hill of Edinburgh while a late fifteenth-century Irish ring bears a similar inscription.[51] One notable English example is that of the Coventry ring, dated to the late fifteenth century. It depicts the risen Christ with the instruments of the Passion and his five wounds. On its inside it has the inscription *Caspar Melchior Baltazar ananyzapta tetragrammaton*.[52] *Tetragrammaton*, the Greek word for 'four letters', is a word used to represent the unwritable name of God while *ananyzapta* is 'a magical word that was used as a charm against epilepsy or the falling sickness'.[53]

There are also inscriptions with the names of the Magi on English, Irish, and Scottish brooches. A solid brooch of c.1360, found in London, contains the inscription CASPER MELCHIOR B[A]PTIS[AR] on its border.[54] A fourteenth–fifteenth century ring-brooch found at Trim in County Meath contains the inscription 'ihc nri' (an abbreviated version of the *titulus*) on its front and IACPAR : MELCHAR : BALTICAR on its reverse.[55] There are a number of Scottish silver brooches that are inscribed with the formula 'Jesus of Nazareth, king of the Jews'

47 Copenhagen, Nationalmuseet, drinking horn with gilded bronze mount, MDLXXIV.

48 George F. Black, 'Scottish Charms and Amulets', *PSAS* 27 (1892–3), 433–526, at 485–6 note.

49 *ibid.*, 485 note. The Oldenburg horn is on display in the Treasury of the Rosenborg Palace in Copenhagen.

50 Mary B. Deery, *Medieval Ring Brooches in Ireland: A Study of Jewellery, Dress and Society* (Bray, Co. Wicklow, 1998), 72.

51 Black, 'Scottish Charms and Amulets', 486; Ellen Ettlinger, 'British Amulets in London Museums', *Folklore* 50 (1939), 148–75, at 167.

52 *Gothic Art for England 1400–1547*, ed. Richard Marks and Paul Williamson (London, 2003), 333 no. 211; *The Image of Christ. The Catalogue of the exhibition SEEING SALVATION*, ed. Gabriele Finaldi (London, 2000), 162–3. From at least 1323 until Elizabeth I's reign English monarchs distributed 'cramp rings' on Good Friday and, according to a fifteenth-century medical treatise, the insides of these were to be marked with the names of the Three Kings: Olga Pujmanová, 'Portraits of Kings depicted as Magi in Bohemian Painting', in *The Regal Image of Richard II and the Wilton Diptych*, ed. Dillian Gordon, Lisa Monnas and Caroline Elam (London, 1997), 247–66, at 265, 348 n. 63; Hutton, *Stations of the Sun*, 188.

53 *Gothic Art for England*, ed. Marks and Williamson, 233 no. 98.

54 Spencer, *Pilgrim Souvenirs and Secular Badges*, 265–6; 264 no. 260. Spencer considers that this brooch is likely to be of English origin and to have been made as an amulet rather than as a pilgrim souvenir.

55 Deery, *Medieval Ring Brooches in Ireland*, 109–10.

or some variation of this.[56] There are a few, though, that combine reference to Christ and His Passion with the names of the Magi. The Glenlyon brooch has the inscription IASPAR . MELCHIOR . BALTAZAR . CONSVMATVM . on its reverse side.[57] The Islay gold ring brooch has been dated to the mid-thirteenth century. On one side it has IESVS n(?) NAZARENSVS RX and on the other IASPER X MELD(?)HITR : ATROP.[58] It is noticeable that only two of the Kings' names are given. The third name Atropa is that of the eldest of the Three Fates.

The Kames gold ring-brooch also dates from the mid-thirteenth century and is thought to be from the same workshop as the Islay ring brooch. On its back on the ring is the talismanic inscription IhESVS : NAZARENVS : CRUCIFIIXVS : REX / IVDEORM : IASPER : MEL : PChIOR : (Lombardic) A, while the back of the pin has ATROPA engraved on it. Virginia Glenn claims that the inspiration for the front of the brooch – the dragons – may have been manuscript illumination and cites English and French examples. She also states that the combination of the two Kings' names with that of Atropa 'is most unusual and thought to be peculiar to this brooch and E20 [the Islay brooch], probably indicating a common origin for both in Bute or southern Argyll'.[59]

Nevertheless, from the *Liber de Diversis Medicinis* copied into the Lincoln Cathedral Thornton manuscript comes this recipe:

> Take the blode of the litill fynger of hym that is seke and wryte thir thre names in his forhed of the iij kynges of Colayn, that is to say: Jasper fert aurum, thus Melchior, Attro pamirram. he that beris thir names of thir iij kyngis with hym, he sall be lesid thurgh the petee of God of the falland evyll. Or write tham with the sam blode & hynge tham abowt his nek in a writ.[60]

Julia Boffey notes that Robert Thornton, a Yorkshireman, who included this recipe in the Lincoln Cathedral manuscript (MS 91), also compiled another manuscript collection (BL Additional MS 31042) that contains the sole witness of the verse edition of the *Historia Trium Regum*.[61] From a Scottish point of view what is

56 Virginia Glenn, *Romanesque & Gothic Decorative Metalwork and Ivory Carvings in the Museum of Scotland* (Edinburgh, 2003), 56 (E1), 57 (E3) (E4), 58 (E6), 59 (E7), 60 (E9), 61 (E11), 63 (E14), 66 (E19), 70 (E25), 72 (E28), 75 (E31) (E32), 76 (E33), 77 (E35), 78 (E37); J. Graham Callander, 'Fourteenth-century Brooches and other Ornaments in the National Museum of Antiquities of Scotland', *PSAS* 58 (1923–4), 160–84, at 169–72.

57 'Consumatum' represents the last words of Christ on the cross. For the brooch, see D. H. Caldwell, *Angels, Nobles and Unicorns. Art and Patronage in Medieval Scotland* (Edinburgh, 1982), 90 (E71); Graham Callander, 'Fourteenth-century Brooches', 183–4; Black, 'Scottish Charms and Amulets', 487; Ettlinger, 'British Amulets in London Museums', 168.

58 Glenn, *Romanesque & Gothic*, 66 (E20); Caldwell, *Angels, Nobles and Unicorns*, 41 (C40); Graham Callander, 'Fourteenth-century Brooches', 170.

59 Glenn, *Romanesque & Gothic*, 67–8 (E21). See also Caldwell, *Angels, Nobles and Unicorns*, 38–9 (C32); R. B. K. Stevenson, 'The Kames Brooch', *PSAS* 95 (1961–2), 308–9; Graham Callander, 'Fourteenth-century Brooches', 170.

60 Quoted in Boffey, 'Reading and Circulation of the Middle English Prose *Three Kings of Cologne*', 39.

61 *ibid.*, 39.

interesting too is that the recipe contains the Jasper, Melchior and Atropa combination. One can't help wondering whether the compiler of the recipe was familiar with some talisman with these words on it, mistaking Atropa as the name of one of the kings. It is significant, though, that in this combination it is the king who brought myrrh – the gift that can represent mortality – who is replaced by Atropa – the Fate who cut the thread of life.[62]

Charms containing the names of the Three Kings can be found in the Gaelic manuscript NLS, Adv. MS 72.1.2, a collection, dated to the sixteenth–seventeenth century, which includes medical items and was brought together by the Beatons of Mull. It had links to Ireland (Ossory and Howth) before coming to Scotland. On fol. 99v it contains a charm beginning *Cara caduca veni pura ... paracli(ti?) guthatus Amen X f ... aurum thus Belsisar Meilsisar ...*, while on fol. 97v there is the beginning of a treatise on epilepsy that includes the prescription *sgribh na focail so .i. Iasper Meilsisar Balsisar.*[63] In this context it is also worth mentioning the Irish verses on the Magi in the Gospels of Máel-Brigte and in the *Leabhar Breac*. In the former source, dated 1138, three names (in Greek, Latin and Arabic) are given for each Magus.[64] In the latter source, compiled in the early fifteenth century but containing earlier material, they are called Casper or Hiespar, Melcisar or Malcus, and Balcisar or Patifaxat.[65] The Three Kings are also commemorated in two poems on the Epiphany in the sixteenth-century Book of the Dean of Lismore, although earlier versions of these poems exist in other manuscripts.[66]

In comparison to other countries there is little visual material extant from medieval and early modern Scotland.[67] The Murthly Hours is a thirteenth-century book

62 In his account of the Epiphany Jacobus de Voragine provides several explanations of what the gifts symbolised: de Voragine, *The Golden Legend*, ed. Ryan, I.83.

63 Ronald I. M. Black, 'The Gaelic Manuscripts of Scotland', in *Gaelic and Scotland*, ed. William Gillies (Edinburgh, 1989), 146–74, at 154 no. 7; John Mackechnie, *Catalogue of Gaelic Manuscripts in Selected Libraries in Great Britain and Ireland*, 2 vols (Boston MA, 1973), I.123–4. See also *ibid.*, 129. I am grateful to Simon Roy Innes for informing me of the charms in this manuscript and for supplying me with these references.

64 Whitley Stokes, 'The Irish Verses, Notes and Glosses in Harl. 1802', *Revue celtique* 8 (1887), 346–69, at 346–9; James F. Kenney, *The Sources for the Early History of Ireland: Ecclesiastical. An Introduction and Guide* (Dublin, 1979), 648 no. 483.

65 Stokes, 'The Irish Verses', 360–1; Kenney, *Sources for the Early History of Ireland*, 25, 739 no. 616.

66 I am grateful to Simon Roy Innes for alerting me to the two Epiphany poems in the Book of the Dean of Lismore and for kindly supplying the following information. The poem 'Triúr ríogh táinig go teach nDé' is acephalous in the Book of the Dean of Lismore. For a version of this poem, although not from the Book of the Dean of Lismore, see *The Irish Liber Hymnorum edited from the MSS., with translations, notes and glossary*, ed. J. H. Bernard and R. Atkinson, Henry Bradshaw Society 13, 14, 2 vols (London, 1898), I.194; II.90–1. For a version of the poem 'Fuigheall beannacht bru mhuire', see *Aithdioghluim Dána: A Miscellany of Irish Bardic Poetry, Historical and Religious, including the Historical Poems of the Duanaire in the Yellow Book of Lecan*, ed. Lambert McKenna, Irish Texts Society 37, 40, 2 vols (Dublin, 1939–40), I.190–4; II.112–14. Information concerning both of these poems can be found in the Bardic Poetry Database at http://bardic.celt.dias.ie/main.html

67 In part this may be due to destruction at the time of the Reformation: David McRoberts, 'Material Destruction Caused by the Scottish Reformation', *IR* 10 (1959), 126–72.

of hours that was put together for use in England and illuminated in Paris in the 1280s. Its illuminations include in the hours of the Virgin historiated initials of a Nativity scene and an Adoration scene.[68] The book also contains full-page miniatures that originated in England. Three of these depict the Journey of the Magi, the Magi before Herod, and the Adoration of the Magi.[69] John Higgitt has dated these miniatures by the 'Infancy Artist' to the 1260s or 1270s and has suggested that they, along with the other full-page miniatures, were probably intended as the preface for a psalter or separate picture-book.[70] By the fifteenth century the Murthly Hours was owned by the Stewarts of Lorne.[71]

A rare survival is a late fifteenth-century oak misericord that is regarded as being from the south of Scotland, although no precise provenance is known. It has carvings of the Virgin Mary and on her lap the Christ Child, who sits facing two of the Kings. The ox and ass look over Mary's shoulders while there is a star at the top. According to Richardson, the third king and Joseph may have been depicted on the surrounding supporters.[72] It is quite an unusual subject for a misericord. In their survey of nearly 8,000 misericords, Dorothy and Henry Kraus calculated that only 3 per cent had subjects drawn from scripture and that more than half of this category were found in France.[73] Furthermore, they state that 'the use of scriptural subjects was extremely sparse' owing to clerics being 'delicate about allowing the lower body to be in contact with the effigies of Christ, Mary, or the Apostles'.[74]

Other wooden objects that survive are the pre-Reformation panels in St Mary's

68 The authoritative work on the Murthly Hours is John Higgitt, *The Murthly Hours: Devotion, Literacy and Luxury in Paris, England and the Gaelic West* (London and Toronto, 2000). For discussion of these two historiated initials, see *ibid.*, 134–8. For these images (on fols 82r and 91v of the manuscript), see http://www.nls.uk/digitallibrary/murthly/folios/images (accessed 30 June 2006).

69 Higgitt, *Murthly Hours*, 250–1. For these images (on fols 11r, 12r, and 13r of the manuscript), see http://www.nls.uk/digitallibrary/murthly/folios/images (accessed 30 June 2006).

70 Higgitt, *Murthly Hours*, 5, 212–13. For the 'Infancy Artist', see *ibid.*, 199–202.

71 *ibid.*, 2, 19.

72 Caldwell, *Angels, Nobles and Unicorns*, 112–13; James S. Richardson, 'Unrecorded Scottish Wood Carvings', *PSAS* 60 (1925–6), 384–408, at 386–8. Supporters (wing carvings) are a particular feature of British misericords: Dorothy Kraus and Henry Kraus, *The Hidden World of Misericords* (London, 1976), 171. Christa Grössinger notes that an exception to this is the late fourteenth-century misericords with supporters in Barcelona Cathedral. She also comments that a 'close iconographic relationship between centre and supporters can be established in English misericords': Christa Grössinger, *The World Upside-Down. English Misericords* (London, 1997), 15.

73 Kraus and Kraus, *Hidden World of Misericords*, x. See also E. C. Block, *Corpus of Medieval Misericords in France XIII–XVI Century* (Turnhout, 2003), 195–6. In Lincoln Cathedral there survive misericords from the second half of the fourteenth century. One of these depicts the Nativity and the Adoration of the Magi. It is different in style from the Scottish example as the Virgin is lying in bed holding the Child, and the ox and ass are in the foreground. It also contains the Three Kings, Joseph, and the star: G. L. Remnant, *A Catalogue of Misericords in Great Britain with an essay on their iconography by M. D. Anderson* (Oxford, 1969), 90–1 (no. 23); Grössinger, *The World Upside-Down*, 126–8.

74 Kraus and Kraus, *Hidden World of Misericords*, ix.

crypt in St Nicholas church, Aberdeen, which were apparently once the door of a cupboard in Ruthven.[75] A mid-sixteenth-century panel from the Franciscan nunnery in Dundee depicts the Adoration of the Magi.[76] An example in stone is that of the fifteenth-century roof boss of the Adoration in the Lady chapel of Rosslyn chapel.[77]

Far less likely to survive from the medieval period is tapestry and embroidery. Two English survivals are the Chichester-Constable chasuble and the Butler-Bowdon cope. They are likely to be from the same set of vestments, thought to have been made between 1330 and 1350, and include the scene of the Adoration of the Magi.[78] Record evidence survives, though, of tapestries that are no longer extant. For example, a charter of Robert III, dated 4 May 1403, records a grant to Gilbert Greenlaw, bishop of Aberdeen, royal chancellor, of various items that had come to the king through the death of Walter Danielston, bishop of St Andrews. These included two cloths, one of Arras of the *historia oblationis trium regum de Colonia ad beatam Virginem.*[79] The tapestry was still extant in 1436 as it is recorded in the cathedral inventory for that year.[80]

The Three Kings was a popular subject of tapestry, being found in the collections of the dukes of Burgundy and English kings.[81] An inventory of the tapestries of Henry VIII shows that he had '2 peces of the Three Kinges of Colleyn' in the Tower of London. He also had Arras work of the Kings at Westminster and Richmond.[82] At a less exalted level, among the possessions listed in the will of the

75 J. G. Grant Fleming, *The Story of St. Mary's Chapel. The Ancient 'Lower Church' or Crypt of St. Nicholas* (Aberdeen, 1935), 11–12.

76 John Shiell, 'Notice of Carved Oak Panels which were formerly in the chapel of the Franciscan Nunnery in Dundee', *PSAS* 20 (1885–6), 108–25; Caldwell, *Angels, Nobles and Unicorns*, 110 (F13).

77 Earl of Rosslyn, *Rosslyn Chapel* (Rosslyn, 1997), 21.

78 Bonnie Young, 'Opus Anglicanum', *The Metropolitan Museum of Art Bulletin*, new series 29 (1971), 291–8.

79 *Registrum Episcopatus Aberdonensis. Ecclesie cathedralis Aberdonensis regesta que extant in unum collecta*, ed. Cosmo Innes, Maitland Club 63, 2 vols (Edinburgh, 1845), I.208. There has been some confusion about this 'gift' of Robert III. Hofmann claims erroneously that Robert III gifted the panels of the Three Kings in St Mary's chapel, St Nicholas kirk, Aberdeen: Hofmann, *Die Heiligen Drei Könige*, 299 n. 483. Walter Danielston was elected as bishop of St Andrews around June 1402 following the resignation of Thomas Stewart, an illegitimate brother of the king, who had been elected to the bishopric in July 1401 but had not received papal confirmation. Danielston was not confirmed either but acted as bishop until his death around Christmas 1402, following which the chapter of St Andrews sought Greenlaw's translation from the bishopric of Aberdeen. Papal confirmation of the translation was not gained, however, and Henry de Wardlaw received papal provision to the see of St Andrews on 10 September 1403: *Fasti Ecclesiae Scoticanae Medii Aevi Ad Annum 1638*, ed. D. E. R. Watt and A. L. Murray, rev. edn, Scottish Record Society (Edinburgh, 2003), 382–3.

80 *Registrum Episcopatus Aberdonensis*, II.141.

81 W. G. Thomson, *A History of Tapestry. From the Earliest Times until the Present Day* (London, 1906), 77, 165, 263, 265, 273. Among the tapestries presented to the Lord Chamberlain of England by Archduke Maximilian of Austria and his wife Marie of Burgundy (purchased by them in Bruges in 1478) was a church-hanging depicting the Three Kings: *ibid.*, 126, 170.

82 *ibid.*, 263, 265, 273.

fifteenth-century Beverley merchant John Brompton was a bed of arras that was worked with a picture of the Virgin Mary and the Three Kings.[83]

In the reign of James IV evidence of royal devotion in the form of offerings to the Three Kings can be found in the Treasurer's Accounts. On 6 January 1505, the feast of Epiphany, James IV gave an offering of three French crowns, a sum equivalent to 42 shillings, in honour of the Three Kings. This is likely to have occurred in the Carmelite priory of Luffness where he had made a payment of 28 shillings to the friars on the previous day.[84] At Epiphany 1507 James likewise made an offering of 42 shillings in honour of the Three Kings. Again this seems to have occurred at Luffness.[85] At Epiphany 1512 the sum of three French crowns (or 42 shillings) was offered to the 'three Kingis of Culane', although the location of the offering is unclear.[86]

The probable location of the priory of Luffness for at least two of these offerings suggests that James IV's devotion to the Three Kings should be assessed within the context of Carmelite devotion. As with other Carmelite houses in Scotland, Luffness was dedicated to the Blessed Virgin Mary.[87] The Carmelite order enjoyed 'firm royal support' in Scotland,[88] and as an order was particularly devoted to St Anne in whose honour James IV regularly made offerings, particularly on her feast day, from 1503 onwards.[89] Furthermore, Scottish visitors to Bruges tended to worship in the Carmelite church where there was a Scottish aisle chapel dedicated to St Ninian. This was receiving financial support from Edinburgh and Aberdeen by the fifteenth century and its chaplain was appointed by the king.[90] It is perhaps significant too that John of Hildesheim belonged to the Carmelite order.

James IV's practice can be compared also with the English kings' practice of offering gold, frankincense, and myrrh at Epiphany. For example, Edward III, Richard II and Henry VII are all known to have done so.[91] It is noticeable that the

83 'Medieval Beverley: The Townspeople', in *A History of the County of York East Riding: Volume 6: The borough and liberties of Beverley*, ed. K. J. Allison, VCH (Oxford, 1989), 57–62, at http: // www.british-history.ac.uk/ report.asp?compid= 36410 (accessed 12 Sept. 2006).

84 *TA*, II.268.

85 *TA*, III.285. The next payment in the register is for 14 shillings to the 'Freris of Lufnes'.

86 *TA*, IV.181. Corresponding entries suggest a likely location of Edinburgh or Leith.

87 For houses of the Carmelite friars in Scotland, see Ian B. Cowan and David E. Easson, *Medieval Religious Houses: Scotland*, 2nd edn (London and New York, 1976), 134–9.

88 Macfarlane, *William Elphinstone*, 255.

89 *TA* II.253 (26 and 30 July 1503), II.260 (26 April 1504), II.263 (26 July 1504), III.76 (26 July 1506), III.292 (26 July 1507), IV.43 (26 July 1508), IV.190 (26 July 1512). The Carmelites had a special devotion to the cult of the conception of Mary and first kept the feast day of St Anne in the thirteenth century: Marina Warner, *Alone of All Her Sex. The Myth and the Cult of the Virgin Mary* (London, 1976), 243; Kathleen Ashley and Pamela Sheingorn, 'Introduction', in *Interpreting Cultural Symbols: Saint Anne in Late Medieval Society*, ed. Kathleen Ashley and Pamela Sheingorn (Athens GA and London, 1990), 21.

90 Stevenson, 'Medieval Scottish Associations with Bruges', 100.

91 Shelagh Mitchell, 'Richard II: Kingship and the Cult of Saints', in *The Regal Image of Richard II and the Wilton Diptych*, ed. Gordon, Monnas and Elam, 115–24, at 123; Hutton, *The Stations of the Sun*, 16.

Scottish records of James IV's offerings to the Three Kings at Epiphany begin only after his marriage to Margaret Tudor. This might suggest English influence on James's actions, even if the practice was more widespread; royal offerings of gold, frankincense, and myrrh were prepared at the time of the visit of Emperor Charles V to the French king Charles V in 1378, for example.[92] Unfortunately the lack of extant Treasurer's Accounts for earlier reigns, for the most part, does not confirm when the practice began in Scotland. However, the fact that James's devotion to St Anne also becomes apparent at around the time of his marriage does suggest that Margaret may have had some influence on royal devotional practice, and this is supported, to some extent, by the evidence that English monarchs were receptive to the devotional practices of their spouses.

Although not the first English king to show an interest in the cult, Richard II is the English king who is probably most associated with the cult of the Three Kings of Cologne.[93] Born on Epiphany 1367, he was attended by three kings at his baptism, and a contemporary chronicler drew a parallel between this and the Adoration.[94] As Nigel Saul has noted, this story was possibly alluded to in a speech by Chancellor Houghton when Prince Richard was introduced to parliament in January 1377, and in the Wilton Diptych, which shows a kneeling Richard being presented to the Virgin and Child by the royal saints Edmund and Edward, and John the Baptist.[95] Richard was also the owner of a ewer that had the names 'Jasper, Melcheser, Balteser' engraved on it.[96]

Saul has written of the influence that the wives of Edward III and Richard II may have had on their husbands' devotion to the Virgin Mary.[97] In addition, Richard's wife Anne of Bohemia is regarded as being responsible for the increase in popularity of the cult of St Anne in England where papal recognition of her feast day came in 1382 after the royal marriage.[98] It is possible that as a child Anne of Bohemia inherited from her father an interest in the cult of the Three Kings, which she may have shared with her husband. In 1357 her father Charles IV had visited the shrine with his third wife, Anne of Swidnica, and the Hungarian queen mother,

92 Trexler, *Journey of the Magi*, 85, 87.

93 A mandate of Henry III, dated 8 November 1256, instructed Philip Lovel, treasurer 'that he provide for the king three of the most precious cloths of gold that he can find in London and deliver them to Drogo de Barentyn, to offer in the king's name at the tomb of the Three Kings, buried at Cologne, as a gift of the king': Webb, *Pilgrims and Pilgrimage in the Medieval West*, 169. As mentioned earlier, Edward II and Edward III both visited the shrine at Cologne while Edward III may have expressed a wish to be buried there before opting to be buried at Westminster Abbey: *Chronica Johannis de Reading et Anonymi Cantuariensis 1346–1367*, ed. James Tait (Manchester, 1914), 132–3 and note at 275–6; Diana Webb, *Pilgrimage in Medieval England* (London and New York, 2000), 112.

94 Nigel Saul, *Richard II* (New Haven and London, 1997; repr. 1999), 12.

95 Saul, *Richard II*, 12 n. 15, 304–7. See also Mitchell, 'Richard II: Kingship and the Cult of Saints', 122–3.

96 Saul, *Richard II*, 12 n. 15.

97 *ibid.*, 307–8.

98 David Hugh Farmer, *The Oxford Dictionary of Saints*, 5th edn (Oxford, 2004), 25; H. M. Bannister, 'The Introduction of the Cultus of St. Anne into the West', *EHR* 18 (1903), 107–12, at 107; Saul, *Richard II*, 308, 324.

Elizabeth Piast.[99] Two years earlier on his visit to Italy, Charles had been crowned at Milan on the feast of Epiphany.[100] Furthermore, Olga Pujmanová has discussed the likely influence of the Luxembourg Epiphanies on art in Europe. In the case of the English court she speculates that 'their impact on the art of the English court may have been due to Richard II's first wife, Anne of Bohemia …'[101]

When considering the development of the cult of the Three Kings of Cologne in late fifteenth-century Scotland, then, it is tempting to look for possible influences that may have occurred through the royal marriages. In the case of James IV, as well as possible English influence from his marriage, Danish influences should be borne in mind too. He was the son of Margaret of Denmark, who was officially appointed as tutor to Prince James for five years from Whitsuntide 1478.[102] Wife of James III, Margaret of Denmark was the daughter of King Christian I and Queen Dorothea of Denmark.[103] As mentioned earlier, King Christian had visited the shrine of the Magi in Cologne on his return from Rome. He had timed his visit to the Kings' shrine so as to be present on the feast of Epiphany in 1475. Danish interest in the cult was already well established by this time. For example, Waldemar Atterdag of Denmark had visited the shrine in Cologne in 1364 while Queen Margaret I (1353–1412), in her will of 1410, had provided payment for a number of men to go on various pilgrimages on her behalf. These included three men to go to the Three Holy Kings in Cologne.[104]

Of most significance in a Scottish context, though, is the foundation, by Christian I and Dorothea, of the chapel of the Three Kings in Roskilde Cathedral in 1464. The chapel is dedicated to St Anne, the Holy Trinity, the Virgin Mary, and the Three Kings, and its fifteenth-century decoration reflects these dedications.[105] At the time of the foundation of the chapel Christian and Dorothea's daughter Margaret was still in Denmark and would presumably have had direct knowledge of it. The upper chapel was the meeting place of the Danish Order of the Elephant, whose members included James III.[106] Thus through his marriage and his

99 Gábor Klaniczay, *Holy Rulers and Blessed Princesses. Dynastic Cults in Medieval Central Europe*, trans. Éva Pálmai (Cambridge, 2002), 342; Diana Webb, *Medieval European Pilgrimage* (Basingstoke, 2002), 102. Anne of Bohemia was the daughter of Charles IV and his fourth wife Elizabeth of Pomerania.

100 Klaniczay, *Holy Rulers and Blessed Princesses*, 341.

101 Pujmanová, 'Portraits of Kings depicted as Magi in Bohemian Painting', 264.

102 Norman Macdougall, *James IV* (Edinburgh, 1989; repr. 1997), 1; Thomas Riis, *Should Auld Acquaintance Be Forgot … Scottish-Danish relations c.1450–1707*, 2 vols (Odense, 1988), I.252.

103 For Margaret of Denmark, see S. B. Chandler, 'An Italian Life of Margaret, Queen of James III', *SHR* 32 (1953), 52–7.

104 Webb, *Pilgrims and Pilgrimage in the Medieval West*, 141–2. I owe this reference to Dr Steve Boardman.

105 J. O. Arhnung, *De hellige tre Kongers Kapel ved Roskilde Domkirke 1459–1536* (Copenhagen, 1965). An English summary of this book can be found at 236–9. Christian I and Dorothea are buried in the chapel.

106 For the Order of the Elephant, see D'Arcy Jonathan Dacre Boulton, *The Knights of the Crown. The Monarchical Orders of Knighthood in Later Medieval Europe 1325–1520*, 2nd edn (Woodbridge, 2000), 399–402; see also Boardman, 'Cult of St George', above. James III was also a member of the Order of St Michael, founded in 1469, along with

membership of this chivalric order, James III is likely to have been aware of the existence of the chapel of the Three Kings at Roskilde and Danish devotion to the cult of the Three Kings more generally.

Danish influences could have spread to Scotland through other means, however. In the reigns of James III, IV and V there are examples of Scots in Denmark and Danes in the Scottish court. These include the eight ambassadors on the diplomatic mission to Copenhagen to arrange the marriage treaty (ratified on 8 September 1468) between James III and Margaret of Denmark; Christian, nephew of King Hans of Denmark, who was at the Scottish court from early 1505 until 1508, and in July 1512; and Alexander Kinghorn who held office in the university of Copenhagen, at the royal court of King Christian II, and in the cathedral chapter of Roskilde, before becoming Christian II's ambassador to Scotland.[107] Like Kinghorn, there were other Scots who had direct associations with Roskilde Cathedral in the early sixteenth century: several Scots, including Walter Mortimer *dictus* Grøn, were members of St Lucius's guild.[108] In addition, there was a Scottish altar dedicated to St Ninian at St Olaikirke in Elsinore and a Scottish altar in the church of St Mary in Copenhagen.[109]

Despite these connections between Scotland and Denmark, with regard to the cult of the Three Kings, one notable difference is the lack of depictions of Scots monarchs as Magi, unlike their Danish counterparts. An altarpiece, made in Antwerp around 1520, shows the Adoration of the Magi. The eldest king in the centre, who is kneeling, is probably a portrait of King Hans of Denmark (1481–1513), son of Christian I and brother of Margaret of Denmark, while the figure on the right, who is standing, is thought to be his son Christian II (1513–23).[110] It was not an unusual practice for monarchs to be depicted as Magi. Other examples include Charles IV, king of Bohemia (1347–78) and Holy Roman Emperor (1355–78). He was depicted as one of the Magi in panel and wall paintings, and in book illuminations.[111] Monarchs associated themselves with the Three Kings in imagery: one of the most pertinent examples in discussing the cult is that of Otto IV joining the Three Kings on their shrine at Cologne.[112] In a similar way

Christian I and his son Hans (brother of Margaret of Denmark): Katie Stevenson, *Chivalry and Knighthood in Scotland 1424–1513* (Woodbridge, 2006), 81–2 and n. 88.

107 Ranald Nicholson, *Scotland. The Later Middle Ages* (Edinburgh, 1989), 415–16; Norman Macdougall, *James III. A Political Study* (Edinburgh, 1982), 78; Riis, *Should Auld Acquaintance Be Forgot*, I.257, 259, 260. Christian was son of Princess Elizabeth, daughter of Christian I: *ibid.*, II.283. For details of Kinghorn's career, see *ibid.*, II.65.

108 Mortimer was admitted to the guild in 1516–17 and was canon of Roskilde Cathedral by 1520 and until at least 1534. He also served as headmaster of the cathedral school: *ibid.*, II.259. Other examples include William Skotte who was admitted to the guild in 1510; Robert 'Boen' Scotus and his spouse who were admitted to the guild in 1513; Thomas Lumsdale and his spouse, admitted to the guild in 1515; and Thomas Skotte admitted by 1517: *ibid.*, II.258–9.

109 Ditchburn, *Scotland and Europe*, 247.

110 Poul Grinder-Hansen, *Danish Middle Ages and Renaissance*, trans. Philip Ronald Davies, Guides to the National Museum (Copenhagen, 2002), 105.

111 Pujmanová, 'Portraits of Kings depicted as Magi in Bohemian Painting', 252–4.

112 Sumption, *Pilgrimage*, 159–60.

the Three Kings are depicted on one side of a gold coin that contains a portrait of Pope Leo X on the other side.[113]

There is a Scottish connection in an image from the Book of Hours of Étienne Chevalier, constable of France. An illumination by Jean Fouquet depicts an Adoration scene and encompasses a number of features that have been mentioned above.[114] The first king is a representation of the French king Charles VII. In the background is a scene in which a castle is being attacked. This has been identified as a representation of part of an Epiphany celebration, a royal pageant in which a fortress is stormed. For the purposes of this chapter, though, a third element is important. The retinue of the kings featured in this image includes the *Garde Ecossaise* (or Scots Guard) of Charles VII, depicted in the livery of the king. Thus Scots themselves are seen to play a significant role in the Adoration of Christ.

Although Scots monarchs do not appear as Magi themselves, they are found associated with them in armorials and on a painted ceiling. For example, the Lindsay armorial of 1542 contains the arms of the Scottish royal family and nobility along with those of European monarchs. It also depicts the arms of the nine worthies, the Three Kings – Balthasar, king of Saba, Caspar, king of Tharsis, Melchior, king of Arabia – and Prester John.[115] In the sixth century there arose the claim that the Three Kings had been baptised by St Thomas the Apostle in India.[116] From the twelfth century they also became linked with stories of Prester John.[117] Thus Scottish royalty and nobility are linked to the Kings and traditional elements of their legend as well as taking their place among the ranks of European nobility.

This tradition continued into the seventeenth century, as evidenced by the painted decoration on the Earlshall ceiling of 1620. The ceiling displays the arms of the Three Kings and nine worthies along with those of European monarchs and Scottish nobles.[118] It should be noted, though, that the better-known ceiling of the nave of St Machar's Cathedral in Aberdeen, the decoration of which dates to the previous century, does not include the Three Kings or Prester John among its

113 Hofmann, *Die Heiligen Drei Könige*, 390 illustration 23: 'Goldmünze des Papstes Leo X (1513–1521)'.

114 For discussion of this illumination and reproductions of it, see Sandro Lombardi, *Jean Fouquet* (Firenze, 1983), 208–9 and plate 79; Norman Macdougall, *An Antidote to the English: The Auld Alliance, 1295–1560* (East Linton, 2001), plate 7.

115 Michael Bath, *Renaissance Decorative Painting in Scotland* (Edinburgh, 2003), 152; Andrea Thomas, *Princelie Majestie: the Court of James V of Scotland, 1528–1542* (Edinburgh, 2005), 204.

116 Harris, 'The *Historia Trium Regum*', 23.

117 Bernard Hamilton, 'Prester John and the Three Kings of Cologne', in *Studies in Medieval History Presented to R. H. C. Davies*, ed. Henry Mayr-Harting and R. I. Moore (London and Ronceverte, 1985), 177–91, at 180–1. See also Sumption, *Pilgrimage*, 25, describing Joos van Ghistele's carrying of gems that had been in contact with the relics of the Magi at Cologne 'in the belief that, should he discover the land of the legendary Prester John, they would make an acceptable gift to that potentate'.

118 Bath, *Renaissance Decorative Painting*, 147, 253–6. Bath discusses the likelihood that the Earlshall ceiling may be the work of a herald painter. He notes, however, that the Lindsay armorial is not the direct source of the ceiling's scheme and that a number of other Scottish heraldic manuscripts have similar coats of arms: *ibid*., 152–4.

displays of the arms of Scottish royalty, nobility, bishops, European monarchs and Aberdeen institutions.[119]

Scottish dedications to the Three Kings of Cologne all relate to altars and date to either the end of the fifteenth century or early sixteenth century. One record relates to an agreement made by Beatrice Douglas, dowager countess of Errol, with the Franciscans of Dundee in 1481 regarding the building of an altar to the Three Kings of Cologne in Greyfriars' church. However, as Torrie points out, this did not necessarily happen as 'such endowments were not welcomed in friary churches'.[120] In the parish church of St Mary's, Dundee, George Brown, bishop of Dunkeld (1483–1515) founded the altar and perpetual chaplainry in honour of St Mary and the Three Kings. Brown had family connections with Dundee, having being born there as son of a burgh treasurer and baptised in the parish church.[121] In Haddington, in the church of St Mary's, an altar dedicated to the Three Kings of Cologne was founded by the burgess David Forrest in October 1522.[122] In the 1550s the patronage was still in the family's hands, being held by his heir John.[123] In the early 1550s the chaplainry of the altar was held by Master Alexander Forrest, provost of the collegiate church of St Mary of the Fields.[124] Family support of an altar dedicated to the Three Kings of Cologne can also be found in Aberdeen. There an altar was founded before 1524 in the parish church of St Nicholas by Patrick Leslie senior, burgess of Aberdeen, with Master Gavin Leslie as the first chaplain.[125] It appears that the Leslie family continued to be associated with it up until the Reformation.[126]

It is noteworthy that these foundations all occurred in east coast burghs,

119 Bath, *Renaissance Decorative Painting*, 5, 224. See also David McRoberts, 'The Heraldic Ceiling of St Machar's Cathedral Aberdeen', Friends of St Machar's Cathedral Occasional Papers 2 (Aberdeen, 1976); Helena M. Shire, 'The King in his House: Three Architectural Artefacts belonging to the Reign of James V', in *Stewart Style 1513–1542: Essays on the Court of James V*, ed. Janet Hadley Williams (East Linton, 1996), 62–96, at 63–72.

120 E. P. D. Torrie, *Medieval Dundee. A Town and its People* (Dundee, 1990), 66. Following Maxwell, Torrie states that 'it is possible that it was erected in St Mary's where there was an altar of that dedication'. See Alexander Maxwell, *Old Dundee, Ecclesiastical, Burghal, and Social, prior to the Reformation* (Edinburgh and Dundee, 1891), 33. However, the St Mary's dedication was a sixteenth-century one by Bishop George Brown. See below.

121 See Boardman, 'Cult of St George', above.

122 Edinburgh, National Archives of Scotland [hereafter NAS], GD1/39 Documents relating to properties in and about Haddington, GD1/39/1/21.

123 NAS, GD1/39/1/37 (16 July 1553), GD1/39/1/40 (29 June 1557), GD1/39/5/3 (15 July 1553).

124 NAS, GD1/39/5/3 (15 July 1553), a notarial instrument of resignation of the chaplainry by Master Alexander Forrest into the hands of the patron John Forrest. On the following day Forrest presented the chaplainry to dene John Anderson: GD1/39/1/37.

125 For the foundation charter, see *St Nich. Cart*, II.297–9. Unfortunately the charter is imperfect and has no date.

126 *ibid.*, II.321 n. 1, which refers to a transcript of a 'Presentation to the Chaplaincy at the Altar of the Three Kings by John Leslie of Balquhane, undoubted patron thereof, in favour of Mr Andrew Leslie, canon of Aberdeen and prebendary of Ellon'. The presentation is dated 27 July 1559 but the transcript gives no source.

suggesting that there may have been a mercantile factor involved in the spread of the cult of the Three Kings. What appears to have been the only medieval church dedication to the Three Kings in Britain was that of Foster's almshouse and chapel in Bristol, which was founded by the merchant and mayor John Foster before 1492.[127] Certainly a possible mercantile connection has been noted in the transmission of Christocentric devotion in late medieval Scotland.[128]

In addition to the growing popularity of Christocentric and Marian cults in late medieval Scotland, David Ditchburn has written of the growth in devotion to other members of Christ's family; in particular, his maternal grandmother, St Anne, and royal offerings to her in the sixteenth century have been discussed above.[129] Two of the Scottish altar dedications to the Three Kings have connections with the cult of St Anne. Bishop George Brown who founded the altar of the Three Kings in the parish church of Dundee was also responsible for the foundation of a parish church dedicated to St Anne in Dowally.[130] In a grant of land on 5 March 1524 by sir William Philipson, chaplain and stipendiary of the altars of St John the Baptist and the Three Kings in the church of St Nicholas, Aberdeen he stipulated that during his lifetime an anniversary mass be celebrated annually (a sung mass with trental throughout the week following) on the second Sunday of Lent and also that a mass of St Anne be said at the altar of the Three Kings, or at the high altar, every Tuesday.[131] Interestingly, Philipson is numbered among the Scots who owned a copy of the *Golden Legend*.[132]

In this same church of St Nicholas too can be found one of the few dedications in medieval and early modern Scotland to another member of Christ's family: his father, St Joseph. A notarial instrument of 16 May 1518 mentions the altar of the Blessed Virgin Mary and St Joseph.[133] There is also a reference to a dedication to St Joseph in Perth in 1498 when John Tyrie, provost of Methven, made a grant to the chaplainry of the Annunciation of the Blessed Virgin Mary and St Joseph, confessor, father of Christ, at the altar of St Michael in the parish church.[134]

The cult of the Three Kings of Cologne was commemorated throughout medieval and early modern Europe, as Hofmann's study has demonstrated.[135] As a

127 W. K. Jordan, 'The Forming of the Charitable Institutions of the West of England: A Study of the Changing Pattern of Social Aspirations in Bristol and Somerset, 1480–1660', *Transactions of the American Philosophical Society*, new series 50 no. 8 (1960), 1–99, at 26; Clive Burgess, ' "By Quick and by Dead": Wills and Pious Provision in Late Medieval Bristol', *EHR* 102 (1987), 837–58, at 846–7. See also Roger H. Leech, *The Topography of Medieval and Early Modern Bristol Part 1: Property Holdings in the Early Walled Town and Marsh Suburb North of the Avon*, Bristol Record Society 48 (1998), 54, 157.

128 Ditchburn, *Scotland and Europe*, 52.

129 *ibid.*, 52–4.

130 *Rentale Dunkeldense: being accounts of the Bishopric A.D. 1505–1517, with Myln's 'Lives of the Bishops' A.D. 1483–1517*, trans. and ed. Robert Kerr Hannay, Scottish History Society, 2nd series 10 (Edinburgh, 1915), 311, 313.

131 *St Nich. Cart.*, I.140–1 (text of charter); II.125–6 (abstract).

132 Durkan and Ross, *Early Scottish Libraries*, 135.

133 *St Nich. Cart.*, II.267.

134 *RMS*, II.525 no. 2470. For St Joseph, see also Ditchburn, *Scotland and Europe*, 54 and n. 87; Richardson, 'Unrecorded Scottish Wood Carvings', 387–8.

135 Hofmann, *Die Heiligen Drei Könige*.

universal cult it is not surprising to find evidence of it in Scotland, and indeed evidence that shows similar characteristics to the cult elsewhere. At the same time it is not always possible to prove unquestionably the manner in which the cult was transmitted to, or throughout, Scotland. This is partly owing to the fragmentary nature of the Scottish evidence, which does not allow firm conclusions to be drawn. A few features can be highlighted, however. Throughout the period under review the names of the Kings were inscribed on talismanic objects, and there is a hint that this might have been a more significant feature in the Gaelic west. On the other hand, an assortment of evidence is linked to the burgh of Aberdeen in which there were plays, an altar dedication and imagery. One striking feature is the late date of much of the evidence, in particular the royal offerings and the altar dedications. While the former may be attributable to the royal marriages of either James III or James IV, whose wives both came from realms in which the cult was commemorated by royalty, the late date of the dedications to the Three Kings is probably best regarded in the context of the increased growth in Christocentric and Marian devotion in Scotland in the later middle ages.[136]

136 An earlier version of this chapter was presented at the Traditional Cosmology Society's 'Saints' Days and other Markers in the Ritual Year' conference, held at the University of Edinburgh on 23 April 2007. I am grateful to Professor John J. McGavin and Dr Steve Boardman for reading a draft of this essay and suggesting improvements.

10

THE MEDIEVAL AND EARLY MODERN CULT OF ST BRENDAN

Jonathan M. Wooding

In early Irish tradition St Brendan (feast day 16 May) is ranked among the 'twelve apostles of Ireland' (*dá apstol decc na hÉrenn*), the generation of sixth-century Irish monastic founders who followed St Finnian of Clonard.[1] St Brendan is also immortalised as the most famous voyager to the legendary 'Promised Land of the Saints'.[2] Dedications to St Brendan, as we will see, are found throughout the medieval Celtic world, including Brittany, and on a more limited basis in England, while outliers of his cult in the middle ages are found as far away as the Faroe Islands and possibly north-east Germany. Brief surveys of the extent of his cult were made by John O'Hanlon in 1875, and by Sabine Baring-Gould and John Fisher in 1907, but these pioneers – whose fieldwork remains indispensable – saw the journeys of the saint himself as an explanation for the distribution of his cult, whereas we would now assume that the distribution of a cult has many causes and

1 *Dá apstol decc na hÉrenn* is the title of one of the Irish texts concerning St Brendan: *Bethada Náem nÉrenn: Lives of Irish Saints*, ed. Charles Plummer, 2 vols (Oxford, 1922), I.96–102. The twelve are listed, for example, in the *Vita S. Finniani* § 19: *Vitae Sanctorum Hiberniae: Ex codice olim Salmanticensi, nunc Bruxellensi*, ed. W. W. Heist (Brussels, 1965), 96–107, at 101.

2 For a complete bibliography for the legend of St Brendan, see Glyn S. Burgess and Clara Strijbosch, *The Legend of St Brendan: A Critical Bibliography* (Dublin, 2000). The voyage is described in the *Nauigatio Sancti Brendani* § 28 (ed. G. Orlandi, Florence, forthcoming – I would like to thank Giovanni Orlandi for generously sending me his new edition of this text in advance of publication) and in the various recensions of *Vita S. Brendani* (see below). The feat was acknowledged in other texts, for example in *Vita S. Carthagi siue Mochutu* § 3: '... *qui inuenit terram repromissionis sanctorum*': *Vitae Sanctorum Hiberniae*, ed. Charles Plummer, 2 vols (Oxford, 1910), I.170–99, at 170. It is clear from texts such as the Litany of Pilgrim Saints that other saints were believed to have sought the same destination: *Irish Litanies: Text and Translation*, ed. Charles Plummer, Henry Bradshaw Society 62 (London, 1925), 60–75, at 62–3. Other voyages to this specific destination are attributed to SS Barrind and Mernóc, in the *Nauigatio*, and, in the *Vita Fintani seu Munnu* § 31 to SS Munnu, Cainnech and Columba, as well as Brendan: *Vitae*, ed. Heist, 208.

chronological strata.[3] St Brendan became a popular symbol for the travels of Irish clergy and religious and remains so into the modern era.[4] The wide circulation of the ninth-century tale *Nauigatio Sancti Brendani abbatis* (henceforth *Nauigatio*), especially in the high middle ages, encouraged a process by which both existing dedications and suggestively similar toponyms were drawn into the cult, no doubt in a similar process to many early Irish cults, if perhaps on a greater scale. Brendan's cult is one amongst a number of international cults of Irish saints that are case studies of how the cult on the ground is subject to more than one process of promulgation. These processes can be separated and include: travels of individual persons, travels of groups, travels of texts, and philological convergence.[5] What Gwenaël Le Duc has said about the cult in Brittany holds true for the cult as a whole: 'the story is rather detailed than complicated'.[6]

The dossier *of St Brendan*

The *dossier* of an insular saint typically centres on co-ordinates such as a known feast day, resting-place, miracles and genealogy.[7] St Brendan is recorded as being the son of Findlug of the Munster sept of Altraige. St Brendan's feast day appears in the ninth-century martyrologies as 16 May.[8] His resting-place is recorded in hagiography as Clonfert, Co. Galway (see below). The earliest reference to

3 *LBS*, I.233–62; John O'Hanlon, *Lives of the Irish Saints with special festivals and the commemorations of holy persons*, 10 vols (Dublin, 1875–1907), V.389–472. On the saint's travels as the basis of cult geography, see Owen Chadwick, 'The Evidence of Dedications in the Early History of the Welsh Church', in *Studies in Early British History*, ed. Nora K. Chadwick (Cambridge, 1954), 173–88; Jonathan M. Wooding, 'The Figure of David', in *St David of Wales: Cult, Church and Nation*, ed. J. Wyn Evans and Jonathan M. Wooding (Woodbridge, 2007), 1–19, at 8–10; John Reuben Davies, 'The Saints of South Wales and the Welsh Church', in *Local Saints and Local Churches in the Early Medieval West*, ed. Alan Thacker and Richard Sharpe (Oxford, 2002), 361–95, at 363 – but see also J. W. Hunwicke, 'Kerry and Stowe Revisited', *Proceedings of the Royal Irish Academy* [hereafter *PRIA*] 102C (2002), 1–19, at 2, for an expression of the older view.

4 See, for example, P. S. Cleary, *Australia's Debt to Irish Nation Builders* (Sydney, 1933), 66.

5 For a recent case study, see Karen Jankulak, 'Fingar/Gwinear/Guigner: An "Irish" Saint in Medieval Cornwall and Brittany', in *Studies in Irish Hagiography: Saints and Scholars*, ed. John Carey, Máire Herbert and Pádraig Ó Riain (Dublin, 2001), 120–39.

6 Gwenaël Le Duc, 'Irish Saints in Brittany: Myth or Reality?', in *Studies in Irish Hagiography*, ed. Carey, Herbert and Ó Riain, 93–119, at 96.

7 Hippolyte Delehaye, *Cinq leçons sur la méthode hagiographique* (Brussels, 1934), 13. On genealogy as a co-ordinate in the Irish context, see Paul Grosjean, 'Déchiffrement d'un groupe de *Notulae* du Livre d'Armagh sur S. Patrice (numéros 28–41)', *Analecta Bollandiana* 77 (1959), 387–411, at 389.

8 *Félire Óengusso Céli Dé. The Martyrology of Oengus the Culdee*, ed. Whitley Stokes, Henry Bradshaw Society 29 (London, 1905), 132; *The Martyrology of Tallaght, from the Book of Leinster and MS. 5100–4 in the Royal Library, Brussels*, ed. Richard Irvine Best and Hugh Jackson Lawlor, Henry Bradshaw Society 68 (London, 1931), 43.

Brendan, in *Vita Columbae*, refers to his making a sea-voyage;[9] a number of mystical encounters with beasts and persons who lived in the ocean were already attached to his name prior to the writing of the *Nauigatio* (see below). The main features of his *dossier* were thus certainly established by around the early to mid-ninth century. I have discussed in a separate study claims that have been made concerning the conflation of his identity with St Brendan of Birr – these conflations have no demonstrable impact on the medieval cult.[10]

At what point there was first a *Vita* of St Brendan is a key question. The number of extant Irish *Vitae* that can be presumed to have had earlier medieval versions, and the extent to which extant *Vitae* might be comparable to these putative earlier counterparts, remain contentious questions. Richard Sharpe has argued that some *Vitae* preserved in the Salmanticensis collection represent early medieval texts, while Pádraig Ó Riain takes a minimalist view of the scale of literary evidence prior to the arrival of the reformed religious orders.[11] The problems of the *Vita S. Brendani* can only serve to fuel such debates. That most, if not all, of the extant *Vitae* reflect a common original is likely, but for different reasons none of the extant texts give a clear picture of its nature. The *Vita S. Brendani* survives in four main versions in Latin: two in the Brussels Salmanticensis collection (henceforth VBSi and VBSii), one in the Marsh's Library (Dubliniensis) collection (henceforth VBD) and Rawlinson B485 (Oxoniensis: henceforth VBO). There are also two versions in Irish (O'Clery and Lismore). Only VBSii and Lismore are not subsequently conflated with the *Nauigatio*, and these texts are heavily abbreviated.[12] The unconflated Lives, especially VBSii, have the best claims to represent the original *Life*, but the matter needs more systematic study. Ó Riain is right to observe that there is little in the stemma of the extant versions to require the putative common original to be as early as the first millennium.[13] For reasons that have been set out more fully elsewhere, however, our working hypothesis should be that a *Vita* did exist by at least AD 800, and contained accounts of foundations and voyages by the saint.[14] Some episodes in the *Nauigatio* are best explained as

9 Adomnán, *Vita Columbae*, III.17: *Adomnán's Life of Columba*, ed. A. O. and M. O. Anderson (Oxford, 1991), 207.

10 See Jonathan M. Wooding, 'St Brendan, Clonfert and the Ocean: Charting the Voyages of a Cult', in *Navigatio: A Voyage of Research in Search of Clonfert*, ed. C. Cunniffe and J. Higgins (Galway, forthcoming).

11 On the early *Vitae* in Codex Salmanticensis, see Richard Sharpe, *Medieval Irish Saints' Lives: An Introduction to Vitae Sanctorum Hiberniae* (Oxford, 1991), 318–32; see recent critique by Caoimhín Breatnach, 'The Significance of the Orthography of Irish Proper Names in the Codex Salmanticensis', *Ériu* 55 (2005), 85–101. On the minimalist case, see Pádraig Ó Riain, 'Towards a Methodology in Early Irish Hagiography', *Peritia* 1 (1982), 146–59.

12 Burgess and Strijbosch, *The Legend*, 4–12.

13 Pádraig Ó Riain, 'Hagiography without Frontiers: Borrowing of Saints across the Irish Sea', in *Scripturus Vitam: Festgabe für Walter Berschin zum 65. Geburtstag*, ed. Dorothea Walz (Heidelberg, 2002), 41–8, at 47 n. 12.

14 Séamus Mac Mathúna, 'The Structure and Transmission of Early Irish Voyage Literature', in *Text und Zeittiefe*, ed. Hildegard L. C. Tristram, ScriptOralia 58 (Tübingen, 1994), 313–57, at 318–37; Charles Plummer, 'Some New Light on the Brendan Legend', *Zeitschrift für celtische Philologie* 5 (1905), 124–41; Wooding, 'St Brendan, Clonfert', forthcoming.

derived from versions of episodes in the *Vita*.[15] The Irish Litany of Pilgrim Saints (c.900) includes episodes that are closer to those in the surviving *Vita* than those in the *Nauigatio*.[16] These sources all suggest the existence of a primitive *Vita*, which, though including episodes from the extant *Vita*, may still have been remote in form from the extant *Vita* – perhaps more closely resembling Brendan episodes in the Breton *Vita S. Machutis* (Life of St Malo), or even the tale *Immram Brain*, which may be based on a lost Brendan narrative.[17] Whether the sites of the extant *Vita* featured in the earlier *Vita* is arguable; Ó Riain, for example, would suggest they reflect the pattern of a later medieval cult.[18]

The *Nauigatio* (which is confusingly termed *Vita S. Brendani* in some medieval manuscripts) is probably derived from the primitive *Vita*, developing the voyage element more fully in the context of more recent Irish voyages in the North Atlantic.[19] It is probably a Clonfert product of the mid-ninth century.[20] Unlike the *Vita* it provides only occasional witness to the extent of the cult, but its evidence is crucial on a number of points where the *Vita* is deficient, as we will see.

The above questions are discussed at length elsewhere. For the present purpose it is worth noting the probable relationship of these texts to the promulgation of the cult. The *Vita S. Machutis* (865 × 872, discussed below) along with the episodes in the Litany, being distinct from the *Nauigatio*, suggest that there was already a popular tradition of Brendan as a voyager well before the *Nauigatio*. The manuscript evidence for the popularity of the *Nauigatio* is not strong before the end of the first millennium, though this might be more a measure of manuscript survival than it is of reception of the tale.[21] There is clearly much that did not survive. Dauvit Broun has posited the existence of a now lost Anglo-Latin *Legenda S. Brandani* in medieval Scotland with a component of pseudo-historical material.[22] This would be clearly unlike any surviving version of the legend. The nature of this no longer extant stratum of *Vita*/*Nauigatio* legends, whether of literary or oral character, and its relationship to early medieval promulgation of the cult is a major complicating factor in the study of the dedication evidence.

15 Jonathan M. Wooding, 'Fasting, Flesh and the Body in the St Brendan *Dossier*', in *Celtic Hagiography and Saints' Cults*, ed. Jane Cartwright (Cardiff, 2003), 161–76; Mac Mathúna, 'The Structure', 331–4.

16 *Irish Litanies*, ed. Plummer, 62–3; Bili, *Vita S. Machutis* §§ 1–23: *Mélanges d'histoire Bretonne (VIe–XIe siècle)*, ed. Ferdinand Lot (Paris, 1907), 353–68.

17 J. Carney, Review of *Navigatio Sancti Brendani Abbatis*, ed. Carl Selmer (Notre Dame, 1959), *Medium Ævum* 32 (1963), 37–44, at 44.

18 Ó Riain, 'Hagiography without Frontiers', 47 n. 12.

19 Michaela Zelzer, 'Philological Remarks on the so-called *Navigatio S. Brendani*', in *The Brendan Legend: Texts and Versions*, ed. Glyn S. Burgess and Clara Strijbosch (Leiden, 2006), 337–50, at 337; Jonathan M. Wooding, 'The Date of *Nauigatio S. Brendani abbatis*', *Journal of Celtic Studies*, forthcoming.

20 Wooding, 'The Date', forthcoming.

21 See list of MSS with dates in Burgess and Strijbosch, *The Legend*, 13–20.

22 Dauvit Broun, *The Irish Identity of the Kingdom of the Scots* (Woodbridge, 1999), 13.

The cult of St Brendan in Ireland

St Brendan's main monastery was at Clonfert in eastern Co. Galway.[23] According to the annals – though for this period they are likely to be retrospective – Clonfert was founded by St Brendan in the year 558.[24] The annals record St Brendan's death there in AD 575.[25] Those versions of the *Vita* that refer to Brendan's death all have him buried at Clonfert (see below).

The *Saltus Virtutum* where St Brendan resides at the outset of the *Nauigatio* is clearly Clonfert.[26] When St Brendan visits St Enda (§ 3), this requires a journey westward (*contra occidentalem*) to an island.[27] St Enda is traditionally associated with Aran, which is more or less due west of Clonfert. These details reinforce the reading of *Saltus Virtutum* as a calque of *Clúain Ferta*.[28] A competing case has been made for the identification of the centre of Brendan's cult being at Ardfert, which also incorporates the *-fertae* element, but this is not supported by the evidence.[29]

The annals place the *comarba* of Brendan at Clonfert in 766, 992 and 1036.[30] The first *comarba* named as buried at Ardfert is only in 1074,[31] six years after 'Clonfert was abandoned and its seniors came into west Munster' (*Cluain Ferta Brenaind do fássugud & a sruithe do thichtain i n-Iarmumain*).[32] The eleventh-century relocation of the *comarba* to Munster was presumably on account of the despoiling of Clonfert by Ua Ruairc with the men of Bréifne and the Connachta,

23 VBSii § 17: *Vitae*, ed. Heist, 324–31, at 331; VBD § 29: 'Vita S. Brendani Clonfertensis e codice Dublinensi', ed. Paul Grosjean, *Analecta Bollandiana* 48 (1930), 99–123, at 121; VBO § 105: *Vitae*, ed. Plummer, I.98–151, at 151.

24 'The Annals of Tigernach. The Continuation, AD 1088–AD 1178', ed. Whitley Stokes, *Revue celtique* 18 (1897), 150–97 [hereafter *AT*], 142; *The Annals of Inisfallen* (*MS Rawlinson B.503*), ed. Seán Mac Airt (Dublin, 1951) [hereafter *AI*], 73; *AU*, 80; calibration after Daniel P. McCarthy, 'The Chronology of the Irish Annals', *PRIA* 98C (1998), 203–55. See also online concordance at https://www.cs.tcd.ie/Dan.McCarthy/chronology/synchronisms/annals-chron.htm (accessed 18 Dec. 2007).

25 *AT*, 152; *AI*, 76; *AU*, 88.

26 Dónall Mac Giolla Easpaig, 'Early Ecclesiastical Settlement Names of County Galway', in *Galway: History and Society*, ed. Gerard Moran and Raymond Gillespie (Dublin, 1996), 795–815, at 791; Jonathan M. Wooding, 'The Munster Element in *Nauigatio Sancti Brendani abbatis*', *Journal of the Cork Historical and Archaeological Society* 110 (2005), 33–47, at 35.

27 *Nauigatio* § 3 (ed. Orlandi).

28 Wooding, 'The Munster Element', 44 n. 16.

29 Denis O'Donoghue, *Brendaniana. St Brendan the Voyager in story and legend* (Dublin, 1893), 111. Also see T. Charles-Edwards, 'Connacht, Saints of (*act. c.* 400–*c.* 800), holy men and women believed to have been buried within the province of Connacht', *ODNB*, XII.960–3, at 961. Charles-Edwards does not claim that Ardfert is *Saltus Virtutum*, but he suggests that Ardfert competed as the main foundation with Clonfert at the time of the *Nauigatio*. See Wooding, 'St Brendan, Clonfert', forthcoming.

30 *AI*, 112, 168, 202; *AU*, 218, 423, 475.

31 *AI*, 225. Though the *comarba* of Brendan of Clonfert is mentioned in 1094, this entry is ambiguous as to whether he is *at* Clonfert.

32 *AI*, 230.

mentioned three years previously in the annals – it had also been plundered in 1035, 1043, 1045 and 1065. The extant cathedral at Clonfert, with its distinctive west door of c.1180, post-dates the Synod of Ráth Bressail (1111), at which Clonfert was named as an episcopal see. An Augustinian priory was founded at Clonfert in the twelfth century.

The rulers of Connacht promoted the cult of St Brendan in the middle ages – for example, the *Lex Brendani* was enforced by Forgus mac Cellach in 744.[33] That Clonfert was not central to their territory may account for its links with Munster dynasties, as well as its frequent destruction. Clonfert was under the control of an Éoganacht Locha Léin *comarba* in the seventh century.[34]

Annaghdown, Co. Galway (Eanach nDúin), is one of the foundations of Brendan according to the *Vita* tradition. Annaghdown is mentioned in VBO and VBD versions of the *Vita*.[35] These state that Brendan's sister Brig governed a convent at Annaghdown under the direction of Brendan, 'in the province of Connacht and in the district of the Uí Briúin';[36] Annaghdown is the setting for the death of the saint, though he is then buried at Clonfert – VBSii gives this same episode without naming the monastery, but we should probably assume this, heavily abbreviated text of the *Vita*, reflects a source that once specified Annaghdown.[37] The three episodes suggest an origin in a common source – perhaps from Annaghdown.

AI s.a. 578 (575) records the 'death of Aed son of Eochaid, King of Connacht, who granted Annaghdown to Brendan', though this entry is certainly retrospective.[38] The genealogical tract *Comainmniguid Nóem nÉrenn* refers to a 'Ciarán Enaigh Dúin',[39] and Donal Mac Giolla Easpaig argues that the original affiliation was to this Ciarán, not to St Brendan,[40] but this seems a slight basis from which to argue the prior claims of this Ciarán over Brendan as the original dedication. St Brendan's cathedral at Annaghdown was the centre of a see from 1188/9 to 1325/6.[41] The oldest structures on the site are twelfth-century in date. In the twelfth century the monastery adopted the rule of the Augustinian canons. A convent of Augustinian nuns and Praemonstratensian *Parva Cella* was also founded.[42]

33 *AU*, 198.

34 Wooding, 'The Munster Element', 37–8.

35 VBO § 102: *Vitae*, ed. Plummer, I.149–50; VBD § 29: 'Vita', ed. Grosjean, 121.

36 ... *qui locus est in prouinchia Connachtorum, in plebe Hua Briun*: VBD § 29: 'Vita', ed. Grosjean, 121.

37 VBSii § 17: *Vitae*, ed. Heist, 331; VBD § 29: 'Vita', ed. Grosjean, 121; VBO § 102: *Vitae*, ed. Plummer, I.149–50. VBSi does not give any details of the saint's death and the version in *Nova Legenda Anglie* simply specifies Clonfert as his place of death.

38 *Mors Aeda m. Echdach, ríg Connachta, qui obtulit Enach nDúin do Brennainn*: *AI*, 76–7.

39 *Corpus Genealogiarum Sanctorum Hiberniae*, ed. Pádraig Ó Riain (Dublin, 1985), 145–53, at 145.

40 Mac Giolla Easpaig, 'Early Ecclesiastical Settlement Names', 812.

41 Aubrey Gwynn and R. Neville Hadcock, *Medieval Religious Houses: Ireland* (London, 1970), 60–1; Pádraig Ó Riain, 'Sanctity and Politics in Connacht c.1100: The Case of St Fursa', *Cambridge Medieval Celtic Studies* 17 (1989), 1–14, at 12–13.

42 *Pontificia Hibernica: medieval papal chancery documents concerning Ireland, 640–1261*, ed. Maurice P. Sheehy, 2 vols (Dublin, 1962–5), II.129–30.

Also in Co. Galway, Inchiquin (Inis Moccu Cuínn), an island in Lough Corrib, figures in VBD and VBO, warranting two episodes in the former, one featuring the hostility of the King Aed whom *AI* (see above) record as the patron of Annaghdown.[43] In view of its proximity to Annaghdown, it is probable that it is an early foundation linked to that site.

The Uí Briúin was the dominant dynasty in Connacht after c.700. Brendan's rule is given to him on the plain of Mag Ai by an angel, which again suggests a cult promulgated in the heart of Connacht.[44] Clonfert was the resting-place of Brendan and thus the cult centre, but it would not be surprising that cult sites to the north-west, such as Annaghdown, were promoted to rival Clonfert. The same is probably true of Tuam, which features in the *Vita*, and *AU* s.a. 882 records the death of Cormac son of Ciarán, 'prior of Cluain Ferta Brénainn and superior of Tuaim dá Gualann' (*secnap Cluana Ferta Brenainn & princeps Thuama Da Ghualann*).[45] Of indeterminate date but consistent with the geography of the Uí Briúin, which stretched to the edge of Roscommon, is the cult in the parish of Ballygar (Galway). Here Doranstown has a well dedicated to St Brendan with a pattern on 16 May. Brendan is acknowledged as the patron of the small church in Tohergar (Roscommon) in the same parish.[46] There is also a townland of St Brendan's (or Cregganagrogy) in the same parish.

Inis Gluaire (Mayo) is another significant Brendan dedication in Connacht.[47] The scale of the cult on this site is considerable, with more than one dedication to the saint: St Brendan's chapel, St Brendan's cell and St Brendan's well. The chapel contains a statue to St Brendan. John O'Donovan recorded that fishermen lowered their sails in honour of St Brendan.[48] Giraldus Cambrensis refers to a story of an island off the coast of Connacht, dedicated to St Brendan, where corpses left on the ground do not decay and there are no mice. The island is not named in the earliest recension;[49] later recensions locate the story on Aran, but John Lynch in *Cambrensis Eversus* (1662) attributed it to Inis Gluaire.[50] As there is no dedication to St Brendan on Aran, Inis Gluaire is the more likely subject of Giraldus's reference, though a primary voyage to Aran features consistently in many of the related texts to the St Brendan legend.[51] Also of interest is the fact that the *Vita Columbae* (I.6) records that *Eirros Domno* was the starting-point for Cormac's first voyage.[52]

43 VBD § 18: 'Vita', ed. Grosjean, 114–15; VBO § 88: *Vitae*, ed. Plummer, I.143.

44 VBD § 10: 'Vita', ed. Grosjean, 108.

45 VBSii § 6: *Vitae*, ed. Heist, 326; VBO § 9: *Vitae*, ed. Plummer, I.102; VBD § 9: 'Vita', ed. Grosjean, 108; *AU*, 338.

46 Francis Beirne, *The Diocese of Elphin: People, Places and Pilgrimage* (Dublin, 2000), 214.

47 Gwynn and Hadcock, *Medieval Religious Houses*, 387.

48 *LBS*, I.258.

49 Gerald of Wales, *The History and Topography of Ireland*, trans. John J. O'Meara (Harmondsworth, 1982), 61–2.

50 Text of the longer recension and Lynch reference in *Giraldi Cambrensis Opera*, ed. J. S. Brewer *et al.*, 8 vols, RS 21 (London, 1861–91), V.83.

51 See Wooding, 'St Brendan, Clonfert', forthcoming.

52 Adomnán, *Vita Columbae* I.6: *Adomnán*, ed. Anderson, 30–1; Nollaig Ó Muráile, 'An Outline History of Co. Mayo', in *Mayo: Aspects of its Heritage*, ed. Bernard O'Hara (Galway, 1982), 10–35, at 12–13.

Eirros Domno (*Irrus Domnann*) refers to the Mullet Peninsula, off which Inis Gluaire is located.[53] In addition, this island plays a significant role in the story of the Children of Lir.[54] Irrus Domnann was in the territory of the Uí Fiachrach, who contended with the Uí Briúin for control of Connacht in the later first millennium. Though the cult in this region is the cult of a Connacht saint we might, in the light of the evidence for the separate significance of coastal sites in the cults of voyaging saints, seek an explanation of this cult in theological rather than political tensions (see below).

Holy wells dedicated to St Brendan in Kilmeena and in Roskeen are further evidence of the cult in Mayo, though they are further to the south.[55] The site at Roskeen is very impressive with a *leacht* and bullaun stone.

In Co. Clare Inis-dá-Dromma ('island of two backs') is a small island in the estuary of the River Fergus; the toponym is variously equated with Coney Island, or a part thereof. It is described as a settlement of Brendan in VBSii § 13 and in VBO § 77, where it states that the saint stayed there for seven years.[56] There are two ruined churches on the island, which are the 'backs' of the name. Samuel Lewis reports it as a parish, returned with a mainland parish, 'but it is stated in the late report of the Ecclesiastical Commissioners that the parish is withheld from the precentor, although mentioned in his titles'.[57] This suggests a separate status consistent with a monastic origin and thus may be an early dedication – perhaps linked to the Munster cult rather than the Connacht. In southern Clare there is also a holy well dedicated to St Brendan in Cluain-na-gCarnán, Clonmore Co. Clare (Tober Brenaill). Whether the original patron was Brendan is uncertain in view of the name.[58]

Though genealogists in time came to link his ancestry to Connacht families, St Brendan's Munster origins appear clear from his earliest genealogical affiliations.[59] The reference to St Brendan in Adomnán's *Vita Columbae*, where he is named as *Brendenus mocu Alti*, appears to associate him securely with the Altraige of northern Co. Kerry, a sept roughly centring on Tralee. Brendan's birth among the Altraige is either explicitly stated or not contradicted in the versions of the

53 N. Stalmans and T. M. Charles-Edwards, 'Meath, Saints of (act. *c.*400–*c.*900)', *ODNB*, XXVII.671–8, at 675.

54 P. W. Joyce, *Old Celtic Romances* (repr. Dublin, 1961), 6, 19; also T. J. Westropp, 'Folk Lore and Legends from the Coasts of Counties Mayo and Galway', *Folklore* 27 (1916), 99–106, at 105. In this story the island is the last place in which the children of Lir are in swan form. This is arguably another 'otherworld' tradition tied to the site – albeit a comparatively modern one – and one with parallels to the Island of Birds in the *Nauigatio* (§ 11).

55 Patrick Logan, *The Holy Wells of Ireland* (Gerrard's Cross, 1980), 76; Noel O'Neill, 'St Brendan's Well, Roskeen' (2004): http://www.castlebar.ie/mayo_historical_and_archaeological_society/mhas-20040601.shtml (accessed 18 Dec. 2007).

56 VBSii § 13: *Vitae*, ed. Heist, 329; VBO § 81: *Vitae*, ed. Plummer, I.140.

57 Samuel Lewis, *County Clare: A History and Topography* (repr. Ennis, 1995), 55–6.

58 Eugene O'Curry, Ordnance Survey Letter regarding Parish of Killard, 1839: http://www.clarelibrary.ie/eolas/coclare/history/osl/killard2_cill_na_gclochan.htm (accessed 19 Dec. 2007).

59 Ó Riain, 'Sanctity and Politics'.

Vita/*Betha*.[60] The genealogical information at the opening of the *Nauigatio* says: 'St Brendan, son of Findlug of the sept of Altraige, was born of the Éoganacht of Loch Léin in the region of Munster' (*Sanctus Brendanus, filius Finlocha nepotis Althi, de genere Eogeni stagni Len regionis Mumenensium ortus fuit*).[61] This Éoganacht attribution is probably an attempt to associate him retrospectively with a group who controlled Clonfert after his time.[62]

Cnoc Bréannain Co. Kerry (Brandon Mountain) has been the principal cult site for St Brendan since at least the high middle ages and remains so in the present day.[63] In the thirteenth century Giraldus Cambrensis described the mountains of south-west Munster (which he places slightly too far to the south) as *Montes Brendanici*.[64] The first actual reference to the mountain is apparently in *Nauigatio* § 4 where the saint visits 'a distant part of his native region' (*in ultimam partem regionis suae*) 'where he pitched his tent at the edge of a mountain stretching far out into the ocean, in a place called Brendan's Seat, at a point where there was entry for one boat' (*in cuiusdam summitate montis extendentis se longe in oceanum, in loco qui dicitur Sedes Brendani, fixit tentorium ubi erat introitus unius navis*).[65] This seems to describe the mountain, its location and the creek to the west, Cuas an Bhodaigh or Brandon Creek, which is the likely setting for Brendan's departure in the *Nauigatio*.

The remains on the mountain include two sites dedicated to the saint. Teampaillín Bréannain is the name attached to a ruined drystone structure on the summit.[66] Nearby is Tobar Bréannain, now little more than a depression in the ground. The area between the Owenmore River and Arraglen was known as Paróiste Bhréannain. There are various toponyms in this area to the north and north-west of the mountain: Brandon Point (Sron Broin), Brandon Head (Pointe an Choma Dhóite) and Brandon (Cé Bhréanainn). The mountain has three pattern days: 16 May; 29 June (feast of SS Peter and Paul); and Domnach Chrom Dubh (last Sunday in July). The first is Brendan's correct feast day and the third is claimed by Máire Mac Néill to be the likely pre-Christian pattern day.[67] The Papal

60 Wooding, 'St Brendan, Clonfert', forthcoming. The Irish Lives attribute his ancestry to the Ciarraige, but only insofar as they hold the Altraige to be a subset thereof.

61 *Nauigatio* § 1 (ed. Orlandi, forthcoming).

62 Wooding, 'The Munster Element', 37–8.

63 See O'Donoghue, *Brendaniana*, 341.

64 The other material given in some recensions of *Topographia Hibernica* is of doubtful authenticity, though still medieval evidence for the mountain: *Opera*, ed. Brewer *et al.*, v.125. The mountain also finds reference in the Norman French *Song of Dermot and the Earl* as the lordship of Miles de Cogan: *The Song of Dermot and the Earl: An Old French Poem about the Coming of the Normans to Ireland*, ed. Goddard Orpen (Oxford, 1892), 122–3, lines 1653–5; it is described there as the 'wildest place in the world'. It is also the lordship of Ceryd, the foster-father of Gruffydd ap Cynan, in the Latin Life of Gruffydd: *Vita Griffini filii Conani* § 14: *Vita Griffini Filii Conani: The Medieval Latin Life of Gruffudd ap Cynan*, ed. Paul Russell (Cardiff, 2005), 64–5. These references imply that the mountain was a notable place, in the high middle ages, perhaps on account of the fame of St Brendan.

65 *Nauigatio* § 4 (ed. Orlandi).

66 Judith Cuppage *et al.*, *Archaeological Survey of the Dingle Peninsula* (Ballyferriter, 1986), 263.

67 Máire Mac Néill, *The Festival of Lughnasa: A Study of the Survival of the Celtic Festival*

Taxation List of 1302–7 refers to the *Collis Sancti Brendani* ('hill of St Brendan') as paying the third highest revenue in the diocese of Ardfert.[68] In the 1540s Primate Dowdall of Armagh referred to it as among fifteen main penitential stations of Ireland.[69]

In the *Nauigatio* St Brendan's journey takes him to the western edge of Altraige and, if the creek is correctly identified with Cuas an Bhodaigh, into the territory of the neighbouring Corco Dhuibhne. The Ciarraige took over the Altraige and Corco Dhuibhne around the time of the writing of the *Nauigatio*, and the extension of Brendan's cult into Corco Dhuibhne is usually attributed to the Ciarraige.[70] At Kilmalkedar, two miles to the west of Brandon Mountain, are found three Brendan dedications.[71] Three hundred metres from the church is located Teampall Brénnain, a drystone oratory of 'Gallarus' type. Nearer to the church is a seventeenth-century house known as St Brendan's house, which also has a holy well dedicated to St Brendan.[72] Maolchéodar, the main dedication, is a saint of the Corco Dhuibhne and, as Tomás Ó Carragáin has observed, the continuance of his cult is probably evidence that it had sufficient weight that it could not be displaced by that of the incoming Brendan – whose cult was thus forced to the periphery, but is the most numerous in terms of dedications in the parish.[73]

The other significant complex in Corco Dhuibhne is on Inis Tuaisceart in the Blasket Islands. Here is a site known as St Brendan's monastery, with a drystone oratory, Teampall Bréanainn, and the supposed remains of a holy well (Tobar Bréanainn).[74] Inis Tuaisceart might be the site of that name referred to in the Lismore Life of St Senan, when the saint, aiming to land at an *Inis Mór* near the coast of Clare (presumably the Aran Islands), was blown past it and landed on an island named Inis Tuaisceart. This is often taken to relate to the Fergus estuary, and *Inis Tuaisceart* simply means 'northern island' so the specifics of the island are unclear. The Lismore Life of Senan is concerned with voyages around Corcomroe, however, which as we have seen has potential links with Brendan, so it is conceivable that there is some Brendan-related story tied up with this episode.[75] Gwenaël Le Duc speculated that the legend – inspired by the shape of the island – that Inis

of the Beginning of Harvest (Dublin, 1962), 101–5. O'Donoghue, *Brendaniana*, 81–3; Doncha Ó Conchúir, *Corca Dhuibhne i Aos lorruis tuaiscirt agus Uí Fhearba* (Dublin, 1973), 115.

68 *Calendar of Documents relating to Ireland 1171–1307*, ed. H. S. Sweetman and G. F. Handcock, 5 vols (London, 1875–86), at v.296.

69 Aubrey Gwynn, *The Medieval Province of Armagh 1470–1545* (Dundalk, 1946), 268.

70 Donncha[dh] Ó Corráin, 'Studies in West Munster History: II Alltraighe', *Journal of the Kerry Archaeological and Historical Society* 2 (1969), 27–37, at 27.

71 Cuppage *et al.*, *Dingle Peninsula*, 308–23.

72 *ibid.*, 310; Tomás Ó Carragáin, 'A Landscape Converted: Archaeology and Early Church Organisation on Iveragh and Dingle, Ireland', in *The Cross goes North: Processes of Conversion in Northern Europe, AD 300–1300*, ed. Martin Carver (Woodbridge, 2002), 127–52, at 143–6.

73 Ó Carragáin, 'A Landscape Converted', 146.

74 Caoimhín Ó Danachair, 'The Holy Wells of Corkaguiney, Co. Kerry', *Journal of the Royal Society of Antiquaries of Ireland* 90 (1960), 67–78, at 77.

75 *Betha Sénain*, lines 2155–7: *Lives of Saints from the Book of Lismore*, ed. Whitley Stokes (Oxford, 1890), 65.

Tuaisceart is a sleeping giant found its way early into the literary tradition, whence it appears in the *Vita S. Machutis* as the story of the giant Milldu. This appears a little far-fetched.[76]

The other major complex in Munster is the major church at Ardfert, which was linked in the later middle ages to Brandon Mountain, by the location of the chancellor of Ardfert's prebend at Kilmalkedar.[77]

In some of the Lives, St Brendan's birth is associated with the region around Tralee. Ardfert is not referred to in the Latin *Vita*, however, nor in the *Nauigatio*. VBD refers to his birth by *Litus Ly*, a calque of *Tragh Li* (Tralee). Fénit, Co. Kerry, on the coast near to Ardfert, where local tradition places his birth, is named (*Fiannain*) in the Lismore Life, but in the O'Clery Life the reading is *an fheorann* ('the shoreland').[78] The reference to Fénit in the Irish text may arise from the misreading *stagnili* ('swampy') for *stagni Len* (Loch Léin) in the *Nauigatio* – though notably Lismore is not conflated with the *Nauigatio*.[79] The antiquity of the Fénit tradition must be regarded as uncertain.

Though early medieval burials have been found at Ardfert, its early connection to the cult, however, remains uncertain.[80] Charles-Edwards suggests that Ardfert and Clonfert were linked by the interests of the Éoganacht Locha Léin, who claimed authority over West Munster and who, as we have already seen, also ruled the church of Clonfert in the seventh century.[81] Ardfert's main *floruit* in the sources is only around the eleventh century onwards, however, when it was for a time clearly the main house of the *familia* of Brendan. The first datable reference to a cult of Brendan at Ardfert, among many to Ardfert in *AI*, is only in 1031–2 when 'Mac Mara ... fasted "against" Brénainn at Ard Ferta' and an '*erenagh* of Ard Ferta Brénainn' is mentioned.[82] After 1068 the *familia* of Brendan abandoned Clonfert for West Munster for a short period, and the *comarba* of Brénnain was buried at Ardfert in 1074. The shift may have been short-lived as the stone church (*damhlaig*) of Ardfert was destroyed by Rory O'Connell of Munster in 1089 and the Synod of Rath Breasil (1111) did not accord the status of a cathedral to Ardfert. In 1152, at the Synod of Kells, the church at Ardfert was judged the most suitable in the diocese to be the cathedral. Consistent with this, the standing church reflects major investment only from around the third decade of the twelfth century.[83]

76 Le Duc, 'Irish Saints in Brittany', 96; Gwenaël Le Duc, 'La Bretagne, intermédiaire entre l'Aquitaine et l'Irlande', in *Aquitaine and Ireland in the Middle Ages*, ed. Jean-Michel Picard (Dublin, 1995), 173–87, at 184–5.

77 Marie O'Sullivan, 'A History of the Development of St Brendan's Cathedral, Ardfert', *Journal of the Kerry Archaeological and Historical Society* 21 (1988), 148–65.

78 *Betha Brénnain* (Lismore), line 3368: *Lives*, ed. Stokes, 101; *Betha Brénnain* (O'Clery) § 2: *Bethada Náem nÉrenn*, ed. Plummer, I.45.

79 *Navigatio*, ed. Selmer, xvii; *Acta Sancti Brendani: original Latin documents connected with the life of Saint Brendan*, ed. P. F. Moran (Dublin, 1872), 85; Carney, Review of *Navigatio*, ed. Selmer, 37–44; David N. Dumville, 'Two Approaches to the Dating of *Nauigatio Sancti Brendani*', *Studi Medievali*, 3a serie 29 (1988), 87–102; Wooding, 'The Munster Element', 37–8.

80 Caroline Toal, *North Munster Archaeological Survey* (Dingle, 1995), 24; Wooding, 'The Munster Element', 41–2.

81 Charles-Edwards, 'Connacht, Saints of', 962.

82 *AU*, 198.

83 Toal, *North Munster*, 259.

How a saint's cult was established in his or her place of origin remains one of the more complex questions in the study of saints. The fact that many early Irish saints deliberately pursued the monastic life *away* from their places of origin suggests that the establishment of the cults of such saints in their places of origin was a subsequent, probably posthumous, action – perhaps by the family of the saint, or by monks from the saint's main cult centre. It is worth noting that the medieval evidence for Ardfert control of Kilmalkedar would, without the *Nauigatio*, inspire the view that the cult in Corco Dhuibhne was taken there during the Ciarraige takeover. This still leaves one with the feeling that Ardfert's specific acquisition of a Brendan cult, as distinct from a cult in West Munster, is later than the writing of the *Nauigatio* or it would have featured in some way in that text. The Altraige no doubt honoured a saint who was of their own kin, but we can say with certainty only that, at least on the evidence of the *Nauigatio*, the mountain was the main centre of Brendan's cult in the ninth century, as it remains to the present day.

The *Nauigatio* indicates that Brandon Mountain was a cult site by the ninth century – unless we entertain the idea that the *Nauigatio*-author himself made the first connection of this mountain with the cult of Brendan. Máire Mac Néill makes the persuasive suggestion, in the light of the referent of local place-names, that the eponym of the mountain is Bran, not Brendan.[84] Irish *Sron Broin* (lit. 'Bran's nose'), for example, refers to *Bran* or *Bron*, not Brendan. The *Sedes Brendani*, which the *Nauigatio*-author gives as the *pre-existing* name for a place on the mountain, or the mountain itself, might be only an interpretation of a name such as **Suidhe Broin*.[85] This would not be the only point at which Brendan and Bran were compared in the Brendan *dossier* and such loose equations of names are fairly typical of cults (see below).[86] Those versions of the *Vita* that present a different opening sequence to the voyage from the *Nauigatio* associate Brendan's vision of the Promised Land and subsequent departure with a mountain in Connacht, named in VBSii as *Mons Aitche*.[87] If this is the older motif, its replacement by the Munster scene could have various causes; perhaps evidence gathered by the *Nauigatio*-author on a visit to his patron's homeland, or perhaps a desire to contrive, by bringing him so near and yet not to his homeland, to show how Brendan could prove that he had truly left his family to follow Christ.

There are a number of minor dedications to Brendan in the area around Brandon Mountain. Holy wells dedicated to St Brendan are at Cloghane (Tobar Bréanainn [site of]),[88] Kildurrihy West (Tobar Bréanainn),[89] and on the north slopes of Cruach Mhárthain (Tobar Bhréanainn).[90] Elsewhere in west Kerry is Tobar ola

84 Mac Néill, *The Festival*, 101–5.

85 Cf. Suidhe Ailbhe in Clare: Edmund Hogan, *Onomasticon Goedelicum locorum et tribuum Hiberniae et Scotiae* (Dublin, 1910), 605.

86 The idea that the tale *Immram Brain* is based on a version of the Brendan legend is set out briefly by Carney, Review of *Navigatio*, ed. Selmer, 44. I discuss this in detail in a forthcoming paper.

87 VBSii § 8: *Vitae*, ed. Heist, 327.

88 100m north-west of the medieval church. Pattern day is Crom Dubh Sunday: Cuppage *et al.*, *Dingle Peninsula*, 354.

89 Ó Danachair, 'The Holy Wells', 76; Cuppage *et al.*, *Dingle Peninsula*, 355.

90 Cuppage *et al.*, *Dingle Peninsula*, 353.

Brénnain, on Valentia Island, Co. Kerry. This is a substantial site, with a holy well and large medieval cross. The name 'Well of Brendan's Anointing' is explained in a local legend of indeterminate date, in which St Brendan is called into the shore to administer the sacraments to two dying men.[91] Further west in Munster is Tobar na Croise (Caherpierce), near Castlemaine.[92] Tober na Molt, near Ardfert, Co. Kerry is linked to St Brendan's baptism by Erc.[93] The *Taxatio* of Ardfert in 1300 lists an *Antrum Brendani* ('Brendan's Cave'), now the churchyard of 'O'Brennan' (< *Uaim Brénnain*) in the parish of Trughanacme – O'Donoghue claims the 'cave' was once visible as an outcrop nearby but the truth of this story is hard to establish.[94] This was associated with an episode in the Life in which the young Brendan does penance in a cave (VBSii: *specus*, VBD/O: *spelunca*) in the course of a journey with Erc.[95]

Brendan's cult is thus represented in many sites across Munster, major and minor. It is notable that the *Nauigatio* suggests a cult only on Brandon Mountain and, possibly, spilling over to the *western* side. This is at odds with the cult as it is seen today, which is found extensively throughout the territory of Altraige and Corco Dhuibhne. The *Nauigatio*-author, in view of the needs of his story, may have simply gone out of his way not to refer to anything within the territory of the Altraige. There is also the possibility that there was no cult in Kerry at all until the *Nauigatio* included Brandon Mountain in the story. Hence the cult as we see it today may be an artefact of the period after the two septs had been united under the Ciarraige, while the cult on the mountain is a separate matter.

A cult of St Brendan in Kilkenny represents an outpost with no obvious early medieval cause. Clonamary, or Cloone, Co. Kilkenny is an early monastic site, lying at the bottom of the valley of the Nore, one mile south-east of Inistioge. It has a variety of structures of medieval date.[96] The dedication is to 'Broondawn/ Bronndan/ Broonahawn'. The dedications include a holy well, with a pattern on St Brendan's day (16 May). The nearby Brandon Hill is a further toponymic reference to the same 'Brendan'. Killenney More (Toberboe), Co. Laois was formerly a separate parish of 'Killiny and Cahir' and the parish church of Killiney now stands in ruins in the townland of Killennymore, or Toberboe.[97] The first reference to a

91 O'Donaghue, *Brendaniana*, 278–90; Paul Grosjean, 'Catalogus codicum hagiographicorum Latinorum bibliothecharum Dubliniensium', *Analecta Bollandiana* 46 (1928), 91–148, at 101–2 n. 2.

92 Cuppage records visits in recent times on St Brendan's day, *contra* An Seabhac: Cuppage *et al.*, *Dingle Peninsula*, 354; An Seabhac, *Triocha-Céad Chorca Dhuibhne* (Dublin, 1939), 203.

93 Toal, *North Munster*, 232–3.

94 O'Donaghue, *Brendaniana*, 59; Paul MacCotter, 'The See-Lands of the Diocese of Ardfert: An Essay in Reconstruction', *Peritia* 14 (2000), 161–204, at 187.

95 VBSii § 4: *Vitae*, ed. Heist, 326; VBD § 6: 'Vita', ed. Grosjean, 106–7; VBO § 5: *Vitae*, ed. Plummer, I.100.

96 Gwynn and Hadcock, *Medieval Religious Houses*, 154; Henry S. Crawford, 'Notes on the Church of Cloone or Cloneamery, County Kilkenny', *Journal of the Royal Society of Antiquaries of Ireland* 55 (1925), 54–7; J. J. Hughes, 'Clonamery Church', *Old Kilkenny Review* 9 (1956–7), 27–31.

97 P. David Sweetman, *et al.*, *Archaeological Inventory of County Laois* (Dublin, 1995), No. 808.

Brendan dedication is in the List of Bishop James Phelan (1669–95): *Patronus Ecclesiæ de Killeen et Cahir, S. Brandanus, Abbas, 16 Maii.* At the Reformation the church and parish of Killiney belonged to the Augustinian canons of the priory of Inistioge, established c.1150–80.[98] The most recent dedication of the church is unknown. The name may be *Cill-finnce* 'Church of St Finneach' or *Cill-finci* the 'Church of St Fainche'. On this basis William Carrigan suggested a dedication to an early bishop Finneach Duirn, or one of a number of SS Fainche. Carrigan rejected the connection of Clonamery with St Brendan of Clonfert, presumably considering the acquisition of the 16 May pattern as antiquarian.[99] There is no reason to agree. As the Augustinian house of Inistioge, a mile to the north-west, had a church in Killiney where the 16 May pattern is recorded at least as early as the seventeenth century, the Clonamery dedication is possibly its work, but in any event was at least acknowledged as a Brendan dedication in the early modern era.[100]

Processes for the establishment of St Brendan's cult in Ireland

Our examination of the cult thus far has accepted the premise that the distribution of the cult is likely to reflect political groupings. St Brendan should be presumed to have moved to Connacht as an act of *peregrinatio*: consciously moving outside his home territory. Whether this movement was undertaken as part of some relationship between the regions – such as for example is implicitly the case with St Columba's migration to Scottish Dalriada – is uncertain. One branch of the Altraige was evidently located around Corcomroe in west Co. Clare, a site with undoubted connections to the Brendan legend.[101] Whether, or how, such migrations may have influenced the cult in Connacht is unclear. The presence at Clonfert of Cuimmíne Fota in the seventh century is presumed to indicate control of the site by the ascendant Éoganacht Locha Léin, but whether this was effected through Munster politics, such as a claim over St Brendan's own sept, or simple political expansion is unclear.[102]

St Brendan's departure in the *Vita S. Brendani* is located somewhere more or less west of Clonfert, as his departure for Aran in the *Nauigatio*, prior to his main voyage. Voyages by SS Ailbe and Mac Creiche, as well as by the voyager Máel Dúin, all focus on Corcomroe and Aran, likely in relationship to the Brendan

98 William Carrigan, *The History and Antiquities of the Diocese of Ossory*, 4 vols (Dublin, 1905), at II.227.

99 Carrigan, *The History and Antiquities*, II.227. Peter Harbison disagrees with Carrigan, but only on the basis of the pattern day of the holy well and on account of the presence of drystone structures, which he implies suggests a western coastal connection of the cult: Peter Harbison, *Pilgrimage in Ireland* (London, 1991), 182.

100 C. A. Empey, 'County Kilkenny in the Anglo-Norman Period', in *Kilkenny: History and Society*, ed. William Nolan and Kevin Whelan (Dublin, 1990), 75–95, at 80.

101 Donnchadh Ó Corráin, 'Studies in West Munster History: IIa: A Further Note on the Alltraighe', *Journal of the Kerry Archaeological and Historical Society* 3 (1970), 19–22; *idem*, 'The Families of Corcumroe', *North Munster Antiquarian Journal* 17 (1975), 21–30.

102 Charles-Edwards, 'Connacht, Saints of', 962.

legend.[103] The west coast, then, is a place in which the voyaging saints appear to be jostling with each other for space, often departing from the same locations. There are several ways to read this evidence. Máire Herbert sees the rise of the Éoganachta, who are linked to Brendan, Ailbe and Máel Dúin, as playing a part in the commemoration of these figures on coastal sites. Implicitly the interaction of cults is here made a matter of shifting politics, but Herbert is rightly wary of tying the promulgation of cults simply to political expansion, noting that the interaction could be mainly on a literary level.[104] The work of Thomas O'Loughlin in particular has drawn attention to theological causes that might influence these processes, eschatological ideas of Ireland as the last nation.[105] We might, for example, interpret Brendan's cult in Mayo as a product of links between the Uí Fiachrach and the other peoples of Connacht, but Brendan's departure from Irrus Domnann, as Stalmans and Charles-Edwards observe, also takes him to a very significant place: the place of Patrick's vision by the western sea.[106] Corco Dhuibhne, as Harbison observes, with its unusual density of monuments and especially ogham stones, has definite claims to be considered as a place with a special status as a religious landscape, and one imagines there must have been similarly very special associations to Corcomroe to account for the range of voyagers associated with it in literature.[107] To what extent might these places of departure for voyages into the ocean have been able to attract cults regardless of secular politics? Such a model might explain the relationship between St Brendan's journey into Corco Dhuibhne and the probably later promulgation of his cult there by the Ciarraige.

Ó Riain has noted another possible model of which we must take note. Both Clonfert and Annaghdown, as well as Tuam, are sites taken over by the Augustinians in the twelfth century, part of a wider pattern of occupation of early sites by the Augustinians in Ireland.[108] Ó Riain – who is inclined to attribute a great part of our hagiographical evidence to the Augustinians – sees the selection of dedications in the extant *Vita S. Brendani* as reflecting an Augustinian interest in promoting the cult.[109] The circumstantial evidence for the cult in Ossory suggests that the Augustinians were active in promoting the cult of St Brendan, and this must give pause in considering other Brendan dedications on the basis of the *Vita*. Circumstantial associations might, however, be all that are at work.

103 Máire Herbert, 'Literary Sea-Voyages and Early Munster Historiography', in *Celtic Connections, Proceedings of the Tenth International Congress of Celtic Studies*, ed. Ronald Black, William Gillies and Roibeard Ó Maolalaigh (East Linton, 1999), 182–9.

104 *ibid.*, 188.

105 Thomas O'Loughlin, *Celtic Theology: Humanity, World and God in Early Irish Writings* (London, 2000), 25–47.

106 Stalmans and Charles–Edwards, 'Meath, Saints of', 675.

107 Peter Harbison, 'Early Irish Pilgrim Archaeology in the Dingle Peninsula', *World Archaeology* 26 (1994), 90–103, at 93–4.

108 See in general, Geraldine Carville, *The Occupation of Celtic Sites in Ireland by the Canons Regular of St Augustine and the Cistercians* (Kalamazoo, 1982).

109 Ó Riain, 'Hagiography without Frontiers', 47 n. 12.

The cult of St Brendan in Scotland and the Atlantic Islands

The *Vita Columbae* describes a visit of *Brendenus mocu Altai* to Columba on the mysterious island of *Hinba*. There is also a reference to a man who had once been a follower of St Brendan.[110] These references imply that by c.700 St Brendan had a considerable cult, which was known in Scotland. This is made more likely in the light of the western coastal occurrences of St Brendan's cult in Ireland, which can be seen as forming one province with western Scotland at times in the early middle ages.

The island of A'Chuli in the Garvellochs was earlier named *Culbrandon*, and the peak of neighbouring Eileach an Naoimh is named Dún Bhrennain.[111] These names have prompted the identification of Eileach an Naoimh with an episode in the *Vita*. The *Vita S. Brendani* has St Brendan visit *Britannia*, where, in the VBSii account, he founds 'two monasteries, one in the island of *Ailech*, the other in *Terra Ethica*, in a place named *Bledua*' (*duo monasteria, unum in insula Ailech, alterum in terra Ethica, in loco nomine Bledua, fundauit*).[112] *Ethica terra/insula* is the name of Tiree in Adomnán's *Vita Columbae*.[113] W. J. Watson found this case compelling, and certainly it is significant that what is possibly the most archaic of the *Vitae* preserves the closest forms to the Scottish names,[114] though it is possible that the names in VBSii were simply subject to reinterpretation in an Ulster context.[115] The topographical details from the Irish Life suggest that its author had Eileach an Naoimh in mind. *Ailec* is in this case an island. In one episode, 'One day Brendan was on a high rock in this island' (*Araile la boi Brénnain for carraic aird isin inis sin*). This would be consistent with an interest in accommodating the place-name Dún Bhrénnain into the author's interpretation of the Latin Life.[116]

The main cluster of medieval dedications to St Brendan is adjacent to the Firth of Lorn, in which lie the Garvellochs. Brendan is the dedicatee of the parish of Kilbrandon and Kilchattan, on the island of Seil, in Lorn.[117] There is also a cemetery site Kilbrenan in Mull and a lost chapel of Kilbraenan in Islay.[118] This cult in and around Lorn is, by its adjacence with Eileach an Naoimh, the most likely to be appreciably early, though it is still a challenge to ascribe an early medieval date to

110 *Vita Columbae* I.26: *Adomnán*, ed. Anderson, 52.

111 RCAHMS, *Argyll: An Inventory of the Ancient Monuments*, 7 vols (Edinburgh, 1971–92), V.No. 354 and n. 22.

112 VBSii § 15: *Vitae*, ed. Heist, 330. VBO (§ 86–7: *Vitae*, ed. Plummer, I.143) gives the variant *Auerech* for *Ailech*, names the monastery *Bledach* and the district *Heth*. The O'Clery Life names the monastery *Bleit*, in the district of *Letha*: *Betha Brénnain* § 56: *Bethada Náem nÉrenn*, ed. Plummer, I.85.

113 *Vita Columbae* I § 9, II § 15: *Adomnán*, ed. Anderson, 44, 114.

114 W. J. Watson, *The History of the Celtic Place-Names of Scotland* (Edinburgh, 1926), 81.

115 Pádraig Ó Riain, 'Codex Salmanticensis: A Provenance *inter Anglos* or *inter Hibernos*?', in '*A Miracle of Learning': Studies in Manuscripts and Irish Learning*, ed. Toby Barnard, Dáibhí Ó Cróinín and Katharine Simms (Aldershot, 1998), 91–100.

116 *Betha Brénnain* § 56: *Bethada Náem nÉrenn*, ed. Plummer, I.85.

117 RCAHMS, *Argyll*, II.No. 254.

118 RCAHMS, *Argyll*, III.Nos 361 and 291.

any site. Eileach an Naoimh has a range of typologically early stone structures, but hard dating is lacking. All the other sites have churches of twelfth-century or later date. At Kerrowmore, Glenlyon, Perthshire, a chapel dedicated to St Brendan was, according to Charles Stewart in 1880, 'built by a McDougal who "dedicated it and the burying ground to St Brandan, the patron saint of his native county, Lorn in Argyleshire" ' in the twelfth century. This is plausible, but no source is given for this explanation.[119]

Scottish cults are characteristically difficult to trace before the later middle ages. Tracing early cults through later evidence one hits the obstacle of the fact that cults of iconic Irish saints are subject to reintroduction from learned antiquarian activity – sometimes a 're-gaelicisation' of existing sites by either incomers or locals. In the case of Lorn, the sites in question all fell within the purview of the Augustinian house on Oronsay at some point in the middle ages, and a case could be made that they were all culted on the basis of a reading of the *Vita* during that period.[120] This would be hypersceptical, but such possibilities do give pause for reflection. We can at least say that the evidence for the cult of Brendan in Scotland is mostly limited to clusters, which might suggest individual promulgations. St Brendan is absent from the Aberdeen Breviary of William Elphinstone (1509–10).

Kilbrannan chapel, Skipness, Argyllshire, is dedicated to St Brendan. The structure is of late thirteenth- to early fourteenth-century date. The site is adjacent to Kilbrannan Sound. The castle contains a chapel dedicated to St Columba, which is arguably earlier than this chapel.[121] John of Fordun states that the island of Rothesay was known as Bute because: *sanctus Brandanus in ea botham ydiomate nostro .bothe. i. cellam construxit* ('St Brendan built a hut on it, *bothe* in our language, i.e. a cell.').[122] The inhabitants of Bute subsequently became known periodically as 'Brandans'. Fordun's *Chronica Gentis Scottorum* (c.1385) ascribes much of its contents to a lost *Legenda Sancti Brendani*, which appears to have included a substantial pseudo-historical account of Scottish/Irish origins, perhaps reflecting a requirement to contextualise an early Irish story for an Anglo-French audience.[123] We do not know how many of the St Brendan dedications in Scotland may have been inspired by this text, but it is one known stimulus for the cult in the later middle ages. Virginia Glenn notes the appearance of St Brendan in an early thirteenth-century psalter from Paris, which appears to have been produced for a patron interested in the saints with cults in the Clyde.[124] Steve Boardman points out that the appearance of Brendan in these Scottish sources is coincident with the

[119] Charles Stewart, *The Gaelic Kingdom of Scotland* (Edinburgh, 1880), 76; James Murray Mackinlay, *Ancient Church Dedications in Scotland: Non-Scriptural Dedications* (Edinburgh, 1914), 69.

[120] RCAHMS, *Argyll*, III.254.

[121] RCAHMS, *Argyll*, I.No. 277.

[122] Broun, *The Irish Identity*, 56, 130. Also note *Chronicle of Scotland* at Database of Dedications to Saints in Medieval Scotland http://www.shca.ed.ac.uk/Research/saints/ Entry EN/EW/1776 (accessed 18 March 2008) and the recorded name from 1450/1 of a mill, 'St Brane', at Methven: *ibid.* Entry EN/EW/651 (accessed 18 March 2008).

[123] *ibid.*, 13, 18, 63–5, 83–8.

[124] Virginia Glenn, 'Court Patronage in Scotland 1240–1340', in *Medieval Art and Architecture in the Diocese of Glasgow*, ed. Richard Fawcett, British Archaeological Association Conference Transactions 23 (Leeds, 1998), 112–21, at 112–14.

settlement of the Stewart lordship in Bute and Cowal, and suggests that the cult of Brendan became promoted in contrast to the devotion to St Columba among their more northerly opponents.[125] What presents itself as a problem from the evidence is how we might take the cult of St Brendan back with any confidence beyond this substantial thirteenth-century promulgation.

Bishop Forbes ascribed Kilbirnie in Ayrshire to St Brendan and St Birinus. St Brennan's or Brinnan's fair was held there on 28 May – at least the same month as the feast of St Brendan.[126] Dunbarney, Perthshire, is attributed to Brendan, though the earliest name (c.1150) is *Drumbirnen*. James Mackinlay assigns it on the basis of a well, in the adjacent parish of Abernethy, known now as Brendi Well.[127] In these cases the fair and well are possible corroborative evidence for a cult of St Brendan of medieval date, though not necessarily of its primary status vis-à-vis a namesake. Birnie (1200 *Brennach*) in Moray is also claimed as a Brendan dedication and has a twelfth-century church.[128] In all these cases a separate *Birinus* or a formation from *braonaigh*, dat. sing. of *braonach* (a 'moist place') could be the cause of association with Brendan.[129]

Forbes lists a range of other sites, only some of which have been documented more extensively by Mackinlay and W. J. Watson. These sites include Balbirnie (Fife), Cullen (Banff), Boyndie (Banff) and Essie (Forfar).[130] A 'St Brandan's Haven' in Banff (*portu nuncupato Sanct Brandans hawyn*) is referred to in a c.1527 charter in the Register of the Abbey of Arbroath.[131] The Calendar of David Camerarius (1631) also presents St Brendan (16 May) with the epithet: *Apostolus Orcadum & Scoticarum insularum*.[132] The claim is a unique one, though echoed in the *Vitae anonyma* of Malo.[133] A Breton origin for the putatively Anglo-Norman *Legenda* would be a plausible explanation. One other possibility should be entertained. Cormac's visit to Orkney suggests, along with his seeming association with Inis Gluaire, that a Brendan narrative – which would therefore likely be the source of the *Vitae anonyma* – was the original source of his voyage tale, in which the more Columban figure of Cormac has displaced Brendan. This may appear an elaborate explanation, but it would explain the otherwise unique association of Cormac with Inis Gluaire, a place otherwise linked to Brendan. Both models are plausible and one is left with only balance of probability to choose between one or the other.

On his visit to St Kilda in 1697, Martin Martin recorded the existence of a St

125 Stephen Boardman, 'The Gaelic World and the Early Stewart Court', in *Mìorun Mòr nan Gall, 'The Great Ill-Will of the Lowlander'? Lowland Perceptions of the Highlands, Medieval and Modern*, ed. Dauvit Broun and Martin MacGregor (Glasgow, 2007), 83–109. Online version at: http://www.arts.gla.ac.uk/scottishstudies/ebooks/miorunmor.htm (accessed 19 Dec. 2007).

126 Mackinlay, *Ancient Church Dedications*, 68–9.

127 *ibid.*, 69.

128 *ibid.*, 69.

129 Watson, *Celtic Place-Names of Scotland*, 189.

130 A. P. Forbes, *Kalendars of Scottish Saints* (Edinburgh, 1872), 284–7.

131 Ed. Cosmo Innes and Patrick Chalmers, *Liber S. Thome de Aberbrothoc* (Edinburgh, 1856), 467.

132 *ibid.*, 237.

133 *Vita anonyma longior* § 7: *Mélanges*, ed. Lot, 304.

Brianan's chapel.[134] This he describes as a stone building with thatched roof in its own churchyard.[135] The name *Brianan* is acceptable as a variant of *Brénnain*, but since the site itself is now almost invisible, no firm conclusions can be drawn from it.[136] Further into the Atlantic, Kirkjubøur, the medieval episcopal centre of Stremoy in the Faroes contains three ruined churches. The church of St Brendan, first built in the eleventh century, was rebuilt around 1420, when it was dedicated to St Brendan and Bishop Erlendur. A pew-carving in the extant church is said to depict St Brendan. A nearby creek is named Brandarsvík (Brendan's Creek).[137] There is also one dedication at Braddan in the Isle of Man.[138]

The cult in Brittany

The dedications to St Brendan at foundations in Brittany of probable medieval origin fall into three clusters. The first centres on Saint-Malo, where we have literary evidence for a cult of Brendan as early as at least 865 × 872, when the earliest firmly datable *Vita* of St Malo, that of Bili, was written. The second is on the western border of Côtes d'Armor. The third is in northern Finistère. A later medieval chapel in Morbihan is an isolated dedication that extends the distribution further south. Many, if not most, of the dedications represent cases in which it is uncertain that the original patron was Brendan of Clonfert.

Five versions survive of Malo's Life, *Vita S. Machutis*. There is controversy over which of the two clearly early Lives is the earlier. Ferdinand Lot argued that the text known as the *Vita anonyma longior* is the earlier version. Bernard Merdrignac, by contrast, has set out the case in detail for the priority of the version by Bili, which is datable, through its dedication to Bishop Ratwili, to 865 × 872.[139] In the *Vita S. Machutis* St Malo is a companion of St Brendan, and studies under him at Nantcarfan in Wales (see below).[140] In Bili's version Malo makes a seven-year sea voyage along with Brendan, with some encounters similar to those in the *Vita S. Brendani*, before becoming the bishop of Alet (Saint-Malo).

The association of Brendan and Malo suggests a cult at or near Saint-Malo in the first millennium. There was a chapel of St Brendan on the island of Cézambre,

134 Martin Martin, *A Description of the Western Islands of Scotland Circa 1695; and A Late Voyage to St Kilda* (Edinburgh, 1999), 264–7.

135 *Ibid.*, 266.

136 David A. Quine, *St Kilda Island Guide* (Grantown-on-Spey, 2000), 74; Harbison, *Pilgrimage*, 183; Geoffrey Stell and Mary Harmon, *Buildings of St Kilda* (Edinburgh, 1988), 17.

137 I have unfortunately been unable to consult Knud J. Krogh, *Kirkjubøur Benches and the Cathedral* (Tórshavn, 1988).

138 George Broderick, *Placenames of the Isle of Man*, 7 vols (Tübingen, 1994–2005), V.111: *Kirk Bredon* (1595), *Sancti Bradarni* (c.1600), *St Brandon* (1693).

139 Lot, *Mélanges*, 100–6, 166ff; Bernard Merdrignac, 'La "desacralisation" du mythe celtique de la navigation vers l'Autre Monde. L'apport du dossier hagiographique de saint Malo', *Ollodagos* 5 (1993), 13–43.

140 It is also claimed that St Gurval was educated with St Brendan in Britain, no doubt as an extension of the story in the *Vita S. Machutis*: O. J. Padel, 'Gudwal', *ODNB*, XXIV.165–6.

just to the north of Saint-Malo; three other chapels were dedicated to St Michael, St Joseph and Notre-Dame.[141] The early tradition that Brendan founded a monastery in *Britanniam* at *Ailech*, which we have seen above in connection with Eileach an Naoimh, has been identified with Alet by modern interpreters, and Baring-Gould and Fisher energetically trace the other names from this episode in Plouaret.[142] This is less likely than the Scottish alternative. Le Duc, while rejecting the idea that the Latin Life is concerned with Brittany, suggests that the Middle Irish forms of the names in the British episode visit are an interpretation of the Latin Life in terms of Breton place-names. Plummer, certainly, regarded the reference to *Letha* as indicating Brittany.[143]

The parish of Saint-Brandan, near Quintin, lies just 2 km south of the ancient road between Carhaix and Alet. The patron is nowadays identified with St Brandan and his identity as patron of Clonfert.[144] Fourteenth- and fifteenth-century attestations of the name, however, indicate the forms *Bedan* (1459, 1468, 1508, 1535, 1543, 1598) and *Brandan* (1543, 1599).[145] It is likely that St Bédan was the original patron and that Brandan is a conflation. Trégrom is one of two dedications to St Brandan in the west of Côtes d'Armor.[146] Here a restored medieval church, located south of Lannion in the valley of Leguier, has St Brandan as its patron. Preserved in the churchyard is a stone coffin – either prehistoric or medieval – which in legend is the boat by which Brandan travelled to Brittany.[147] Lanbellec, Côtes d'Armor, is a second dedication in the area.[148] There is also a sixteenth-century chapel at Langonnet (nr Gourin) that is well to the south of the other occurrences.[149] Here a family connection with a cult site in Côtes d'Armor may be the most likely explanation.[150]

In Finistère two sites are associated with Brendan in tradition, though in clear conflation with a separate saint, Brévelaire. At Loc Brévelaire the earliest references to the site are in the following forms: *Loprevalarz* (1467), *Loc Brevalazre* (1516), *Locprevalazre* (1664), and *Locprevalayre* (1680).[151] The nineteenth-century author Pol de Courcy stated that Loc Brevelaire was '*Monasterium Sti*

141 Nathalie Molines and Philippe Guigon, *Les églises des îles de Bretagne* (Rennes, 1997), 56–7, include a photo of the chapel before all traces of it and the other three chapels disappeared after the Second World War; G. H. Doble, *The Saints of Cornwall*, 5 vols (Truro and Oxford, 1960–70), IV.118; *LBS*, I.246.

142 *LBS*, I.246.

143 Le Duc, 'Irish Saints in Brittany', 96; *Bethada Náem nÉrenn*, ed. Plummer, II.375.

144 Jean Le Retif, *Si Saint Brandan m'était Conté* (Saint-Brieuc, 1989), 5.

145 Bernard Tanguy, *Dictionnaire des noms de communes, trèves, et paroisses des Côtes d'Armor: origine et signification* (Douarnenez, 1992), 268–9.

146 Baring-Gould (*LBS*, I.247) claims that VBSii's *Ethica* corresponds to the *'-et'* in *Plouaret*, i.e. *plou-ar-et[h]*, but this seems fanciful.

147 Tanguy, *Côtes d'Armor*, 334.

148 *ibid.*, 123–4.

149 *LBS*, I.251.

150 For example, three members of the Marboeuf family of Trégrom were abbots of Langonnet in the seventeenth/eighteenth century: see 'Ancienne noblesse de Tregrom' at http://www.infobretagne.com/tregrom htm (accessed 19 Dec. 2007).

151 Bernard Tanguy, *Dictionnaire des noms de communes trèves et paroisses du Finistère* (Douarnenez, 1990), 117.

Brendani' in the middle ages, but gave no source for this.[152] His ascription is probably based on a false attribution of two references to *Ecclesia Loci Bridanni* (1185) and *Locus Brendani* (1330) to Loc Brévelaire, which actually refer to Lopreden in Plouenan.[153] Doble was prepared to accept the possibility of the Brendan dedication being primary, but on the basis of the Lopreden reference being to Loc Brévelaire; without this evidence the Brévelaire dedication is clearly likely to be the original. A sixteenth-century chapel at Botsorhel, now completely ruined, was ascribed to St Brandan, but located in the manor of *Brévara*, again indicating Brévelaire as the primary cult.

The conflation of Brévalaire with Brendan is clearly a common one, but it is unclear as to its antiquity. Albert Le Grand records the equation of the two saints in Brittany in the early seventeenth century, although it is not clear how much earlier the conflation dates.[154] St Brévelaire is recorded in The *Breviary of Tréguier* for 1 June as *S. Brangualadri confessoris*. He figures (*Brangualadre*) in litanies of *Missel Saint-Vougay*, around the end of the eleventh century. He is clearly the saint known in Britain as Branwalader or Breward, an obscure but clearly once influential cult, recorded in the *Martyrology of Exeter* under 6 June and 9 February.[155] His feast is 6 June in Jersey (St Brelade).

Kerlouan, Guisseny, Finistère, has a ruined medieval church and a modern church dedicated to Brévelaire.[156] Here there is no specific reference to Brendan and the pattern is the first Sunday in June; again this provides a link to the cult of Branwalader. The Fishermen's Chapel in Saint Brelade, Jersey, a building of eleventh- to twelfth-century date, evinces a conflation of Branwalader with the cult of St Brendan from at least 1914–15, the date being the design of several suggestive windows: the north window ('St Brelade en voyage') depicts the saint among icebergs, the south transept window (untitled) has him saying mass on the Paradise of Birds. This link, which also appears in a church pamphlet of 1932, may be simply the antiquarian speculation of the incumbent of the early twentieth century, J. Balleine.[157] The earliest reference is to *Broladri* (1053), again Branwalader and not St Brendan the Navigator.[158]

The Breton cult is the only significant dedication evidence on the Continent. The large number of *Nauigatio* MSS in France and Italy do not find a corresponding material cult east of Brittany, except in areas where suggestive place-names might be adopted.[159] Carl Selmer, the twentieth-century editor of the *Nauigatio*, tried to identify St Brendan with the origins of the name Brandenburg in Germany and a cult in the cities around it. His attempts are not convincing, but his identification of the cult in the region is plausible.[160]

152 *LBS*, I.251.

153 Tanguy, *Finistère*, 118, 192 – *contra* Doble, *The Saints of Cornwall*, IV.118.

154 Doble, *Saints of Cornwall*, IV.118.

155 Tanguy, *Finistère*, 117–18.

156 *ibid.*, 95.

157 J. A. Balleine, *The Story of St Brolade Church, Jersey* (Gloucester, 1932); Doble, *The Saints of Cornwall*, IV.116–27.

158 Warwick Rodwell *et al.*, *The Fishermen's Chapel, Saint Brelade, Jersey* (Stroud, 1990), 161, also 13–14, 123–4.

159 Burgess and Strijbosch, *The Legend*, 13–20.

160 Carl Selmer, 'The Origin of Brandenburg (Prussia), the St Brendan Legend and the

The cult in Britain

The Breton and Scottish cults of St Brendan combine early literary references by writers located in these countries with probable later culting of the saint by medieval enthusiasts. The earliest datable Brythonic cult is that suggested by *Vita Machutis* of Bili (865 × 872), but it in turn is probably relying on a British source inasmuch as it places Brendan at Llancarfan, in Wales. In Wales there are no dedications to St Brendan, but the *Vita S. Machutis* makes Brendan abbot in *Nantcaruan* (and *uallis Caruan*), which we know to be an older name for Llancarfan (Glamorgan).[161] The claim that Brendan was an abbot in Wales is unique; the cult is otherwise unattested in Llancarfan – Brendan does not, for example, feature in the considerable documentary record, known as the Llancarfan 'archive', at the close of the *Vita S. Cadoci*.[162] Nonetheless it is plausible that a cult of St Brendan once existed in Wales and on the Welsh border. Brendan features among the Irish saints mentioned in Rhygyfarch's *Vita S. David*. Ó Riain sees Rhygyfarch's references to Irish saints as fuelled by later Irish textual imports – though he has oscillated on the chronology of this process – but Rhygyfarch's Irish saints include ones already culted in Wales.[163] A *Vita* of St Brendan (based on the *Nauigatio*) exists in the collection of *Vitae* in BL Cotton Vespasian A.xiv, and there was once a *Vita* of Brendan at Leominster Priory.[164] In 1199/1200 Ludlow Priory claimed the discovery of the bodies, identified with a label, of Brendan's father and mother.[165] There is also a Brendan chapel dedication in Bristol that

Scoti of the Tenth Century', *Traditio* 7 (1949–51), 416–33. On the cult in Mecklenburg, see *ibid.*, 428–9.

161 *Vita S. Machutis* §§ 2 & 4: *Mélanges*, ed. Lot, 354–5; *Book of Llan Dâv*, 145.

162 *Vita S. Cadoci: Vitae Sanctorum Britanniae et Geneaologiae*, ed. and trans. A. W. Wade-Evans (Cardiff, 1944), 110–41. See also Wendy Davies, 'Property Rights and Property Claims in Welsh *vitae* of the Eleventh Century', in *Hagiographie, cultures, et sociétés, IVe–XIIe siècles*, ed. Evelyne Patlagean and Pierre Riché (Paris, 1981), 515–33, at 519.

163 Pádraig Ó Riain, 'The Irish Element in Welsh Hagiographical Tradition', in *Irish Antiquity*, ed. Donnchadh Ó Corráin (Cork, 1981), 291–303, at 294–5; Ó Riain, 'Hagiography without Frontiers', passim; Wooding, 'The Figure', 12–13.

164 Richard Sharpe, 'Which Text is Rhygyfarch's *Life* of St David?', in *St David of Wales*, ed. Evans and Wooding, 90–106, at 103 n. 51. Layamon, a west country man, also refers to St Brendan in his *Brut*, but the context here (with Columcille and Brigit) suggests a direct Irish source: Layamon, *Brut*, line 11180: *Brut edited from British Museum MS Cotton Caligula A.IX and British Museum MS Cotton Otho C.XIII*, ed. G. L. Brook and R. F. Leslie, Early English Text Society 250, 277, 2 vols (London, 1963–78), II.585. There is a useful discussion of this and the direct sourcing of the English cult in general in J. S. P. Tatlock, 'Greater Irish Saints in Lawman and in England', *Modern Philology* 43.1 (1945), 72–6.

165 John Leland, *De Rebus Brittanicis Collectanea*, ed. Thomas Hearne, 6 vols (London, 1774), III.407, where Brendan's father (Findlug) is named St Fercher and his mother St Corona (cf. *Cara* in VBSii) – who is also here claimed as aunt to St Columba. There is a brief discussion in Robert Bartlett, 'Cults of Irish, Scottish and Welsh Saints in Twelfth-century England', *Britain and Ireland 900–1300: Insular Responses to Medieval European Change*, ed. Brendan Smith (Cambridge, 1999), 67–86, at 77.

might be linked to a west country cult. In 1174 William, earl of Gloucester gave the outcrop of Brandon Hill (now topped by Cabot's Tower) to the monks of St James, Tewkesbury, where they dedicated a chapel to St Brendan.[166]

How might the cult have reached the west country? It may only have been a literary enthusiasm, but the cult is found across more or less the same geographical range, though on an extremely more limited scale, as David's cult through South Wales and into western England. While this is thin evidence on which to speculate that Brendan was to some extent culted as a companion of David across South Wales, this is an attractive explanation.[167]

There appears to have been no significant cult of St Brendan in the heartland of Anglo-Saxon England.[168] Relics are claimed from the Benedictine abbeys of Reading, Hyde and Thorney, but in these cases the relics are plausibly explained as post-Reform assemblages collected from various sources.[169] At Reading the relics are listed among a collection that Denis Bethell would see as drawing upon Anglo-Saxon collections including Leominster, where we have already noted the previous existence of a *Vita* of St Brendan.[170] A further relic list claiming St Brendan is that of the canons of St Mary at Warwick.[171] Brendan was commemorated in the cathedral at Exeter by the twelfth century – where he was not equated with Branwalader, as in Brittany – but his feast was removed at the revision of the cathedral's martyrology at the direction of Bishop Grandisson c.1337.[172] Further evidence of his cult in western Britain comes from Perranzabuloe (Cornwall), which claimed to possess one of his teeth in the visitation of 1281, and from two dedications in Devon: the parish church of Brendon and the chapel at South Prawle, in the parish of Stokenham.[173] Brendon parish church has been held to be a

166 *William Worcestre: The Topography of Medieval Bristol*, ed. Frances Neale, Bristol Record Society 51 (Bristol, 2000), 227. Nearby to the east is an area named 'Broomhill', but this is apparently a separate toponym. Interestingly, though coincidentally, modern St Brendan's College is in Broomhill Rd.

167 There is also the tradition in the *Catalogus Ordinum Sanctorum in Hybernia*, that Brendan was among the early Irish saints to receive their order of the Mass from David, Cadoc and Gildas: *Catalogus sanctorum Hiberniae* § 4: ed. Paul Grosjean, 'Édition et commentaire du *Catalogus sanctorum Hiberniae secundum diversa tempora* ou *De tribus ordinibus sanctorum Hiberniae*', *Analecta Bollandiana* 73 (1955), 197–213, 289–322, at 206, 209–10, and commentary, 292–6.

168 He appears under 16 May in the late eleventh-century calendar, probably written at Evesham c.1064–95, in Bodleian Hatton 113, iii*r*–viii*v*: Rebecca Rushforth, *An Atlas of Saints in Anglo-Saxon Calendars* (Cambridge, 2002), 33. See also John Blair, 'A Handlist of Anglo-Saxon Saints', in *Local Saints and Local Churches*, ed. Thacker and Sharpe, 495–565, where St Breward appears (519), but not Brendan.

169 I. G. Thomas, 'The Cult of Saints' Relics in Medieval England' (unpublished PhD thesis, University of London, 1974), 374.

170 D. Bethell, 'The Making of a Twelfth-century Relic Collection', in *Popular Belief and Practice*, Studies in Church History VIII, ed. G. J. Cuming and Derek Baker (Cambridge, 1972), 61–72, at 65.

171 Thomas, 'The Cult of Saints' Relics', 374.

172 *Ordinale Exon.*, ed. J. N. Dalton and G. Doble, 4 vols (London, 1909–40), IV.12. On Branwalader, see *ibid.*, IV.42.

173 Nicholas Orme, *The Saints of Cornwall* (Oxford, 2000), 73.

Brendan dedication since the first reference in 1742, though the parish feast was Whit Tuesday in the 1700s.[174] The place-name 'Brandon' is possibly from OE *brōm dūn* 'broom hill' or 'bramble hill' and the dedication to Brendan was probably inspired by the toponym.[175] At Prawle, on the south coast of Devon, a *capella Sancti Brendani* was licensed by Bishop Lacey in 1421.[176] A subsequent licence of 1425, however, calls it *capellis sanctorum ... Brendoci*, leading Orme to speculate that there was a cult of separate saint Brandoc/Brendoc, which became conflated with that of Brendan.[177] The place-name *brōm dūn* also gave cause for the dedication to St Brandon of the medieval church at Brancepeth, Co. Durham (*Brentespethe* 1085). The name is from OE *Brōmdunes-pæþ* ('path to 'broom hill').[178] These dedications give clear cause to believe that they are toponymic in origin. Their appropriation to the cult of Brendan reflects the continuing fame of the saint in the later middle ages and early modern period.

Processes for the spread of the cult outside Ireland

Pre-modern scholars were credulous in their reading of travels in hagiography as giving form to the medieval cult. There is cause to see the cult in Scotland and Brittany as having arrived there in the early middle ages. The evidence of *Vita S. Machutis* should be given great weight. Its association of St Brendan with South Wales probably identifies an early theatre for the reception of the cult and a path of transmission of the cult to Brittany. This, and the possibly early cult in Argyll, suggests transmission through early Irish links to Wales and Scotland – on the chronology of *Vita S. Machutis* this should be earlier than Ó Riain posits for the transmission of cults to Wales.[179] More than likely the earlier transmissions were interpreted and extended by much later promulgations in a period, after c.1100, when St Brendan was thoroughly the saint of the *Nauigatio*. At this point a clue to the fact that the 'literary cult' is influential are some associations with other saints linked to St Brendan – a phenomenon of 'recurrent adjacency'?[180] A cult of St Marnock (Mernóc) is found in Bute and a cult of St Barnitus (Barrind) in Argyll.[181] Both of these saints are associated with St Brendan at the opening of the *Nauigatio*

174 Nicholas Orme, *English Church Dedications: with a Survey of Cornwall and Devon* (Exeter, 1996), 137.

175 J. E. B. Gover *et al.*, *The Place-Names of Devon*, 2 vols (Cambridge, 1931–2), I.58–9.

176 *Episcopal register of Edmund Lacy*, II.fol. II*r*: *The Register of Edmund Lacy, Bishop of Exeter, 1420–1455: Registrum Commune*, Devon and Cornwall Record Society, new series 7, 10, 13, 16, 18, 5 vols (Torquay, 1963–72), I.34.

177 Orme, *The Saints of Cornwall*, 73: he notes a bequest of 1431 to a *capelle Sanct Brandoci*, which is unlocated. This also could be Prawle or possibly Braunton, N. Devon.

178 Eilert Ekwall, *The Concise Dictionary of English Place-Names*, 4th edn (Oxford, 1960), 60.

179 Ó Riain, 'The Irish Element'; *idem*, 'Hagiography without Frontiers'.

180 See Karen Jankulak, 'Adjacent Saints', above.

181 Watson, *Celtic Place-Names*, 187, 292; D. E. Thornton, 'Barinthus', *ODNB*, III.857; Boardman, 'The Gaelic World', 94 n. 32.

– a clue that this tale in particular is the one involved, as these figures are probably unique to the *Nauigatio*.[182]

A problem for the study of the British and Breton cult is the British episode in the *Vita*. This seems to indicate the sites in Argyll, but the sites named could also be in Brittany. The British episode also involves a visit to Gildas, which could originally have indicated Wales or south-west Britain, but could also be set in Brittany or conceivably Scotland. Only further study of the *Vita* might resolve this question.

Conclusion

St Brendan's cult is unusual for the scale of the literary impetus that sustained it beyond its early medieval promulgation. Both the limitations of the early sources and the almost overwhelming impact of *Nauigatio* upon pre-existing evidence of the cult make identification of early dedications often a matter of circumstantial, rather than conclusive, argument. The evidence is, however, as Le Duc has observed, more detailed than complicated. There seems little cause to doubt the coherence of the story of a cult founded at Brendan's own house in Connacht, being posthumously taken to his home region and, at an early date, further afield to places, such as Scotland and South Wales, where early Irish cults are otherwise known.[183]

182 St Brendan's parish, Coolock, Co. Dublin, also claims a holy well to St Brendan, connected to the cult of Mernóc in Co. Dublin: http://www.stbrendanscoolock.org/index.php?sid=history/h2&sidep=history (accessed 19 Dec. 2007).

183 For assistance in the completion of this survey I would like to thank especially Karen Jankulak for her help with many matters, including numerous references and company on field visits. Pat Jones also assisted in digging up numerous items and Steve Boardman, John Carey, Bernadette Jordan, Kevin Murray, Breandán Ó Ciobháin and Donnchadh Ó Corráin all provided invaluable references. All responsibility for any errors lies with the author. I would also especially thank Glyn Burgess, Tomás Ó Caoimh and Thomas O'Loughlin for much encouragement.

INDEX

Aberdeen, 127, 156, 163, 165–6, 172, 177, 179; Breviary, 24, 67, 196
Aberdour, 26
Abernethy, 3, 197
A'Chuli, 195
Acts of Andrew and Matthias, 7
Ada, countess, 124
Adam, 139
Adomnán, 15, 20, 67, 74, 187, 195
Adoration, 170–1, 173, 175–6
Aebbe, saint, 121
Aed son of Eochaid, King of Connacht, 185–6
Áed mac Máel Mithig, 4, 9
Aelred of Rievaulx, 125, 130–4, 136–40, 142–5
Aeneas Sylvius Piccolomini, 161
Ailbe, saint, 193–4
Ail Cluaide, 27, 28, 36, 37, see also Dumbarton, Dumbarton Rock
Ailech, 195, 199
Aird, William, 120
Airedale, 58
Alan, monk of Durham, 119, 123–4
Alba, 26, 49, 50, 54
Alchfrith, king of Deira, 10
Aldhun, bishop, 52
Alet, 198–9
Alexander, bishop of Lincoln, 85
Alexander III, pope, 78
Alexander I, king of Scots, 8, 9, 67, 121, 144
Alexander son of Hugo, 39
Alexandria, 154
Alfred, king of England, 139–42, 144
Alfred Westou, 125
Allerdale, 55–6, 75–6, 79
Altarnun, 101, 104–5
Altraige, Munster sept, 181, 187–9, 191–3
Alwin, mormaer of Lennox, 40
Ambrose, 133
Ambrosius, 85
Anderson, Marjorie, 2, 52
Andrew, apostle and saint, 1, 4, 5, 6, 7, 8, 10, 13, 17, 114
Anecol, 40
Anglo-Saxon Chronicle, 28, 46, 73
Angus, 23
Angus, earls of, 149
Annaghdown, 185–6, 194
Annales Cambriae, 68–9, 71, 87, 88
Annals of Ulster, 28, 73
Anne, saint, 172–4, 178
Antioch, 8
Antonine Wall, 32
Antwerp, 175
Aran, 184, 186, 189, 193
Arbroath, 197
Arbuthnott, 24
Ardbraccan, 24–5
Ardfert, 184, 189–92, *Taxatio* of, 192
Arendal, 167
Argyll, 29, 73, 168
Arkil, 57–9
Armagh, 25, 26, 31
Armagh, book of, 20, 22, 27
Armes Prydain, 28
Armorica, 27, 36, 38, 97
Arraglen, 188
Arthur, king, 111
Arwystli, 84
Asaph, bishop and saint, 66, 83–4, 86–7
Ash, Marinell, 3, 16
Aspatria, 75, 79
Athelstan, King, 139, 142, 144
Athgal, king of the Britons of Strathclyde, 28
Atropa, 168–9
Augustine, 6, 9, 12, 14, 70
Augustinians, 82, 185, 194
Austol, saint, 100, 109, 113–14, 116
Ayr, parish kirk of, 39
Ayrshire, 73
Baithenus, saint, his relics, 33
Balbirnie, 197
Balliol, Edward, 150
Ballygar, 186
Baltic Crusade, 151, 153
Balthasar, 162, 166–8, 173, 176
Bamburgh, 13, 14, 44, 46; house/dynasty of, 43–6, 51–2, 54–5, 57–8, 61, 77, 78
Bampton Patrick, 61, 77
Banchory-Ternan, 24
Bangor, bishopric of, 83–4
Baring-Gould, Sabine, 87, 94, 106, 180, 199
Barnabas, saint, 34
Barrfind, 15
Barrow, Geoffrey, 45, 56, 81–2, 120
Barry, Charles, 66, 90
Bartrum, Peter, 107
Baxters' Guild, 156
Bay of Biscay, 154
Beatons, of Mull, 169
Beauly river, 15
Beda Ferdan, 32, 39–40
Bédan, saint, 199

Bede, 5, 6, 7, 8, 9, 10, 11, 13, 14, 17, 25, 66, 69
Bergen, 167
Bernard of Clairvaux, 133–4
Bernicia, 10, 12
Berwickshire, 121
Beunans Meriasek, 108
Beverley, 172
Bewnans Ke, 111
Bieler, 33, 34
Bili, 198, 201
Birinus, saint, 197
Birnie, 197
Blackadder, Robert, archbishop of Glasgow, 80
Black Isle, 15
Boardman, Steve, 196
Boffey, Julia, 168
Boethenus, island of, 34
Bohemia, Anne of, 173–4
Book of the Dean of Lismore, 169
Books of Epistles, 36
Boquhanran, see Monachkenneran
Bonedd y Saint, 106
Bonkill, Edward, 157
Borthwick, 79, 82
Bothmael, 110
Botsorhel, 200
Bowen, Emrys George, 91–6, 99, 117
Bower, Walter, 129, 130, 162–3
Boyndie, 197
Braddan, 198
Bran, 191
Brandarsvík, 198
Brandenburg, 200
Brandon (Cé Bhréanainn), 188
Brandon Creek (Cuas an Bhodaigh), 188–9
Brandon Head (Pointe an Choma Dhóite), 188
Brandon Hill, 192, 202
Brandon Mountain, 188–92
Brandon Point (Sron Broin), 188
Branwalader, see Brévelaire
Briac, saint, 109
Brechin cathedral, 155
Bréifne, 184
Brendan, saint, of Clonfert, 180–204; his various *Lives*, 182–6, 188, 190–1, 193–6, 198
Brendan, saint, of Birr, 182
Brendan's Cave (*Antrum Brendani*)
Brendan's Seat (*Sedes Brendani*), 188, 191
Brendi Well, 197
Breock, saint, 98
Brévelaire, saint, 199–200
Breviary of Tréguier, 200
Bridei, son of Der-Ilei, 15
Bridget of Sweden, saint, 154
Brieuc, saint, 98
Brig, sister of St Brendan, 185
Brigid, saint, 69
Brioc, saint, 100, 109
Bristol, 201
Britain, 4, 6, 8, 12, 38, 42, 51, 69–70, 72, 75–6, 83, 88, 90, 91, 122–3, 126, 201–3
Britons, 28, 30, 31, 32, 36, 37, 38, 58, 89 38, 73, 86
Brittany, 48, 50, 51, 71–2, 91–2, 93, 94, 96–101, 103, 106–8, 110–12, 114–15, 117, 180–1, 198–200
Bromfield, 75, 79
Brompton, John, 172
Brooke, Christopher, 86
Brooke, Daphne, 60
Broun, Dauvit, 2, 3, 8, 16, 26, 30, 49, 183
Brown, George, bishop of Dunkeld, 156, 177–8
Bruges, 172
Buchedd Ieuan Gwas Padrig, 45
Budoc, saint, 110–11
Budock, parish of, 111
Buez Santez Nonn, 103, 105
Burghead, fort of, 13, 14, 16
Burgundy, 54, 171
Bute, 168, 196–7
Butler-Bowdon cope, 171
Byrne, Francis John, 20, 22, 26, 27, 30, 31, 33, 34
Cabot's Tower, 202
Cado, saint, 108
Cadoc, saint, 95, 100, 108–10, 117; *Life* of, 108
Cadwallon, king, 84
Caelian Hill, 6, 7
Caerleon, 86
Caernarvonshire, 51
Caldbeck, 75, 79
Calpurn, father of St Patrick, 36, 38
Camborne, 107
Cambrensis Eversus, 186
Camerarius, David, 197
'Campus Taburniae', 32, 37
Candlemas, 165
Cane, Meredith, 48
Canterbury, 9, 11, 12, 161; archbishop of, 83–4
Caradog of Llancarfan, author of Book of Llandaf, 86, 88
Carantec, 97–8
Carantoc/Carantec, saint, 96–9, 116
Cardigan, 94
Carey, John, 117
Carham, battle of, 54, 74, 78
Carhaix, 199
Carlisle, 55, 82, 122, 125, 131; priory, 79; bishopric, 81
Carmelites, 172
Carrick, 129
Carrigan, William, 193
Castlemaine, 192
Castle Sowerby, 75
Cartwright, Jane, 103
Caspar, 166, 176
Celestine I, pope and saint, 33, 34, 35
Celestine III, pope, 72
Cell Fine, church of, 33, 34–5, see also Finte

Cennrígmonaid, 1–4, 6, 8–9, 13, 16–17
Ceredigion, 98, 101–2
Cerrigydrudion, 45
Cézambre, 198
Charles IV, Emperor, 173–5,
Charles V, Emperor, 173
Charles V, king of France, 173
Charles VII, king of France, 176
Charles-Edwards, Thomas, 14, 18, 22, 190, 194
Chester, 70; earl of, 83–4; bishopric of, 83
Chevalier, Étienne, 176
Chichester-Constable chasuble, 171
Children of Lir, 187
Chlodomer of Orléans, 54
Christ, 7, 9, 70, 133, 160, 162–3, 166–8, 170, 173, 178, 191
Christian I, king of Denmark, 161, 167, 174–5
Christian II, king of Denmark, 175
Christian, nephew of King Hans of Denmark, 175
Chronica Gentis Scottorum, 196
Chronicle of Ireland, 3
Church of St Fainche, *Cill-finci*, 193
Church of St Finneach, *Cill-finnce*, 193
Ciarán Enaigh Dúin, 185
Ciarán, founder of Clonmacnoise, 69
Ciarraige, 189, 191–2, 194
Citeaux, 126
City of the Legion (see Chester)
Clancy, Thomas, 5, 50, 60, 77, 88, 126
Clark, Cecily, 44, 55.
Cleder, saint, 95
Cléder, 113
Cloghane, 191
Clonamary/Cloone, 192–3
Clonfert (*Clúain Ferta*), 181, 183–6, 188, 190, 193–4
Cluain-na-gCarnán, 187
Clwyd, river, 83
Clyde, Firth of, 30
Clyde, river, 29, 30, 31, 32, 39, 60, 73, 196
Clyde Rock (see Dumbarton)
Clydesdale (also Clyde Valley), 44, 73
Cnoc Bréannain, see Brandon Mountain
Cnut, 140, 143–4
Cochno, 39
Cóeti, bishop of Iona, 15
Colan, saint, 98
Coldingham, priory of, 121
Coldinghamshire, 121
Colgan, John, 21
Collen, saint, 98
Colmán na mBretan, abbot of Sláne, 22, 30, 31
Colodoc, saint, 111
Cologne, 161–3, 167, 174–5
Columb of Cornwall, saint, 96–7, 109
Columba of Iona, saint, 15, 29, 30–1, 69–70, 74, 88, 193, 195, 197; *Life* of, 67, 182, 186–7, 195; bell named, 156
Columba of Sens, saint, 96–7
Columbanus of Luxeuil, saint, 97
Colum Cille, (see Columba)
Comainmniguid Nóem nÉrenn, 185
Concess/Concessa, mother of St Patrick, 36, 38
Coney Island, 187
Confession, of St Patrick, 18
Congar, saint, 95
Congresbury, 95
Connacht, 185–7, 191, 193–4
Connachta, the, 184
Constantine V, of Byzantium, 9
Constantine of Govan, saint, 29, 73, 77, 81
Constantine the Great, 163
Constantinople, 8, 10, 12, 13, 161–3
Conveth, 25
Conwy, river, 83
Copenhagen, 175
Corco Dhuibhne, 189, 191–2, 194
Corcomroe, 189, 193–4
Corentin, saint, 109–10
Cormac son of Ciarán, 186
Cormac ua Liatháin, saint, 186–7, 197
Cornwall, 48, 50, 51, 91–2, 93–4, 96–101, 104, 105, 107–17
Corpus Christi, feast of, Aberdeen, 156; Dublin, 165; Hereford, 165; Lanark, 165
Côtes d'Armor, 198–9
Coventry, 166; ring from, 167
Coulm of Brittany, saint, 97
Cowal, 29, 197
Craigbanzo, 39
Cramond, William, 160
Crantock, 96, 98
Crete, 152, 154
Crichton, 79
Crínán of Dunkeld, 56
Crinan tein, 56
Cristinus, son of Beda, 39
Crosthwaite, 82–3
Cubert, 98
Cubert, saint, 98
Cuby, saint, 104–5
Cuimmíne Fota, 193
Culbrandon, 195
Cullen, 197
Cullen Bay, 160
Culross, 80
Cumberland, 44, 73, 75–6, 77, 81, 82, 83, 88, 131
Cumbria, 29, 44, 50, 53, 54, 56, 72–3, 75, 77–8, 82, 88, 142
Cumbrians, 53, 141
Cumin, William, 121
Curetán, bishop of Ross, 15, 16
Cury, 109
Custantín, king of the Picts, 9
Cuthbert, abbot of Monkwearmouth, 69
Cuthbert, saint, 49, 98, 119–29, 141; *Life* of, 10, 67
Cyndeyrn (see Kentigern)

Cynog, bishop and saint, 70
Dál Cais, 22
Dalpatrick, 29
Dalriada, 193
Dalziel, 29
Dalziel, Sir John, 153
Damon, John Edward, 145
Danes, 140–2
Daniel of the Bangors (see Deiniol)
Daniel, Walter, 131
Danielston, Walter, bishop of St Andrews, 171
Daoulas, abbey of, 103
David, Old Testament king, 14, 133, 136
David I, king of Scots, 77–82, 121–2, 125, 128, 130–9, 144–5
David II, king of Scots, 129, 149–50, 152–3
David, Earl, brother of William I, 40
David, bishop and saint, of Wales, 70, 84–6, 94, 100–5, 108, 202; *Life* of, 101–4, 201
Davidstow, 101, 105
Dearham, 75
de Culwen, Sir Patrick, 77
Decuman, saint, 109–10
Deer, 26
Deiniol, saint and first bishop of Bangor, 70
Deira, 10, 12, 14
Denbighshire, 45, 51, 83
Denmark, 160, 174–5
de Mezieres, Phillipe, 154
De obsessione Dunelmi, 51, 58
De primo Saxonum adventu, 51
de Puiset, Hugh, bishop of Durham, 119–21, 123
Derwent, river, 76
de St Calais, William, bishop of Durham, 120–1
de Vaux, Hubert, 49, 50
Devon, 91, 94, 105, 112–13
de Voragine, James/Jacobus, 154, 163
de Worde, Wynkyn, 68, 164
Dirinon, 101, 103, 105
Ditchburn, David, 178
Doble, Gilbert Hunter, 91–100, 104, 106–10, 112–14, 116–18, 200
Dol, archbishop of, 86
Dolfin, 123
Dolfin, son of Gospatrick son of Maldred, 56
Dolfin, son of Thorfinn, 58
Domesday survey, 46, 57, 59, 104, 111–12
Domnach Arte/Airte, 33, 35 see also Dominica Archa,
Domnach Chrom Dubh, 188
Dominica Archa, 34
Domus Romanorum, 34, see also Thech na Róman
Donnchad/Duncan I, king of Scots, 53, 54, 56
Doranstown, 186
Dorothea, queen of Denmark, 174
Douglas, Beatrice, countess of Errol, 177
Douglas, George, earl of Angus, 153
Douglas, James, lord of Dalkeith, 153
Douglas, William, earl of Douglas, 153
Dowdall, primate of Armagh, 189
Down, abbey, 125
Driscoll, Steve, 76
Drostan, saint, 24, 25–6
Drumelzier, 56
Dryburgh, abbey, 80
Dublin, 59
Duffus, parish of, 13
Dufgall, son of Mormaer of Lennox, 39–40
Duine, François, 112–13, 116
Dull, 126
Duloe, 104
Dumbarton, 19, 20, 27, 28, 29, 30, 31, 36, 73; kingdom of, 44, 60
Dumbarton Rock, 28, 31, 73–4, 88
Dumfriesshire, 29, 44, 75, 83
Dumville, David, 92
Dunbar, 45
Dunbar, George, earl of March, 152
Dunbar, Sir Patrick, 152–3
Dunbar, William, 165–6
Dunbarney, 197
Dunbartonshire, 29
Dún Bhrennain, 195
Duncan II, king of Scots, 121
Duncan, Archibald A.M., 5, 53
Dundee, 155–6, 177, Franciscan nunnery of, 171, Franciscans of, 177
Dunfermline, 119, 124, 128
Dunkeld, 126, 156
Dunod, King, 70
Dunstan, archbishop of Canterbury and saint, 140, 142
Duntiglennan, 39
Durham, 46, 51, 54, 82, 120–4, 127–8, 146; *Liber Vitae* of, 47, 121, 128; bishops of, see Hugh de Puiset; William de St Calais
Dyfed, 68, 101
Dyffryn Clwyd, 84
Dyfrig, bishop and saint, 68–9, 71, 81, 86–7
Eadmer of Canterbury, 8, 9
Eadred, King, 139, 142, 144
Eadwulf, son of Uhtred, earl of Northumbria, 52, 57
Eadwulf Rus, 53
Ealdgyth, Queen, 52,
Ealdgyth, daughter of Earl Uhtred, 57
Ealdred, son of Uhtred, earl of Northumbria, 52
Eamont, river, 73
Earlshall, 176
Ecgfrida, 57
Edgar, Aethling, 144
Edgar, king of England, 139, 142–3
Edgar, king of Scots, 121, 144
Edinbarnet, 39
Edinburgh, 172; Castle Hill of, 167
Ediunet, saint, 109
Edmonds, Fiona, 29, 77, 78, 88
Edmund, King, 139, 142, 144, 173
Edmund Ironside, 139, 143–4

Edward II, king of England, 161, 166
Edward III, king of England, 147, 150, 153, 161, 172–3
Edward, Prince, 166
Edward the Confessor, king of England and saint, 139, 173
Edward the Elder, king of England, 139, 141–2, 144
Edward the Exile, 139
Edward the Martyr, 139–40
Edwin (d.632–3), King, 10
Edwin, King, 139–40, 142
Éguiner, saint, 107
Eileach an Naoimh, 195–6, 199
Einion ap Maredudd, bishop, 84
Eirros Domno, 186–7
Ekwall, Eilert, 60
Elfoddw, archbishop of Venedotian kingdom (Gwynedd), 69
Elgin, 163
Eliud, 86 (see Teilo)
Elphinstone, William, bishop of Aberdeen, 162, 196
Elwy, river, 83–4
Enda, saint, 184
Engelram, bishop, 78
England, 6, 9, 44, 46, 58, 75, 95, 119–20, 122, 125, 127, 129, 136–7, 146–7, 150, 173, 180, 202
English, 44, 70, 83, 89, 136, 142
Enoder, saint, 98
Entenin, saint, 112
Éoganacht Locha Léin, 185, 188, 190, 193–4
Epiphany, 163, 166, 167, 169, 172–4, 176; Luxembourg Epiphanies, 174,
Erc, 192
Ercilingus, 105
Ercilius, 105
Erlendur, bishop, 198
Ervan, saint, 98
Essie, 197
Ethbin, saint, 109
Ethelred, King, 139–40, 144
Ethelwulf, king of England, 139–40
Eubonia (see Man, isle of)
Eulogium (for David I), 131–2, 134, 137, 139, 144–5
Euny, saint, 109
Eusebius of Caesarea, 5
Eustorgius, saint, 162–3
Eval, saint, 98
Exeter, 116
Faifley, 39
Fainche, saint(s), 193
Fal, river, 111
Falaise, treaty of, 75
Farmer, David, 8
Farne Island, 123
Faroe Islands, 180, 198
Fechtmaide, king of the Britons, see Sechtmaide
Fénit, 190
Fergus, Pictish bishop, 25, 30
Fergus, river and estuary, 187, 189
Fergus of (?) Cunningham, 40
Ferrocinctus, bishop of Évreux, 72
'Fiacc's Hymn', 35
Findlug, 181, 188
Fingar, saint, 107; *Life* of, 107
Fili, saint, 100, 109, 111–13
Filleigh, 112
Finistère, 198–9
Finneach Duirn, bishop and saint, 193
Finnian of Clonard, saint, 180
Finte, church of, 34
Fisher, John, 87, 94, 106, 180, 199
Flambard, Ranulf, 121
Fletcher, Richard, 52–3
Flintshire, 83
Forbes, Bishop, 197
Fordoun, 19, 20, 22, 23, 24, 25, 34, 35
Fordun, John of, 130, 162, 196
Forgus mac Cellach, 185
Forrest, Master Alexander, provost of St Mary of the Fields, 177
Forrest, David, 177
Forrest, John, 177
Forth, firth of, 17, 119, 122
Fortriu, 14, 15, 16; kings of, 13
Fortrose, 15
Foster, John, 178
Foster's almshouse, Bristol, 178
Fotid, see Potitus
Fouquet, Jean, 176
France, 200
Francis, Padraig, 22, 26, 33, 34
Frankia, 88
Franks, the, 36
Fraser, James, 30
Frederick Barbarossa, 161
Frisians, 8
Furness, 124–5
Gaels, 5, 88
Gall-Gháidheil, 30
Galloway, 126
Garde Ecossaise, 176
Garvellochs, 195
Gaskel, Thomas, 39
Gaul, 20, 71–2, 76
Gens Pictorum, see Picts
Génair Pátraicc i nNemthur, 20, 21, 22–3, 35, 36
Genealogia regum Anglorum, 125, 131–2, 137–9, 142–3, 145
Geoffrey of Monmouth, 57, 85–7, 90, 112
George, saint, 146–59; bell named for, 156
Gerald of Wales, 102, 186, 188
Gerard, brother of Bernard of Clairvaux, 133–4
Gerent, saint, 112
Germanus, saint, 33, 34, 35
Germany, 180
Gilbethoc, 40

Gilbert son of Samuel of Renfrew, 39–40
Gildas, 70, 88–9, 106; *Life* of, 88
Gille-Conaill mantach, brother of earl of Carrick, 40
Gillemihhel queschutbrit, 49
Gillemor, 40
Gillepatrick, 59–60
Gilon, 40
Gilsland, 49, 50
Giraldus Cambrensis (see Gerald of Wales)
Girgin, plain of, 34
Giric, bishop of St Andrews, 8, 9
Glasgow, 53, 66, 67, 72, 74, 76–80, 81, 82, 83, 85, 88, 90; bishopric/diocese of, 74–5, 80, 81, 82–3, 88, 90; cathedral, 53, 67, 72, 77, 81, 163; bishops of, see Herbert; Jocelin; John; Michael
Glenlyon brooch, 168
Glenn, Virginia, 168, 196
Glywysing, 109
Golant, 116
Golden Legends, see *Legenda Aurea*
Gonotiern, bishop of Senlis, 71–2, 88
Gorton, lordship of, 153
Goscelin, 24
Gospatrick, 29
Gospatrick, earl of Lothian, 79
Gospatrick of Worthington, 77, 79
Gospatrick, sheriff of Roxburgh, 45
Gospatrick, son of Arkil, 43, 52, 55, 57–9, 64
Gospatrick, son of Maldred, 43, 45, 52, 54–8, 63–4
Gospatrick, son of Uhtred , 43, 51, 52–5, 63
'Gospatrick's writ', 54–5, 58
Gospels of Máel-Brigte, 169
Govan, 73, 77, 79
Great Crosthwaite, 75–6
Greenlaw, Gilbert, bishop of Aberdeen, 171
Gregory the Great, 6, 7, 70, 136
Grinsdale, 75–6
Groome, Francis, 160
Guelders, Mary of, 157–8
Guigner, saint, 107
Gunthar, son of Chlodomer of Orléans, 54
Gunwalloe, 109
Gwas-Mungho, 49
Gwas-Oswald, 49
Gwbert, 98–9
Gwbert, supposed saint, 98–9
Gwinear, saint, 100, 107–8
Gwinear, parish, 107
Gwynedd, 69
Gwynog, saint, 106–7
Haddington, 124
Hadrian's Wall, 14
Haliburton, Walter, lord of Dirleton, 153
Hans, king of Denmark, 175
Harbison, Peter, 194
Hassendean, 80
Heavenfield, 14
Helen/Helena, saint, 125, 161, 163
Henderson, Charles, 109
Henderson, George, 13
Henderson, Isabel, 13
Henfynyw (*Vetus Rubus*?), 101–2
Hengist, 9
Henry I, king of England, 55–6, 79, 81, 82, 131, 136, 144
Henry II, king of England, 75, 124, 131, 133, 135, 138–9, 143–4
Henry VII, king of England, 172
Henry VIII, king of England, 166, 171
Henry of Huntingdon, 137
Henry, son of David I, 121
Herbert, bishop of Glasgow, 67, 82, 85
Herbert, Máire, 194
Hernin, saint, 95
Herod, 162–3, 170
Hexham, 6, 7, 8, 10, 11, 12, 14, 45
Hexhamshire, 45
Heysham, 60
Higgitt, John, 170
Hilarius, 40
Hildesheim, John of, 163–4, 166, 172
Hinba, 195
Historia Brittonum, 20, 22, 85, 92
Historia de sancto Cuthberto, 122
Historia ecclesiastica, 5
Historia regum, 51, 73–4
Historia Regum Britanniae, 85–6, 112
Historia Trium Regum, 163–4, 168
Hoddom, 53, 78, 80
Hofmann, Hans, 178
Holy Sepulchre, 154
Holy Trinity, 33, 34, 174; church in Edinburgh, 157
Horsa, 9
Houghton, Chancellor, 173
Howlett, David, 89
Howth, 169
Hudson, Benjamin, 49
Huel, saint, 98
Hull, Vida, 164
Ia, saint, 109
Ieuan, saint, 45
Île Lavret, 110–11
Île Maudez, 111
Immram Brain, 183
Inber Déa, 34
Inchiquin (Inis Moccu Cuínn), 186
India, 176
Inis Baitheni, 33, see also Boethenus
Inis-dá-Dromma, 187
Inis Gluaire, 186–7, 197
Inistioge, 192; priory of, 193
Inis Tuaisceart, 189–90
Insley, John, 45
Inverness, 15
Iona, 11, 25, 73

Ireland, 4, 9, 25, 26, 28, 29, 30, 31, 33, 34, 35, 36, 38, 43, 59, 92, 94, 125–6, 184, 189, 194–5
Irish, the, 34, 38, 89
Irrus Domnann, 194
Irthington, 75
Irvine, 162; parish kirk, 39
Islay brooch, 168
Isidore of Seville, 5
Italy, 76, 174, 200
Ivar, king, 73
Ivi, saint, 103
James I, king of Scots, 130, 155
James II, king of Scots, 157
James III, king of Scots, 157, 162, 174–5, 179
James IV, king of Scots, 80, 158–9, 162, 172–5, 179
James V, king of Scots, 175
James, Heather, 102
James the Greater, saint, 161
Jarman, Alfred Owen Hughes, 57
Jasper/Jaspar, 162, 167–9, 173
Jeremiah, 133
Jerome, 8
Jersey, 200
Jerusalem, 8, 133, 152
Jews, the, 36
Jocelin, bishop of Glasgow, abbot of Melrose, 67, 90
Jocelin of Furness, 59, 67–8, 72, 74–5, 78, 80, 81, 82, 84–6, 88–90, 125
John, abbot of Furness, 124
John, bishop of Glasgow, 81–2
John Duns Scotus, 162
John II, king of France, 152
John of Beverley, saint, 142
John the Baptist, saint, 7, 173, 178; festival of, in Florence, 166
John, saint, 95
Jonathan, 133
Jonathan, abbot of Abergele, 69
Joseph, saint, 170, 178, 199
Judea, 5, 36
Judicaël, saint, 115
Just, saint, 112
Kachconnen, 40
Kalendars of Scottish Saints, 127
Kalfurnus, see Calpurn
Kames brooch, 168
Kapelle, William, 58
Kay, 111
Ké/Kea, saint, 95, 100, 109, 111–13
Kedicus, 84
Kells, Synod of, 190
Kent, 9, 13
Kentigern, bishop and saint, 29, 31, 56, 66–9, 71–83, 84–90, 125; *Lives* of, 67–8, 72–5, 78, 80, 82, 83, 84, 85–6, 88, 125
Ker, Neil, 47
Kerlouan, 200
Kerrowmore, 196
Kerry, 192
Kerian, saint, 111
Keswick, 82
Keyne, saint, 109–10
Kilbrandon and Kilchattan, 195
Killellan, 29
Kilbarchan, 29
Kilbraenan, 195
Kilbrannan chapel, 196
Kilbrannan Sound, 196
Kilbrenan, 195
Kilbowie, 39
Kilburnie, 197
Kildurrihy West, 191
Kilkenny, 192
Killiney, 192–3
Kilmacolm, 29
Kilmahew, lost place-name, 29
Kilmalkedar, 189–91
Kilmeena, 187
Kilpatrick (Old Kilpatrick), 27, 29, 31, 32, 39–40, 60
Kilpeter (now Houston), 29
Kingarth, 30
Kinghorn, Alexander, 175
Kinneddar, 13
Kirkcudbright, 125
Kirkjubøur, 198
Kirkmahoe, 80
Kirkpatrick-Fleming, 29, 60
Kirkpatrick-Iuxta, 29
Königsberg, 151, 153
Kraus, Dorothy, 170
Kraus, Henry, 170
Lailoken, 56–7, 85
Lagenenses (Leinstermen), 33, 34
Lanark, 80, 156, 165–6
Lanarkshire, 60, 75
Lanbellec, 199
Lancashire, 59, 61
Landévennec, 110
Landkey, 112
Langolen, 98
Langonnet, 199
Lanmérin, 98
Lannion, 199
Largillière, René, 97
Lawrence, saint, of Canterbury, 24
Lawrence, saint, martyr, 24, 25
Lawrencekirk, 24, 25
Leabhar Breac, 169
Legenda Aurea, 154, 163, 178
Legenda Sancti Brendani, 196–7
Legends of the Saints, 154
Leguier, 199
Leinster, 23, 25, 34; Fortuatha of, 35
Lebor Bretnach, 23, 35
Lebor Gabála Érenn, 92
Le Duc, Gwenaël, 111, 181, 189, 199

Legenda S. Brandani, 183
Le Grand, Albert, 111, 200
Leland, John, 111
Lelant, 109
Lennox, mormaerdom of, 40
Leo X, pope, 176
Leominster Priory, 201
Leonard, confessor and saint, 155
Leslie, Master Gavin, 177
Leslie, Norman, 154
Leslie, Patrick, 177
Leslie, Walter, 154
Lewis, Christopher, 46
Lewis, Samuel, 187
Lex Brendani, 185
Lex innocentium, 15
Libellus de admirandis beati Cuthberti virtutibus, 122–8
Libellus de exordio, 51
Libellus de nativitate sancti Cuthberti, 126–7
Liber de Diversis Medicinis, 168
Liber Hymnorum, 21, 23, 27, 35
Life of St Cathroe, 26
Life of St Guénolé, 110
Life of St Senan, 189
Lifris of Llancarfan, 108
Lindisfarne, 123, 128
Lindsay, Alexander, brother of David, 154
Lindsay, Alexander, father of David, 154
Lindsay, Alexander, 2nd earl of Crawford, 155
Lindsay, David, 1st earl of Crawford, 154–5
Lindsay, William, 154
Linkinhorne, 116
Lithuanians, 151
Lives of the British Saints, 94
Lixtune, 125
Llancarfan, 84–6, 198, 201
Llandaf, 81, 82, 84, 86–7; Book of, 84, 86, 87
Llandyfaelog, 87
Llanelwy, 66, 75, 83–7, 90
Llangollen, 98
Llangrannog, 98–9
Llangyndeyrn, 87
Llanilar, 87
Llanon, 101–2
Llwngwm Dinmael, 106
Llyfr Coch Asaph (see Red Book of St Asaph)
Loc Brévelaire, 199–200
Lochwarret, see Borthwick
London, 84, 167; Bridge, 155; Tower of, 171
Lopreden, 200
Lorn, 195–6; Firth of, 195
Lot, Ferdinand, 198
Loth, Joseph, 98, 106, 108
Lothian, 75, 79, 83, 88, 119, 124, 126–7
Lough Corrib, 186
Louis, duke of Orléans, 154
Ludlow Priory, 201
Luffness Priory, 172
Lupait, 36
Lynch, John, 186
Lytham, 125
Mac Bethad, 53, 78
Mabon, saint, 95
MacCraken, Henry, 164
Macence, king, 107
Mac Creiche, saint, 193
Mac Giolla Easpaig, Donal, 185
Mackinlay, James, 197
Macquarrie, Alan, 24, 27, 49
MacNéill, Máire, 188, 191
Máel Coluim/Malcolm, probably son of Owain the Bald, 53, 56, 78
Máel Coluim/Malcolm III, king of Scots, 45, 53, 79, 120–2, 128, 131, 144
Máel Dúin, 193–4
Maelgwn Gwynedd, 84–5
Mag Ai, 186
Magi, the (see Three Kings)
Magloire, saint, 116
Malcolm Beg, 39–40
Malcolm IV, 121, 124
Maldred, son of *Crinan tein*, 56–7, 64
Malginus, 84
Malo, saint, 198; his various *Lives*, 183, 190, 197–8, 200–1
Man, isle of, 70
Maolchéodar, 189
Marcan, saint, 100, 109
March, earls of, 149
Margaret of Denmark, wife of James III, 157–8, 174–5
Margaret I, queen of Denmark, 174
Margaret, saint and queen of Scots, 120, 124, 128, 131, 139, 144
Martin, saint, 36; feast of, 39
Martin Martin, 197–8
Martyrologium Romanum, 5
Martyrology of Aberdeen, 24
Martyrology of Exeter, 200
Martyrology of Oengus, 24
Martyrology of Tallaght, 15
Mary, sister of David I, 144
Massen, King, 107
Mathafarn, 37
Matilda, Empress, 131, 139, 144
Matilda (Edith), sister of David I, wife of Henry I, 139, 144
Matilda, of Senlis, 139, 144
Matthew, saint, feast of, 39
Maudez, saint, 110–11
Maugan/Mawgan, saint, 95, 100, 108
Maurice, vicar of Cléder, 111
Maye, king of Powys, 84
Mayo, 194
Mawes (see Maudez)
Mearns, 25, 35
Meehan, Bernard, 52
Méen, saint (see Mewan)
Meirionydd, 51

Melchior, 162, 166, 168–9, 173, 176
Melconde Galganu, 84
Mellitus, 70
Melor, saint, 116
Melrose, 10; abbey of, 80, 126–7
Memling, Hans, 164
Menn Bairenn, abbot of Aghaboe, 15
Menologium Scoticum, 127
Mercia, 11
Meriadoc/Meriadec, saint, 100, 107–8; *Life* of, 107–8
Merlin, 85–6
Merryn, saint, 98
Meschin, Ranulf, 55
Mewan, saint, 100, 109, 113–16
Michael, saint, the Archangel, 159, 178, 199
Michael, bishop of Glasgow, 80
Milan, 161–3, 174
Milldu, 190
Missel Saint-Vougay, 200
Modaibeg, 23, 35
Monachkennaran [mod. Boquhanran], 39–40
Montgomery, 51
Montgomeryshire, 83
Morbihan, 198
Morgan, David, 147, 149
Morgan Wood, 109
Morken, king of Cumbria, 84
Morland, 81
Mortimer, Walter, called Grøn, 175
Mounth, the, 17
Muir, Lynette, 166
Muirchú maccu Machthéni, 19, 20, 21, 22, 25, 27, 28, 30, 31
Mulchrone, 34, 36
Mulet peninsula, 187
Mungo (see Kentigern)
Munster, 184–5, 187–8, 190–2
Murdoch, Brian, 107–8
Murthly Hours, 169–70
Mwnt, 99
Naiton son of Der-Ilei, 14, 16
Nantcarfan (*Nant Carvan*) see Llancarfan
Nathi son of Garrchon/Garrchú, 33, 34
Nativity, 170
Nationalmusset, Copenhagen, 161, 166–7
Navigatio Sancti Brendani abbatis, 181–4, 188, 190–3, 200
Nectan, saint, 94, 95, 100, 106–7
Neizan, 106
Nelson, Janet, 134
Nemias (Nehemiah?), 40
Nemthor, 20, 26, 27, 28, 31, 36, 37
Neville's Cross, battle of, 129, 150, 152
Newcastle, 82
Newquay, 94
New Statistical Account, 160
Nicholas of Verdun, 161
Nicolaisen, Bill, 29
Nidd, River, 58
Niduari, 122
Ninian, saint, 172, 175
Noethon, saint, 106–7
Non/Nonita/Nonna, saint, 94, 100–5
Nore, river, 192
Norham castle, 121
Northumberland, 82, 131
Northumbria, 10, 13, 14, 25, 42–4, 46, 47, 58, 121; earls of, 44, 54
Northumbrians, 51, 54, 61, 141
Norway, 160
Notre-Dame, 199
Nynnid, saint, 104
O'Brennan, churchyard of, 192
Ocbass of Gaul, 38 (see also Ocmus)
Ocmus, 36 (see also Ocbass)
Ó Carragáin, Tomás, 189
O'Connell, Rory, 190
Ó Cróinín, Dáibhí, 18
Ó Cuív, Brian, 59
O'Donoghue, Denis, 192
O'Donovan, John, 186
Ogilvy, Sir Walter, 155
Ogstoun, parish of, 13
O'Hanlon, John, 180
Oise, 71
Olaf, King, 73
Oldenburg Horn, 167
O'Loughlin, Thomas, 194
Olson, 112, 115
Onamasticon, 46, 56
Onuist son of Vurguist, king of Picts (820–34), 1, 2, 3
Onuist son of Vurguist, king of Picts (732–61), 1, 2, 3, 4, 13, 16, 17
Oronsay, 196
Order of the Elephant, 174
Order of the Garter, 147, 150
Order of the Passion, 154
Ordnance Gazeeter of Scotland, 160
Ó Riain, Pádraig, 102, 182–3, 194, 201
Origen, 5
Orkneys, 26, 197
Orléans, council of, 71
Orme, Nicholas, 107, 112
Ossary, 169, 194
Oswald, 11, 14, king and martyr saint
Otto IV, Emperor, 175
Our Lady, church of, Bruges, 164
Our Lady of the Snow, confraternity, 164
Owain ap Gruffudd ap Cynan, ruler of Gwynedd, 83–4
Owain the Bald, king of Strathclyde, 53, 78
Owenmore, river, 188
Padel, Oliver, 48, 56, 85, 91, 97, 104, 112, 115
Padstow, 117
Paisley, abbot of, 39
Paisley Register, 32; translation from, 39–40
Palladius, saint, 18, 19, 20, 21, 22, 23, 24, 25, 31, 32, 33, 34, 35, named Pledius, 35

Paris, 166, 170, 196; council of, 71–2
Paróiste Bhréannain, 188
Paschal II, pope, 81
Patrick Brompton, 59–60
Patrick, saint, 18, 19, 20, 21, 22, 23, 26, 27, 28, 29, 30, 31, 32, 33, 34, 35, 36, 37, 38, 39, 40, 42–6, 51, 58–61, 77, 88–9, 125, 194; his various *Lives*, 19–23, 25–8, 30–2, 36, 59, 125; translations from, 33–38
Patrick's Rock, 32
Patrik Keld (Patrick's Well), 59
Paul, saint, 6, 7, 8, 9, 33, 34, 35, 161, 188
Paulinus, 10
Pelynt, 104
Pembrokeshire, 94, 102–3
Pennines, 58
Penrith, 73
Persia, 161
Perth, 119, 124, 178
Peter, saint, 6, 7, 8, 9, 10, 13, 14, 17, 26, 29, 33, 34, 35, 161, 188
Petroc, saint, 95, 99, 108–10, 115, 117
Phelan, Bishop James, 193
Philipson, Sir William, 178
Philleigh, 112
Phythian-Adams, Charles, 54–6
Piast, Elizabeth, 174
Picken, W.M.M., 109
Pictavia/Pictland, 14, 15, 17, 20, 25, 26, 31, 34, 35
Picts, the, 5, 31, 32, 33, 34, 35
Pius II, pope, see Aeneas Sylvius Piccolomini
Plévin, 109
Pleucadeuc, 108
Plouaret, 199
Plonéour-Lanvern, 106
Plougoulm, 97–8
Plouhinec, 106
Plouyé, 109
Plumbland, 125
Plummer, Charles, 199
Pluvigner, 107
Poitiers, battle of, 152
Poitou, 20
Pol de Courcy, 199
Portmahomack, 13
Potitus, grandfather of St Patrick, 36, 38
Prat, Thomas, 156
Praemonstratensians, 185
Prester John, 176
Preston, George, of Gorton, 153
Preston, Simon, of Gorton, 153
Preston Patrick, 61
Prosopography of Anglo-Saxon England, 46, 56
Prosper of Acquitaine, 18, 19
Pugin, Augustus, 66, 90
Pujmanová, Olga, 174
Quimper, 110
Quintin, 199
Radnor, 51
Ramsay, Sir Alexander, 152
Ráth Bressail, Synod of, 185, 190
Rathel, 40
Ratwili, bishop, 198
Red Book of St Asaph, 68
Redon Cartulary, 48
Rees, Rice, 94
Reginald of Durham, 122–8
Reims, 71
Renfrewshire, 29
Renpatrick, 29
Ressin, 40
Revello, 166
Rhine, river, 163
Rhoscrowdder, 87
Rhuddlan, 84
Rhydderch ap Tudwal, king of 'Clyde Rock', 74, 81, 85
Rhygyfarch, author of *St David's Life*, 101–4, 201
Ricatus, 105
Richard I, king of England, 121
Richard II, king of England, 146, 154, 172–4
Richard, bishop of Llanelwy, 84
Richard of Hexham, 137
Richardson, James S., 170
Richmond, 171
Ripon, 10, 11, 12
Robert, earl of Gloucester, 85
Robert I, king of Scots, 80
Robert III, king of Scots, 171
Rochester, 6 , 7, 8, 9, 10, 11, 12
Romans, 36
Rome, 6, 8, 10, 12, 13, 25, 30, 33, 34, 75, 124, 161, 174
Ronald, earl of Orkney, 128
Roscarrock, Nicholas, 111, 114–15
Roscommon, 186
Rosemarkie, 15, 16, 17
Roskeen, 187
Roskilde cathedral, 174–5
Rosneath, 28
Ross, Alasdair, 13
Ross, 15
Rosslyn chapel, 171
Rotheric Beg of Carrick, 40
Rothesay, 196
Roxburghshire, 75
Rumon, saint, 112
Ruthven, 171
Ryedale, 58
St Andrews, 1, 3, 8, 9, 13, 17, 119, 124; bishop of, 82, diocese of, 82
St Anne's, Dowally, 178
St Asaph, 83–4, 87
St Austell, 114
St Brandan's Haven, 197
St Brandan, parish of, 199
St Brelade, Fisherman's Chapel in, 200
St Brendan, hill of, 189

St Brendan's house, 189
St Brendan's townland, 186
St Breock, parish of, 109
St Brianan's chapel, 198
St-Cado, island of, 108
St Columb Major, 96–8
St Columb Minor, 96–8
St Columba's chapel, Skipness Castle, 196
St Davids, 68–9, 75, 84–6, 101
St-Divy, 101, 103
St Enoder, 98
St Eustorgius, church of, Milan, 161
St George's altar, Dundee, 155
St George's chapel, Windsor, 150
St-Gildas-de-Rhuys, 88
St Ives, 109
St James, priory of, Bristol, 202
St Just-in-Roseland, 111
St Kea, church of, 111
St Kilda, 197
St Lucius, guild of, 175
St Machar's cathedral, Aberdeen, 176
St-Malo, 198–9
St Mariengraden, Cologne, 162
St Mary's Abbey, York, 79
St Mary's Copenhagen, 175
St Mary's, Dundee, 155–6, 177–8
St Mary's crypt, Aberdeen, 171
St Mary's, Haddington, 177
St Magnus's cathedral, 128
St Méen, abbey of, 114–15
St Mewan, parish and church of, 114, 116
St Nicholas, Aberdeen, 156, 171, 177–8
St Non's chapel, 102
St Olaikirke, Elsinore, 175
St Peter, cathedral of, Cologne, 161
St Petrock's Priory, 48
St-Quay-Portrieux, 112–13
St Stephen's Cloister, 66
St Winnow, parish of, 106
Saints, Seaways and Settlements, 94
Saltus Virtutum (see Clonfert)
Samson, saint and bishop of Dol, 72, 86, 116
Sanctus, putative father of St David, 101–2
Santiago de Compostela, 161
Satan, 141
Satyrus, 133
Saul, 133
Saul, Nigel, 173
Scammell, Geoffrey, 120
Scandinavians, 59, 73; of Dublin, 59
Scofili/Scophili/Scubilion, saint, 112–13
Scone, 82
Scotland, 2, 4, 26, 29, 31, 32, 58, 75, 88–9, 119–20, 122, 125–7, 129, 142, 147–8, 160, 164, 174–5, 179, 195
Scotichronicon, 82, 129, 162
Scots, 122, 141
Scythia, 5, 6, 8
Searle, William George, 46
Sectmaide, king of the Britons, 36
Sedulius (see Siadal)
Seil island, 195
Segitius, 33, 34
Selby, 128
Selmer, Carl, 200
Serf, saint, 80; *Life* of, 67, 80
Serk, isle of, 116
Sharpe, Richard, 55, 182
Siadal, bishop of the Britons, 30
Sigen, wife of Uhtred, earl of Bamburgh, 52
Sigrida, 57
Silvester, 33, 34, 35
Simeon, archdeacon of Teviotdale, 67
Simeon of Durham, 51, 67, 73–4, 122
Simon, friend of Aelred of Rievaulx, 133–4
Siward, of York, earl of Northumbria, 52–4, 78
Skene, William, 16
Sláne, 22, 26, 30, 31
Slitrig, 123
Smithfield, 154
Smyth, Alfred, 3
Solomon, 11, 142–3
Solonius/Solinus, 33, 34, 35
Solway, 54, 78
Somerled, 67
Somerset, 93, 95
Somerset Herald, 158
Southill, 116
Spennithorne, 59
Sprouston Breviary, 67
Squire, Aelred, 133
Sron Broin, 191
Stalmans, Nathalie, 194
Standard, battle of the, 131, 137
Stephen, author of the *Vita Sancti Wilfrithi*, 6, 7, 10, 11, 12
Stephen, king of England, 82, 131, 144
Stewart, Charles, 196
Stewart, Margaret, 153
Stewarts of Lorn, 170
Stobo, 49, 50
Stoddart, Robert, 162
Stokes, 34, 35, 36
Strachan, 35, 36
Strathclyde, 20, 26, 27, 28–29, 30, 31, 32, 36, 42–4, 46, 49, 50, 53–9, 60–1, 73–4, 76–8, 88, 89
Strathtay, 127
Stremoy, 198
Suidhe Broin, 191
Swale, river, 58
Swein of Denmark, 140
Swidnica, Anne of, 173
Tanguy, Bernard, 103, 106, 109, 113
Tanners'/Saddles' Guild, Bruges, 164
Tarbat, 15
Tay, river, 122–3
Taylor, Simon, 2, 3
Teampaillín Bréannain, 188

Teampall Brénnain/Bréanainn (two sites), 189
Tedda, saint, 95
Tees, river, 82, 122–3
Teilo, saint, 81, 82, 86
Ternan, saint, 24, 25
Teudar, see Theodoric.
Teutonic Order, 151, 153
Teviotdale, 80
Tewkesbury, 202
Thacker, Alan, 105
Thames, river, 162
Théarnec, saint, 97
Thech/Tech na Róman/Rómanach, 33, 35
'The Dangerous Fortress', 166
Theobald of Bec, archbishop of Canterbury, 84
Theodore, Archbishop of Canterbury, 12
Theodoric, king, 107
Thesaurus Palaeohibernicus, 36
Thomas, apostle and saint, 156, 163, 176
Thomas Becket, saint, 127
Thomas II, archbishop of York, 80
Thorfinn, 58
Thornton, Robert, 168
Three Fates, 168
Three Kings, of Cologne, 156, 160–79; of Cullen, 160
Tinidor, saint, 98
Tiree, 195
Tobar Bhréanainn, 191
Tobar Bréanainn, 189, 191 (three separate sites)
Tobar Bréannain, 188
Tobar na Croise, 192
Tobar na Molt, 192
Tobar ola Brénnain, 191–2
Tohergar, 186
Tolley, Tom, 157–8
Torannán, see Ternan
Torrie, Pat, 177
Tostig, earl of Northumbria, 52, 53
Tralee, 187, 190
Trégarantec, 97–8
Tregony, 104–5
Trégrom, 199
Trim, 167
Trinity triptych, 157–8
Trondheim, 128
Trughanacme, 192
Tuam, 186, 194
Túathalán, abbot of Cennrígmonaid, 2, 3
Tudor, Margaret, 158, 165, 173
Turgot, 120–1, 124
Tweed, river, 82
Tynedale, 50
Tynemouth, John of, 67
Tyrie, John, 178
Tyrrhene Sea, 36
Tyssilio, saint, 116
Tywardreath Priory, 114
Ua Ruairc, 184
Uhtred, earl of Bamburgh, 52, 54
Uí Briúin, 185–7
Uí Fiachrach, 187, 194
Uí Garrchon, 35
Ungus filius Urguist (see Onuist son of Vurguist), 1
Ure, river, 58
Uvel, saint, 98
Valentia Island, 192
van der Goes, Hugo, 157
Vauclair, 126
Ventre, 20
Vetus Rubus, see Henfynyw
Vikings, 28
Virgin Mary, 112, 121, 151, 155, 157–8, 161, 164, 170, 172–4, 178; bell, 156
Vita anonyma longior, see Malo
Vita Columbae, see Columba,
Vita Merlini, 57, 85
Vita Sancti Brendani, see Brendan
Vita Sancti Cadoci, 201
Vita Sancti Cuthberti, see Cuthbert
Vita Sancti Machutis, see Malo
Vita Sancti Wilfrithi, 6, 7, 11
von Dassel, Rainald, archbishop of Cologne, 161–2
Waldemar Atterdag, king of Denmark, 174
Waldeve, son of Gospatrick, 79
Waleran, count of Meulan, 85
Wales, 20, 22, 28, 30, 48, 50, 51, 57, 66, 68–9, 82, 83–4, 86, 88, 91, 92, 93, 94, 96–7, 99, 101, 108, 110, 112, 117, 142, 201–2
Waltham, 128
Waltheof, abbot of Melrose, 125
Waltheof, son of Gospatrick son of Maldred, 55–6
Watson, William, 15, 195, 197
Weem, 126
Wells, Lord, 155
Welsh, 30, 73, 83, 89, 141
Welsh (language), 74
Wensleydale, 58, 59, 60
Wessex, 28
Westminster, 66, 90, 171
Westmorland, 131
West Saxon, 95
Wetheral Priory, 55, 77, 78
Wharfedale, 58
Whitby, 7, Synod of, 12, 17
Whithorn, 122, 125
Whitelaw, Archibald, 162–3
Whitelock, Dorothy, 47
Wick, 127
Wight, sea of, 36
Wilfrid, bishop of York, 6–12
William, author of *Carmen de morte Sumerledi*, 67
William, earl of Gloucester, 202
William Rufus, 56, 144
William I of England, 'the Conqueror', 57, 139, 144

William the Lion, king of Scots, 75, 80, 121, 123–4
Willibrord, 7
Wilton Diptych, 173
Winnoc, saint, 94, 106–7
Winnow, saint, 100
Wimwaloe, saint, 106, 109–10
Wmffre, Iwan, 102
Woden, 139
Woolf, Alex, 53, 56
Worcestre, William, 104
Wormald, Patrick, 7
Wrdisten, abbot of Landévennec, 110
Wyntoun, Andrew of, 4, 16
Yates, Nigel, 87
Y Ferwig, 99
Y tri brenin o Gwlen, 166
York, 8, 10, 11, 12, 14, 53, 90; archbishops of, 75, 78, 83; diocese of, 81
Yorkshire, 58, 59, 61

STUDIES IN CELTIC HISTORY

Already published

I · THE SAINTS OF GWYNEDD
Molly Miller

II · CELTIC BRITAIN IN THE EARLY MIDDLE AGES
Kathleen Hughes

III · THE INSULAR LATIN GRAMMARIANS
Vivien Law

IV · CHRONICLES AND ANNALS OF MEDIAEVAL IRELAND AND WALES
Kathryn Grabowski and David Dumville

V · GILDAS: NEW APPROACHES
M. Lapidge and D. Dumville (edd.)

VI · SAINT GERMANUS OF AUXERRE AND THE END OF ROMAN BRITAIN
E. A. Thompson

VII · FROM KINGS TO WARLORDS
Katherine Simms

VIII · THE CHURCH AND THE WELSH BORDER IN THE CENTRAL MIDDLE AGES
C. N. L. Brooke

IX · THE LITURGY AND RITUAL OF THE CELTIC CHURCH
F. E. Warren (2nd edn by Jane Stevenson)

X · THE MONKS OF REDON
Caroline Brett (ed. and trans.)

XI · EARLY MONASTERIES IN CORNWALL
Lynette Olson

XII · IRELAND, WALES AND ENGLAND IN THE ELEVENTH CENTURY
K. L. Maund

XIII · SAINT PATRICK, AD 493–1993
D. N. Dumville and others

XIV · MILITARY INSTITUTIONS ON THE WELSH MARCHES:
SHROPSHIRE, AD 1066–1300
Frederick C. Suppe

XV · UNDERSTANDING THE UNIVERSE IN
SEVENTH-CENTURY IRELAND
Marina Smythe

XVI · GRUFFUDD AP CYNAN: A COLLABORATIVE BIOGRAPHY
K. L. Maund (ed.)

XVII · COLUMBANUS: STUDIES ON THE LATIN WRITINGS
Michael Lapidge (ed.)

XVIII · THE IRISH IDENTITY OF THE KINGDOM OF
THE SCOTS IN THE
TWELFTH AND THIRTEENTH CENTURIES
Dauvit Broun

XIX · THE MEDIEVAL CULT OF ST PETROC
Karen Jankulak

XX · CHRIST IN CELTIC CHRISTIANITY:
BRITAIN AND IRELAND FROM THE FIFTH TO
THE TENTH CENTURY
Michael W. Herren and Shirley Ann Brown

XXI · THE BOOK OF LLANDAF AND
THE NORMAN CHURCH IN WALES
John Reuben Davies

XXII · ROYAL INAUGURAON IN GAELIC IRELAND c.1100–1600:
A CULTURAL LANDSCAPE STUDY
Elizabeth FitzPatrick

XXIII · CÉLI DÉ IN IRELAND: MONASTIC WRITING AND IDENTITY
IN THE EARLY MIDDLE AGES
Westley Follett

XXIV · ST DAVID OF WALES: CULT, CHURCH AND NATION
J. Wyn Evans and Jonathan M. Wooding (ed.)

XXV · SAINTS' CULTS IN THE CELTIC WORLD
Steve Boardman, John Reuben Davies and Eila Williamson (ed.)

XXVI · GILDAS'S *DE EXCIDIO BRITONUM* AND
THE EARLY BRITISH CHURCH
Karen George

XXVII · THE PRESENT AND THE PAST IN MEDIEVAL IRISH CHRONICLES
Nicholas Evans

XXVIII · THE CULT OF SAINTS AND THE VIRGIN MARY IN MEDIEVAL SCOTLAND
Steve Boardman and Eila Williamson (ed.)

XXIX · THE TRANSFORMATION OF THE IRISH CHURCH IN THE TWELFTH CENTURY
Marie Therese Flanagan

XXX · HEROIC SAGA AND CLASSICAL EPIC IN MEDIEVAL IRELAND
Brent Miles

XXXI · TOME: STUDIES IN MEDIEVAL CELTIC HISTORY AND LAW IN HONOUR OF THOMAS CHARLES-EDWARDS
Fiona Edmonds and Paul Russell (ed.)

XXXII · NEW PERSPECTIVES ON MEDIEVAL SCOTLAND, 1093–1286
Matthew Hammond (ed.)

XXXIII · LITERACY AND IDENTITY IN EARLY MEDIEVAL IRELAND
Elva Johnston

Printed and bound by CPI Group (UK) Ltd, Croydon, CR0 4YY

09/06/2025

14685716-0002